Urban and Community Politics

William A. Schultze

San Diego State University

W9-BII-817

Duxbury Press

North Scituate, Massachusetts
A division of Wadsworth Publishing Company, Inc., Belmont, California

Duxbury Press
North Scituate, Massachusetts
A Division of Wadsworth Publishing Company, Inc.

ISBN-0-87872-063-4

L. C. Cat. Card No.-74-75717

Printed in the United States of America

1 2 3 4 5 6 7 8 9 10—78 77 76 75 74

Urban and Community Politics was edited and designed by Jane Lovinger. Photographs and cover design were provided by Marshall Henrichs.

Contents

Preface

Most of us will spend most of our lives in cities. Yet many of us — citizens, politicians, and scholars alike — are far from appreciating or even understanding that fact. As presently constituted, American cities do not seem hospitable to human life. Though economically vital, they tend to be physically overpowering, socially unfulfilling, and personally alienating. Like so many human creations, our cities threaten to become the Frankenstein's monsters of civilization. Since a responsive political process is crucial to achieving and maintaining control of the city, there seems to be no need for further justification of a book on urban politics.

In organizing and writing this book, I have attempted to provide a synthesis of the materials of contemporary scholarship which define and explain the politics of the American city. I emphasize this point because genuine synthesis is taken too lightly by American political scientists. Synthesis as an intellectual activity is fundamentally different from analysis. Just as human beings are more than the simple sum of their parts, political synthesis necessarily adds perspective and life to the process with which it deals. Necessarily, then, a synthesis of the materials on urban politics requires much more than merely setting side by side several analytical studies within a loose-fitting general framework. It has been my highest aim to provide in this book a provocative and readable synthesis of reliable information about urban politics which will enable the citizen to find ways to positively affect the city, will help the politician to gain a more complete overview of that chaotic and recalcitrant creature he is called upon to govern, and will suggest to the scholar a number of hypotheses worth testing in pursuit of a fuller theoretical understanding of that dangerous, majestic beast — the American city.

There are many long-standing personal and professional debts that I should like to acknowledge. Certain former teachers have had more impact on this work than they will recognize; nonetheless, each has contributed to my state of mind as I wrote this book: Jack Mueller, Harold Hall, Nixon Mumper,

E. Glenn Callan of Nebraska Wesleyan University; and Ardath W. Burks, Eugene Meehan, Gerald Pomper, and Robert Gutman, who were members of the Rutgers University faculty while I was there; I should especially like to thank two members of the Rutgers faculty whose dedication to sound scholarship and humane values were exemplary: Benjamin Baker and Edward McNall Burns.

Many personal friends have provided me with the stimulus, encouragement, emotional support, and some of the concrete experience upon which I have drawn, and I thank them. They include: James L. Jorgenson, James Forrest, Richard Peterson, Harry Huge, Darrel Seng, Duane Hubbard, and Hess Dyas.

A number of colleagues have provided both specific and general help with this book, among them: Al Trost of Valparaiso University; Victor Hoffman of the University of Wisconsin, Milwaukee; E. Terrence Jones of the University of Missouri, St. Louis; David N. Chamberlin of Grossmont College; as well as James Conniff, Henry Janssen, Harlan Lewin, Dwight Anderson, Charles Andrain, and James Clapp, all of San Diego State University. Two other of my colleagues at San Diego State deserve special thanks: E. Walter Miles, for his careful and helpful comments on the chapter on urban justice; and Kenneth R. Keiser, for his continuing helpful discussion of a wide range of topics and research from which I freely drew over the years I was writing this book.

Thomas R. Dye read the entire manuscript and made a number of suggestions which were consistently perceptive and helpful. Since so much of the research on the city was originally done by Professor Dye, my debt to him is double. I am happy to acknowledge a similarly heavy debt to Bernard Hennessy, whose recommendations and encouragement have improved this manuscript considerably. In working with Professor Hennessy, I discovered that there is substance to the appellation "gentleman and scholar." Several other colleagues rendered helpful commentary on the entire manuscript, and I am particularly grateful to Michael C. LeMay and G. Thomas Taylor.

I should also like to take this opportunity to thank several people who helped me with tasks ranging from research assistance to typing. They include Patricia Perrin, Robert W. Larkins, Joan Weschler, Jan Slanczka, Diane Burtless, Genevieve Offner, and Veva Link.

The Duxbury people are a pleasure to work with. Robert Gormley is a fine publisher and person, and Jane Lovinger is an extremely able copy editor. I should also like to thank John Ochse for his early encouragement with this project. Despite all this help from competent people, I must acknowledge the possibility that they may have in important matters failed to save me from myself. I therefore accept full responsibility for what errors of fact and judgment remain.

It is a shame that acknowledging wife and family has been reduced to a formality — because it makes sincere thanks seem hollow. Sharon, my wife, and Blair, David, and Carol deserve much more than a courtesy nod. Sharon has more practical political experience than I and considerable ability as a writer. As a result, her reading and typing of the several drafts of this book improved its content. The encouragement and emotional support my family provides has, in a fundamental way, made this book possible.

Urban
and
Community
Politics

Chapter 1

Urbanism
and Politics

Look at the curve in Figure 1.1. It sums up the story of our efforts to "Go forth and populate the earth." Another way to make the same point — that human population has grown radically in the modern age — is to look at what is called the *doubling time* of population, the time necessary for the world population to double. It is estimated that the human population of 6000 B.C. was about 5 million people, taking perhaps one million years to get there from 2½ million. The population did not reach 500 million until almost eight thousand years later, about A.D. 1650: this means it doubled roughly once every one thousand years or so. It reached a billion people around 1850, doubling in some two hundred years. It took only eighty years or so for the next doubling, as the population reached 2 billion around 1930. We have not completed the next doubling to 4 billion yet, but we now have well over 3 billion people. The doubling time at present seems to be about 37 years. This is an impressive reduction in doubling time; 1,000,000 years, 1000 years, 200 years, 80 years, 37 years.[1] Of course, all those people have never been uniformly distributed across the landscape. For whatever reasons — personal economic advantage or pathological togetherness — people have migrated to the city.

Urbanism is a world-wide phenomenon. To illustrate briefly, approximately 80% of the United Kingdom's population live in urban areas, 67% of the Danes, 62% of the Chileans, and 39% of the Japanese. Even those areas of the world which you might expect to be much less urbanized have surprising proportions of their population living in the cities: 24% of the Philippines, 43% of the Mexicans, and even 11% of the residents of mainland China. Despite our mythology, that we are a nation of Tom Sawyers and Easy Riders, the United States is no exception to world population trends. As of this writing, America's population is approximately 70% urban.

Still, American experience with the city is relatively recent. In 1790, there were only twenty-four urban places of 2500 or more, and only about one-twentieth or 5% of our population lived in them. American population growth was slow but steady during the 1800's. With the turn of the twentieth century, the rate of population increase quickened so that by 1920 for the first time more than half the American people lived in urban areas. Urbanization

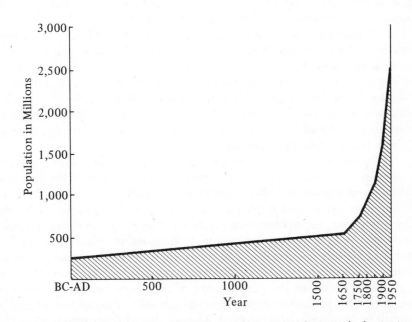

Figure 1.1. Graphic representation of world population growth since the beginning of the Christian era. Source: Adapted from estimates of the United Nations in The Determinants and Consequences of Population Trends. *(ST/SOA/ Series A-17) (New York 1954), pp. 8-11.*

slowed to a virtual standstill during the thirties, but it accelerated again in the forties and has continued to increase since then. Small wonder that a great many Americans have not yet accepted the fact that we are a nation of city dwellers. But population figures tell us very little of significance about urban life. Most of us, if we know the city at all, know it in much more personal ways. We know its sounds, its smells, its feel, its capacity to create anxiety or satisfaction. What we know is not always pleasant.

Cities Make Problems

There can be no denying that our cities manifest major symptoms of social, physical, and political illness; many Americans can't say the word "urban" without adding "problem." How valid is that perception of city life?

Air pollution is an example of how cities can make problems. The city has accelerated the development of the forces that create air pollution and has maintained conditions which make it very hard to cure.

A billboard just outside San Diego reads, "Avoid L.A."; and while it turns out to be an ad for an airline, it expresses a sentiment that is national. Los Angeles smog has become not only intolerable for the residents of that city, but a national symbol of the evils of urbanism. It is a symbol equally understood and agreed on by the most conventional middle-class surburbanite and by his children who have dropped out and are growing pot and potatoes in a Colorado commune. Smog is nature's own billboard: "WARNING: this area is becoming unfit for human habitation."

Symbols, of course, need only partially correspond with reality, but the realities of air pollution are sufficient to anyone's vision of the doom man is bringing on himself and his environment. A report of the staff to the Senate subcommittee on air and water pollution matter-of-factly observed in 1968, "There is ample quantitative evidence of acute air pollution effects on public health and welfare during air pollution episodes in which persons with chronic bronchitis, lung cancer and other respiratory and cardio-pulmonary diseases have suffered aggravated distress and death. There is evidence that air pollution decreases the performance of otherwise healthy individuals." New York City, for instance, experienced high sulfur dioxide levels for about a month in January-February, 1963. During that critical period, 809 excess deaths took place from all causes. "When the effects of other biological stresses than air pollution were removed, an estimated 200 to 400 of the 809 excess deaths experienced were attributed to air pollution."[2]

Certain forms of cancer have been closely associated with air pollution. Former surgeon general, Dr. LeRoy E. Burney has observed, "There is a very definite association between community air pollution and high mortality rates due to cancer of the respiratory tract, cancer of the stomach, esophagus and arteriosclerotic heart disease."[3]

Air pollution is not totally an urban creation, but its development correlates with concentration of population and industry; the four most common sources of air pollution have been found to be (1) the combustion of fuels, (2) motor vehicles, (3) industrial and manufacturing effluents, and (4) miscellaneous commercial and community activities including burning of solid wastes, solvent losses, pesticides and agricultural chemicals.[4]

Industry-originated air pollution poses a visible threat to urban residents

The thought of Los Angeles smog conjures up visions of other urban distresses. For example:

Riot and Disorder   Over 200 American cities experienced major civil disorder from 1965 through 1968. Over 250 persons were killed in these disorders, $500 million in property damage was inflicted, and 50,000 persons were arrested.

Crime   The urban crime rate more than doubled during the 1960s. There is on the average a murder every ten minutes in every large city of the nation, an aggravated assault or rape every five minutes, and a grand larceny every minute.

Housing   One out of every three urban dwelling units is classified as substandard by the U.S. Census Bureau. This means that the unit is "dilapidated" or without heating, running water, or toilet facilities.

Inequality   Three times as many urban blacks are unemployed as urban whites. The infant death rate for black children is twice as high as for whites. The average income of blacks is only 60 percent of the income of the average white.

Less concretely, the city manifests symptoms of physical and social ugliness, exploitation of both land and people, depersonalization and loneliness. Tales of urban tragedy and sad, sad nostalgia for a lost rural utopia are so familiar they border on platitude. Yet the protest and the ever-more obvious symptoms of urban decline have not produced massive reaction. Most Americans seem strangely unaroused; as Raymond Vernon has commented, "Each year they buy a few hundred thousand more picture windows, seed a few hundred thousand more lawns."[5]

There seem to be two general explanations for this lack of concern. One is the often-used refuge of the traditional democrat — it holds that there is a gutsy wisdom in the Middle American: if he is not aroused, it must be because the problem is not nearly so extensive or profound as the criers of alarm would have us believe. The other reaction is grounded in moral indignation; it reasons that if Middle Americans cannot be stirred to action by the dramatic developments of the last decade, it is because they have been thwarted in their attempts to find levers for effective action and consequently have become either blunted and insensitive or frustrated and withdrawn.

Since no writing is without viewpoint, I do not hesitate to acknowledge that my personal dispositions move me toward the latter view. However, moral indignation could turn us to several undesirable paths: withdrawal, detachment, physical escape, drug or alcohol escapes, or endless actionless contemplation of the problem. Neither can I endorse the advice of those spokesmen of the pop culture, the Beatles, who have urged us to "get back to where you once belonged." This is a particularly unattractive alternative if you once belonged in a small, rural town, populated with a Huck Finn or two, and gossipy petty people who excluded nigger Jims. The creation of a viable urban policy must begin with the recognition that most of us have a love-hate relationship with our cities. We want to be near but not in them. The city offers advantages of higher paying jobs, theaters, museums, better shopping and the exhilaration of diversity; while the suburbs offer fresh air, greenery, a sense of detachment, and escape. The opening assumption of this book, then, is that cities are here to stay, that a return to pastoral bliss is impossible, and that, even if possible, most of us would not be content there without the advantages of the city that have become the "givens" in our lives. Our future is urban. The real question is: Can our cities be tailored to human scale? Can man bend the city to his needs and desires? Can he personalize his environment or will that environment depersonalize and dominate us all?

It is almost too obvious to state that we should approach such a grand and complex question with all humility. No man, no book, no field of study, no active organization has *the* answer. Moreover, there probably are several possible workable arrangements. Consequently, each of us must affirm his limitations as well as his capacities to comprehend and prescribe for urban needs. Political analysis and political activism are not the universal solvent.

However, knowledge of politics is a vital component in achieving most alternatives. Political inquiry at the least can provide a body of verified knowledge of the dimensions of the situation. At the most, politics is itself a humanizing activity in which knowledge produces understanding, understanding facilitates empathy, and empathy motivates and focuses action. If our knowledge is good enough, perhaps our action will be effective, nor merely cathartic.

Political Analysis Can Help Solve Urban Problems

Usable political knowledge has no single source. There is a vast storehouse of political theory in our long history of speculation on political matters in the Western tradition. There are the thoughts of contemporary philosophers and activists. There is knowledge derived from participants in ongoing events. And there is a body of useful insights derived from scientific inquiry into the political process. Though all sources provide useful perspective and none alone can claim to be sufficient, still, we must make some operational choice. Here I opt for careful, systematic study of the political process. I acknowledge that social scientific study is relatively recent and its findings scarce in some areas; as a result, I shall find it necessary to speculate, often broadly, beyond verified findings.

Careful, systematic analysis requires a frame of mind that is alien to many Americans. Most of us grow up with what could be called a "Tinker's mentality." When confronted with a problem, we like to think that we are people of action and begin immediately trying this or that ad hoc solution. When our car breaks down, for example, we don't formulate an overall strategy of examination. We begin poking and prodding, pulling a wire, adjusting the carburetor, checking the battery cables, etc. Our hope is that we will stumble across the solution. Undoubtedly in many situations this is an effective mode of action. When dealing with complex social, economic and political situations, however, the tinker can create more problems than he solves. Tinkering with the traffic problem by building more and bigger freeways has contributed to the unanticipated consequences of air pollution, traffic congestion, more crowded downtown areas, and more sprawling and wasteful land use. As our population grows and becomes even more interdependent, it becomes gradually clearer that more comprehensive solutions are necessary; and comprehensive solutions are dependent on comprehensive understanding.

Both comprehensive understanding and careful political analysis begin with the inelegant but quite necessary task of careful definition of central terms and concepts. To fail to define is to open the way to faulty communication. If I use the word "cow" and you think of a long slender reptile with no legs that crawls on the ground, which sometimes bites humans and may be poisonous, then we will have some difficulty when I begin to describe how to milk one. So it is with political ideas. If I say democracy and you think of Athenian Greek political practice in the fourth century B.C., we may spend the rest of our time talking past one another. Our task is to find core meaning in political terms; it is made particularly complex by the fact that politicians are the worst enemies of clear usage. They seem forever intent on expanding the meaning of "good" words to include whatever evil practice they have in mind to recommend.

UNDERSTANDING THE CITY

At the highest level of abstraction, an urban area is a complex cultural, economic, demographic, and legal-political configuration. It is most generally described as a "population concentration" or as "an arrangement of people in space."[6] A more complete definition would add the recognition that cities create distinctive modes of human relationship.

> Definition 1. A *city* consists of a dense human population concentration on the land, the members of which have distinctive modes of social, economic, and political interaction.[7]

This definition contains three major elements: it emphasizes that the city contains large numbers of people. More than that, they are located close together; there is relatively high population density. And finally, the people of a city are heterogeneous; that is, different from one another in ways which are important to them and which affect how they relate to one another.

Let me clarify this general definition and extend it by discussing three different ways of defining the city: (1) as urban culture, (2) as a legal entity, and (3) as an operational unit for census and research purposes.

Urban Culture

This definition emphasizes that a city is more than a dense settlement of people on the land, that it is different from an overgrown village. It must be understood that the forces of industrialism and technology have reshaped the entire setting in which we live. This reshaping is pervasive, affecting everything from economic structure to patterns of personal relations. The differences between the culture of cities (the urban-industrial culture) and the preurban (or preindustrial) culture are differences of kind, not just of degree. To clarify these differences, some scholars have found a number of grounds

Table 1.1   Some Points of Comparison Between Preindustrial and
Urban-Industrial Cultures

Characteristic	Preindustrial Culture	Urban-Industrial Culture

Integration:
    Division of
    Labor
	Mechanical Solidarity
	Little; self-sufficiency
		Organic Solidarity
		    Complex; specialization;
		    heavy interdependency

Interpersonal relations	Face-to-face; personal	Secondary group (role) relationships dominate; impersonal
Institutional Proliferation:	Single; dominant institution	Many semiautonomous institutions
Role of Religion:	Dominant; major source of moral values; spiritualism	One among many sources of values; secular sources dominate; rationalism

Authority:
    Source
    Structure
	Religious; unitary
	Centralized
		Secular; multiple
		Decentralized; pluralistic

of contrast between urban and preurban cultures. Notably, there are
differences in the nature of integration; in the character of institutions; in the
role of religions; and in the source and structure of authority.[8] These
differences are summarized in Table 1.1.

Integration

The division of labor and specialization which has attended industrialism has produced far-reaching, and many unanticipated consequences. These principles, of course, make a great deal of economic sense:
specialization allows the person with the greatest skill in a particular job to
concentrate his time and attention on perfecting his performance. As
specialization becomes a general organizing principle, as it does in the urbanization process, it creates a distinctive form of social integration; the
French sociologist, Emile Durkheim, described this pattern over seventy years
ago as *organic solidarity*. Briefly, organic solidarity is a complex and subtle
form of social organization in which the modes of interdependency of the
constituent units are an outgrowth of the differences between their specialized
functions: for example, the apartment dweller becomes dependent on the garbage collector because the garbage collector performs a function that the
apartment dweller does not, one he needs performed. There is no necessary
friendship between the two, but there is functional dependence.[9]

Durkheim distinguishes organic solidarity from *mechanical
solidarity*, which is the social organization of simpler cultures. Similarities
rather than difference characterize the organization of these simpler cultures

— similarities in physical type, basic values, and occupations. Relationships in this setting tend to be personal rather than related to the performance of the specialized role.

Two important transformations occur with the emergence of organic solidarity as the dominant form of social organization: with specialization there occurs a loss of the personal self-sufficiency which attended mechanical solidarity. As a result the virtues of self-reliance and individualism become increasingly out of joint with the realities of urban life. A crisis of self-confidence and a sense of estrangement from others easily develop in the transition.[10]

A second change worth emphasizing is that relationships with others cease to be personal: "Urbanism may be described as a life style characterized by social impersonality rather than intimacy. It is characteristic of a society that is too large and complex for pervasive face-to-face interaction."[11]

Institutional proliferation and secularization

In the preurban setting there tends to be one dominant institution which serves a variety of functions. The religious, governmental, and economic functions in particular are unified in the person of the leader or a council of elders. Religions provide the code of ethics and standards of judgment of behavior. The specialization and division of labor that attend urbanization cause these functions to become vested in separate, semiautonomous institutions. No single institution is able to remain dominant. The high place of religion in the culture gives way to secularism.[12] Theologian Harvey Cox puts it succinctly, "When man changes his tools and techniques, his ways of producing and distributing the goods of life, he also changes his gods."[13]

Although religion continues to be the dominant source of cultural values, the emerging urban society is strongly influenced by other forces as well — the forces nurtured by the growth of secular institutions. Each institution attempts to create and enforce its own value system; in so doing, it strives to match action to belief more effectively than traditional religion has done. Urban secularism, by permitting the growth of semiautonomous institutions, facilitates the emergence of multiple sources of value and thereby opens the possibility of conflict between, for example, religious and educational values. Finally, it should be noted that religious values have encouraged spiritualism — the doctrine that emphasizes man's immortal spirit and his moral relations to his fellow man and to the universe — as a mode of thought. Urbanism and industrialism have proved more congenial to rationalism and materialism.

Source and structure of authority

In the urbanization process, "truth" loses its hallowed ring; urban culture creates the disposition to believe that there are several sources of truth.

Marshall Henrichs

A vista like this one is bound to influence the lives of its residents.

Absolutes are viewed with skepticism. Appeals to authority as a means of social control are thus undercut. Which authority is *genuinely* authoritative is the kind of question which the urban-industrial culture is hard pressed to answer. Not even governmental institutions can promote a single value system and thus become supreme authority. In fact, pressure develops for governmental authority to become less absolute and to recognize and accommodate the competing versions of "good" contained in a pluralistic urban culture.

> Whether we like it or not, we have long ceased to live in a world in which the faith in the Judeo-Christian myth of creation is secure enough to constitute a basis and source of authority for actual laws. . . .
>
> Our new difficulty is that we start from a fundamental distrust of everything usually given, a distrust of all laws and prescriptions, moral or social, that are deduced from a given, comprehensive, universal whole.[14]

As pluralism becomes the cultural norm, the urbanite is called on to discover and accept secular authority as a basis for the creation of law and the settlement of disputes. In the transition, individuals are likely to feel that authority, like religious values, is in crisis.[15] Those who had been psychologically dependent on authority may find that they feel cut off from certainty and even from meaning.

America seems to contain elements of both preindustrial and urban cultures, as well as many symptoms of transition. Some segments of America seem just now to be responding to urbanism. Other segments give evidence of moving to a new era — a postindustrial culture perhaps. This diversity leads me to emphasize that this discussion is more a device than a description of any real, particular historical setting. Discussion should be seen as an aid to examining the original contention — that the city is a wholly transformed environment for man — and to establishing some important reference points to clarify the nature of the transition.

The City in Law

Even though we are compelled to think of the city in these broad cultural terms, we must at the same time recognize that the city for the purposes of contemporary American law is much more narrowly conceived. Legally the city has no existence unless the state creates it in fact or in law (de facto or de jure). A city or "municipal corporation" comes into being only through an act of the legislature in the state in which it is located. The old axiom is still true that "the city is a creature of the state." A municipal corporation has been defined as a

. . . body politic and corporate, established by public law, or sovereign power evidenced by a charter with defined limits and a population, a corporate name, and a seal (although a seal is not essential), and perpetual succession, primarily to regulate the local or internal affairs of the territory or district incorporated by officers selected by the corporation, and secondarily, to share in the civil government of the state in the particular locality.[16]

This authorization of the right to local self-government is not unqualified, however. In many states, cities cannot extend their own powers to meet unanticipated problems. If, for example, a city wants to use its zoning powers to leave certain lands undeveloped to assure open space, that city may find it necessary to get specific authorization from the state legislature. The "home rule" city may exercise more autonomy, but it, too, is restricted in the exercise of its powers.

A further complication produced by the legal status of the city is generally referred to as the boundary problem. The physical boundaries of the municipal corporation are generally defined at the time the city is created. As American cities have grown, they have generally spilled over the boundary, leaving city governments unable to deal with problems and needs that result from that overgrowth.

Whatever the strengths and weaknesses of this legal definition of the city, there seems little likelihood of major change. As one commentator on local government has put it, the doctrine of legislative supremacy over the city "has not been seriously questioned since the federal government was established."[17]

An Operational Definition: The SMSA

It could be argued that the cultural definition of the city just discussed makes the city synonymous with the American culture generally, and therefore permits no drawing of physical boundaries. For some purposes I am prepared to accept that. It could be successfully argued, I think, that cities are the physical points at which the tendencies of our urban culture are most advanced. A clear implication of this view would be that even the most agricultural of American regions could not be fully understood except in their relation to the activities of urban centers.

For other purposes, however, in order to have a clear focus for our attention, we may desire to fix the physical boundaries of a city. We need to know the boundaries in order, for example: to apply for state and federal aid programs, to assign responsibility for particular services, and to undertake a scientific research project for which the precise subject of interest must be specified. The Bureau of the Census is charged with designating such boundaries; their definition, which they call the Standard Metropolitan Statistical Area (SMSA) is widely used.[18]

According to the Bureau of the Census definition, each SMSA must contain at least one city of not less than 50,000 population or two contiguous cities constituting for general economic and social purposes a single community with a combined minimum of 50,000. In general, the SMSA will include the entire county in which this central city is located. In addition, adjacent counties will be included in the SMSA if they meet two criteria: they must be "metropolitan in character," and they must be "economically and socially integrated" with the county containing the central city.

1. *Metropolitan Character.* To qualify as "metropolitan in character," an adjacent county must meet certain specific criteria. At least 75 percent of its labor force must be engaged in nonagricultural work. In addition, the county must meet at least one of three other conditions: (1) It must have not less than one half its population living in minor civil divisions with a density of at least 150 persons per square mile in an unbroken chain of minor civil divisions from a central city in the area. ("Minor civil divisions" are the primary divisions of a county such as a township, election precinct, etc.) (2) Its number of nonagricultural workers must equal at least 10 percent of the number of nonagricultural workers employed in the central county or the county must be the place of employment of at least 10,000 nonagricultural workers. (3) Its nonagricultural labor force must equal 10 percent or more of the number of nonagricultural workers living in the central county, or the county must be the place of residence of a nonagricultural labor force of 10,000 or more.

2. *Economic and Social Integration.* For an adjacent county to qualify as "economically and socially integrated" with the central city, either of two criteria must be met: (1) At least 15 percent of the workers living in the county must work in the central county. (2) At least 25 percent of those working in the county live in the central county. When these measures of integration produce inconclusive information about an adjacent county, the Bureau of the Census has more detailed criteria which can be applied. They include, for example, average monthly telephone calls per subscriber from the county to the central county, audited newspaper circulation reports, and number of charge accounts held by members of the adjacent county in central city retail stores.[19]

Operational definitions seldom leave us applauding wildly and cheering "encore." This one is no exception. And, while no one believes that it is a perfect definition, it is nonetheless widely used and provides a useful starting point for many careful analyses.[20]

A DEFINITION OF POLITICS

There is no single definition of politics on which all political scientists agree. Traditionally, American political scientists relied chiefly on historical sources and normative philosophy to decide which were political questions. Traditional political scientists fastened their attention on governmental institutions and on the specific content of constitutions and laws; and they often concerned themselves with "reform."

After World War II there emerged a group of political scientists commonly referred to as behavioralists, who disputed the focus of traditional political scientists.[21] As a prominent behavioralist, Robert Dahl has summarized the "behavioral mood." Its major thrust was "to make the empirical component of the discipline more scientific."[22] Behavioralism moved our attention toward more careful observation of the canons of science. Behavioralism, according to Dahl, exhibits (1) a decided preference for quantitative analysis of objectively selected data, (2) an insistence on the need for an explicit conceptual framework, (3) a demand for a research design that permits replication, and (4) a strong emphasis on the need to evolve theories of political behavior.[23]

Still more recently there has arisen a group of political scientists who fear that our concern for scientific analysis has led us away from political relevancy. This movement has been dubbed the "postbehavioral revolution" and is closely associated with what has been called New Left Scholarship — that group of scholars in all disciplines who are critical of many of the fundamental values and institutions of the Western culture and are attracted to ideologies of the political Left. The postbehavioral revolutionaries emphasize these tenets: (1) Substance is more important than technique. "For the aphorism of science that it is better to be wrong than vague, postbehavioralism would substitute a new dictum, that it is better to be vague than non-relevantly precise."[24] (2) Behavioral science often masks an ideology of conservatism. (3) Behavioral inquiry does not consistently aid in exposing the realities of contemporary politics. (4) The intellectual should take action, when necessary, to protect and promote humane values of our civilization. According to the postbehavioral indictment, behavioralism has in no way made that obligation clear.[25]

Each of these three perspectives on the study of politics — traditional, behavioral, and postbehavioral — offers us a different conception of politics. Among the several definitions that have been offered and used are: the study of legal government,[26] of power,[27] of decision making,[28] of that system which authoritatively allocates values in society,[29] communications control in organizations,[30] and a number of others. Since there is little agreement as to what the core concern of our study is, we must leave this a somewhat open question. Tentatively, I shall use a definition of politics which has been found useful in organizing and presenting an overview of the American political process.

> Definition 2. *Politics* is the most inclusive process by which social conflict is managed.[31]

We Assume Conflict

This definition begins with the assumption that conflict is a fundamental fact of human social existence, and that out of conflict politics arises. This observation is made without prejudging whether conflict is, in itself, good or bad. I say this because there is a marked tendency for Americans to presume that conflict is a bad thing, evidence of original sin, or of fundamental animal nature. But that is not an unchallenged interpretation. For example, when we think of that form of conflict which we call competition, most Americans think it is good; competition is expected to produce social progress and personal maturity for the individual competitors. For present purposes then, we merely assume that human conflict is pervasive, whether we like that fact or not.[32]

Social conflict develops when participants, whether individuals or groups, realize that their desires differ from those of others, and when those desires seem to be incompatible. If preferences are held intensely enough, and if resources are scarce enough so that both participants cannot get what they want, and if there is an unwillingness to compromise, then social conflict breaks into war or violence. Not all social conflicts must go to this extreme for resolution. Disputes within the American society characteristically have been among participants who have enough in common to make compromise possible.[33]

We are all aware that we have a series of procedures and practices for dealing with war and violence. Images of bombs exploding in Vietnam and Korea, of nightsticks swinging in Chicago, and of exchanges of gunfire in Newark rioting are recent reminders of these procedures. But there are other procedures and processes which we rely on when compromise is possible. By "political process" we have in mind a pattern of human activities leading to the adjustment of social disputes.

We Assume Pattern

The assumption that we are dealing with a process or pattern is important for several reasons. Primarily, it emphasizes that we are not interested

Marshall Henrichs

Some have chosen to buck the trend toward urban living, but at what cost?

in isolated political acts but instead assume that politics occur within the context of other acts. This necessarily means that a given act is understandable only in context. To make that point clear, let's consider an extreme example: if all we know is the following political act, man A kills man B, we are still a good distance from understanding. We would call that act "murder" if the context is that man A disagreed with man B's political position and shot him dead in the street. We would call the same act "patriotic" if B had been a foreign agent escaping our country with top secret documents and A had shot him down with "007" flare.

We assume politics involves conflict management. The political patterns which are our central concern are distinguished by the function they perform of managing social conflicts. Conflict management here means the process by which ". . . a system attempts to maintain or preserve its identity . . . as it adapts to changing conditions."[34] Two overlapping activities occur in the process of managing conflict in urban America. First, conflicts are represented; that is persons, groups, or corporate interests are led to clarify and define their goals, to confront opponents, and to press their desires on public decision makers. Secondly, once social conflict has emerged and become clarified, the conflict is coped with, adjusted, or managed in order to settle the controversy. Such activities aim at the management of conflict by adjusting interest disputes.[35] Let us examine these two processes more fully.

Conflict Representation

People disagree. As we live closer together and become more dependent on each other — that is, as we become a more urban culture — social disagreements multiply. In this process, even those who like things the way they are must become contestants. Conflict representation, then, refers to the activities of persons or groups who publicly acknowledge their disagreements and move toward public resolution. When an irate citizen phones the mayor, when the chairman of a local conservation group testifies before the city council, when a business takes an ad in a newspaper to decry the excesses of contemporary youth, and when black renters march in protest of substandard housing conditions — in all of these cases conflict is being represented.

Conflict representation occurs within any governmental form, even though the cost of representing conflict under totalitarian forms can be extraordinarily high — confinement or death. A "democratic" political process generally reduces drastically the potential costs of representing a conflicting position; it creates and maintains regular channels for such expression. Presumably American democracy makes it axiomatic that no one will have to remain silent who feels that he cannot accept things as they are. That is, no one should be forced to "love it or leave it." Generally speaking, Americans have preferred to believe that any position should be able to be represented, no matter how incredibly deviant or seemingly unacceptable that position might appear to be. We have endorsed the ideal that all views should be submitted to the "free market of ideas" — there to be discussed, debated, and burnished or tarnished as they are clarified.

Conflict representation includes various patterns of activity. Instead of trying to trace all such patterns, I have instead decided that four are crucial and have allowed them to provide the organizational scheme of Parts One and Two of the book. Focus will be on the following topics: (1) the development and expression of differing cultural values, interests, and opinions, (2) the role and strategies of leadership in the presentation of conflict, (3) the function of groups, and (4) political parties. Broadly then, we will be observing and describing the processes of *issue formulation and aggregation* leading from individual opinion to presentation of broad questions of public policy.

By putting the emphasis on political process, I do not intend to avoid political substance. Most of us would agree that it is equally important to ask which issues arise and why it is those issues and not others. Fortunately, we have a growing body of literature which describes the debate, discussion, and resolution of specific urban issues — ranging from freeway location to urban

WE are students asking we don't want to do o'

THIS IS THE HOUR FOR MOTHER POWER

Marshall Henrichs

Participation in the urban political process takes diverse forms.

renewal controversies. The substance of political conflict is discussed in Part Four.

Conflict Management

The presentation of conflicting positions on substantive social questions does not exhaust the concern of the student of politics. Our definition of politics also calls our attention to the analytically distinct patterns of activity by which conflict may be managed. Such resolution occurs when *legitimate public policy* concerning a dispute is pronounced. Of course, the term *management* need not mean definitive settlement of the controversy. Most of us view "final solutions" with some alarm. Instead, conflict management implies the more modest goal of "moderating social tensions to avoid destructive competition."[36] If urban social conflicts were characteristically struggles between "good guys" and "bad guys" then we could expect definitive resolutions — in which good would triumph over evil. In a great many American urban social conflicts, however, good (some would say God) is on both sides. In these cases, the goal of resolution means accommodation rather than victory. By emphasizing *legitimate* community policy, I necessarily imply that there is a willingness to accept particular decisions as binding. The subjective feeling that one ought to obey is crucial to the process. Obviously if a citizen has perceived the conflict as one between good and evil, he will find it impossible to afford legitimacy to a public policy which in any way rewards evil. If, on the other hand, he perceives that a given public policy reflects an accommodation between two goods, then his sense of obligation to obey is going to be much greater.

There seem to be two fundamental reasons for compliance with public policies. First, people may obey out of fear if they anticipate that severe deprivations would result if they refused. Force alone, however, is likely to produce only short-term resolutions of conflict. Real or threatened force used over long periods of time tends to (1) create and reinforce the perception that authority is morally bankrupt, (2) fan the flames of dissent and protest, and (3) provide the justification for responses ranging from disrespect to bloody revolution.

More enduring obedience is elicited when compliance results from citizen consent.[37] Willed consent may be forthcoming for a number of reasons: as a result of empathy between citizens and officials where the citizen is rewarded (either materially or symbolically) for his compliance; or where the citizen feels he has significantly participated in the making of the policy.

When decisions are made which manage social conflicts, we call those decisions *public policy*: *policy* because they pronounce a general rule with which compliance is expected and *public* because they affect the society at large, the participants and nonparticipants alike. In general our expectation is that public policy is made by our political institutions. For a great many, the term *institution* conjures up sacred imagery. Social scientists mean nothing so mysterious. An institution, for our purposes, is a pattern of behavior which is highly stable and has endured over a long period of time.[38]

Despite our presupposition that political institutions make public policy, we should not let a definition alone foreclose the possibility that more short-lived behavior patterns might create policy. For example, a small group of businessmen may make the public policy by adopting some course of action that affects the townspeople just as profoundly as any decree ever issued by the Selectmen. Our definition of politics thus prods us to find those decisions which in fact manage conflict and to recognize that those decisions, wherever made, constitute public policy.

As with conflict representation, conflict management as a political activity consists of overlapping patterns. Again for analytical purposes it is convenient to distinguish patterns of resolution. Five such patterns have been central to the organization of Part Three. They are: *policy formulation*, that is the activities by which policies are initiated, negotiated, and defined; *policy leadership*, the role played by individuals in the formulation of policy and the building of support for it; *policy adoption*, the legitimating of policy; *policy application*, the process by which general rules are tailored to specific circumstances and administered; and *policy adjudication*, wherein disputes among individual citizens and challenges to enacted policy are adjusted.

SUMMARY

The City is a fact of life, though many of us would prefer to have it otherwise. Cities have been the locus of what many Americans consider to be our most severe problems — crime, social disorganization, air pollution, and the like. In this opening chapter I have argued that there is much in urbanism which is good and worth saving. In addition, I have suggested that careful analysis of the politics of the city is a necessary prerequisite for making social change that will save the best of urban life while alleviating the problems. To aid in careful political analysis, we defined the key terms "city" and "politics," emphasizing the city as a cultural phenomenon and politics as conflict. In the next chapter we shall turn our attention to two additional definitional questions: what is meant by the terms "democracy" and "community"?

NOTES

1. Paul R. Ehrlich, *The Population Bomb* (New York: Ballantine Books, 1968), p. 18.
2. L. Greenberg et al., "Air Pollution and Mortality in New York City," *Archives of Environmental Health* (1967), p. 430.
3. Michell Gordon, *Sick Cities* (Baltimore: Penguin Books, 1965).
4. Subcommittee on Air and Water Pollution, Committee on Public Works: United States Senate, *Staff Report: Air Quality Criteria* (Washington, D.C.: U.S. Government Printing Office, 1968), p. 12.
5. Raymond Vernon, *The Myth and Reality of our Urban Problems* (Cambridge, Mass.: Harvard University Press, 1966), p. 2.
6. Cf. Edward Banfield and James Wilson, *City Politics* (Cambridge, Mass.: Harvard University Press and the MIT Press, 1963), p. 1.
7. This definition borrows heavily from John C. Bollens and Henry J. Schmandt, *The Metropolis, Its People, Politics, and Economic Life* (New York: Harper & Row, 1965), p. 6. Note that this definition combines the conceptions David Popenoe calls "urbanization" with the "urban process." I recognize the need for certain purposes to make that distinction between the city as a physical entity (urbanization) and urban culture, and will do so when the exposition demands. For elaboration of this distinction, see David Popenoe, "On the

Meaning of 'Urban' in Urban Studies," *Urban Affairs Quarterly* 1 (September 1965): 30; also John Friedman, "Two Concepts of Urbanization: A Comment," *Urban Affairs Quarterly* 1 (June 1966): 78-84; John Friedman and John Miller, "The Urban Field," *Journal of the American Institute of Planners* 31 (November 1965): 312-320.

8. These points of contrast and comparison are suggested by the following sources: Gideon Sjoberg, *The Pre-Industrial City* (New York: Free Press of Glencoe, 1960); Robert Redfield, *The Folk Culture of Yucatan* (Chicago: University of Chicago Press, 1941); Robert Redfield, *The Little Community* (Chicago: University of Chicago Press, 1955); and Louis Wirth, "Urbanism as a Way of Life," *American Journal of Sociology* 44 (July 1938): 1-24. In general, folk cultures are compared with urban cultures on such dimensions as the basis of overall integration, institutional character, role of religion, and basis of authority. The phrase "folk-urban continuum" is associated with the work of Robert Redfield. I alter the original meaning in the following discussion. However, the dichotomy between folk and urban is best understood as the polarization of "ideal types," not as an empirical description; see Philip M. Hauser, "The Folk-Urban Ideal Type: Observations on the Folk-Urban Dichotomies as Forms of Western Ethnocentrism," in *The Study of Urbanization*, ed. Philip M. Hauser and Leo F. Schnore (New York: John Wiley and Sons, 1965), especially pp. 503-517.

9. Emile Durkheim, *The Division of Labor in Society*, trans. George Simpson (New York: Free Press of Glencoe, 1947), chap. 2 and 3. For a discussion of the application of Durkheim's concept to contemporary urban areas, see Alvin Boskoff, *The Sociology of Urban Regions* (New York: Appleton-Century-Crofts, 1962), pp. 281-293.

10. There is a great deal of literature extending and disputing the implications of this view. For an overview, see Eric and Mary Josephson, *Man Alone: Alienation in Modern Society* (New York: Dell Publishing Co., 1966); Eric Fromm, *The Sane Society* (New York: Holt, Rinehart and Winston, 1955); George Simmel, "The Metropolis and Mental Life" in *The Sociology of George Simmel* (New York: Free Press of Glencoe, 1957).

11. Robert T. and Barbara G. Anderson, "The Village and the City," reprinted in Robert M. French, *The Community: A Comparative Perspective* (Itasca, Ill.: F. E. Peacock Publishers, 1969), p. 308.

12. Cf. Harvey Cox, *The Secular City* (New York: The Macmillan Co., 1965), esp. pp. 1-13. For a discussion of the persistence of sacred forms in preindustrial cities see Gideon Sjoberg, *The Pre-Industrial City* (New York: Free Press of Glencoe, 1960), chap. 9.

13. Cox, *Secular City*, p. 8.

14. Hannah Arendt, *The Origins of Totalitarianism* (New York: Harcourt, Brace, 1951).

15. Henry Kariel, *In Search of Authority* (New York: Free Press of Glencoe, 1964), discusses the implications of this view at greater length, see especially pp. 245-252.

16. Eugene McQuillan, *The Law of Municipal Corporations*, 3d ed., by Clark A. Nichols, et al. (Chicago: Callaghan, 1949), p. 451.
17. Jewell Cass Phillips, *State and Local Government in America* (New York: American Book Co., 1954), p. 364.
18. U.S. Bureau of the Census, *U.S. Census of Population: 1960. Number of Inhabitants*. Final Report PC (1) — 17A (Washington, D.C.: U.S. Government Printing Office, 1960), pp. vii-viii.
19. Bureau of the Budget, *Standard Metropolitan Statistical Areas* (Washington, D.C.: U.S. Government Printing Office), 1961.
20. For a more complete discussion of the considerations involved in fixing urban boundaries, see Jack P. Gibbs, *Urban Research Methods* (Princeton: D. Van Nostrand Co., 1961), Part I.
21. See especially David Easton, *The Political System* (New York: Alfred A. Knopf, 1953).
22. Robert Dahl, "The Behavioral Approach in Political Science: Epitaph for a Monument to a Successful Protest," *American Political Science Review*, 55 (December 1961): 763-772. Empiricism, most simply, involves reliance on systematic observations as the primary data on which generalizations are based.
23. Ibid., The term *theory* is popularly misused to mean something like ideal. That misuse should be carefully avoided. I intend *theory* to mean a generalized explanation of reality.
24. David Easton, "The New Revolution in Political Science," *American Political Science Review* (December 1969), p. 1052.
25. Ibid.
26. Charles Hyneman, *The Study of Politics* (Urbana: University of Illinois Press, 1959).
27. Charles E. Merriam, *A Study of Power* (Glencoe, Ill.: Free Press, 1950); George E. G. Catlin, *The Science and Method of Politics* (Hamden, Conn.: Archon Books, 1964); Robert A. Dahl, *Modern Political Analysis* (Englewood Cliffs, N.J.: Prentice-Hall, Inc., 1963).
28. Richard C. Snyder, et al., *Foreign Policy Decision-making* (New York: Free Press of Glencoe, 1962); Donald Matthews, *The Social Background of Political Decision-makers* (New York: Random House, 1954).
29. David Easton, *A Systems Analysis of Political Life* (New York: John Wiley and Sons, 1965); see also Gabriel Almond and G. Bingham Powell, *Comparative Politics: A Developmental Approach* (Boston: Little, Brown, 1966).
30. Karl Deutsch, *The Nerves of Government* (London: Free Press of Glencoe, 1963).
31. Dan Nimmo and Thomas Ungs, *American Political Patterns: Conflict and Consensus* (Boston: Little, Brown, 1969), p. 14. See also Edward C. Banfield and James Q. Wilson, *City Politics* (Cambridge, Mass.: Harvard University Press and the MIT Press, 1963), p. 1.
32. Ibid., p. 8. See also Lewis A. Coser, *The Functions of Social Conflict* (Glencoe, Ill.: Free Press, 1956); Raymond W. Mack and Richard G. Snyder, "The Analysis of Social Conflict," *The Journal of Conflict Resolution* I (June

1957), pp. 212-248; Elton B. McNeil, ed., *The Nature of Human Conflict* (Englewood Cliffs, N.J.: Prentice-Hall, 1965); Ted Gurr, *Why Men Rebel* (Princeton: Princeton University Press, 1970); and Stanford Lyman and Marvin Scott, *The Sociology of the Absurd* (New York: Appleton-Century-Crofts, 1970).

33. Grant McConnel, *Private Power and American Democracy* (New York: Alfred A. Knopf, 1966).

34. Morton A. Kaplan, *System and Process in International Politics* (New York: John Wiley and Sons, 1957), p. 89.

35. These postulates and much of the discussion of the definition of politics borrows heavily from Nimmo and Ungs, *American Political Patterns*, especially pp. 14-23.

36. Nimmo and Ungs, *American Political Patterns*, p. 18.

37. Robert A. Dahl, *Modern Political Analysis* (Englewood Cliffs, N.J.: Prentice-Hall, 1963), p. 50.

38. The definition of "Institution" is from Gary Steiner and Bernard Berelson, *Human Behavior* (New York: Harcourt, Brace and World, 1967). For a good brief review of alternative conceptions of "public policy," see Robert Lineberry and Ira Sharkansky, *Urban Politics and Public Policy* (New York: Harper & Row, 1971), Chap. 6.

Chapter 2

The Aspiration for
Democratic Community

Most Americans have a strong commitment to a vision of democratic community. Despite that commitment, however, most of us really do not understand what we or anyone else means by either "democracy" or "community." This seeming contradiction can be understood if we recognize that those key terms function as symbols. Symbols stand for something other than themselves and they evoke " . . . an attitude, a set of impressions, or a pattern of events associated through time, through space, through logic, or through imagination with the symbol."[1] Symbols can convey rather precise meanings. Numbers, for example, are symbols. But other symbols draw an emotional response. They condense into one term (or event or act) such feelings as patriotic pride, anxiety, remembrances of past glories or defeats, promises of future greatness: some one of these or all of them.[2] These *condensation symbols* may convey little common meaning to different individuals. For example, the American flag has long been a symbol of national pride and of unity. To a great many American citizens, it still is. But to a number of others, that same symbol calls up a vision of racial bigotry, wasteful use of natural resources, and excessive concern with "law and order." The physical symbol is constant; the symbolic content varies.

THE MEANINGS OF DEMOCRACY

In general use, we expect the term democracy both to convey accurate meaning and to evoke appropriate emotions. That expectation is obviously too high and results in much confusion and misunderstanding. For example, you would receive quite different responses from a cross-section of Americans if you asked them whether democracy necessarily includes

The trappings of "the American way of life" are showy but insubstantial.

Marshall Henrichs

capitalism, or a belief in Judeo-Christian teachings, or a particular institutional arrangement like constitutionalism, separation of powers,
federalism, or political parties.

Philosophical discussion of the concept of democracy has provided
some clarity but not universal agreement. George Sabine, for example, has
seen the history of democracy as composed of a dynamic tension between two
ideals, liberty and equality.[3] Speaking more specifically, the sociologist Robert
MacIver has conceived democracy as ". . . not a way of governing, whether by
majority or otherwise, but primarily as a way of determining who shall govern
and, broadly, to what ends . . ."[4] Henry Mayo, moving toward a conception of
institutionalized democracy, distinguishes four fundamental principles of a
democratic system: popular control of policy makers; political equality;
political freedom; and majority rule.[5] Within this diversity can be discerned at
least one element of agreement, that democracy requires a pattern of managing conflict which assures a close association between what the citizens want
and the decisions that are made.

To be useful in an examination of urban political patterns, however, a
definition of democracy must be more complete, accounting for patterns of
institutionalization. It has seemed to me for some time that Americans operate
with two competing conceptions of a democratic process — sometimes implicit
and sometimes explicit. One cluster of beliefs, commitments and expectations
is in the form of an idealization. I will call that *individualist democracy*. The
other democratic cluster emerges from the work of contemporary behavioral
political scientists and is by contrast largely descriptive. Other political scientists have labeled that concept *pluralist democracy*.[6]

Both the individualist and the pluralist visions of democracy are composed of patterns of attitudes, beliefs, value commitments, and institutional
arrangements. Such clusters are invariably complex. To simplify and to
facilitate comparison I will state the assumptions and certain major implications of those assumptions regarding three political questions: (1) Who is
the basic actor in the political process? (2) What is the function of the party
system? (3) What is the function of the public decision maker?

Individualist Democracy

Anyone who has listened to a Fourth of July oration or read a junior
high school civics text will recognize the assumptions of individualist
democracy. Its precepts are an idealization and most of us realize that there is
a yawning gulf between these ideals and our political practices, — and most of
us yawn about the gulf. Still, it is useful to try to make explicit what so many
of us think ought to be the case.

Definition 3. *American Gothic Democracy* is that mode of democracy which is based on the assumption that the basic political unit is the individual actor, that the political parties reflect distinguishable and contrasting philosophies of governing, and that the public decision makers' principal rule of decision is to implement their party's philosophy of governing.

The basic actor

Each citizen, acting as an individual and expressing himself primarily through the vote, is assumed to be the sovereign and the actuator of the political process — sovereign because he is the ultimate authority and actuator because his positive action is what is needed for the process to work. Some additional assumptions must be made about that individual voter to justify the initial one. It must be assumed that each citizen will behave rationally.[7] It is generally assumed that this rational individual will formulate goals which are largely self-interested, but that — and this is important — when his self-interest conflicts with the "greater public good" he will be willing to subordinate self-interest. For example, a hypothetical voter faced with the necessity to vote on additional money for schools might calculate that his self-interest would best be served by voting against it, thus keeping his taxes low. After further deliberation, however, that voter could be expected to recognize the broad community interest in maintaining high educational standards and decide to take the short-run loss in income as perferable to the long-run decline of educational standards among residents of the next generation. The traditional assumption is that the individual voter can and often will make the "public interest" choice. This rational, public-interested individual is also assumed to be highly interested in electoral politics. Finally, these assumptions make it necessary that the individual voter have access to sufficient information to permit his rational calculation. Without all the relevant political facts, he can scarcely be expected to make a reasoned choice.

Function of the party system

Political parties are often assumed to be intimately associated with the development of democracy.[8] Both the individualist and the pluralist democratic models assume the important role of the party, and both tend to see the party's function as aggregating the desires of the basic actors in the political process for the purpose of electing officials. As we define the core function of the parties more specifically, however, the individualist assumptions diverge from the pluralist by making the important addition that the parties should and do express an ideological position which is based on a reasonably coherent philosophy of governing.[9] It is widely assumed that the party specifically appeals to the ideology agreed on by party members. This, of course, leads to the further expectation that the candidates nominated for public office should be chosen because they embrace the common ideology of the party. If these prerequisites are met, then the individualist version of the party system enables two such ideological parties to provide contrasting positions on most major issues. A clear statement of these beliefs regarding the party system can be found in a report of the American Political Science Associates, titled *Toward A More Responsible Two-Party System.* That report consistently assumed the need for parties with programs, the reason being

> Unless the parties identify themselves with programs, the public is unable to make an intelligent choice between them. The public can understand the general management of the government only in terms of policies. When the parties lack the capacity to define their actions in terms of policies, they turn irresponsible because the electoral choice between the parties becomes devoid of meaning.[10]

Since the individualist assumptions lay heavy stress on voting as the route to political power it becomes necessary for the parties to present a clear contrast on all issues for the voters' options to be meaningful. For example, a choice between two "law and order" city council candidates would rob the voter of choice.

Function of public decision maker

In both the individualist and the pluralist versions of democracy, public decision makers are presumed to function to manage conflict by establishing binding public policy. To be consistent with its earlier assumptions, however, the individualist pattern must add that the public decision maker is guided by the ideology and platform of the party from which he was elected. That is, when the decision maker is faced with a particular issue, his principal rule of decision should be to refer to his ideology or to the platform. This implies that each decision is related to the desires of a majority of citizens, since the individual vote is interpreted as a statement of ideological commitment. The assumption is made that the majority ideology must have elected the decision maker, and if he acts in conformity with the ideology, he must be enacting majority desires on each public policy question he decides.

Another implication of the assumption that the public decision maker is guided by his ideology is that each officeholder is consistently engaged in *comprehensive evaluation;* that is, a full range of alternatives are systematically examined. And further, this means that each decision is made with some calculation as to how compatible the decision will be with the established pattern of rules and procedures.[11]

If this total individualist pattern operates, the linkage between individual political goals and public policy is assured. If there is some interruption of the pattern — for example, if the officeholder turns his back on the party after he is elected — there develops a democratic short circuit. For suddenly the basic actor is cut off from his policy objectives.

Just this simple rundown of the assumptions of the individualist style probably leaves most of you realizing how difficult they would be to implement and recognizing how far they are from what we actually do in this country. Recent empirical studies of American urban, state, and national politics provide little comfort to those who believe that we act in the individualist democratic mode. A number of studies leave seriously in doubt, for example, the voter's rationality.[12] The two parties have come to look increasingly alike and in local politics have often been entirely eliminated in favor of nonpartisan election systems. Clearly we need to revise the individualist concept to be more realistic. If we can agree that the individualist democrat's assumptions, as a whole, are at present either naive or unrealized or both, can we then go ahead to describe a political process which is a closer fit with what we do? And once we have accurately described our practices, we then must ask, is that process democratic?

Pluralist Democracy

Contemporary behavioral political scientists have made significant steps toward accurate description of our political life. If we take behavioral findings, together with some speculation and extrapolation, it is possible to conclude that seemingly isolated empirical findings point some common directions. For the sake of simplicity I will refer to one such direction as the finding of pluralism. Pluralist perspective begins with the assumption that ours is a diverse culture composed of a large number of groups and individuals, each having its own version of the good life and each pursuing different strategies to obtain its goals. Applied politically, that conception leads to the conclusion that there are "multiple centers of power in the U.S., none of which is or can be wholly sovereign."[13] Or put another way "pluralism is a system in which political power is fragmented. . . . It is moreover shared between the state and a multitude of private groups and individuals."[14] With this vision of pluralism in mind and with the whole series of empirical findings in hand — it is possible to construct an alternative conception of our political process. The pluralist democratic vision assumes quite different responses to those three questions: Who is the basic actor in the process? What is the function of the party system? What is the function of the public decision maker?

Definition 4. *Pluralist democracy* is that mode of democracy based on the assumption that the basic political unit is the group and/or activist, that the

Marshall Henrichs

A pluralist democracy emphasizes that diverse value systems can coexist.

political parties are nonideological and primarily power seeking and that the public decision maker's principal rule of decision is that he should be guided by the coalition of the most powerful actors who are attentive to the specific issue.

The basic actor

The level of voter and citizen interest and the level of knowledge of the political process are both low in this country. (Studies that confirm that statement are taken up in greater detail in Chapter 3. For now, I simply assume the validity of those findings.) However, lack of citizen interest has not caused the political system to stop working. In seeking explanation, some contemporary researchers have assumed that another basic actor must be driving the process. In the pluralist version, the rank-and-file citizen is replaced by a relatively smaller number of political *activists* or by *groups*. Activists are those who are both interested in and attentive to specific areas of public policy. As a result of their selective attentiveness, these actors become knowledgeable, and they develop contacts with public officials which can be translated into influence. For example, a local bank president or political party official or well-known resident of a black community might be such an activist. In other cases, groups and their representatives are the political attentives — groups like the Chamber of Commerce, the local Teamsters Union or the Minister of Information of the Black Panther Party. By mobilizing the power which their resources make possible these actors become the presentors of conflict.

The activist or group is assumed to have many of the attributes ascribed in the individualist democratic mode to the individual voting citizen, the basic actor. It is assumed (1) that the activist or group will be *rational* — able to formulate goals and choose strategies appropriate to obtaining them, (2) that it will be *highly motivated* to participate in all aspects of politics which affect its particular interest, (3) that it will have *access to necessary information*, and (4) that it will act in a fundamentally *self-interested* way. However, and this is an important difference from the assumptions of the individualist style, the activist need have *no operating concept* of a public interest. What we call the public interest is more properly understood as a dynamic equilibrium among the contending forces.

Function of the party system

Not only is the pluralist political actor different from the idealized actor of the individualist model but so is the operation of the party system. A number of authorities have come to feel that political parties are best conceived as power-seeking aggregations. As one commentator says, "The first goal of the political party is to win. The second goal of the party is to win. The third goal of the political party is to win, etc." As a result, emphasis on party philosophy has been subordinated to winning. Since both parties desire to win and both parties must court the same constituency of groups and activists to do so, they come to look increasingly alike in their ideologies. As Harvey Wheeler has put it, the two major national parties have "adhered to the same basic values and sought the same basic goals . . . even though they have differed over the best means of achieving those goals."[15] Given the non-ideological character of the political party, the first axiom in choosing a candidate becomes: find one who will be appealing to the largest number of basic actors. Do not worry about his ideology; that can be blurred, altered, or manipulated to assure his attractiveness to a mass audience.[16]

The contrasts between the function of the political party in the individualist model and the view of the party in the pluralist version are great. Whereas the individualist assumption is that philosophy predetermines a candidate's views, in the pluralist model it is the need to win that determines the candidate's philosophy. An important byproduct of nonideological parties, then, is that they come to look alike in philosophy. Thus, no longer can it be simply assumed that two parties provide a contrast to one another on major issues. Ideological sameness has not been lost on many of our recent ideological presidential candidates. For example, Barry Goldwater wanted to offer a "choice, not an echo" and George Wallace found "not a dime's worth of difference" between the two national parties. In many cities local parties offer little ideological contrast, sometimes because only one party exists.[17] However, let us not close this subject too soon. It remains an ongoing question as to whether local parties, in fact, tend toward the pluralist model.

Function of public decision maker

Elected on a vague platform, the decision maker, once in office, could not be expected to manufacture a party philosophy out of whole cloth and follow it carefully. Instead, many pluralists assume that the official is likely to continue anticipating and accommodating responses of the activists or groups on particular issues. He becomes a broker of power. If he finds, for example, that when he must decide issue A there are only two activists interested in that issue, and further that those activists agree as to what they want, his job is quite simple. But on the other hand, if every group and activist in the city is attentive to issue A and they are equally divided, his difficult task is to discover the coalition of interests which represent the most powerful actors. The most powerful and effective coalition, pluralists assume, generally gets the public policy it wants. The further implication is that a minority of the total electorate may get what it wants on many public questions: the principle of majority dominance gives way to minority rule. And finally, this view of the function of public decision makers implies that no comprehensive evaluation of public policy is likely to take place; instead, individual decision makers do as much or as little as they think they have to in the face of pressure. Rather than asking what are the long-range values to be served, decision makers are more likely to ask what ad hoc modifications can be made. Put quite simply, incrementalism means that "policies result from the reciprocal adjustments of leaders to one another rather than to long-range community goals."[18]

These two views of what constitutes the democratic process by no means exhaust the possibilities of putting together empirical findings into intelligible patterns. Probably no one researcher in the area of urban politics who thinks of himself as a pluralist would approve of the way I have arranged and related these assumptions. That fact in no way detracts from the usefulness of this particular patterning, however. What is always needed at the outset of any discussion of "democracy" is to fix some standard, however imperfect, so that we will have at least some point of reference in our discussion. Discourse can then proceed by comparing the variety of the world with the relatively greater simplicity of the abstract standard.

Criticism of Pluralistic Democracy

There are at least two directions that have been taken in criticizing pluralistic democracy. One direction is to argue that the description is not accurate — that is, that this is not the way our political processes work. I've already acknowledged the lack of agreement about assumptions regarding pluralist democracy. But even if we grant the basic accuracy of description, a second kind of criticism is possible. A number of political scientists — especially those labeled postbehavioral — argue that this vision of democracy is inadequate to the high ideals they associate with the democratic process. The most central elements of this latter kind of criticism are three: (1) Pluralist democracy tends to accept inequality of political power as a "given." (2) That fact produces a bias in behalf of the status quo. (3) The status quo retards the emergence of social and political changes which would facilitate expanded citizen participation.

Pluralism accepts unequal power

The research findings that individual American citizens are most accurately described as "apolitical clay" can easily be taken as evidence that, for democratic systems to operate, they "must rely on the wisdom, loyalty and skill of their political leaders, not on the population at large."[19] Robert Dahl has affirmed his acceptance of this view, putting it succinctly: "It goes without saying that except in exceedingly small groups, specific decisions must be made by a relatively few people acting in the name of the polity."[20] While Dahl, as a liberal democrat, is sympathetic to the idea of equality of political power, he nonetheless believes that it is impossible to realize in any large political system. In this view he is fairly representative of a number of pluralists.

Pluralism accepts the status quo

Though it does not *necessarily* follow from the assumption of inequality of power, there is nonetheless a strong tendency among pluralists to affirm the fundamental fairness of the current political process. Christian Bay, for example, finds many of the implications of behavioral research "antipolitical." "What is anti-political is the [behavioralists'] assumption, explicit or implicit, that politics, or at any rate American politics, is and must always remain primarily a system of rules for peaceful battles between competing private interests, and not an arena for the struggle toward a more humane and more rationally organized society."[21] Thus, concludes Jack Walker "Contemporary [behavioral] political scientists have stripped democracy of much of its radical elan and have diluted its utopian vision, thus rendering it inadequate as a guide to the future."[22]

Pluralism stunts participation

One implication of pluralism is that the political process can operate democratically without massive citizen participation; this idea has been severely, and to me convincingly, criticized. Robert Pranger has contended that the civilizing, educating functions of political participation are lost in a process which reduces politics to mere power seeking: "Political power promotes the distinctive values of power."[23] A political culture which acquiesces in the conclusion that political activity is essentially a contest for power ". . . becomes lopsided and human potential is short-circuited."[24] The reasoning on which these conclusions rest borrows heavily from Eric Erikson's theories of individual identity formation.[25] Pranger asserts that participation at various stages of personality development is necessary if the individual is to "mature" — that is, to become a reasonably autonomous person, capable of independent judgment, without excessive reliance on authority, and capable of empathy with others. Simplified somewhat, the analysis contends that persons have to be tutored by the results of their own actions to mature; they have to have personal successes and failures in order to form an identity. If, for some reason, they are retarded in their participation, particularly at the stages of adolescence and young adulthood, their sense of identity and their capacity for ongoing participation is correspondingly weakened. Pranger concludes, "The relevant issue is whether adults will continue to make political judgments as children make them, relying on hierarchial authority. . . . The politics of power tends to encourage such childlike dependence . . . but participation does not."[26]

To summarize this overview of democracy, it seems clear that the era of individualist democracy is gone. Pluralistic democracy seems a better description of our current political realities, but when judged by the high aspirations for a democratic process, it too seems inadequate. (The two modes of democracy are compared in summary in Table 2.1.) I am left with the conclusion that the words of Walt Whitman are as true today as when he wrote them in Democratic Vistas in 1871:

> We have frequently printed the word democracy. Yet I cannot too often repeat that it is a word the real jist of which still sleeps, quite unawakened, notwithstanding the resonance and the many angry tempests out of which its syllables have come, from pen or tongue. It is a great word, whose history, I suppose, remains unwritten, because that history has yet to be enacted.

THE ASPIRATION FOR COMMUNITY

I should now make explicit what I have been assuming throughout this section — that the assumptions of the preindustrial culture are congenial to individualist democracy and that urban-industrialism has been attended by the development of pluralistic democracy. What underlies the discontent of so many with urban-industrial pluralism is the feeling that important elements,

Table 2.1   **Comparison of the Assumptions of Individualist and Pluralist Democracy**

	Individualist	*Pluralist*
Basic Actor	Individual voting citizen assumed to: 1. be rational. 2. be fundamentally self-interested. 3. be willing and able to temper self-interest. 4. be highly motivated to know and participate in politics. 5. have access to necessary information.	Activists or groups which are politically attentive assumed to: 1. be rational. 2. be self-interested. 3. be without concept of public interest. 4. be highly motivated to know and participate in politics. 5. have access to necessary information.
Function of Party System	In both constructs: the party aggregates the desires of the basic actors for the purpose of electing officials.	
	Expressly ideological: based on a philosophy of governing and conviction that: 1. candidates should embrace ideology. 2. two ideological parties provide a contrast on all major issues.	*Nonideological:* groups are power seeking; result is that: 1. candidate is chosen on ability to win; ideology can be altered. 2. two parties become ideologically alike.
Function of Public Decision Makers	In both constructs: public decision maker manages conflict, creating binding policy.	
	Public decision maker *guided by ideology* he was elected to serve. This implies: 1. majority sentiment is served by officeholder. 2. content of policy is consistent with ideology. 3. comprehensive evaluation.	Public decision makers *guided by coalition* of most powerful actors attentive to the particular issue. This implies: 1. minority of electorate served by officeholder on most issues. 2. content of policy is linked to particular configurations of power; not ideologically consistent. 3. incremental evaluation.

especially the sense of community and the opportunity for face-to-face contact with other human beings has been retarded in this transition. Since a return to the culture in which individualist democratic assumptions might be recovered is impossible, and since so many of the elements of democratic pluralism seem unworkable, the task seems to be to find grounds on which to restore a sense of democratic community within an urban-industrial setting. There are those who would argue that this is an impossible task. And they may yet be right. Still, it would be premature to reach that conclusion since so little attention has been focused in precisely these terms. For present purposes, I am content merely to suggest the centrality of the question and to provide some preliminary insights which might aid us in the development of a *humanized pluralism*.

The term *community* like the term *democracy* has been used so variously that its popular meaning has become rather vacuous. We have all heard such diverse uses as community of Saints, community of scholars, world community, community of orangutans, and the community of Levittown. It seems there are at least two major ideas which are intertwined in these uses. One conception is that community occupies a definite physical location. This ecological conception guided Robert Park, a founder of the study of human ecology, when he described the characteristics of community as (1) a population, territorially organized; (2) a population that is more or less completely rooted in the soil it occupies; (3) a population whose individual units are living in a relationship of mutual interdependence that is symbiotic rather than societal.[27] There are a good many problems with this conception for our purposes. In the first place, not every common territory produces a sense of common destiny — a component many of us associate with human community. Residents of a suburban community like Levittown, for example, may share certain *interests*, but that they share a sense of common destiny and overall goals is questionable. A second problem with this conception of community is that it ignores our capacity to develop mutual understanding and social organization over broad expanses of territory. "Our communications system make possible a kind of unity over great space, our educational systems in our affluence make possible a kind of interaction among highly differentiated people never before known."[28] This is simply to say that you might have more in common with a fellow student in Japan than with the electrical engineer who lives next door.

The other conception of community is more social than geographic. Community is pictured in both empirically descriptive and normatively prescriptive meaning. In this usage, community becomes indivisible from human actions, goals, and values. It expresses our vague yearnings for commonality ". . . a communion with those around us, an extention of the bonds of kin and friend to all those who share a common fate with us."[29] This vague "we" feeling is generally fleeting unless it is reinforced by ongoing interaction. The opportunity for face-to-face contact and discussion is only the most obvious kind of interaction. Long-distance communication through the written word or via telephone or television is also a form of interaction which can build and sustain the sense of community.

In the remainder of this book I will use two terms to describe these two disparate uses of the term *community*. When the emphasis is on shared territory, I will use the term *neighborhood*. This reserves for the term *community* the more elaborate conception based on communal feelings.

> Definition 5. *Community* is a shared sense of common life and destiny, reinforced by ongoing interaction and characterized by many shared beliefs and values.

Contemporary history is full of indications that the sense of community is being lost.[30] Personal and cultural disintegration is a bright thread through the fabric of American urban life. This perception is a perplexing contrast to our understanding that the American society is increasingly well organized. Indeed we have become accustomed to thinking of ourselves as living in an "organizational" society, one in which our functional interdependence is clear and accepted. As our definition of community indicates, however, mere functional interdependence is not a sufficient condition of community. There are a number of conditions which, when present within interdependence may, in fact, become destructive of the sense of community. For example, excessive concern with individualism and competitiveness can serve to decisively divide humans from one another. Preoccupation with rationality can lead individuals in a search for standards of behavior which, while internally consistent, may become anti-human.[31] Extraordinary concern for the proper performance of one's specialized role can inhibit full understanding of the impact of one's actions on others. The lack of access to communications channels can prevent continuing interaction, thus allowing the long-run demise of common perceptions, beliefs, and values. And gross inequalities of wealth and power may disrupt mutual trust.

One of the ongoing concerns of this book, then, is with the state of community in the American city.

SUMMARY

Starting with the assumption that the city is here to stay, even though it is the source of major problems, I have offered the argument that systematic analysis, coupled with imaginative exploration of alternatives, are hopeful routes to useful knowledge of urban America. To facilitate analysis, I have defined and discussed five key concepts:

1. A *city* consists of a dense human population concentration on the land, the members of which have a high degree of social and economic interaction.

2. *Politics* is the most inclusive process by which social conflict is managed in a society.

3. *Individualist democracy* is that mode of democracy which is based on the assumptions that the basic political unit is the individual voter, that the political parties reflect distinguishable and contrasting philosophies of governing, and that the public decision maker's principal rule of decision is to implement that philosophy of governing.

4. *Pluralist democracy* is that mode of democracy which is based on the assumptions that the basic political unit is the group or the activist, that the political parties are nonideological and primarily power seeking, and that the public decision maker's principal rule of decision is that he should be guided by the coalition of the most powerful actors which are attentive to the specific issue.

5. *Community* means a shared sense of common life and destiny, reinforced by ongoing interaction, and characterized by many shared beliefs and values.

I have also elaborated in this section the normative and speculative perspective of this book. To briefly summarize the two major interpretations that have guided my concern and which organize this text:

1. *As presently constituted, American cities are incapable of creating and maintaining community.* The deterioration of the sense of community prevents the realization of a humane pluralism, so that pluralistic democracy has become almost wholly a power exchange process, retarding full individual and social development.

2. *The modern American city is best understood as a creation of economic forces.* The emergence of industrialism corresponds well with the development of urban centers. The forces which continue to transform our cities are heavily intertwined with economic development, from changes in land uses to the introduction of new technologies. Politics, while able to operate somewhat apart from these forces, I have assumed, is crucially linked to the economic life of the city. That interpretation is more fully explored in Part One.

NOTES

1. Murray Edelman, *The Symbolic Uses of Politics* (Urbana, Ill.: University of Illinois Press, 1964), p. 6.
2. Ibid.
3. George H. Sabine, "The Two Democratic Traditions," *The Philosophical Review*, 61 (1952): 451-474.

4. Robert M. MacIver, *The Web of Government* (New York: Macmillan, 1947), p. 198.

5. Henry B. Mayo, *An Introduction to Democratic Theory* (New York: Oxford University Press, 1960), Chap. 4.

6. Pluralist democracy is also put together from several sources, most notably from the work of Robert Dahl and Seymour Lipset. I should underscore that I have taken a great many liberties with their ideas and the ideas of others who contribute insight in this frame of reference. In order to simplify I have chosen to arbitrarily reconcile some contradictions, clarify some ambiguities and extend certain interpretations to what seem to me consistent conclusions. The major sources on which I drew are the following: Jack L. Walker, "A Critique of the Elitist Theory of Democracy," *American Political Science Review* 60 (June 1966): 285-295; also Robert Dahl's reply in the same volume, pp. 296-305; Robert A. Dahl, *A Preface to Democratic Theory* (Chicago: University of Chicago Press, 1956); Seymour Lipset, *Political Man* (New York: Anchor Books, 1960).

   See, in addition to the sources cited in this section, J. Ronald Pennock, *Liberal Democracy* (New York: Rinehart, 1950); A. Lawrence Lowell, *Public Opinion and Popular Government* (New York: Longman, Green and Co., 1962).

   The distinction between individualist democracy and pluralist democracy was written independently from Thomas Dye and Harmon Zeigler's work, but is parallel to their distinction between "democracy" and "pluralism." Cf. *Irony of Democracy*, (Duxbury, Mass.: Duxbury Press, 1971), pp. 14-18.

7. This and many of the following assumptions regarding the individual citizen are paraphrased from William C. Mitchell, *The American Polity* (New York: Free Press of Glencoe, 1962), pp. 74-76. The term *rational* is itself a thorny one. Here I mean only a minimal concept of rationality which would include: (1) the ability to stipulate a goal, and (2) the capacity to make choices which are consistent with that goal.

8. E. E. Schattschneider, *Party Government* (New York: Farrar and Rinehart, 1942).

9. By *ideology* I mean "systems of belief that are elaborated, integrated and coherent, that justify the exercise of power, explain and judge historical events, identify political right and wrong, set forth the interconnections (causal and moral) between politics and other spheres of activity, and furnish guides for action." From Herbert McClosky, "Ideology and Concensus In American Politics," *American Political Science Review* 58 (June 1964): 362.

10. The Committee on Political Parties of the American Political Science Association, *Toward a More Responsible Two Party System* (New York: Rinehart and Co. 1950), p. 22.

11. A more complete discussion of comprehensive evaluation is to be found in Charles E. Lindblom, "The Science of 'Muddling Through,'" *The Public Administration Review* 19 (1959): 79-88.

12. Angus Campbell et al., *The American Voter* (New York: John Wiley and Sons, 1960). For a review and criticism of this view, see V. O. Key, *The Responsible*

Electorate (Cambridge, Mass.: Belknap Press of Harvard University, 1966). Whether the American voter in Presidential elections is, in fact, issue oriented and in that sense rational, has been subject to important reinterpretation. Gerald Pomper has found growing issue orientation since the Eisenhower years. See his "From Confusion to Clarity: Issues and American Voters, 1956-1968," *American Political Science Review* 66 (June 1972): 415-428. Whether, and in what sense, and with what variations, local voters are issue oriented awaits similar analysis.

13. Robert A. Dahl, *Pluralist Democracy in the United States: Conflict and Consent* (Chicago: Rand, McNally, 1967), p. 24.

14. Robert Presthus, *Men at the Top* (New York: Oxford University Press, 1964).

15. Harvey Wheeler, " 'Duocracy' or the Imperfect Competition in Our Party System," in *The American Political Arena*, ed. Joseph R. Fiszman (Boston: Little, Brown, 1962), pp. 302-306.

16. Stanley Kelley, *Professional Public Relations and Political Power* (Baltimore: Johns Hopkins University Press, 1956); James Perry, *The New Politics* (New York: Potter, 1968). For contrary views, see Pomper, "From Confusion to Clarity."

17. See, for example, Charles E. Gilbert and Christopher Clague, "Electoral Competition and Electoral Systems in Large Cities," *Journal of Politics* 24 (1962): 323; and Duane Lockard, *The Politics of State and Local Government*, (New York: The Macmillan Co., 1963), pp. 239-240.

18. Lindblom, "Science of 'Muddling Through.' " See also Nimmo and Ungs, *American Political Patterns: Conflict and Consensus* (Boston: Little, Brown, 1969), pp. 388-390.

19. Jack Walker, "Critique of the Elitist Theory." For additional critical materials, succinctly summarized, see Dye and Ziegler, *Irony of Democracy*, pp. 14-18.

20. Robert Dahl, "Power, Pluralism and Democracy: A Modest Proposal," (Paper delivered at the 1964 Annual Meeting of the American Political Science Association, Chicago, September 9-12, 1964). As quoted in Peter Bachrach, *The Theory of Democratic Elitism: A Critique* (Boston: Little, Brown, 1967), p. 86.

21. Christian Bay, "Politics and Pseudo-Politics: A Critical Evaluation of Some Behavioral Literature," *American Political Science Review* 59 (March 1965): 39-51.

22. Jack Walker, "Critique of the Elitist Theory."

23. Robert Pranger, *The Eclipse of Citizenship: Power and Participation in Contemporary Politics* (New York: Holt, Rinehart and Winston, 1968), p. 91.

24. Ibid.

25. Especially *Childhood and Society* (New York: W. W. Norton, 1950), Chap. 7.

26. Ibid., pp. 99-100.

27. Robert E. Park, "Human Ecology," *The American Journal of Sociology* 42 (July 1936): 1.

28. David W. Minar and Scott Greer, *The Concept of Community* (Chicago: Aldine Publishing Co., 1969), p. xi.

29. Ibid., p. ix. It should be noted that this use differs markedly from that of Bert E. Swanson, *The Concern for Community in Urban America* (New York: Odyssey Press, 1970).

30. Cf. James Q. Wilson, "The Urban Unease: Community vs. City," originally published in *The Public Interest* 12 (Summer 1968): 25-39, reprinted in Henry J. Schmandt and Warner Bloomberg, *The Quality of Urban Life* (Beverly Hills: Sage Publications, 1969), pp. 455-472.
31. This discussion draws heavily on Robert Nisbet, *The Quest for Community* (New York: Oxford University Press, 1953), Chapt. 1.

PART ONE

Urban Environment
and Politics

Politics is crucially shaped by the environment in which it is set. Hence, knowledge of the environment is necessary to a full understanding of how politics works. Knowing the environment enlightens us in three important ways: First, it heightens our sense of *ordinary politics*, as distinct from the more dramatic and visible events which many think of as the central concerns of politics. By packaging political news, the media provide the service of concise summary but at the cost of making events often appear unconnected with the broader social, economic, and political processes. By contrast with the dramatic and newsworthy, ordinary politics has to do with the thousands of established patterns of thought and behavior, sometimes considered to be so unimportant that they are not really even seen; environments tend to be invisible. A large number of actual and potential conflicts are handled by the established pattern of reflex responses. This is because human skills are consciously learned, but later, through repetition, become reflexive in nature.[1] It is true that what most humans regard as most important and interesting in their lives are the novel and nonrepetitive activities; however, most social scientists understand that even the novel cannot be understood except in the context of the ordinary.

Second, the *environment imposes constraints*. Many of us, imbued as we are with that can-do attitude which is so prevalent in American society, seem to think that any new direction can be taken at any time. If a faucet leaks, fix it; if cars cause smog, ban them. However, such easy alternatives often have a hard time in the political system because the broader environment is not that pliant. Edward Banfield has put the position in extraordinarily bold form. In discussing the "logic" of metropolitan growth, he discerns three environmental factors which he chooses to call "imperatives" — demographic, technological, and economic.

> The word "imperatives" is used to emphasize the *inexorable, constraining character* of the three factors that together comprise the logic of metropolitan growth. . . . Given a rate of population growth, a transportation technology, and a distribution of income, *certain consequences must inevitably follow*; that the city and its hinterland must develop according to a predictable pattern. . . . The argument is not that nothing can be done to improve matters. Rather, it is that only those things can be done which lie within the boundaries — rather narrow ones to be sure — fixed by the logic of the growth process.[2]

Without accepting the strong determinacy of Banfield's formulation, we must still understand that we are not given the luxury of absolute free choice; the particular environment of the city already exists and its growth follows a kind of logic of its own.

Finally, by examining the setting of the urban politics, we learn something of *the sources of political change*. To fail to examine the environment of politics is to leave the impression that the political process is disembodied and autonomous, which is a distortion of the relationship it bears to the other processes of the culture. As David Easton has put it, without examining the environment, "we could not proceed to suggest a kind of analysis designed to shed light on the way in which political systems are able to persist and change or cope with the stresses to which they are constantly exposed."[3]

In short, in Part One, we shall examine the efforts that have been made to characterize the American urban environment — with special emphasis on (1) those components of the environment which aid our understanding of the shape of ordinary politics, (2) some of the constraints on political action and policy, and (3) the sources of pressure for change. In other words, the nature of the urban environment aids our understanding of the first of the functions of conflict representation which was discussed in the first chapter — that is — the development and expression of differing cultural values, interests, and opinion. Thus, Chapter 3 selects materials from the fields of urban ecology, sociology, economics, and geography which aid our understanding of the physical and social environment of the city. Chapter 4 reviews briefly the ordinary political patterns of Americans and reviews the role of the intellectual in shaping American perspectives on the city.

Since Part One is based on an incomplete research tradition, much of it will necessarily be speculative and suggestive. Indeed, much of the material used in this section is included to stimulate additional study of the "linkages" between political life and the environment in which it occurs.[4]

NOTES

1. Arthur Koestler, *The Act of Creation* (New York: The Macmillan Co., 1964), p. 38.
2. Edward Banfield, *The Unheavenly City* (Boston: Little, Brown, 1970), p. 24.
3. David Easton, *A Framework for Political Analysis* (Englewood Cliffs, N.J.: Prentice-Hall, 1965), p. 71. It should be noted that the systems analysis framework which Professor Easton has formulated is characterized by a much more careful effort to distinguish the political system from the environment. In my view this is an unnecessary and potentially misleading distinction, disposing us to emphasize the relative autonomy of the political process.
4. As Robert Lineberry has pointed out, this is a necessary effort at this stage in the development of urban political inquiry if we are to avoid the "ecological fallacy." Most simply, this means that "in the analysis of social units, the whole is greater than the sum of its parts." To illustrate: if the median income of Superior City is $50,000 a year, we are not justified in assuming that any particular resident of Superior City has such an income. One cannot simply extrapolate from part to whole or from whole to part. Instead, the actual connections must be adequately characterized. This makes our job of understanding more difficult, but our theories will be more reliable once we create them. Robert Lineberry, "Approaches to the Study of Community Politics," in *Community Politics*, ed. Charles Bonjean, Terry Clark, and Robert Lineberry (New York: The Free Press, 1971), p. 17.

Chapter 3

The Physical and Social
Environment of the City

The physical form of cities is shaped by ongoing human behavior. Obviously no two environments are precisely the same. As a result, each urban area in America seems superficially to be unique. Fortunately, sociologists and geographers have for many years been engaged in a search for patterns in the physical development of urban areas.

Ecology is the study of organisms "at home," in interaction with their living and nonliving environments. Systematic ecological reasoning was first applied to the study of plants in the late nineteenth century,[1] to animal life early in the twentieth century, and to human beings beginning in the 1920s. The earliest and most influential development in the field of human ecology is found in the work of two Chicago sociologists, Robert E. Park and Ernest W. Burgess.[2] Through the study of ecology — plant, animal, and human — we have come to realize how intricate and carefully balanced is that web of relationships which make up an ecosystem.

Robert Park put the fundamental postulate of human ecology succinctly when he said, "Most, if not all, cultural changes in society will be correlated with changes in territorial organization, and every change in the territorial and occupational distribution of the population will effect changes in the existing culture."[3] In adopting the ecological frame of reference in this chapter, we shall assume that there is an intimate congruity between the social order and physical space, between social and physical distance, and between social differentiation and residential proximity.[4] As a result, a map of a contemporary American city can be understood as "a dramatic example of a geographical division of labor."[5] That map is separated into component parts that are located at different points; yet the components are coordinated. As a result of this spacial differentiation, Scott Greer notes, "Where you live tells those persons with information about a city such things as your general in-

46

come level, the kind of people you live among, your probable prestige or social honor, and any number of less basic matters."[6] Of course, that's a long way from knowing you intimately, but it's a beginning.

What has all this to say to the study of politics? Most simply, I am assuming that the physical layout of the city affects social relationships, leading to social tensions, which create urban conflict, which necessitates the creation of public policy. We can examine that proposition (and don't forget that propositions are less binding than proposals) by reviewing selectively certain of the theories and findings of the field of ecology. Two questions will guide the organization of this review: (1) Why do cities locate where they do? and (2) What patterns of growth characterize American cities?

URBAN LOCATION THEORY

Why do cities locate where they do? Earlier in the Western tradition when cities were more self-sufficient, a need for defense was an important rationale for city location. Cities were located on hilltops, islands, or other protected sites. Walls and moats were added as further protection against attack.[7] Later, the best site for the capitol city of an emergent nation or empire was usually determined to be one of the commercial cities which had emerged along major transportation routes, often at the mouths of navigable rivers. In nineteenth- and twentieth-century industrial America, the most important locational factors have been "those associated with the production, distribution, and sale of goods."[8]

Just how central these economic factors are in determining the location of American cities is apparent in the work of White, Foscue, and McKnight.[9] They describe thirteen major variables influencing the location of manufacturing and thus the sites of modern cities. Those variables follow:

1. Proximity to market. Being close to distributors and consumers reduces transportation costs and is especially important for those industries that make products that are bulkier than their raw materials (e.g., pianos, capital goods, fragile or perishable products).

2. Proximity to raw materials. Minimizing transportation costs is especially important for industries that process perishables (e.g. canning) and those that involve considerable loss of weight in manufacturing (e.g. cement making and smelting).

3. Proximity to power. This is particularly important for those industries which require a large and constant input of power (e.g. textile mills).

4. Proximity to skilled manpower.

5. Transportation. Access to the appropriate mode of air, water, or ground transport, as well as the cost of each, can be determinative location factors.

6. Climate. This factor is increasingly important in this era of job mobility because it affects laboring and executive personnel.

7. Water supply. This can be an important factor since water is essential for such industries as chemical manufacture, rubber, iron and steel, pulp and paper.

8. Capital. Money is currently quite mobile, showing hesitancy only to cross certain international barriers or to enter regions of political disruption or social unrest.

9. Availability and cost of land.

10. "Human factor." The head of the company may have personal and idiosyncratic preferences, say, to be near his childhood home.

11. Taxation. Understandably, industries are attracted to areas with low tax rates.

12. The cost of living. This has a direct impact on wages and employee satisfaction.

13. Disposal of waste. This is not just a requirement for certain industries; it is becoming a consideration for all industries as public sensitivity to industrial pollution increases.

Gary, Indiana, is a near-perfect illustration of these locational factors. Gary is located in the midst of a large steel market, has easy access to necessary raw materials via the Great Lakes, and is in a central location where the cheapest direct route between coal and iron ore regions is crossed by rail lines linking Chicago and the West with the Atlantic seaboard. Gary's proximity to Chicago provides both access to business and financial institutions and a large labor supply.[10]

A number of other American cities — and especially the younger ones — were located for reasons that are less overtly economic. Los Angeles, for example, is difficult to explain in simple economic-geographic terms. Besides its partly sunny year-round climate, a few oil wells, and the mountain pass routes to the central valley of California and the Imperial Valley, L.A. has few economic locational advantages. Still, between 1925 and 1960, L.A.'s population tripled. To comprehend modern L.A., we must take account of technology and, specifically, the advent and impact of the automobile.

In general, technology makes topography, time, space, and distance less decisive in determining the location of cities. Technology enables us to substantially control our physical environment; we can compensate for poor climate with heat and air conditioning, remove the physical and economic barriers of distance with air flight over the most forbidding terrain, com-

A river, the railroad, and coalfields inspired the location of Kingsport, Tenn. Photograph courtesy of Eastman Chemical Corp., Kingsport, Tenn.

municate by telephone or television almost instantly, and even transport bulky materials thousands of miles in a short time. For the first time in history, man is able to locate cities where he chooses. However, it is interesting to note that technology has produced few startling departures in urban location patterns. The tendency has been to use technology to ratify and extend the essentially economic forces. Speaking of the impact of technology on contemporary urbanism, Lewis Mumford has said, "The important thing to recognize about this whole process is that although rapid transportation and instant communication have altered the scale of urban development they have not so far altered the pattern. This whole vast change has in fact been taking place within an obsolete urban framework."[11]

There are a number of more specific theoretic explanations of urban placement, nearly all of which rely on economic locational forces. Charles Cooley suggests that cities develop at those points at which the form of transportation must change: say from rail to highway, or from sea to land.

Cities locate at these points essentially because of the need to reload finished goods and raw materials, making it economical to process and sell them.[12] Other location theorists say large cities form so as to serve the needs of a cluster of smaller cities. The large city develops to provide services, banking, regional shopping, and manufacturing to the less developed rural area and small towns.[13] A third explanation of urban location patterns also focuses on the central city which serves smaller towns and rural area, but this theory emphasizes the roles of technology and communications in the location. Central Place Theory, as it is called, also assumes that a large city develops at an intermediate location which is central to the various productive enterprises it serves. However, the central place of a region need not be the largest city, but it *will* be the city which has taken on the functions that are the core of the region's economy. That central place may locate anywhere the communications and transportation technology permits; it is central in function, rather than central geographically.[14] There are a number of other attempts to explain city location. But with few exceptions they give primacy to the needs of business, services, and manufacturing in determining where a city will locate and develop.[15]

URBAN GROWTH AND DIFFERENTIATION

What patterns of growth characterize American cities? At a casual glance, urban growth often appears random and chaotic. However, the more careful city watcher quickly learns that the apparent disorderliness of urban growth is deceptive — that in fact there is a rather clear "logic" which has created patterns of land use.

A simple, almost simple-minded, explanation of urban growth is *demographic*. That is, cities grow because more people come there. At first the migration to American cities was from abroad. In the half century following the Civil War, 25 million immigrants — over a million during each of six years shortly after 1900 — came to the United States. Most of them settled in the cities. Since the immigration acts of the 1920s slowed the flow of "foreigners," migration to the city has been primarily internal, or from South to North and West, from Midwest to East and West, from farm to city. The principal participants in the new urban migration have been blacks along with a number of poor rural whites and a sprinkling of Mexicans in the West and Puerto Ricans in the East.[16] That people migrate to the city is, however, of less immediate interest to us than why they migrate there. The city is "where the action is," the most likely place to find a good job, good opportunity to advance one's social and economic position. For those opportunities to be there, presumably there must be a viable local economy. Consequently, the factors that facilitate the growth and development of the economic base of the city are crucial determinants of the shape the city takes. This point can be illustrated, and properly qualified by examining first some of the materials of urban growth and analysis undertaken by urban economists and second, some of the theories produced by urban ecologists to explain the developmental patterns of urban areas.

The Urban Economic Base

One of the most widely used analytical frameworks for examining the urban economy is the export-base construct.[17] Export-base theory assumes that it is the basic economic activities that build cities. A basic activity is one that brings income into the city from outside, whereas nonbasic activities supply goods and services within the local area but do not bring money from outside. Thus the urban area is depicted as a wide open economy which is heavily dependent on external trade, very much like the small industrially advanced nation in the world market. Both Switzerland and Wichita, it is assumed, must export or die. The best examples of basic activities are, of course, factories that sell their products outside the city.

Economic geographers have undertaken a number of studies of the basic/nonbasic ratios of American cities.[18] For example, a study of the economic base of Oshkosh, Wisconsin, found six nonbasic employees for every ten basic ones; Madison, Wisconsin, has eight nonbasic for every ten basic.[19] Relatively higher employment in basic industries has been found in most of the studies of small or medium-sized cities, which implies the necessity of large basic industry employment in the early stages of urban growth. As cities become larger and, economically speaking, more mature, it has been found that the basic-to-nonbasic employment ratios tend to approach equality. "With greater urban size comes a tendency toward greater local self-sufficiency."[20]

While export-base theory is by no means universally accepted by urban economists[21] it has come to be accepted in its most immediate implication, that is "the export industries clearly generate a net flow of income into the local economy, from which the necessary imports can be financed. In this most immediate sense of current money flow, the export sector is basic and the local service sector is derivitive in origin."[22] The centrality of basic industries to the life of the city raises fundamental political questions: Does "good" policy protect and promote basic industry? Must it be protected at all stages in the history of the city? To what extent must the needs of basic industries be given priority over other competing interests? How much political conflict is generated by the needs of basic industry? These are undeniably important questions, but they are, as yet, only partially answered by the experts.

Dynamics of Urban Growth

A number of additional political questions are suggested by the particular land-use patterns that result as cities grow. Although the internal structure of each city is in some degree unique in its particular combination of details, most American cities at the very least have business, industrial, and residential districts.

Let us review some of the most basic theories of urban land use to clarify the forces of internal differentiation in the city. Why is it, say, that the poor tend to concentrate in particular areas of a city? Why is the central business district located where it is? Locations of particular urban functions are partially the result of conscious governmental decisions, of course, but primarily they result from the tendency of urban land to be put to "its highest use" — highest, in this case, meaning the use which yields the largest dollar return.

Concentric zones

The Concentric Zone Hypothesis is undoubtedly the best known ecological construct. It was the formulation of the founders of the "classical" school of ecology, Ernest W. Burgess and Robert E. Park.[23] While it has been decisively criticized in many of its particulars, it still provides useful introductory insight into the urban shaping forces. The hypothesis states that the pattern of growth of cities can best be understood as producing five concentric zones, each zone defining an area of distinctive land use. (See Figure 3.1.)

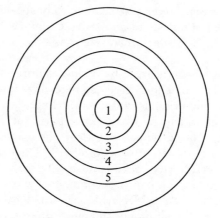

Concentric Zone Theory

Figure 3.1.

1. *The central business district.* The physical center of the city, this zone is the site of the focal activities of urban life. It is the retail district with its department stores, shops, office buildings, banks, hotels, theaters.

2. *The zone in transition.* Encircling the downtown area is a zone of mixed uses: some business and light manufacturing, but primarily deteriorating residences and rooming houses — slums, to put it indelicately. Here are the regions of poverty and of organized and unorganized crime and vice. In many American cities, the zone in transition has been inhabited primarily by colonies of recent immigrants who must have low-cost housing and close proximity to work.

3. *The zone of independent workingmen's homes.* This area is inhabited by industrial workers who have escaped from the zone in transition but who desire to live within easy access of their work. In American cities, the second generation of immigrant families have lived here.

4. *The zone of better residences.* Here are more expensive, usually single-family dwellings, upper income apartment buildings, and occasionally exclusive restricted neighborhoods.

5. *The commuter's zone.* In this zone are located spotty developments of satellite cities connected to the central city by lines of rapid transit. Park and Burgess assumed that these satellite cities would be populated largely by upper income residents who could afford the relatively high costs of commuting.

These physical divisions of the city were obviously also social areas: as the classical ecologists noted, the central business district, for example, is predominantly a homelessman's area, the rooming house district is the habitat of the working-class family, the area in which the first immigrants settled is the locus of the patriarchal family transplanted from Europe, and so on.[24]

The concentric zone model is a particularly useful formulation of urban growth patterns because it emphasizes the intimate connections between physical differentiation and social differentiation. Social differentiation, by its nature, creates basic political cleavages.

The classical ecologist formulation is also of interest to students of urban politics because it links social differences in the city with growth itself. Growth creates the five zones of the model. Economic and technical advances permit mobility, that is "change of residence, change of employment, or change of location of any utility or service."[25] Growth creates the tendency for each zone in the model to extend its area by invading the next outer zone. So as more working-class people move out of the zone in transition into the workingmen's residential zone, that zone becomes larger, creating the conditions which led earlier residents of that area to relocate in the next outward zone. In this way the forces of growth may be said to have a logic of their own. A number of social conflicts are generated in this process. When minority-group residents begin to invade a previously homogeneous area, for example, the conflict can be violent.

The zone in transition is a particularly fascinating element of the concentric circle model. Here are the "problem" groups, the vice and crime subcultures, the poor, the black, the Bohemian subcultures. When we speak of the "urban problem," most of us are thinking primarily of this area. Many proposed solutions aim at eliminating or rehabilitating slums. Such solutions, however, tend to ignore the insight of the classical ecologists — that the slum is an unintended consequence of urban growth forces. In Burgess' formulation, the zone in transition results when economic men do what comes naturally. Slums develop because the land which is immediately adjacent to the central business district is increasing in value while the buildings on the land are decreasing in value. This happens because the land may be a potential site for high-income-producing uses, but the building on the land will probably have to be torn down to accommodate the new function.

Let us illustrate the process with a hypothetical lot near a central business district: currently on the lot is a large rambling old home, built 100 years ago by a wealthy resident at a time when the city was smaller and the site was on its periphery. The growth of the central business district has made this lot closer and closer to the center of the city. At some point, a local real estate speculator, anticipating that the lot would some day be a possible business site, purchases it, hoping that its value will continue to increase. The purchaser's best strategy is to hold onto the property until he can obtain the highest possible price for it. In the meantime he must minimize his losses by making some use of the house. It is reasonably inexpensive to divide the house into small apartments or rooms to rent. Improvements seem out of the question since our speculator knows that money put into the building comes out of his eventual profit margin when he sells the site for the land. His rational economic strategy is simply to minimize costs while the land increases in value. Thus is born the rat-infested, badly kept-up, inadequately heated tenement so characteristic of slum areas in America. The "heavy" in this drama — the slumlord of popular rhetoric — turns out to be not a hard-hearted Simon Legree, but instead the hero from the urban growth drama: he turns out to be Mr. America doing business as usual. Small wonder one of the slogans of the ecology movement has become, "We have met the enemy and he is us."

We should not take the tenets of classical ecology too literally. They imply unnecessary determinism of economic and biological forces.[26] No area of the city can be assumed to be "natural" in the sense that its location is inevitable.[27] It has been shown that many portions of the city are not put to their

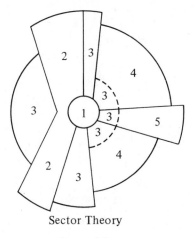

Sector Theory

Figure 3.2.

highest economic use at all. Some are deliberately kept as they are for more symbolic reasons: the scenic old Beacon Hill area of Boston, an upper-middle-income residential area, is an example of symbolic land use. So, too, is Central Park on Manhattan island. Moreover, the classical ecological viewpoint does not help us understand contemporary mid-city blight.[28] It provides insights into the reasons for formation of slums, but tells us little about their dynamics once they are formed. As a result, this particular set of theories provides few workable guidelines for the creation of public policies.

Sectors

Certain criticisms of the concentric zone theory have moved toward the creation of alternative generalizations. One such alternative is a theory of axial development, according to which urban growth takes place along main transportation routes, resulting in pie-shaped wedges or sectors radiating from the central business district. Transportation routes, highways, and freeways tend to create social and land-use barriers and become area boundaries. (See Figure 3.2.) Implicit in this theory of growth pattern is the assumption that a particular axis of transportation usually abuts lands used for a single type of land use: thus, a particular land use originating near the center of the city migrates outward as the city grows. For example, a high-rent residential area in the eastern quadrant of the city would tend to migrate outward, keeping always in the eastern quadrant, resulting in a pie shape.

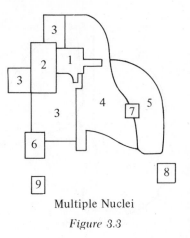

Multiple Nuclei

Figure 3.3

Multiple nuclei

Unlike the two other theories of urban growth, the multiple nuclei theory finds no single center to be the dominant force in urban development. It is founded on the premise that cities develop multiple business, industrial, and residential nuclei. (See Figure 3.3.) These several growth-creating locations tend to develop separately and at different rates; therefore no single generalized land-use pattern is applicable to all cities. Four factors determine the rise of each nucleus: (1) certain activities require specialized facilities, (2) like activities tend to group together, (3) certain unlike activities are incompatible, and (4) some activities cannot afford the high rents of the most desirable sites.[29] Thomlinson has observed that the polinuclear thesis is "less a theory than a negation of all theories."[30] He believes ecologists are able to make more reliable generalizations about the properties of cities than can be asserted by this theory of multiple nuclei.

Summary of Urban Growth Theories

The theories of both urban growth and urban location tend to assume the primacy of economic forces in creating and shaping the city. It has been suggested that certain export industries are especially crucial in activating and maintaining urban growth. As a recent summary of the literature concluded, "Cities are almost always multifunctional, but in almost every instance the principal urban functions are economic in nature."[31]

Technology has permitted the extension of development, facilitating spatial differentiation. The broadest lines of spatial separation seem to be: (1)

the separation of residential from business-industrial sites, which occurs as individuals are able to manage the increased costs of moving away from the central city areas, and (2) initial centralization of business-industrial activities to permit mass production, followed by decentralization as communication and transportation technology have improved.

Growth, then, is a major urban imperative. However, there are a few who would make growth a central political issue. As Sharkansky has commented, "There is no clear division between those who would foster or oppose growth. Growth is a widely supported value that ranks with patriotism and individualism in the pantheon of American symbols."[32] Yet much of this analysis suggests what subsequent discussion will provide additional evidence for — that many urban pathologies and the conflicts over how to deal with them are unintended consequences of economic growth itself. Growth is thus a latent political issue in many cities.[33]

CONSEQUENCES OF URBANISM FOR THE SOCIAL
AND PERSONAL ENVIRONMENT

"Social relations are . . . inevitably correlated with spatial relations. . . ."[34] This simply means that persons sharing similar values, interests, or needs tend to cluster together, and to separate themselves from unlike groups. There are three distinctive bases of urban social segregation: ethnicity, social rank, and life style.[35] First, we note that the larger American cities are mosaics, composed of elements of cultures from other parts of the world. New York City, for example, contains settlements of immigrants from virtually every nationality of any size — Irish, Italian, German, Japanese, etc. This kind of social differentiation is called *ethnicity*. Second, people tend to distinguish among themselves on the basis of their jobs. People in similar occupations receive much the same share of goods and services and of the social advantages. They may attain similar educational levels. Furthermore, when people become accustomed to, or immersed in, the world of their jobs, they come to share ". . . a way of looking at things, of conceptualizing and evaluating, which is unique to (their) kind of job and no other. In other words . . . (they) develop little cultural worlds of their own."[36] Subcultures emerge, based on differences in occupation, income, and education. The term applied to this basis of social differentiation is *social rank*. The third ground of social groupings we call *life style*. There are some who, irrespective of their ethnic origins or social rank, prefer a particular mode of living. They may be prepared to pay the costs of living near the beach, for example, to permit a life style oriented to swimming, surfing, or voyeurism. And in most major cities there is an area like Park Avenue in New York where the wealthy bear ex-

Marshall Henrichs

Multi-unit housing seems the only practical land use for urban areas; the fate of the older homes on the left is quite predictable.

traordinarily high rents to have the advantages of easy access to fine restaurants, theaters, and museums. It is the life style of urbane wealth which determines their location. Such social segregation by ethnicity, social rank, and life style means that people develop differing expectations as to what goals the city ought to serve.

In addition to these patterns of social segregation which we are accustomed to think of as "normal," we also associate urbanization with social pathologies. A brief review of several social manifestations of urban life will serve to heighten our sense of the connection between the social environment and politics as well as to foreshadow some of the political issues cities face. In general, this section deals with some of the highlights of the vast literature dealing with social disorganization, urban personality, anomie, the perceived decline of the family, and the character of "lower-class" behavior.

Theories of Social Disorganization

We are all familiar with the view that cities are sick — that they are, as Thomas Jefferson described them, "hotbeds of vice and crime." Cities, from this perspective, incubate vast and deadly personal and social pathologies, ranging from personal psychoses to organized crime. A whole tradition of sociological study has grown up around the assumption that urban sickness is the result of the social disorganization that has resulted from the breaking apart of society on the reefs of change. Social disorganization generally means "the disruption of relations between the functioning parts of a social system so as to jeopardize the attainment of common goals."[37] Marshal Clinard, among others, specifically traces social disorganization to urbanization: "Urbanism, with its mobility, impersonality, individualism, materialism, norm and role conflicts, and rapid social change appears to be associated with higher incidence of deviant behavior."[38] Others, like Winslow, prefer to think of certain forms of deviant behavior as primarily a result of social transition. As change renders old modes questionable, new modes may emerge. Some individuals may withdraw, still others may engage in violence or politics, in an effort to adapt.[39] Whatever the best explanation — disorganization or transition — deviancy correlates well with the rise of urbanism. The classical ecologists made those associations explicit; Walter Reckless summarized their conclusions:

> Conventional crime, delinquency, mental illness in general and schizophrenia in particular, suicide, prostitution, vagrancy, dependency, illegitimacy, infant mortality, as well as associated problems such as high death and disease rates, have been found to vary with the areas of the city. The highest rates are in Zones I and II (of the concentric zone model) and become successively lower out from this area. The evidence on alcoholism and the manic-depressive psychoses does not show quite this pronounced pattern for, although there are probably higher rates in Zones I and II, the differences are not as marked from one part of the city to another.[40]

The simple formulation was that cities create social disorganization, and social disorganization causes deviancy. This assumption of the classical formulation has been dismissed by subsequent research on deviant behavior; the concept "social disorganization," itself, has not even stood up.[41] William F. Whyte's criticism is typical.[42] Based on his 3½-year observation of an Italian slum district, he concluded that immigrant slums were not disorganized at all. Whyte, along with subsequent students, found subdivisions of informal associations and relationships among those associations in the slum. As he found it, the problem of slum life was not lack of organization but "failure of the slum's own social organization to mesh with the structure — the middle-class structure — of society around it."[43] More recently, Eliot Liebow has drawn much the same conclusions about the streetcorner society of his subjects, the poor black residents of Washington, D.C.[44] These findings press upon us the realization that the city is not disorganized so much as it is the locus of a variety of people with differing goals and interests, and differing abilities to accomplish them.

Urban Personality: Normally Abnormal?

Other scholars have argued that so-called normal urban behavior is, in fact, pathological. Simmel wrote his classical essay, "The Metropolis and Mental Life," over a half century ago. As he saw it, city culture was unhealthy, a money culture. The money economy needs and creates urban dwellers who must become blasé and intellectualized in order to survive. Simmel insisted that there were intrinsic connections between the money economy and intellectualism because they "share a matter-of-fact attitude in dealing with men and things; and in this attitude, a formal justice is often coupled with an inconsiderate hardness."[45] This means, according to Simmel, that the intellectually sophisticated urban dweller comes to be indifferent to the individuality of persons and things around him. The money economy, too, is unconducive to individuality and emotion: "Money is concerned only with what is common to all; it asks for exchange value, it reduces all quality and individuality to the question: How much?"[46]

Obviously, Simmel felt that normal urban behavior was a culturally created problem. In his discussion of "bureaucratic personality," Robert Merton makes much the same point. Urbanism, industrialization, and technology have created large organizations. Merton says individuals adapt to those organizations by assuming bureaucratic personalities. He emphasizes the incapacities which attend bureaucratic personality, incapacities which adversely affect both the person himself and the functioning of the organization.[47] Effective bureaucracy demands reliability of personal response and devotion to regulations. Such devotion to the rules easily results in their being transformed into absolutes. The rule or law, which is initially seen as merely instrumental, thus becomes an ultimate goal. This both stunts individual members of the organization and interferes with the organization's adaptation to circumstances not anticipated by the rules. Emphasis on impersonality in bureaucracies reinforces the matter-of-factness in interpersonal relations that Simmel noted and produces a high level of status anxiety, further alienating members of the organization from one another.

It is not that all theorists of the contemporary society view all normal behaviors as pathological. What this selection of materials from the studies of urban sociology suggests, however, is the difficulty of determining whether any behaviors are so clearly good as to justify compelling others, through an exercise of governmental or private power, to emulate them. These writings of

I love life
And life loves me
I'm as happy as can be
A happier man nowhere
exists
I think I'll go
And slash my wrists

NO EXIT
STAIRWAY 2

Harvey Silver

American urban graffiti: a state of anomie produces uncertainty and despair.

Merton and Simmel are obviously speculative; much of the writing on personal and social pathologies in the city is based on more empirical work — the studies of anomie, for example.

Anomie

A different, though related, explanation of deviance begins with the view that rapid change can produce a loss of individual and social norms.[48] This formulation assumes that *excessively rapid change*, whether produced by urbanization, technological development, or a chain of personal life experiences may leave groups and individuals robbed of their confidence both in themselves and in established norms. In this state, they lack standards of good and bad; as a result, they either flounder in uncertainty, despair, and self-doubt, or compulsively grab for new norms. In their rush to acquire new norms, which they require to give their lives structure — reference points —

these people must settle for whatever is available: either new standards set up by contemporaries whose assertions may well fail to inspire confidence, or older, more rigid and reliable standards which also fail to convince because their irrelevance grows daily more apparent.

Killian and Grigg have modified earlier assumptions that anomie is created entirely by urbanism. In a study of whites and blacks in both small-town and urban settings, they have found that, for the white man, anomie was more closely related to position in the social structure than to urban residence although "urban residence and low status have an additive effect."[49] For blacks, they found the incidence of anomie to be high for ". . . both small town residents and lower class urban Negroes."[50]

There are many versions and applications of the concept of anomie in the literature of social science. Sociologist Robert Merton's formulation of the conception is particularly interesting to students of urban politics. He says that lower-status and minority group members suffer from the despair of anomie and a sense of personal and social isolation. At the same time, however, they hold social values which compel achievement and success.[51] As a result of this uncomfortable personal state, the low-status person may exhibit a variety of tendencies — prejudice, authoritarianism, political apathy, and religious orthodoxy, for example. In a political use of this formulation, Thompson and Horton have found that the sense of alienation among the relatively powerless urban dwellers may be responsible for their consistent voting against a number of local referenda.[52]

However, several political scientists have expressed doubts about the adequacy of the concepts anomie or alienation to explain political behavior. For example, Crain, Katz, and Rosenthal, studying opposition to fluoridating local water supplies, concluded that the cities with the most educated populations "have the most trouble with fluoridation. Yet, from studies of alienation, we might have expected the opposite."[53] They criticize the previous studies of alienation as providing inadequate explanations for any particular outcome, because those studies "tend to assume that there cannot exist a legitimate opposition to the innovation in question."[54]

McClosky and Scharr have reformulated the conception of anomie by emphasizing its psychological rather than its social dimensions.[55] After formulating, testing, and validating a new scale for studying anomie, they suggest that "it may not be defensible to conceptualize anomie as a unique disease that affects man in certain kinds of societies."[56] Instead, they feel that anomie may be one of many symptoms of a "negativistic, despairing outlook" both on one's own life and on the place in which one lives. Reformulated in this way, they suggest further research to clarify the incidence and political impact of anomie. When that is accomplished, we should be in a better position to assess the contribution to anomie of particular urban settings.

The Decline of the Family?

Urbanization has contributed to the transformation of the family.[57] The popular view that urbanism has caused a universal breakdown of the family, however, has not been supported by recent studies. The family has been changed, but precisely how?

The classical ecologists theorized that the heterogeneity and fast pace of large cities would weaken the primary group relationships (i.e., relationships characterized by intimate, face-to-face contacts) within the urban family, thus fostering the emergence of the "mass society" with its attendant personal and social disorganization. A number of studies of American cities cast that conclusion in doubt; Wendell Bell's findings in San Francisco are fairly representative.[58] He studied four areas of the city: Mission, a low-rent, rooming house area; Outer Mission, a neighborhood of low-rent houses; Pacific Heights, composed mostly of high-rent apartments; and St. Francis Wood, which has expensive homes. Bell calculated informal association among neighbors, coworkers, relatives, and friends. Interviewing only men over 21, he found that the majority in each of the neighborhoods got together with some informal group at least once a week: 62% in Mission, 63.4% in Pacific Heights, 71.8% in Outer Mission, and in St. Francis Wood, 73.8%. The figures for informal contact specifically with relatives are contained in Table 3.1. Bell found only a very small percentage of men totally isolated from informal contacts (less than 1% in all but Mission, which had 2.9%). Both Axelrod and Greer report similar findings from studies conducted in Detroit and Los Angeles.[59] These studies led to the conclusion that "the extended family may have lost its function as an economic producing unit in the city, but relatives continue to be an important source of companionship and mutual support."[60]

These findings remain somewhat inconclusive, however, for they leave several key questions unanswered. First, we are unsure whether the reported figures show lower, the same, or higher numbers of informal relationships than the number in nonurban settings. Second, there seems to be no way of determining from these studies what the *quality* of the primary group relationships are. It just could be that families are intensely involved with one another, but enjoying it less.

On this latter point, Richard Sennett has suggested that urban middle-class families exert continued control on each other but that they tend to insulate their members from the diverse realities of city life; "(Families) become, in the words of Theodore Dreiser, little islands of propriety, self-contained, intense and narrow in their outlook, self-restrictive and routine in the tenor of their family activities."[61] As a result, middle-class families tend to perpetuate what Sennett calls a "guilt over conflict" syndrome, teaching

Table 3.1   Frequency of Face-to-Face Family Interactions in Four Sections of the City

Frequency of Interactions, by Group	Low Familism, Low Socioeconomic Status (Mission)	High Familism, Low Socioeconomic Status (Outer Mission)	Low Familism, High Socioeconomic Status (Pacific Heights)	High Familism, High Socioeconomic Status (St. Francis Wood)
About once a week or more	33.1%	45.3%	29.8%	42.3%
A few times a month	10.5	13.0	14.7	13.1
About once a month	12.8	14.1	13.1	11.3
A few times a year	10.5	13.5	16.2	19.0
About once a year	7.5	4.1	11.5	6.0
Never	25.6	10.0	14.7	8.3
Total	100%	100%	100%	100%
No. of cases	172	170	191	168

Source: Adapted from Wendell Bell, "The City, the Suburb and a Theory of Social Choice," in *The New Urbanization*, ed. Scott Greer et al. (New York: St. Martin's Press, 1968, pp. 140-141.

avoidance of conflict — and therefore, we might add, avoidance of politics. Sennett observes that contemporary middle-class families have become "safe places in the city at the cost of becoming suffocatingly dull."[62]

Primary group relationships do not remain similarly intact in all kinds of neighborhoods. Bell found that not as much informal association occurs in lower-income areas, but another study suggests differences as between the races; it found more association among neighbors in certain black neighborhoods than in poor white ones.[63] Another point has been well established — that the black family, like other economically marginal families, has generally become mother centered as it has become urban. The Moynihan

Table 3.2   Father Absent from Home, in Percent

Lower Class		Middle Class		Upper Class	
White	Black	White	Black	White	Black
15.4	43.9	10.3	27.9	0.0	13.7

Source: Adapted from Robert O. Blood, Jr. and Donald Wolfe, *Husbands and Wives: The Dynamics of Married Living* (New York: Free Press of Glencoe, 1960), p. 34.

Report documented this development and set forth some of its consequences. The incidence of fathers absent from the home is summarized in Table 3.2. Females have dominated the black family. This is often so, even in homes where the father is physically present. As with all low-income families, "husbands have unusually low power,"[64] which is a cumulative result of "discrimination in jobs . . . , the segregated housing and the poor schooling of Negro men." In a Detroit sample it was found that in 44 percent of the black families, the wife was dominant, as against 20 percent of white wives.[65]

The consequences of this mother-centered pattern are speculative in many particulars. But the Moynihan Report suggests that lower IQ test results and less satisfactory school and job performance may be partially traceable to the fatherless home, along with high delinquency and crime rates. "Negro children without fathers founder — and fail," he asserts. In making the case for national action, Moynihan acknowledges no special reason that male dominance of the home is inherently preferable. "However, it is clearly a disadvantage for a minority group to be operating on one principle, while the great majority of the population . . . is operating on another."[66]

Can we justifiably create policy to break up black families where they are mother centered? Or are less drastic measures in order? If poverty, not blackness, is what creates mother-centered families, would not a minimum-wage guarantee suffice? The black power movement marked the beginning of renewed efforts of black Americans to revive the male domination of the black family. Blacks have called upon themselves to affirm that "black is beautiful" and for black males to reassert their central position in the family.

But what of the white family? It remains a source of companionship, but Sennett paints the middle-class family as suffocatingly gray and dull; is this the alternate pattern to commend to the minorities, the poor, and each other? Or might not programs to induce acceptance of conflict and tolerance of other life styles aimed at the middle class be equally plausible public policy alternatives?

"I understand you. You understand me. We understand the kids, and the kids understand us. That's why I fall asleep every night after dinner."

The logical, if laughable, end result of middle-class insulation is this all-too-familiar situation. Drawing by Frascino; © 1971 The New Yorker Magazine, Inc.

"Lower-class" Behavior

A strikingly different version of the social-psychological character of the "lower class" emerges from the provocative work of Edward Banfield. Banfield contends that "certain styles of life that are learned in childhood and passed on as a kind of collective heritage operate (within the limits set by the logic of growth) to give the city its characteristic form and most of its problems."[67] These life styles Banfield associates not with race so much as with "class," which he defines in a unique way. He avoids the usual sociological meaning of class as relative social standing measured by attributes like income, education, or occupation; instead he defines class in terms of the individual's "psychological orientation toward providing for a more or less distant future."[68] The upper classes are able, according to Banfield, to imagine a future and to discipline themselves to sacrifice present for future satisfaction; the lower class is not. As a result, the lower class becomes a "problem" population. Banfield's description of "lower" class behavior is worth quoting at length:

> *The Lower Class.* At the present-oriented end of the scale, the lower-class individual lives from moment to moment. If he has any awareness of a future, it is of something fixed, fated, beyond his control: things happen *to* him, he does

not *make* them happen. Impulse governs his behavior, either because he cannot discipline himself to sacrifice a present for a future satisfaction or because he has no sense of the future. He is therefore radically improvident: whatever he cannot consume immediately he considers valueless. His bodily needs (especially for sex) and his taste for "action" . . . take precedence over everything else — and certainly over any work routine. He works only as he must to stay alive, and drifts from one unskilled job to another, taking no interest in the work.

The lower-class individual has a feeble, attenuated sense of self; he suffers from feelings of self-contempt and inadequacy, and is often apathetic or dejected. . . . In his relations with others he is suspicious and hostile, aggressive yet dependent. He is unable to maintain a stable relationship with a mate; commonly he does not marry. He feels no attachment to community, neighbors, or friends (he has companions, not friends), resents all authority (for example, that of policemen, social workers, teachers, landlords, employers), and is apt to think that he has been "railroaded" and to want to "get even." He is a nonparticipant: he belongs to no voluntary organizations, has no political interests, and does not vote unless paid to do so.[69]

Banfield's analysis of class as an urban "given" brings him to the brink of contending that nothing substantial can be done about the problems of the lower class; at one point he reports that "strong correlations have been shown to exist between IQ scores and socioeconomic status, and some investigators have claimed that the correlations are largely attributable to genetic factors."[70] Then, he backs away somewhat, saying that he assumes that *time horizon* (the ability to anticipate the future) is a trait passed on to an individual early in childhood — still implying strong determinism. The policy implications of Banfield's interpretation obviously call for measures designed to *control* the worst behaviors of the problem groups, since the prospects for changing them are remote. Some of his many recommendations are: paying "problem families" to send infants to day schools designed to "bring the children into normal culture," permitting the police to "stop and frisk" in high-crime areas, abridging the freedoms of those who are extremely likely to commit violent crimes by preventative detention, and "prohibition of live television coverage of riots and/or incidents likely to provoke them."[71] Banfield, along with many average Americans, seems to have given up on programs to change the conditions which create the problems and, instead, has come to concentrate on treating their symptoms.

SUMMARY

Urban politics is defined and shaped by the physical and social setting from which it emerges. The central purpose of this chapter has been to survey this urban environment. The attempt has not been exhaustive; instead, I have selected a number of explanations, theories, and speculations which (1) help us understand the broadest outlines of prevailing urban conflicts and (2) suggest fruitful lines of inquiry to pursue in linking politics with its environment. The broadest outline of the links between the forces that create and cities social conflict which this chapter has suggested is:

1. *The location and physical character of American cities is primarily determined by economic forces, and augmented by technological developments.*

2. *Physical differentiation of the city corresponds with the tendency of persons to segregate within the city on the basis of similarities in their ethnic backgrounds, economic positions, or life styles.*

3. *By minimizing the contact between people with differing backgrounds, values, interests, and ongoing experiences, this social differentiation provides at least one basis for social conflict.*

4. *Thus, some (not all) social conflicts produce some (not all) political conflicts.* "Not all" political conflicts are generated by social conflicts because some social conflicts are handled without recourse to public debate, as when a policeman arrests a rapist; further, not all conflicts result from social differences — some are generated by ideas and ideologies, others by politicking itself.

Several studies have been reviewed which suggest that cities create social and personal pathologies by fostering social disorganization and anomie and by breaking down family and primary group relationships. Still others like Simmel and Merton have suggested that even the patterns of "normal" adjustment to the city lead to the pathological manifestations of a money culture and "bureaucratic personality."

A number of social theorists are impatient with the theories of social disorganization and anomie — and equally impatient with the popular assumptions that cities provide an inherently hostile environment. Some find it difficult to call particular behaviors pathological simply because they deviate from accepted norms. They prefer social theories that recognize that deviancy can result from a changing social setting. George B. Vold's conflict theory of deviant behavior goes one step further and emphasizes that deviance is often political. Vold insists that gangs and many criminals should be seen as interest groups conflicting with other groups which are defending an in-group code.[72] Juvenile gangs conflict with adult society; conscientious objectors conflict with the government; labor groups conflict with management. In Vold's formulation we are asked to view normalcy and its code, the law, as the will of the dominant interest groups. This drives the less powerful and less politically sophisticated into rancorous conflict to obtain what they feel they must have. Vold's perspective leaves us with the clear implication that much of what is conventionally called deviant behavior is better conceived as conflict generated by a pluralistic culture.

The political consequences of these social theories are many. Most broadly we need to recognize that the social setting generates the conflicts which the political process is called on to manage. At the same time, the goal of public policy is to reconcile those conflicts when necessary and possible. The urban environment is both the subject and the object of the political process. More specific connections of these phenomena will be made in subsequent chapters.

There are also broad political questions raised by the nature of the urban physical environment. Economic growth is the central feature of the physical city and many believe that to make policy which would assure that cities become liveable would necessitate challenging the value of continued growth.[73] Policies to provide necessary open space, manageable population densities, etc. are possible but require politics which confront the fundamental, root issues. If economic growth is a root issue, then it can be legitimately raised as a subject for political dispute. Henry Kariel has called for reopening what many think of as closed systems of political thought and action — that is, processes and structures which some think are beyond further questioning.[74] Kevin Lynch was responding to that same concern when he wrote that the

> disability of the city is its rigidity, its lack of openness. For his satisfaction and growth, an individual needs opportunities to engage in active interchange with his environment: to use it, change it, organize it, even destroy it. His physical surroundings should be accessible and open-ended, challenging, wayward, responsive to effort. Individual action is a road to personal growth; cooperative action leads to satisfying interpersonal relations. These require a plastic physical setting, with opportunities for seclusion and for risk, and with a degree of ambiguity and waste. Woods, water and lonely places work this way, but so do empty buildings, back alleys, waste heaps, vegetable gardens, pits, caves and construction sites. They are not usually regarded as being beautiful, but this is a narrow view. They are the physical bases of an open society.[75]

NOTES

1. Ernst H. Haeckel, *The History of Creation*, II (New York: Appleton, 1884). This work by the biologist Haeckel appears to be the earliest statement from the ecological perspective.
2. See particularly Robert E. Park, Ernest W. Burgess, and Roderick D. McKenzie, eds., *The City* (Chicago: University of Chicago Press, 1925).

3. Robert Park, *Human Communities* (New York: The Free Press, 1952), p. 14.

4. Ralph Thomlinson, *Urban Structure* (New York: Random House, 1969), p. 9.

5. Scott Greer, *Governing the Metropolis* (New York: John Wily and Sons, 1962), p. 31.

6. Ibid.

7. Max Weber, *The City* (Glencoe, Ill.: The Free Press, 1958); and Gideon Sjoberg, *The Pre-Industrial City?* (Glencoe, Ill.: The Free Press, 1960).

8. Thomlinson, *Urban Structure*, p. 118. See also Richard L. Morrill, *The Spatial Organization of Society* (Belmont, Calif.: Wadsworth Publishing Co., 1970), pp. 18-19.

9. See Langdon White, Edwin J. Foscue, and Tom L. McKnight, *Regional Geography of Anglo-America* (Englewood Cliffs, N.J.: Prentice-Hall, 1964), pp. 23-29.

10. Ibid. p. 30.

11. Lewis Mumford, *The City in History* (New York: Harcourt, Brace and World, 1961), p. 553.

12. Charles Horton Cooley, "Theory of Transportation," *Publications of the American Economics Assn.* 9 (May 1894): 1-148; reprinted in Cooley, *Sociological Theory and Research* (New York: Holt, 1930), pp. 17-118.

13. This model of urban location is usually referred to as Geometric Pattern theory because of the shape of the theoretic urban region which results. See Walter Christaller, *Central Places in Southern Germany*, trans. Karlile W. Baskin (Englewood Cliffs, N.J.: Prentice-Hall, 1966); August Losch, *The Economics of Location*, trans. W. H. Woglom and W. F. Stolper (New Haven: Yale University Press, 1954); Walter Isard, *Location and Space-Economy* (Cambridge, Mass.: M.I.T. Press and John Wiley, 1956).

14. Christaller, *Central Places in Southern Germany*.

15. Simple technology can play a role in city location, for example, apart from strictly economic considerations. Governmental decisions can also explain the location of certain cities — county seat towns in the Midwest, for example. For some other location theories, see George K. Zipf, *Human Behavior and the Principle of Least Effort* (Reading, Mass.: Addison-Wesley, 1949); Herbert A. Simon, *Models of Man* (New York: John Wiley and Sons, 1957), pp. 145-164.

16. Leo F. Schnore and Harry Sharp, "Racial Changes in Metropolitan Areas, 1950-1960," *Social Forces* 41 (March 1963): 247-253.

17. This framework and its precepts were first set forth in Robert M. Haig, *Major Economic Factors in Metropolitan Growth and Arrangement*, Vol. 1, *Regional Survey of New York and Environs*, New York: City of New York, 1928. For a review and critique of the export-base concept, see Wilbur R. Thompson, *A Preface to Urban Economics* (Baltimore: Johns Hopkins Press, 1965), pp. 27-60.

18. Cf. Richard Hartshorne, "Twin City District: A Unique Form of Urban Landscape," *Geographical Review* 22 (July 1932): 431-442. Hartshorne's study was the first attempt to calculate the proportion of basic to nonbasic workers.

19. John W. Alexander, "The Basic - Non-Basic Concept of Urban Economic Functions," *Economic Geography* 30 (July 1954): 246-261.
20. Wilbur Thompson, "Internal and External Factors in the Development of Urban Economics," in *Issues in Urban Economics*, ed. Harvey Perloff and Lowden Wingo, Jr. (Baltimore: Johns Hopkins Press, 1968), p. 45.
21. For example, Harvey Perloff and his associates found "no positive correlation between the proportion of workers in 'growth industries' and the relative rates of increase in total economic activities among the many states." Harvey S. Perloff et al., *Regions, Resources, and Economic Growth* (Baltimore: Johns Hopkins Press for Resources for the Future, 1960).
22. Wilbur Thompson, "Factors in Urban Economics," p. 43.
23. Robert Park, Ernest Burgess, and Roderick McKenzie, *The City* (Chicago: University of Chicago Press, 1928).
24. Robert Park, "Urban Areas," in *Chicago: An Experiment in Social Science Research*, ed. T. V. Smith and L. D. White (Chicago: University of Chicago Press, 1929), pp. 114-123.
25. R. D. McKenzie, "The Scope of Human Ecology," *Publications of the American Sociological Society* 20 (1926): 141-154.
26. Milla Alihan, *Social Ecology: A Critical Analysis* (N.Y.: Columbia University Press, 1938). An excellent collection of articles defining and critiquing the classical, neo-orthodox, social-area analysis, and sociocultural approaches is found in George Theodorson, *Studies in Human Ecology* (New York: Harper & Row, 1961); See also Warner E. Gettys, "Human Ecology and Social Theory," *Social Forces* 18 (May 1940): 469-476.
27. "The Concept of Natural Area," *The American Sociological Review* 11 (August 1946): 423-427; Eshrev Shevky and Wendell Bell, *Social Area Analysis* (Palo Alto: Stanford University Press, 1955). These two works describe a technique for designating social areas using census information to determine "social rank," "urbanization," and "segregation" of census tracts within a city.
28. Nan Sigel, "The Unchanging Area in Transition," *Land Economics* 43 (August 1967): 392.
29. Chauncy D. Harris and Edward L. Ullman, "The Nature of Cities," *The Annals of the American Academy of Political and Social Science* 242 (November 1945): 7-17.
30. Thomlinson, *Urban Structure*, pp. 149-150.
31. Harold M. Mayer, "Urban Geography and City and Metropolitan Planning," in *Social Science and the City*, ed. Leo F. Schnore (New York: Frederick A. Praeger, 1968), p. 225.
32. Ira Sharkansky, *The Politics of Taxing and Spending* (Indianapolis: Bobbs-Merrill Co., 1969), p. 8.
33. The meaning of "latent issue" is discussed more fully in Chapter 13.
34. Robert Park, "The Urban Community as a Spatial Pattern and a Moral Order," in *The Urban Community*, ed. Ernest W. Burgess (Chicago: University of Chicago Press, 1926), p. 18.

35. This formulation is based on the Shevky-Bell typology of *Social Area Analysis.*
36. Scott Greer, *Governing the Metropolis* (New York: John Wiley and Sons, 1960), p. 25.
37. Robert Winslow, *Society in Transition: A Social Approach to Democracy* (New York: The Free Press, 1970), p. 66.
38. Marshal Clinard, *Sociology of Deviant Behavior* (New York: Holt, Rinehart and Winston, 1968), p. 96.
39. Cf. Winslow, *Society in Transition,* Chap. 2.
40. Walter C. Reckless, *Vice in Chicago* (Chicago: University of Chicago Press, 1933).
41. Cf. Ernest Mourer, "Methodological Problems in Social Disorganization," *American Sociological Review* 6 (December 1941): 839-852.
42. William F. Whyte, *Street Corner Society* (Chicago: University of Chicago Press, 1942).
43. Whyte as paraphrased by Winslow, *Society in Transition,* p. 60.
44. Eliot Liebow, *Tally's Corner* (Boston: Little, Brown, 1967).
45. From Georg Simmel, "The Metropolis and Mental Life," as reprinted in Eric and Mary Josephson, *Man Alone* (New York: Dell Publishing Co., 1962), p. 153. Original source is *The Sociology of Georg Simmel* (Glencoe, Ill.: The Free Press of Glencoe, 1950), pp. 409-424.
46. Simmel, "Metropolis and Mental Life," p. 414.
47. Robert K. Merton, "Bureaucratic Structures and Personality," in Robert K. Merton et al., *Bureaucracy* (New York: The Free Press of Glencoe, 1952).
48. The term and concept are originally from Emile Durkheim, *Suicide.* It means the loss of prevailing norms.
49. Lewis M. Killian and Charles M. Grigg, "Urbanism, Race and Anomia," *American Journal of Sociology* 67 (May 1962): 661-665.
50. Ibid.
51. Robert Merton, "Social Structure and Anomie," Chapter 4 in Robert Merton, ed., *Social Theory and Social Structure* (Glencoe, Ill.: The Free Press, 1957). For the full formulation of the theory see Richard Cloward and Lloyd Ohlin, *Delinquency and Opportunity* (Glencoe, Ill.: The Free Press, 1960).
52. John E. Horton and Wayne Thompson, "Powerlessness and Political Negativism," *American Journal of Sociology* 67 (March 1962): 485-493; see also Edward L. McDill and Jean C. Ridley, "Status, Anomia, Political Alienation and Political Participation," *American Journal of Sociology* 68 (September 1962): 205-213.
53. Robert Crain, Elihu Katz, and Donald Rosenthal, *The Politics of Community Conflict* (Indianapolis: The Bobbs-Merrill Co., 1969), p. 215.
54. Ibid., p. 43. They particularly tax Murray B. Levin's *The Alienated Voter: Politics in Boston* (New York: Holt, Rinehart and Winston, 1960) because Levin equates support for Collins for mayor with political alienation.
55. Herbert McClosky and John Scharr, "Psychological Dimensions of Anomia," *American Sociological Review* 30 (February 1965): 14-40.
56. Ibid., p. 40.
57. Cf. Elton B. McNeil, *Human Socialization* (Belmont, Calif.: Brooks Cole Publishing Co., 1969), pp. 75-78.

58. See also Wendell Bell, "The City, the Suburb, and a Theory of Social Choice," in *The New Urbanization*, ed. Scott Greer et al. (New York: St. Martin's Press, 1968), pp. 132-168.

59. Cf. Morris Axelrod, "A Study of Formal and Informal Group Participation in a Large Urban Community," (Ph.D. diss., University of Michigan, 1953); and H. Sharp and M. Axelrod, "Mutual Aid Among Relatives in an Urban Population," in *Principles of Sociology*, rev. ed., ed. R. Freedman et al. (New York: Holt, Rinehart and Winston, 1956), pp. 433-39; and Scott Greer, "Urbanism Reconsidered: A Comparative Study of Local Areas in a Metropolis," *American Sociological Review* 21 (February 1956).

60. Morris Axelrod, "Urban Structure and Social Participation," *American Sociological Review* 27 (February 1956).

61. Richard Sennet, *The Uses of Disorder: Personal Identity and City Life* (New York: Alfred A. Knopf, 1970), p. 60.

62. Ibid.

63. Shigeo Nohara, "Social Context and Neighborliness: The Negro in St. Louis," in *The New Urbanization*, ed. Scott Greer et al., pp. 179-188.

64. Quoted in the "Moynihan Report." Daniel P. Moynihan, *The Negro Family: The Case for National Action*, U.S. Department of Labor, Office of Policy Planning and Research (Washington: U.S. Government Printing Office, March, 1965). Original source is Robert O. Blood, Jr., and Donald M. Wolfe, *Husbands and Wives: The Dynamics of Married Living* (Glencoe, Ill.: The Free Press of Glencoe, 1960), p. 34.

65. Blood and Wolfe, *Husbands and Wives*, p. 35.

66. Moynihan, *The Negro Family*.

67. Edward Banfield, *The Unheavenly City*, (Boston: Little, Brown, 1970), p. 46.

68. Ibid.

69. Ibid, p. 53.

70. Ibid, p. 48.

71. Ibid.

72. George B. Vold, *Theoretical Criminology* (New York: Oxford University Press, 1958).

73. Warren Johnson and John Hardesty, *Economic Growth Versus the Environment* (Belmont, Calif.: Wadsworth Publishing Co., 1971).

74. *Open Systems: Arena for Political Action* (Itasca, Ill.: F. E. Peacock Publishers, 1969).

75. Kevin Lynch, "The City as Environment," in *Cities* (New York: Alfred A. Knopf, 1966), pp. 194-195.

Chapter 4

The Political and Intellectual Environment of the City

The terms *physical* and *social environment* are terms that broadly describe the context in which urban politics functions. We can best understand the political implications of the environment by studying the usual patterns of political behavior of Americans. We shall review some highlights of the extensive literature on political behavior, emphasizing the study of the effects of urbanism. Specifically, in the first section of this chapter, we shall review the major generalizations that emerge from studies of political socialization and opinion, consensus, political participation, and governmental form and public policy. In the second section, we shall scan the intellectual environment of the city — on the assumption that ideas also have an impact on political processes and policy.

THE POLITICAL ENVIRONMENT: A GENERAL OVERVIEW

Unless you are prepared to support the proposition that we are born with special genes that determine our political positions, it must be assumed that our orientations to politics are a product of the combination of our personal characteristics and our learning. To some degree each of us is unique in the way he combines his experiences and background to reach political positions. But we are not nearly so distinctive as we should like to believe. A number of empirical studies of how we learn our political attitudes and what it is we learn have disclosed some reasonably stable patterns.[1]

The Family and Politics

Not surprisingly, the family has been found to have a crucial and enduring impact on the child's political orientation. It is in the family that we learn our most general dispositions — what we are to consider right and wrong, attitudes toward authority, sense of obligation, trust. To be sure, as we grow up we modify and refine these lessons as we apply them, but they are never entirely lost.[2] In the last chapter we noted that urban residence has a strong influence on any family, but it does not destroy family life. Broadly, the white urban middle-class family tends to insulate its members from society; and the poor urban family is frequently found to be without the decisive influence of the father. How, if at all, do these family influences affect what children learn about authority and political authority especially?

Attitudes toward authority

In general, the middle-class, white child embraces the attitudes of his parents. Thus, early studies undertaken to assess the degree of political socialization consistently found a strong sense of trust and affirmation of the society outside the home. Examining the attitudes of 700 Midwestern school children, Easton and Hess report the children's feelings for their political community were ". . . uniformly warm and positive throughout all grades, with scarcely a hint of criticism or note of dissatisfaction."[3] The children's warm feelings toward society were also displaced on "America" as a symbol. The country was also found to be entangled with religion in the minds of the school children: "not only do many children associate the sanctity and awe of religion with the political community, but to ages 9 or 10 they sometimes have considerable difficulty in disentangling God and country."[4]

Similar conclusions have been reached about children's views of authority figures. Greenstein's study of 659 New Haven children revealed that same uncritical view of the mayor and the President.[5] He observed that the children's views developed in the earliest years on purely emotional grounds, without knowledge of what the mayor does. Later, in preadolescent development, children have been found to become somewhat more informed and critical, but not to any great degree.[6]

All this sounds like the making of young authoritarians. The early attitudes of children would seem to be well adapted to the belief "my country right or wrong." And, it has been reported, in a sample of Boston area high school students, one-fifth to one-third of them were "very" chauvinistic politically. Fortunately, later experience alters this pattern — somewhat.[7]

Subcultural orientations to authority

Surely not all children feel this way about political authority. We might expect some variety in attitude among American children of different subcultures, classes, or geographic locations, especially because we know the family to be very important in shaping the child's political orientations. We should expect that poor families with absentee fathers might produce children with distinctive, probably negative, attitudes toward government and authority. There is some evidence for that assumption. One study that supports it was an assessment of children's attitudes in Appalachia. Though not an urban population, Appalachia is distinguished as a subculture of relative poverty and social isolation, much as the urban slum is. Many homes, wracked as they are by poverty, are unhappy places in which to grow up. "In Appalachia there is a high degree of family disruption. The father may well not live at home. Far from providing a glowing prototype of authority, he may be a pitifully inadequate figure, unemployed or absent. . . ."[8] In many important ways, the Appalachian family structure parallels that of the poor urban black family described in the Moynihan Report.

The study in Appalachia (Knox County, Kentucky) used as subjects the children attending 305 rural public schools. In their evaluation of political authority, preadolescent Appalachian children were found to be "dramatically less positive"[9] than the children of the Midwestern research project. Table 4.1 shows a comparison between preadolescents of the Appalachian sample and the Chicago sample of Easton and Hess. Nor does this negative view of political authority change much as the children age; a majority of the high school seniors in the Appalachian sample had negative conceptions of the President.

With these findings in hand, we should expect that a sample of urban blacks would have attitudes similar to those of the Appalachian children. Edward S. Greenberg tested this assumption with a Philadelphia sample of both black and white children.[10] Interestingly, Greenberg's findings do not entirely square with our expectations. However, he does not speak directly to the impact of family structure on political attitudes. Instead he tends to trace black-white attitude differences to "environment and political events." On many dimensions he found no substantial differences between black and white children's scores on indices of "good will" and "role performance," i.e., seeing government as friendly and competent. Only on the dimension of "paternalism-benevolence," the sense that government is caring and trustworthy, do black and white children's attitudes seriously diverge. As Figure 4.1 shows, the black children were much less trusting of government than were the white children.

Greenberg's study is also notable in that it is the only socialization study so far to report children's perceptions of different levels of government. Table 4.2 shows that black students ". . . in the third grade manifest their highest confidence in local government and their lowest in the national government, yet the situation is completely reversed by ninth grade."[11]

Instead of accounting for these changes in terms of early socialization experiences in the family or elsewhere, Greenberg suggests explanations more related to the situation and experiences of the children. He reports that the most perceptive black children see that they live in relatively deprived areas,

Table 4.1   Fifth - Eighth Grade Appalachian Children's Evaluations of the President

	Response	Knox County Data*	Chicago-Area Data†
1. View of how hard the President works compared with most men.	harder	35%	77%
	as hard	24	21
	less hard	41	3
	Total	100%	101%
		(N=128)	(N=214)
2. View of the honesty of the President compared with most men.	more honest	23%	57%
	as honest	50	42
	less honest	27	1
	Total	100%	100%
		(N=133)	(N=214)
3. View of the President's liking for people as compared with most men.	likes most everybody	50%	61%
	likes as many as most	28	37
	doesn't like as many	22	2
	Total	100%	100%
		(N=125)	(N=214)
4. View of the President's knowledge compared with most men.	knows more	45%	82%
	knows about the same	33	16
	knows less	22	2
	Total	100%	100%
		(N=124)	(N=212)
5. View of the President as a person.	best in the world	6%	11%
	a good person	68	82
	not a good person	26	8
	Total	100%	101%
		(N=139)	(N=211)

Source: *The Knox County subjects were provided with a "don't know" option apparently not available to their Chicago-area counterparts. This was done to avoid forcing the subjects, who are relatively undeveloped intellectually, to choose among possibly meaningless options. As expected, choice of the don't know alternative was very frequent. For each of the five items above, approximately 30% responded that they did not know. In the interest of comparability, the data do not include these responses. Reported non-responses (about 1%) to items 4 and 5 are likewise excluded from the Chicago-area data.

†These data are compiled from those reported in Hess and Easton, op. cit., pp. 636-637.

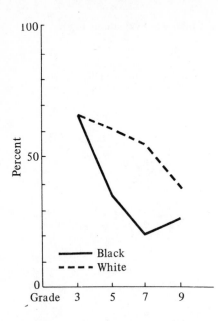

Figure 4.1   *Index of children's perceptions of government on the dimension of paternalism-benevolence; distinguished by race and school grade level. Source: Edward S. Greenberg, "Children and Government: A Comparison Across Racial Lines,"* Midwest Journal of Political Science 14 *(May 1970): 261.*

but that later information about favorable actions of the national government accounts for declining faith in local government. This conclusion is speculative, and much additional study would be necessary to establish its validity. It would also be interesting to know whether these attitudes of black children link with family structure; were these the absent father/dominant mother homes which we have come to associate with both urban and rural poverty?

Table 4.2   Black Children's Perceptions of Whether Government "Makes Things Better for People" by Level of Jurisdiction (Percent Agreeing)

	Third Grade	*Ninth Grade*	*Change*
National Government	60	64	+4
State Government	60	50	-10
Local Government	65	53	-12

Source: Edward S. Greenberg, "Children and Government: A Comparison Across Racial Lines," *Midwest Journal of Political Science* 14 (May 1970): 261.

Growing Up Politically

It would also be interesting and useful to know what proportion of the population develops no further than the grade school syndrome of uncritical acceptance of authority and, specifically, what impact urban living has in retarding or facilitating the development of more tutored views. On these questions the socialization and opinion literature again offers some suggestive materials. Three aspects of socialization have received the particular attention of political scientists — rebellion, the school, and the peer group.

Rebellion

When children rebel against parental authority, they may do so for a variety of reasons, but they usually do it in the teen years. However, that rebellion does not often take the form of *political* rebellion — that is, differences with the parents on political matters. More commonly, rebellion is in terms more immediate to the parent-child relationship — dress, hair length, sexual behavior, obedience to parental wishes.[12]

In those instances in which the child does come to rebel on political matters, it has been found that the family disciplinary climate plays an important part. Both overstrict and overlenient (meaning indifferent rather than permissive) discipline are found associated with political rebellion. Children from lower socioeconomic groups are particularly prone to rebel politically when their parents discipline too strictly.[13] However, in those homes in which political matters are not given much importance, there is little point in the child rebelling politically.[14] Lane suggests that in these cases, the political outcome, especially of damaged father-son relationships, is the child's apathy and despair over the future of the political order.

Much the same outcome has been found where the parents are overprotective, which middle-class, white parents tend to be. Frank Pinner, reporting a study of children in France, Belgium, and the Netherland's, found that parents who attempt to limit and control their children's contacts outside the home implicitly inculcate in the children the belief that politicians are not to be trusted, that political parties are useless, and that politics is generally hostile.[15] There are no directly parallel studies in the United States, but in view of Richard Sennett's conclusions that the American middle-class family (discussed in Chapter 3) tends to isolate its children, Pinner's findings may be broadly applicable in this country as well.

Gary Byrne has found evidence that the family disciplinary atmosphere, by itself, is less a determinative factor than is the degree of congruence between early family experience and later worldly experience. In studying participants in campus disorders at Duke University, he found that students from upper-middle-class homes who had been brought up in an equalitarian family atmosphere expected treatment as equals in their later life experiences, especially in college. Finding themselves subordinated to an administrative and professorial hierarchy, the rebellious students sought to change the structure of the college to bring it more in balance with their expectations.[16]

Rebellion, then, is reasonably rare. It is related, when it occurs, to both overstrict and overlenient child-rearing practices. Rebellion or apathy may also occur where the family atmosphere is overprotective. It is a hypothesis worth testing that urbanization affects families in ways that heighten and intensify all these forces. Byrne's work reminds us that particular situations and institutional settings are at least part of the reason for rebellious responses. Beyond that, we should keep in mind the possibility that people rebel against institutions and political practices because some of them are genuinely untrustworthy, useless, and hostile.

School and the peer group

The formal education process and the informal processes of adjustment to a peer group can also reshape political values, attitudes, and opinions. Hess and Torney state the point more categorically than empirical work has yet demonstrated: "the public school is the most important and effective instrument of political socialization in the United States."[17] What *has* been clearly established is that political party preferences deviate more and more from parental attitudes as formal education increases.[18] What is not yet clear is the role played by the several elements of the educational process. What element has the strongest impact — the teacher, the curriculum, the school "climate," or a less formal influence such as the peer group?[19] The few available studies suggest that teachers who deal with activities which are central to the personal concerns of the students may be quite influential — people like the athletic coach or driver training instructor.[20]

The impact of the curriculum, especially the "citizenship training" courses, also has uncertain effect, although Edgar Litt has found some evidence that civics education courses in the three Boston schools he studied markedly increased support for "democratic" principles and decreased political chauvinism, especially for lower-class students.[21]

It is the influence of *school climate and peer group* which seems most decisive and most directly connected to the urban environment. It is reasonably well established that both school and peer group tend to reinforce existing social and political preferences when the school is composed of students with similar social backgrounds. However, if students with diverse social and economic backgrounds attend a school, it has generally resulted in the resocialization of the working-class students toward attitudes more like their fellow students of higher social status. Neugarten, for example, found the "lower-class" children generally deferred to higher-status students in heterogeneous schools by ascribing more favorable personality traits to them than to students of their own class.[22] Other studies indicate that lower-class students come to share the aspirations of the upper-class students;[23] for example, they tend to reject their parents' party affiliations.[24]

This pattern of yielding political attitudes to the dominant attitude of the school has been referred to as the *breakage effect*. The breakage effect is based on an analogy to gambling; when an individual plays a game like Black Jack, he plays against the dealer. In case of a tie, the dealer, or "house," wins. In political science usage, the dominant climate of opinion is that of the house. The individual who holds a different opinion must have very strong convictions about that opinion if he is to keep from yielding to the prevailing, house, position. The school climate helps to wean people from their parents' political positions. The breakage effect is probably not restricted to school experience either; as the next section suggests, adults, as they associate with groups, are likely to adapt to the dominant norms of those associations.

Urban life, as we saw in Chapter 3, produces social segregation. People who share common life styles, ethnic origins, or social rank tend to inhabit common space in the city. It could be expected that a neighborhood school would normally be composed of students with similar backgrounds. The result would be an educational climate which reinforces the dominant political attitudes of the neighborhood. This appears to occur in many urban middle-class areas and suburban areas. But numerous central-city schools are composed of a relatively greater social mix. Though the term "lower-class" is often assigned to this kind of school, that is a rough designation that masks great heterogeneity. Political cynicism and hostility to authority are common enough in central-city schools to raise doubts about the viability of these school climates as constructive political socializers. As presently constituted, they seem unable to teach middle-class white attitudes or to induce substantial tolerance.

Small Groups as Opinion Makers

Throughout this discussion of political learning, I have been emphasizing that people change attitudes as they adapt themselves to proximate groups. This is probably an offensive assumption to the "rugged individualists" among us. Many Americans like to believe that they must not and do not bend to attempts of groups to make them conform. Are we overemphasizing the ability of groups to achieve compliance? No. The ability of small groups to obtain the conformity of their members is one of the best documented findings of group study.[25] One of the most impressive pieces of evidence is Soloman Ash's experiment in which he demonstrates that an individual will disavow the clear evidence of his senses to comply with the group which unanimously insists that the longer of two objects is really shorter.[26] The opinion-determining character of small groups is connected with physical proximity. A study in a housing development found that those who lived closest together formed informal communication networks and came to share opinions, while those who were physically separate were more likely to be deviant.[27]

That this small-group influence has its political consequences was dramatically demonstrated in a study by Raymond Gorden of thirty-six U.S. citizens from a wide variety of professional backgrounds. Gorden took statements made in private about Russia and compared them with the opinion declared in a public group statement. He found that few of the individuals publicly maintained their private opinions. When they were asked to express opinions they had previously made in private to the assembled group, about half the individuals adapted their opinions to the group norm while a small group of deviants moved away from it.[28]

The capacity of small groups to impel conformity to its norms, nonetheless, has been found to vary with a wide range of conditions. The following propositions — though not universally agreed upon — describe how different factors affect the ability of small groups to gain the conformity of its members.

Group Characteristics

Size: the smaller the group, the stronger the pressure to conform.

Frequency of contact: the more the members of a group interact, the stronger the pressure to conform.

Time: the longer the period during which members of a group have known each other and worked together, the stronger the pressure to conform.

Participation in decisions: the more individuals participate in making decisions, the more likely they are to accept these decisions.

Group-centeredness: group-centered groups compared with leader-centered groups exert stronger pressures to conform.

Cohesiveness (sense of solidarity, feeling of "we-ness"): the higher the cohesiveness of the group, the stronger the pressure to conform.

Group salience: the more salient the basis for group membership in a given context, the greater the pressure to conform.

Clarity of group norm: the less ambiguous the appropriate group norm, the greater the pressure to conform (and ease of conforming).

Homogeneity: the more homogeneous the membership opinion on a given issue, the greater the pressure to conform on that issue.

Issues

Group relevance: the more related the issue to the purpose of the group, the stronger the pressures to conform to group opinion on that issue.

Ambiguity: the more ambiguous the issue and the less relevant the experiential standards of an individual, the greater the pressure to conform.

Individual Characteristics

Feelings of acceptance: members with average, as contrasted with high or low acceptance in the group, are more susceptible to pressures to conform.

Affiliative needs: the more an individual feels the need for acceptance by the group (or perhaps by others generally), the more susceptible he is to group induction.

Group purpose and individual purpose: the more the purposes and goals of the group are congruent with the purposes and goals of the individual, the more he feels the pressure to conform.

Instrumentality: the more the group serves as an instrument for individual goals (advancement, prestige, "contracts"), the more an individual experiences the pressures to conform.

Personality: weaker egos, stronger capacities for group loyalties, other-directedness, lower self-esteem, timidity in intergroup relations, lack of hostility, and other personal factors contribute to greater willingness or need to conform to group standards.[29]

The studies of political socialization to date have not often spoken directly to the relationship of the learning of political attitudes to the urban environment. However, the studies done to date suggest a number of potentially verifiable connections. Urbanism, for example, affects family structure; and family structure, in turn, has been found to have important impact on the learning of political values and attitudes. Middle-class families apparently produce children with an early and often abiding trust in political figures and institutions, but at least two studies indicate that the opposite pattern occurs in certain minority subcultures. Because minority subcultures abound in cities, one can expect urban politics will operate in an environment of higher levels of conflict.

Further, by affecting the quality of family relationships — specifically the closeness of parents and children or the disciplinary pattern — urban life might significantly influence the level of adolescent political rebellion. Schools and peer groups provide climates of opinion which have been found to be critical determinants of political attitudes. The discovery of the breakage effect lends weight to the assumption that the environment can effect opinion

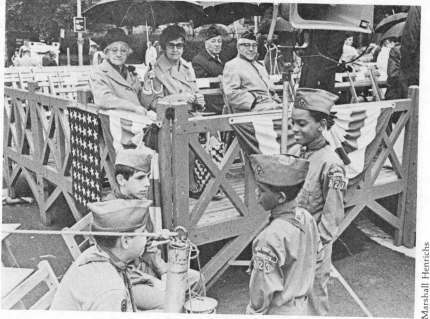

Marshall Henrichs

The Boy Scouts is an organization which transmits traditional values.

change where the individual is in conflict with prevailing climates of opinion.

Finally, the tendency of urban processes to segregate residents in such a way that much of their opinion-forming activity occurs in group settings — primary, secondary, residential, occupational, etc. — makes it extraordinarily important to recognize the great capacity of groups to command conforming opinions, particularly that of small, face-to-face groups. We have reason to believe that we have found in the small group a major opinion-creating force and the taproot of political identity and conflict.

Consensus

So much for generalizations about *how* we Americans learn our political attitudes. Let us now turn to the question: *What* do we learn? It has long been assumed that a high level of agreement on at least some fundamental principles was necessary or the country would fall apart. Most studies that have sought to describe The American Consensus have found, however, that no operative agreement really exists; yet we remain reasonably stable. In this section, I should like to illustrate this point — that stability can exist even without consensus — by describing the findings on an economic consensus and on a political consensus.

Economic consensus

In the preceding chapter I argued that the primary urban-creating forces were economic. A large amount of poll data suggests that Americans share a belief that private economic allocations are to be preferred over public, governmental allocation of economic resources. Even the persistent public doubts about the ethics of business "are quite easily overridden by the powerful cultural tendencies to favor private forms of economic power."[30]

For example, near the end of World War II a Gallup Poll asked, "Is your attitude toward owners and managers of business concerns today more favorable or less favorable than it was before the war?" Thirty-six percent responded that their attitude was the same, 31% were more favorable, and 19% were less favorable.[31] Advertising, seemingly a most vulnerable element of the private economic sector, also enjoys general public confidence. Greyser and Bauer found as late as 1964 that "roughly three quarters of the American public see advertising as an essential economic feature making specific economic contributions, particularly in the form of an improved standard of living."[32] This view persists despite the fact that approximately half the public believe that much advertising is false and 70 to 80% believe that advertising leads people to buy things for which they have no need or desire.

The meager available evidence suggests that public leaders are as agreed on the centrality of private economic forces as are ordinary citizens. Robert Presthus asked a group of small-city leaders to agree or disagree with this statement: "Democracy depends fundamentally on the existence of free enterprise." He found that 90% in one city and 82% in another agreed.[33]

What are the political implications of this confidence in the economic system? The relationship is not direct, and no specific public opinions and actions can be predicted.[34] Economic factors have been shown to relate to political attitudes, but they are often mediated by noneconomic variables, — such as group membership, psychological dispositions, and, especially, educational level.[35] In sum, the relations between economics and political opinion are "much too subtle to be captured by any determinist prescription, and much interwoven by other social and psychological forces."[36]

Political consensus

Our understanding of the political environment in which urban politics develops is sharpened by the several studies of the degree to which we Americans share values, opinions, and attitudes about the political "rules of the game." What the empirical work suggests so far is that no high level of political consensus exists among Americans. The findings of the few studies of consensus point toward the following propositions:

1. The American electorate is often divided on democratic values and procedural rules.
2. The electorate exhibits greater support for abstract statements of democratic values and procedures than for their specific application.
3. Democratic beliefs are more widely shared among political leaders than among the general public.
4. Consensus is far from perfect, even among the politically involved.[37]

Prothro and Grigg, important contributors to these findings, drew their sample from two cities — Tallahassee, Florida, and Ann Arbor, Michigan — and their pioneering study suggests that consensus varies with environment.

> More "correct" responses came from the Midwestern than from the Southern community, from those with high education than from those with less education, and from those with high income than those with low income.[38]

Seemingly, consensus level varies according to the type, size, region, and socioeconomic composition of the city.

Political Participation

Variations in the degree and kind of political participation have also been linked to environmental factors. However, it must be pointed out that political participation has been studied mainly by framing the question in terms of how and why individuals, not groups, get involved in politics. Relatively few studies have used cities or urban subpopulations as the unit of analysis. One of those who has studied differences in participation between cities, Robert Alford, has found "no evidence that a local political culture is created which socializes members of the community into greater or lesser political involvement."[39] Instead, rates of participation in the four Wisconsin cities he examined were associated with more specific population characteristics — education, organizational activity, home ownership and a high sense of civic duty.[40]

Still, it would be premature to dismiss the impact of urban environment as an element of explanation of participation. A number of other studies find that, in the aggregate, city dwellers are more likely to be politically active

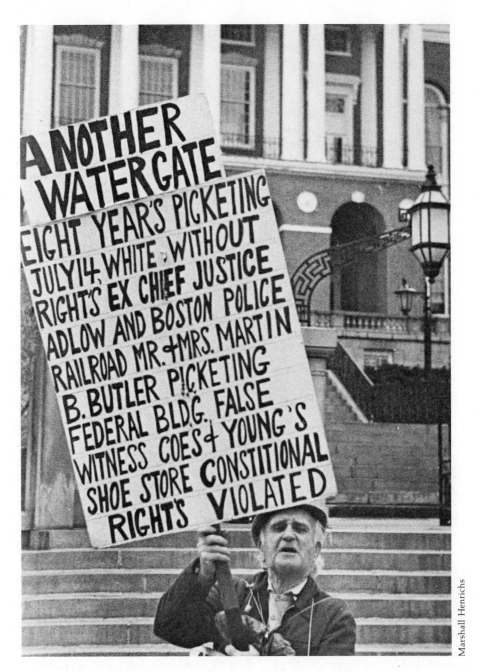

This man participates almost daily in the political process of Boston.

Marshall Henrichs

than are rural people.[41] It has also been shown that rates of participation are affected by city size: the larger the city, the higher the rates of participation.[42] Other connections between the urban environment and its politics emerge as we look more closely at: (1) the several types of political participation and (2) the impact of subculture, group membership, or socioeconomic status on participation. We shall examine the varieties of local political participation in more detail in Chapter 8. In general, that body of literature suggests that (1) voting patterns in national elections are different from those in local elections, and (2) voting patterns in elections of officials are different from those on referenda. In addition, we must recognize that a person may participate in politics in a variety of ways; voting is but one way. For example, besides voting one can talk politics, put on a political bumper sticker, contribute time or money to a cause or candidate, attend meetings, make television appearances, or protest in a variety of ways.[43]

To arrive at a definitive conclusion regarding the connections between environment and political participation would require us to examine each type of participation in relation to urban setting. Needless to say, that much has not yet been accomplished by urban researchers. But a number of recent studies have made necessary first steps. For example, Robert Alford and Eugene Lee have analyzed the data on voting turnout that was collected from about eighty percent of the 729 cities of the country by the International City Managers Association.[44] They were seeking to correlate voting turnout in those cities with *"political structure," "social structure,"* and *"community continuity."* Particularly the latter two variables connect turnout with the kinds of environmental variables we have been examining. As indices of *social structure*, Alford and Lee used the census data to determine the relationship of the ethnic composition of the city (percentage foreign-born) to voter turnout and the relationship of educational level to turnout. To measure *community continuity*, they studied the relationship of the age of the city to the geographic mobility of the population (proportion of population who moved, between specified dates, to the present home from a different county). What they found confirmed some expectations and contradicted others. The correlation between ethnic composition and voting turnout tended to confirm earlier findings — that cities with more ethnic (foreign-born) populations have higher levels of voting turnout, regardless of form of government or type of election system.[45] On the relationship of education to turnout, however, Alford and Lee's findings were a surprise: a large number of studies of individual political participation have found "those with higher education to be more likely to participate in politics."[46] Yet Alford and Lee found voting turnout was *inversely* correlated with the educational level of the city; "we conclude that high educational level of the city as a whole has either no effect or reduces the level of voting turnout."[47] There may be ways of reconciling the apparent contradictions between these conclusions, but that research has yet to be done.

With regard to *community continuity*, Alford and Lee found that the older the city and the less mobile its population, the lower the voting turnout. There was some regional variation in that pattern as well. Mobility was highly correlated with turnout in the East and Midwest but tended not to be related at all to turnout in the South and Far Western cities.[48] Observations about voting participation, of course, may or may not apply to other modes of political participation. Does protest behavior, for example, vary with city size, social structure, political structure, or continuity? And what about the unit we are analyzing? Are we justified in talking about whole cities as environments or should we focus our attention on smaller, more functional units of analysis? (If so, which units? Wards, urban and suburban districts, councilmanic districts, or perhaps more socially grounded units like neighborhoods, social areas, classes, social, occupational or other secondary groups?) Robert Alford and Harry Scoble have already found in their study of four Wisconsin cities that the ward election district did not "exhibit independent influence upon political behavior."[49] Hardly surprising, since few people develop overwhelming loyalty to "Good old Ward #1" anymore. We are far too busy with our loyalties to our toothpaste, hairspray, and cereal.

Subpopulation variations

It is one of the major themes of this book that group conflict is the basis of urban politics; so of course much more will be said about that later, especially in Part Two. For present purposes we can advance our understanding of how urban subpopulations vary in their political participation by reviewing two contrasting illustrations — one of suburban political participation, another of a poverty area in a central city.

Participation in the Suburbs

We have known for some time that the stereotyped picture of suburbia as an area of struggling lawns populated by struggling upward-mobiles is oversimplified. There are many kinds of suburbs and suburban residents: blue-collar residential (like Milpitas, California), industrial (like Woodbridge Township, New Jersey), middle-class residential (like La Mesa, California), and upper-class residential (like Lake Forest, Illinois) as well as some mixed varieties.[50] In general, political participation in the suburb increases with rising levels of income, occupation, and education.[51] In addition, participation increases among those who feel personally and politically effective. In fact, these social and psychological explanations have been found to apply whether we talk about cities, suburbs, or other areas. This has led a number of

Marshall Henrichs

Low levels of participation are usual in conventional urban politics.

observers to question whether there are real differences in the levels of
political participation between cities and their suburbs. At least one careful
analysis of available data shows little significant difference between urban
and suburban political participation.[52] The study on which this conclusion is based used University of Michigan Survey Research Center data on
729 urban and 731 suburban interviews in seven major cities. The responses
of all those in all seven cities were then compared with the responses of all
suburban residents.

> Statistically significant differences appear . . . (only) with regard to party
> identification, party loyalty in past presidential elections, split ticket voting,
> and one of the basic attitude questions (the belief that people in government
> waste a lot of tax money). All of the other comparisons show no significant
> difference between urban and suburban attitude and activity patterns.[53]

Study of individual metropolitan areas has been more successful in
finding urban-suburban differences. Where the suburb is residential and the
men commute, for example, it has been observed that in the middle-income
suburbs, more women participate in politics than men.[54] What this observation suggests is that most of our usual assumptions about suburban political
participation have been made with the middle- and upper-middle-income suburbs in mind. Such suburbs are generally found more participative than
central-city populations. But other kinds of suburbs have been found less ac-

tive in politics. A working-class suburb is likely to have much the same political participation rate as working-class areas in the central city.[55]

Participation by the Deprived

Certain central-city subpopulations composed of the low-income, unskilled workers, the newly migrated black, and the substantially unemployed have been found to have low levels of political participation, as might be expected. A study of a poverty area of Milwaukee is illustrative. Bloomberg and Rosenstock interviewed a sample of Milwaukee's "inner core north" residents. Afterward, they assigned them "political action scores" depending on how many of the following kinds of participation the interviewee claimed for himself:

1. Registering complaints about community or commercial services, politics, or civil rights.
2. Requesting assistance from an alderman.
3. Attending meetings or public hearings.
4. Belonging to a neighborhood committee, civic group, or improvement association.
5. Voting in local elections.[56]

Each respondent was assigned a point for each kind of action he participated in. The expected finding of low participation is shown in Table 4.3. About two-thirds of the residents engaged in none or only one form of political participation. Bloomberg and Rosenstock use a variety of environmental and personal indicators to attempt to explain these relatively low scores: competence, perceived need, home ownership, "group potency," income, residence length, decision means, alienation, education, and others (see Table 4.4). But they concluded that, "So much of the variation in participation remains unex-

Table 4.3   Number of Respondents Receiving Each Action Score

Score	Number	Percent of Total Sample
0	45	27.6
1	66	40.4
2	28	17.3
3	11	6.7
4	7	4.3
5	6	3.7
	163	100.0

Table 4.4   Simple Correlations with Action Score

Competence	.49
Perceived need	.33
Income	.25
Home ownership	.24
Length of residence	.24
Financial dependency	-.20
Group potency	.20
Alienation	.18
Education	.17
Occupation	.16
Decision locus	-.15
Adolescent freedom to complain	.14
Political efficacy	.10
Desire to remain	.09
Perceived commonality	.09
Adolescent family influence	.08
Race	.06
Adolescent decision success	.03
Age	.01

plained that no one model or theory can be held exclusively."[57] Still they found interesting tendencies. For example, greatest participation was by those residents who were more discontent with their lot in life and who also had some political understanding and organizational experience. In addition, an important finding for those who would encourage the poor to participate in local politics was that people with dependent incomes, and especially those on public assistance, tended to withdraw from political involvement. Finally, social and psychological explanations — specifically alienation and sense of efficacy — had a moderate impact on participation.

In other studies, alienation has been found to be a more central explanation of political participation. Thompson and Horton, for example, find evidence that people with low socioeconomic status were likely to be alienated. According to Thompson and Horton, the alienated have the world view of the underdog — that is, "the feeling that the world is a threatening place inhabited by the powerful and the powerless: suspicions of outsiders and of people in general; pessimism about the future; despair; and the tendency to debunk education and other values necessary for success in a competitive society."[58] This orientation may lead to nonparticipation. In Thompson and Horton's study, however, it was suggested that the alienated and powerless participated in order to defeat school bond referenda as a protest to their condition.

Implications of the participation findings

Persons who are well educated, with high income and a professional occupation, generally participate in politics more than persons who are lower on these scales. However, we find that even that well-established generalization fails in the Alford-Lee study of voting turnout. Other evidence suggests that the longer and more permanent the residence, the more likely a person is to participate; but again Alford and Lee's study found that older central-city neighborhoods with static populations had a smaller turnout. Ethnicity has also been found associated with higher voting turnout, yet, when we examine differential participation between poor central-city residents and suburbanites, we find the residents of middle-income suburbs more active in several modes of political action.

The additional research that must be done to reach reliable conclusions will have to take into consideration certain procedural reasons for these inconsistencies. We must, for example, have more comparative study of each variety of political participation: some persons protest by refusing to vote; some show their protest by voting "no" on local referenda. Subtle motivational differences can make greatly complicated explanations. Additional research would profit by some attempt to standardize the unit of analysis used and to reach agreement on definitions and indices of local participation. Two attempts seem most promising — the new reliance on "social areas" and the Alford-Scoble index of political involvement.

Social Areas as a Unit of Analysis

Future research would profit by using more standardized units of analysis. Specific cities or empirically defined, socially homogeneous urban subpopulations are optimal units of analysis. Walter Kaufman and Scott Greer have found that the Shevky-Bell typology for distinguishing "social areas" (see page 57) within the city according to the ethnicity, social rank, and life style of its residents is particularly useful in explaining voting participation. It would probably be useful for additional studies of other forms of political participation as well.[59]

The Index of Political Involvement

Whether the unit of analysis is a particular city or a subpopulation, there is a comprehensive set of categories for the analysis of local political participation.[60] Robert Alford and Harry Scoble constructed an "index of local political involvement" by synthesizing many of the factors discussed in this section. First, they stipulated four separate indices: (1) an index of local *political interest*; (2) an index of local *political information*; (3) an index of *public meeting attendance;* and (4) an index of local *political turnout.* They combined these indices into five types: *Mobilized* (high on all four of the above indicators); *Potentially Mobilized* (high on interest, information and turnout, but low on attendance); *Moderate* (a residual category of mixed cases); *Ritualistic* (low on all except voting); and *Apathetic* (low on all indicators).[61]

Drawing together the several sources of local political involvement, they found six explanations for political participation: social status, organizational activity, the citizen's stake in the local area, religion and ethnicity, political motivations, and the sociopolitical environment. Alford and Scoble used this set of categories in a study of four Wisconsin cities, and in general, found that social status and organizational activity were the most important characteristics associated with local political participation. The impact of the sociopolitical environment was found to exert little independent impact. However, we must realize that Alford and Scoble were using the ward as a unit of analysis, not as an area likely to be socially significant. Additional study using the Alford-Scoble Index and socially connected units would enable us to be more definitive in our assessment of the impact of environment on political participation.

Governmental Forms And Policy Outcomes

A growing body of research has begun to connect the urban environment with public policies. Once again, however, we are not far enough along to claim the research is yet conclusive. Thus far, attention has focused on associating certain social, economic, and political characteristics either with certain policies — like taxing, expenditure, and referenda issues, or with governmental structures — like form of government, type of ballot, or size of election districts.

As with the studies of political participation, the results obtained so far differ with the mode as well as the subject of inquiry. In general, when the research has been in the form of a case study of a set of decisions in a particular city, "political decision-making and interaction processes appear to be the key variables which must be studied in order to understand policy outcomes."[62] By contrast, those studies which have used aggregate data and multivariate statistical techniques of analysis (with some important recent exceptions) suggest that environmental rather than political variables are more crucial determinants of urban policies.[63] Adding to the confusion is the fact that different studies have used different environmental variables, have studied a variety of public policies, and have used several different indicators of political impact.

So, while these studies, like an octopus, point several directions at the same time, it is possible to suggest a main-line interpretation which seems in the process of being developed. First, a number of studies have found that social and economic cleavages in cities directly affect a number of policy outcomes: educational policy, revenue and expenditure policy, policies of cooperation or integration with neighboring municipalities, decisions to change the form of government, and urban renewal policies, for example.[64] Another series of studies of the impact of environment on public policies finds that the political process itself is more important than earlier studies had indicated. The attitudes and actions of the political leaders of the city, the level of voter turnout, the type of proposal and its cost — all have been found to affect referenda outcomes as decisively as environment.[65]

The studies reaching these conclusions will be examined in more detail in Chapter 13, as we discuss the comparative study of urban political issues. For present purposes, we need only recognize that the environment of the city seems to have important impact on the content of the public policies it creates. Whether environment has relatively more impact than specifically political characteristics would appear to vary with the particular policy and, perhaps, the particular city.

What We Have Learned About the Political Environment

This brief review of some of the patterns of Americans' political behavior suggests a number of relationships between urban politics and its environment. The socialization studies find the family a prime transmitter of all attitudes and values, political ones included. City life, by affecting the family, affects, in turn, the political values, attitudes, and behaviors of subsequent generations. Precisely how that behavior is affected remains to be clarified, but it appears that overprotective, overstrict, poor (economically), and mother-dominated family climates produce more than their share of politically rebellious children. Insofar as urbanization fosters these kinds of families, there is evidence that the families produce children who dispute the viability of the political order.

As people become more socially segregated in cities, they come to rely more heavily on a variety of groups — small groups, voluntary associations, political interest groups — to articulate their needs. In turn, groups, and especially small groups, are able to exact conforming behaviors from their adherents. Segregation in the city thus is reinforced and hardens as group consensus forms.

Studies of political consensus indicate that different cities create differing urban environments. But political participation shows relatively less environmental impact than other elements of the political process. Nonetheless, there is great contrast between the levels of participation in middle- and upper-middle-income suburbs and participation in the poverty areas of central cities.

The environment also has its impact on public policy — although we are beginning to qualify the findings of earlier studies that environment is deterministic of public policies. What seems to be emerging is the realization that environmental characteristics like income levels, tax base, city size, and educational level affect some policy areas more than others. Also, we are discovering that the political process itself has an impact on policy which *can be* decisive — crucial, in particular policy areas.

THE INTELLECTUAL MILIEU

There is a history of thought and philosophical discourse about the city which cannot be ignored in any complete examination of the environment of the American city. This is not the place to recount the problem of connecting political thought to concrete political events. I simply accept David Minar's formulation that "political thought . . . both indicates and shapes the culture."[66] Normative political theory is a repository of political ideas and a body of recommendations from past and current generations; it describes (and sometimes prescribes) political patterns. It broadly recommends particular formulations for viewing the meaning and direction of events, helping us define and evaluate the situations we face. As such, normative political theory can be an excellent source of discussion of which political patterns are valuable and which are not.

In the case of the American city, the impact of political thought has been unfortunate because it has overwhelmingly carried the message that *cities are inherently deplorable places*, that rural means virtuous and urban means corrupt. The message has been received and acted on not merely by those who remain in the purity of the countryside but also by those who are themselves urban residents and urban builders — the people who make the decisions that shape the cities. Let me illustrate this admittedly debatable interpretation from representative writings of some important contributors to American cultural traditions.

Historical Anticity Bias

The American literary tradition, as Morton and Lucia White have argued, is filled with caustic condemnation of our cities.[67] Thomas Jefferson

Marshall Henrichs

This sign in front of the Baltimore capitol is truly a sign of the times.

warned against urbanization: "I view great cities as pestilential to the morals, the health and liberties of man."[68] He grudgingly came to accept the growth of cities in America only because of their commercial advantages.[69] Emerson's view was also mixed, but on balance, antiurban: "Whilst we want cities as the centers where the best of things are to be found, cities degrade us by magnifying trifles." Thoreau, always more interested in purity than balance, was more concrete: "The only room in Boston I visit with alacrity is the Gentleman's Room at the Fitchburg Depot, where I wait . . . in order to get out of town."[70]

Herman Melville, Edgar Allan Poe, Nathaniel Hawthorne, Henry Adams, Frank Norris, Theodore Dreiser, and a number of other luminaries of American literature scorned the city. Hawthorne seems to have been the first advocate of his own form of urban renewal: "All towns should be made capable of purification by fire, or of decay, within each half century. Otherwise they become the hereditary haunts of vermin and noisomeness."[71] What would be lost? Little, according to Henry Adams: "San Francisco burned down last week," he noted after the earthquake, "and I have been searching the reports to learn whether the whole city contained one object that cannot be replaced better in six months. As yet, I've heard of nothing."[72]

It is sometimes difficult to determine whether these men were condemning cities in general or specific conditions in particular cities. Everyone knows there are many conditions — crowded housing, congested streets, poverty, crime — that need correcting. The question is whether we must destroy the cities in order to save them. The tone of many intellectuals indicates that they think so. Of course, there is some affection shown for cities in the literary tradition as well, particularly Walt Whitman's and William James' praise of New York, and every schoolboy knows Carl Sandburg's "Chicago." But, as the Whites put it, ". . . the volume of their voices did not compare with the anti-urban roar produced in the national literary pantheon. . . ."[73]

The concrete results of these antiurban impulses are numerous — the move to the suburbs, the move to the rural commune, the insistence on placing trees in the way of users of downtown sidewalks, for example. Public attitudes are generally antipathetic to the city. A 1966 Gallup Poll shows that only 22 percent of our citizens would choose to live in a city if they "could live anywhere in the U.S."; 28 percent chose the suburb; and 49 percent opted for the small town or farm. Only about a third of those already living in cities of 50,000 and over preferred their city residence.[74]

But perhaps the most important manifestation of antiurbanism has been that our cities have been built by architects and planners whose traditions and dispositions have tended to lead them not to the building of workable, humane cities, but to the "sacking of cities."[75] "Whatever changes the American people seem to be seeking, they are not directed toward the enhancement of the facilities that lead to an urbane or citified life, but rather to the introduction into the city of qualities associated with the rural life — whether trees, clearer air and water, larger parks, or new family-style dwellings to reduce the overall density of population."[76]

Planning the Anticity

By far the most important impact of antiurbanism has been on our planners and architects. To be sure, they are not solely or even mainly responsible for the shape of American cities; we have already described the environmental forces that are. But, acting within the range of choice open to them, planners have tended to draw their inspiration from a tradition which is anticity. This is not the place for a detailed review of the intellectual origins of American city planning, but certain highlights will make the point.

Most urban historians trace the origins of American city planning to the Englishman, Ebenezer Howard; he was appalled at the plight of the poor in London and created in 1898 a plan to stop the growth of London and repopulate the countryside. He proposed to do that by creating "garden cities." The garden city was to have a maximum population of 30,000 and was to be encircled by a belt of agriculture. Job-providing industry was to be there, but only in carefully circumscribed areas. So too, schools, housing, and green space were assigned their locations; and at the center were to be clubs, commercial centers, and cultural centers — all owned in common.

However appealing this garden city vision may be, it is severely out of joint with the urban shaping forces (see Chapter 3) and would require massive redistribution of political and economic power. But even if garden city advocates overcame those barriers, there is some doubt that the effort would be worth it. Jane Jacobs, among others, insists that the social diversity of the city is more exciting and fulfilling than life in the garden city would be: "His [Howard's] aim was the creation of self-sufficient small towns, really very nice towns if you were docile and had no plans of your own and did not mind spending your life among others with no plans of their own."[79] Despite such criticisms, variations on the garden city vision influenced the most prominent figures in American planning — Lewis Mumford, Henry Wright, Catherine Bauer, and Clarence Stein.[78] Jacobs catalogs their anticity views:

> New York's midtown was "solidified chaos" (Mumford). The shape and appearance of cities was nothing but "a chaotic accident . . . the summation of the haphazard, antagonistic whims of many self-centered, ill-advised individuals" (Stein). The centers of cities amounted to "a foreground of noise, dirt, beggars, souvenirs and shrill competitive advertising." (Bauer).[79]

The "decentrists," as Bauer sometimes called this group, gradually became dominant in schools of architecture and planning. The "comprehensive plans" for cities which have become so popular since World War II often reflect the philosophical position of the decentrists. "This is the most amazing event in the whole sorry tale," Jacobs concludes, "that finally people who sincerely wanted to strengthen great cities should adopt recipes frankly devised for undermining their economies and killing them."[80] To be sure, a number of contemporary planners have grown skeptical of comprehensive planning and garden city assumptions, but they have not yet had as broad an impact as have the decentrists.[81] It is disconcerting to discover at the bedside of the sick city a doctor who is committed to the practice of bleeding.

NOTES

1. "Political socialization" is the name commonly given a subfield or inquiry that deals with "the way society transmits its political culture from generation to generation." Kenneth Landon, *Political Socialization* (New York: Oxford University Press, 1969), p. 4. "Public opinion" is "an implicit verbal response or 'answer' that an individual gives in response to a particular stimulus situation in which some general question is raised." Carl I. Hovland, Irving L. Janis, and Harold H. Kelley, *Communication and Persuasion* (New Haven: Yale University Press, 1953), p. 6. "Opinion" may be differentiated from "attitude" in that attitudes are general dispositions toward objects, persons, or groups which are not specific to any particular factual situation while opinions may be thought of as sharpened attitudes, specific to the situation. Bernard Hennessy, *Public Opinion*, 2d ed. (Belmont, Calif.: Wadsworth Publishing Co., 1970), pp. 209-210.

2. See especially Robert D. Hess and David Easton, "The Child's Changing Image of the President," *Public Opinion Quarterly* 24 (Winter 1960): 632-644.

3. David Easton and Robert Hess, "The Child's Political World," *Midwest Journal of Political Science* 6 (August 1962): 236-237.

4. Ibid., p. 238.

5. Fred Greenstein, "The Benevolent Leader: Children's Images of Political Authority," *American Political Science Review* 54 (December 1960): 934-943.

6. Cf. Easton and Hess, "The Child's Changing Image."

7. Robert Lane and David Sears, *Public Opinion* (Englewood Cliffs, N.J.: Prentice-Hall, 1964), p. 18. The Boston study was done by Edgar Litt, "Civic Education, Community Norms and Political Indoctrination," *American Sociological Review* 28 (February 1963): 69-75.

8. Dean Janos, Herbert Hirsch, and Fredric Fleron, Jr., "The Benevolent Leader: Political Socialization in an American Subculture," *American Political Science Review* 62 (June 1968): 564-575.

9. Ibid.

10. Edward S. Greenberg, "Children and Government: A Comparison Across Racial Lines," *Midwest Journal of Political Science* 14 (May 1970): 249-275.

11. Ibid., p. 265.

12. Russell Middleton and Snell Putney, "Political Expression of Adolescent Rebellion," *American Journal of Sociology* 68 (1963): 527-535.

13. Eleanor MacCoby, Richard Matthews, and Anton Morton, "Youth and Political Change," *Public Opinion Quarterly* 18 (1954): 23-29.
14. Robert Lane, "Fathers and Sons: Foundations of Political Belief," *American Sociological Review* 24 (1959): 502-511.
15. Frank Pinner, "Parental Overprotection and Political Distrust," *The Annals of the American Academy of Political and Social Science* 361 (September 1965): 58-70.
16. Gary C. Byrne, "Cognitive Inconsistency and Student Protest Behavior," *Summation* 2 (March 1970): 17-35; and Part 2, Vol. 2 (December 1970): 28-61.
17. Robert Hess and Judith Torney, *The Development of Political Attitudes in Children* (Chicago: Aldine Publishing Co., 1967), p. 101.
18. MacCoby, Matthews, and Morton, "Youth and Political Change," especially p. 37; and Gabriel Almond and Sidney Verba, *Civic Culture* (Boston: Little, Brown, 1963), pp. 317-318. Almond and Verba say the more educated: (1) are more aware of the impact of government, (2) are more attentive to politics, (3) have more political information, (4) have a wider range of political opinions, (5) discuss politics more and with a wider range of people, (6) feel more able to influence government, (7) are more likely to be active in organizations, and (8) express confidence in their social environment.
19. This point is underscored in the "Introduction" in James S. Coleman, ed., *Educational and Political Development* (Princeton: Princeton University Press, 1965), pp. 18-25.
20. Cf. Albert D. Ullman, "Sociology and Character Education," in *The Adolescent Citizen*, ed. Franklin Patterson et al. (Glencoe, Ill.: The Free Press, 1960), pp. 206-223. For empirical work casting doubt on the importance of college teachers as an agency of attitude change, see Everett K. Wilson, "The Entering Student: Attributes and Agents of Change," in *College Peer Groups*, ed. Theodore Newcomb and Everett K. Wilson (Chicago: Aldine Publishing Co., 1966), pp. 84-87. Much of the material in this section is drawn from Kenneth P. Langdon and M. Kent Jennings, "Political Socialization and the High School Civics Curriculum," *The American Political Science Review* 62 (September 1968): 852-867.
21. Litt, "Civic Education."
22. Bernice L. Neugarten, "Social Class and Friendship Among School Children," *American Sociological Review* 51 (January 1946): 305-313. See also Mary C. Jones, "A Study of Socialization Patterns at the High School Level," *Journal of Genetic Psychology* 93 (September 1958): 87-111.
23. John Michall, "High School Climates and Plans for Entering College," *Public Opinion Quarterly* 25 (Winter 1961): 583-595.
24. Marvin L. Levin, "Social Climate and Political Socialization," *Public Opinion Quarterly* 25 (1961): 596-606.
25. I am using the term "small group" here to distinguish it from the broader use of the term "group" which will occur in the next chapter. A small group is a group of individuals "of limited number with personal relations, some

duration, and identification of the members of the group — hence some solidarity (cohesion), differentiation from others outside the group, common goals, common symbols, and autonomy in setting up procedures." Thomas W. Madron, *Small Group Methods and the Study of Politics* (Evanston: Northwestern University Press, 1969), pp. xxviii-xxix. Political groups may be small groups but may also be much looser aggregations, bound together by fewer common ties and by relationships that are less personal.

26. "Effects of Group Pressure Upon the Modification and Distortion of Judgements," in *Group Dynamics*, ed. Dorwin Cartwright and Alvin Zandler (Evanston, Ill.: Row, Peterson, 1953), pp. 151-162. Much of the discussion in this section is adapted from the excellent treatment of the subject found in Lane and Sears, *Public Opinion*, Chap. 4.

27. Leon Festinger, Stanley Schacter, and Kurt Black, *Social Pressures in Informal Groups* (New York: Harper & Row, 1950).

28. Raymond L. Gorden, "Interaction Between Attitude and the Definition of the Situation in the Expression of Opinion," *American Sociological Review* 17 (February 1952): 50-58.

29. These generalizations are reprinted from Lane and Sears, *Public Opinion*, pp. 35-36. The original source which identifies specific studies and authors is Paul Hare, Edgar Borgatta, and Robert Bales, *Small Groups: Studies in Social Interaction* (New York: Alfred A. Knopf, 1955).

30. Hennessy, *Public Opinion*, p. 267. Much of the material in this section is drawn from Hennessy. For a more complete discussion, see Hennessy's Chapter 14, pp. 261-279.

31. Ibid., Original source is Hadley Cantril and Mildred Strunk, *Public Opinion 1935-1946* (Princeton: Princeton University Press, 1951), p. 337.

32. Stephen Greyser and Raymond Bauer, "Americans and Advertising: Thirty Years of Public Opinion," *Public Opinion Quarterly* 30 (Spring 1966): 69-78.

33. Robert Presthus, *Men at the Top* (New York: Oxford University Press, 1964), p. 324.

34. Hennessy, *Public Opinion*, p. 268.

35. Cf. Heinz Eulau and Peter Schneider, "Dimensions of Political Involvement," *Public Opinion Quarterly* 20 (Spring 1956): 128-142.

36. Hennessy, *Public Opinion*, p. 279.

37. These are paraphrased from Herbert McClosky, "Consensus and Ideology of American Politics," *American Political Science Review* 58 (June 1964): 361-382.

38. James Prothro and Charles Grigg, "Fundamental Principles of Democracy: Bases of Agreement and Disagreement," *Journal of Politics* 22:276-294.

39. Robert Alford, *Bureaucracy and Participation* (Chicago: Rand, McNally, 1969), p. 160.

40. Ibid., p. 159.

41. Cf. Lester Milbrath, *Political Participation* (Chicago: Rand. McNally, 1965), p. 128 for citations of specific studies.

42. Cf. Ibid., p. 130 and Angus Campbell et al., *The American Voter* (New York: John Wiley and Sons, 1960), pp. 460-464.

43. Milbrath, *Political Participation*, pp. 16-22 provides a discussion of the varieties of political participation. However, he omits discussion of protest forms — a serious omission from the perspective of urban politics.

44. Robert Alford and Eugene Lee, "Voting Turnout in American Cities," *The American Political Science Review* 62 (September 1968): 796-813.

45. Ibid. For an earlier similar finding and some discussion of reasons for it, see John Kessel, "Governmental Structure and Political Environment: A Statistical Note about American Cities," *American Political Science Review* 66 (September 1962): 615-620.

46. Milbrath, *Political Participation*, p. 122, cites much of that literature. Especially strong are the findings of Gabriel Almond and Sidney Verba, *The Civic Culture* (Boston: Little, Brown, 1965); they concluded that education has greater impact on political behavior than any other measure of socioeconomic status.

47. Alford and Lee, "Voting Turnout in American Cities," p. 805.

48. H. Sharp, "Migration and Voting Behavior in a Metropolitan Community," *Public Opinion Quarterly* 19 (Summer 1955): 206-209. Found contradictory evidence.

49. Robert Alford and Harry Scoble, "Sources of Local Political Involvement," *American Political Science Review* 62 (December 1968): 1202.

50. For more systematic classification schemes for suburban types, see particularly Leo F. Schnore, "The Functions of Metropolitan Suburbs," *American Journal of Sociology* 61 (1956): 453-458; Otis D. Duncan and Albert Reiss, Jr., *Social Characteristics of Urban and Rural Communities, 1950* (New York: John Wiley and Sons, 1956).

51. Milbrath, *Political Participation*.

52. Joseph Zikmund, "A Comparison of Political Attitude and Activity Patterns in Central Cities and Suburbs," *Public Opinion Quarterly* 31 (Spring 1967): 69-75.

53. Ibid., p. 71.

54. W. T. Martin, "The Structuring of Social Relationships Engendered by Suburban Residence," *American Journal of Sociology* 21 (1956); 446-453; Milbrath, *Political Participation*, p. 131; Scott Greer, "The Social Structure and Political Process of Suburbia," *American Sociological Review* 25 (1960): 514-526; Frederick M. Wirt et al., *On The City's Rim: Politics and Policy in Suburbia* (New York: D. C. Heath, 1972).

55. Cf. Bennett M. Berger, *Working Class Suburb* (Berkeley: University of California Press, 1960). Chap. 3, 5.

56. Warner Bloomberg, Jr., and Florence W. Rosenstock, "Who Can Activate the Poor? One Assessment of Maximum Feasible Participation," ed. Warner Bloomberg, Jr., and Henry Schmandt in *Power, Poverty and Urban Policy* Vol. II, (Beverly Hills, Calif.: Sage Publications, 1968), pp. 313-314, 317-330.

57. Ibid., p. 330.

58. John Horton and Wayne Thompson, "Powerlessness and Political Negativism: A Study of Defeated Local Referendums," *American Journal of Sociology* 67 (March 1962): p. 493. Recall the criticism of this study made by Crain, Katz, and Rosenthal. Robert Crain, Elihu Katz, and Donald Rosenthal, *The Politics of Community Conflict* (Indianapolis: Bobbs-Merrill Co., 1969), pp. 5-7.

59. Walter C. Kaufman and Scott Greer, "Voting in a Metropolitan Community: An Application of Social Area Analysis," *Social Forces* 38 (March 1960): 196-204.

60. Robert Alford and Harry Scoble, "Sources of Local Political Involvement," *American Political Science Review* 62 (December 1968): 1192-1206.

61. Ibid., p. 1193.

62. James W. Clarke, "Environment Process and Policy: A Reconsideration," *The American Political Science Review* 63 (December 1969): 1172-1182. This section owes much to Clarke's useful summary of this literature. For examples, of these case study findings, see Robert Dahl, *Who Governs?* (New Haven: Yale University Press, 1961); and Robert J. Mowitz and Diel S. Wright, *Profile of a Metropolis* (Detroit: Wayne State University Press, 1962).

63. Much of the pioneering work in this mode was done at state rather than local level; cf. Richard G. Dawson and James A. Robinson, "Interparty Competition, Economic Variables and Welfare Policies in the American States," *Journal of Politics* 25 (May 1963): 265-298; Thomas R. Dye, *Politics, Economics and the Public: Policy Outcomes in the American States* (Chicago: Rand, McNally, 1966); Richard I. Hofferbert, "The Relation Between Public Policy and Some Structural and Environmental Variables in the American States," *American Political Science Review* 60 (March 1966): 73-82. For an exception to the general findings see Ira Sharkansky, "Economic and Political Correlates of State Government Expenditures: General Tendencies and Deviant Cases," *Midwest Journal of Political Science* 11 (May 1967): 173-192.

64. Bibliography and additional discussion is in Chapter 13.

65. James Clarke, "Environment, Process and Policy."

66. David Minar, *Ideas and Politics: The American Experience* (Homewood, Ill.: The Dorsey Press, 1964), p. 10.

67. Morton White and Lucia White, *The Intellectual Versus the City* (New York: The New American Library, 1962).

68. Paul L. Ford, ed., *The Works of Thomas Jefferson* Vol. 9 (New York: G. P. Putnam's Sons, 1904), pp. 146-147.

69. White and White, *The Intellectual Versus the City*, pp. 29-31.

70. From Perry Miller, *Consciousness in Concord* (Boston: Houghton Mifflin, 1958), p. 46.

71. From *The Marble Fawn* in *The Works of Nathaniel Hawthorne* (Boston: Houghton Mifflin, 1882), pp. 346-347.

72. Harold D. Cater, *Henry Adams and His Friends: A Collection of His Unpublished Letters* II (Boston: Houghton Mifflin, 1947), p. 46.
73. White and White, *The Intellectual Versus the City*, p. 14.
74. *Gallup Opinion Index* (Princeton: American Institute of Public Opinion, March 1966), p. 23.
75. Jane Jacobs, *The Death and Life of Great American Cities* (New York: Random House, 1961), p. 4.
76. Daniel Elazar, "Are We A Nation of Cities?" *The Public Interest* (Summer 1966) p. 46.
77. Jacobs, *Death and Life of American Cities*, p. 17.
78. For a good brief review of the works of these writers see ibid., pp. 17-25.
79. Ibid., p. 21.
80. Ibid.
81. For an excellent discussion of an alternative "adaptive" approach, see Melvin Webber et al., *Explorations Into Urban Structure* (Philadelphia: University of Pennsylvania, 1964). See especially Foley's section, pp. 21-78.

PART TWO

Urban
Conflict

Conflict begins when a person feels that things are not as they should be — when someone perceives a "problem." Often that sense of problem is an outgrowth of the realization that he is being wronged by a particular person or condition — or, more positively, that something could be made more right than it is. Conflicts emerge as personal, economic and social conditions change; small wonder that the development of urban America has generated so much conflict.

But not all conflict becomes widespread or severe enough to necessitate public action to manage it. For a conflict to become political, it must move from personal discontent to a more organized and articulated form. The traditional American assumption that we are free to speak our minds on any subject supports the notion that issue taking is acceptable, even laudable. We are less sure that it is all right for persons to organize to take action on behalf of their position. Free speech and association is all right, but right next door? In studying politics we quickly discover that we cannot be squeamish about organized power and conflict — it is pervasive. To ignore it is to miss the show; to condemn it is to join the antipolitics chorus.

In Part One, we outlined some of the sources of conflict in the American urban environment. In Part Two, we shall examine the organization and articulation of urban political conflict. We shall emphasize the conflict-presenting processes of (1) important urban groups and (2) urban political parties. In that examination we shall also learn a great deal about the nature and activity of leadership in articulating conflict.

Chapter 5

The Participants
in Conflict

In the wake of our extension of hostilities into Cambodia and after the killing of four Kent State University students, a group of us — students and faculty — sought a resolution from our city council urging a constitutional test of the President's war powers. As we moved from councilman to councilman, asking their support, the question commonly recurred, "Whom do you represent?" and "What organizations support you?" These questions betray the expectation, based on the public officials' experience, that most petitions directed at governments come from blocks of citizens, not individuals. V. O. Key made the same point in more theoretical language, "At bottom, group interests are the animating forces in the political process, and understanding of American politics requires a knowledge of the chief interests and of their stake in public policy."[1]

GROUPS IN POLITICS

We should never argue that groups entirely replace the individual participant in politics. But characteristically, individuals act collectively when they seek to be politically effective; therefore "when men act in consistent patterns, it is reasonable to study these patterns and designate them in collective terms."[2] In studying groups we are studying the basic actors in the urban political process.

In fact, groups may have a greater impact in local politics than at other governmental levels. One local councilman interviewed in a major study of city councils in the San Francisco Bay area explained:

Pressure groups are probably more important in local government than they are nationally or in the state, because they are right here. You see them and they see you, and what you do affects them. It's not like in Washington, where half the time a businessman doesn't really know what the result will be for him.[3]

The Development of Political Groups

Groups form specifically to pursue the values or interests common to those who either are members or share the interests of the members. Political interest groups, therefore, *are a result of the processes of social differentiation*. This is what Robert Salisbury has called the "proliferation hypothesis," which contends that (1) associations are products of differentiated sets of values or interests, and (2) over time there will develop more and more diverse, specialized groups as the process of social fission continues.[4] However, the formulations of both Salisbury and the economist, Mancur Olson, contradict the assumption that group organization is an automatic development attending social differentiation.[5] They note that some social changes lead to the creation of political groups while others do not. In addition, some potential groups are not organized, or, if organized, do not take political positions. Seeking to explain differences in the political involvement of groups, Olson has carefully examined large economic associations. A crucial distinguishing characteristic of the large economic associations that lobby governmental bodies so effectively, he finds, lies in the fact that the large groups are able to sustain high membership. They are able to do this because they "are also organized for some *other* purpose. . . . They perform some function in addition to lobbying for collective goods."[6] Consequently, the groups that can sustain political organizations are the groups having "selective incentives" (like coercion) or positive inducements (such as group health and insurance plans) to assure continuing membership support. In short, Olson says the political character of the group is a byproduct of its other functions.

Salisbury adds to Olson's formulation the assumption that the organizers of the group may be seen as investing capital to create a set of benefits which they offer to members at a price: "If, and as long as, enough customers buy, i.e., join, to make a viable organization, the group is in business."[7] If group benefits are insufficient, the group collapses. Obviously, Salisbury's development of his "exchange theory" is compatible with the concept of the "rational economic man": groups are bought (joined) by customers (members) if the entrepreneurs (organizers) are able to produce sufficiently useful products (benefits) to justify the costs.

The proliferation hypothesis suggests that groups develop political organization in three stages.[8] First, there is a *latent* stage, in which the sense of problem has developed in the minds of a number of individuals. They may even vaguely recognize that they share that particular interest with a number of others, but there has been no action or organization yet. Pigeon fanciers, fence hole viewers, and auto haters all have common interests to protect, but have not moved beyond the incipient stage of group development. At a second stage there is a *growing consciousness* of the common interest. And finally, there is the *organized* stage. Olson and Salisbury emphasize that the development of groups is not automatic; in particular, the development from the conscious to the organized stage depends on the skill of the organizer in convincing potential members that investment of their time, money, and effort will be adequately rewarded. Inducements in addition to promises of favorable political outcomes are probably necessary to convince potential members of the rewards of their involvement.

Groups and Public Policy

Group theory also ties group action to public policy. Latham put it directly, "What may be called public policy is actually the equilibrium reached in the group struggle at any given moment. . . . "[9] In other words, Latham views the political world as consisting of colliding groups. Once the collisions have occurred and their force registered on, say, the city council, then the council declares the net impact to be law — legitimate policy. Latham qualifies this position somewhat when he adds that the lawmaking body "does not play the part of inert cash register, ringing up these additions and withdrawals of strength; it is not a mindless balancing point."[10] The lawmaking body has a will of its own, according to the group theorists, because it is itself a group; to be sure it is a special kind of group, an *official* group. It possesses the capacity to make rules that bind others because there is a "social understanding" that they may do so. Public decision making, then, as well as public policy, is subsumed into the group theory.

This expansiveness of group-based explanation has received much deserved criticism. In general, criticism adds up to agreement that groups are ubiquitous and powerful, but denial that group process can explain the whole of the political process. Generalizations made about group life do not add up to a general theory of politics, but instead constitute a series of middle-range explanations. This is not the place for detailed explication of these criticisms, but let me suggest some important ones. First, the treatment of legislatures, courts, and bureaucracies as just another group is a distortion. Governing bodies often make decisions which seem to oppose the interests of powerful groups. Forces as shadowy as idiosyncracies of the lawmakers, their intellectual and ideological predispositions, their sense of self-imposed restraints all play a part in the creation of public policy. Second, group theory does not adequately explain the "legitimacy" accorded the official groups.[11] Finally, some critics urge that group theory ignores the need to explain that some policy results from the efforts of individual "activists" who act apart from the enduring political groups.

In sum, groups are a central, but not the sole, phenomenon of politics. To comprehend the political process of a city, students of urban politics probably would do well to make themselves a mental map of major groups, their usual goals, strategies, and potential allies. Groups are prime actors in the urban political system, and to comprehend group processes is to go a long distance toward understanding a city's politics.

Groups serve a variety of important functions. They *help individuals to orient themselves to a complex society* by helping them express their desires and by involving them in actions aimed at realizing those goals. A more politically relevant function is that groups often *act as bargaining agents;* they act as spokesmen for particular interests in a negotiating process. To do so, group leaders help narrow the range of alternatives to be discussed and compromised. By serving these functions, groups become a *major link between individual interests and public policy.* In the terms of our conflict management definition of politics, the group aggregates interests and is a prime articulator of conflict.

Group Power

Participants in politics are not born equal. We almost instinctively know that on most issues the local real estate brokers stand a better chance than the League of Women Voters of influencing the City Planning Commission. Why? The answer cannot be simple or one-dimensional, but let us explore one of the most promising explanations — that the actors with superior resources or superior skill in mobilizing those resources are the most effective urban political actors.

Some groups, like some individuals, simply have more power than others. But as soon as we begin to understand what "power" means we come to realize that it cannot be taken as a fixed attribute of a particular group or person. For instance, we cannot say that in all situations the Fireman's Association has 5 hypothetical power units. It may have 5 when contesting firemen's salaries before the city council, 10 in appearing before the Mayor's budgetary agency (composed of some fellow city workers), and only 1 when appearing before the city board of education to oppose building a new school in a particular area. The point is that the power of the group varies with the particular issue, and with the body of official decision makers being approached. Understanding this variation helps us understand the *relational* character of any group's or individual's power. An adequate conception of power, then, must recognize this relational character. In some ways the definition most appropriate to urban group study is that of Bertrand Russell: power is "the production of intended effects."[12] Nelson Polsby, as a prelude to his examination of community power, defines power in somewhat more specific terms as "the capacity of one actor to do something affecting another actor, which changes the probable pattern of specified future events."[13] So, if in a decision-making situation, where the decision involves choice between courses of action leading to different alternatives, a group or individual can be called powerful if he can change the probabilities that any one outcome will be chosen.

Keeping in mind the qualification that power is relational and not a fixed attribute of a group or individual, we can consider the variety of resources on which power depends.

Political resources

A political resource is an available means of realizing potential power. Political resources are a base on which the capacity to influence may be built, just as iron in the ground is an economic resource which, when mined, processed, and shaped becomes something to be exchanged for value. There are a large number of political resources, many more than casual political commentators recognize. In fact, a large number of interests go unrepresented in American urban politics simply because of a lack of imagination in recognizing and cultivating available resources. How many times have we been in a conversation with a friend, airing a grievance that could have been like this one:

> He: I just don't understand why the city allows unsightly billboards all over my neighborhood. Something must be done.
>
> You: Right on! Let's do it.
>
> He: But you know that the businessmen downtown and the Outdoor Advertising Association have the city council in their pocket.
>
> You: Up the establishment! Damn the power structure!
>
> He: We don't have as much money as those interests, so I guess there's nothing we can do.
>
> You: (after a long pause, wistfully) Yeh, guess you're right.

The assumption that money translates into political power is correct; a rather successful local politician once told me his rule of thumb was "(political) power runs on money. Find where the money's flowing from and to and you'll know how politics in this town works." Money is probably the single most important political resource, but it is not the *only* resource nor is it always the decisive resource in any particular political battle.

The following list contains a variety of resources in addition to money which may be used to explain relative differences in influence on local politics:[14]

1. Money.
2. Control over jobs.
3. Control over information.
4. Social standing.
5. Knowledge, expertness.
6. Organization.
7. Officiality, legality.
8. Leadership skills.
9. Popular appeal, charisma.
10. Popular ideology or values.
11. Ethnic solidarity.
12. The vote.
13. Large numbers.
14. Willingness to disrupt others.
15. Influential allies.

Most of these are self-explanatory, but certain items need to be clarified. Money, for example, need not be possessed to be usable as a resource. Banks and finance companies, by creating policies affecting the flow of money, can affect the shape, development, and social relationships of the city as decisively as governmental decisions, even though the money does not strictly speaking belong to the bank. Money, too, may open access to other resources — television time, experts, organization, full time leaders.

Social standing can be a tricky resource to employ. In general it seems that the higher the social status of the group, the more probable is its ability to be influential. In a broad sense, that often appears to be the case. However, when it comes to the specific issues, the representative of a political position is most likely to be effective if he has roughly the same social standing as those he seeks to influence.

The resources that require the most explanation are those that are used in unconventional and protest behaviors. "Protest is one of the few ways in which a relatively powerless group can *create* bargaining resources."[15] The effectiveness of disruption results from the intricate division of labor of the urban culture. Simply by preventing performance of a single function (for instance, garbage collection), protestors can bring the city to a virtual standstill. Cities, like all highly centralized, specialized systems, tend to be less stable than more decentralized systems. Protest uses threats to disrupt — and actual disruption if necessary — to exploit that potential instability. Saul Alinsky envisions a kind of ultimate vulnerability of our society:

> A while back I attended an Aspen seminar where one guy from IBM was talking about automation. All I could think of as I was listening to him was: These computers are going to put our society in a beautiful, vulnerable spot. Just equip all the people in a community with little punchers that make the same mark that Con Edison's bills have on them. Then you can say either you desegregate or we punch a hole in your cards.[16]

Alinsky means here that a massive automated accounting process can be thoroughly messed up by a few punches in the wrong places on a billing card. Getting thousands of accounts confused can bring a giant corporation to a standstill, or, at least, raise its costs of operation considerably. This is a central aim of a disruptive political strategy — to raise the costs of business-as-usual of your opponents.

Not only have the minorities and young radicals used the resource of protest, but it has been the time-honored base for the union movement, increasingly is being used by public employees, and will undoubtedly be used by others who are "power poor." It is important to realize, then, that protest behaviors are not inherently antisystem. Lipsky makes that point in his very definition of protest; protest is "a mode of political action oriented toward objection to one or more policies or conditions, characterized by showmanship or display[17] of an unconventional nature, and undertaken to obtain rewards from political or economic systems *while working within the systems.*" [emphasis added][18]

Willingness to disrupt may also be used to attract additional resources. It may *activate third parties* to enter the struggle in support of the protest. Of course, it will activate opponents as well. Second, protest may enable *access to mass media* which more conventional strategies would not. Third, activity itself may facilitate group involvement and help *extend and solidify group organization.*

Merely having a variety of resources available, does not ensure influence. Some groups and individuals mobilize their political resources more effectively than others. So, for any given resource, influence is a function of (1) access to it — i.e., how much of it one has to allocate, (2) the rate of exploitation, and (3) the efficiency of exploitation.[19] The dispositions and skills of the leadership of a group are crucial determinants of how political resources will be used. These choices, in turn, determine particular strategies: to choose disruption as the resource makes the strategy a form of protest; to use control over information makes it necessary to cultivate access to media and to develop public relations strategies.

THE PLAYERS AND THEIR GAMES

Specifically, what are the usual resources, strategies, and goals of common urban political participants? Let us consider the motives of the following cast of characters: businesses, unions, real estate brokers, professions, the media, utilities, civic associations, public employees, ad hoc organizations, and blacks and other minorities. In Chapter 7 we will also discuss the political party both as a political participant and as a basis of political coalition.

Business

> Suit the action to the word, the word to the action, with this special observance, that you o'erstep not the modesty of nature; for anything so overdone is from the purpose of playing. . . .
>
> Hamlet, Act 3, Scene 2

In general, business is a quiet but powerful participant in urban politics; carefully observing the need to "suit the action to the word, the word to the action." Businessmen preside over the economic functions which built and shape the city, and they are its prime benefactors. If business interests were singular, agreed on, and organized they could dominate a city's politics. However, business interests are often internally divided: absentee-owned business often defines its interests in local politics differently from locally owned; retailers emphasize different policy needs from manufacturers, small businessmen may often oppose the aims of large businesses. More will be said about that later. But there are some goals common to businessmen; two are particularly important: assuring continuing economic growth and keeping taxes on business low.

Striving for growth

Steady, orderly growth of the population of the city is most businessmen's definition of "progress." More people mean more customers and a supply of employees. All businesses — absentee owned and locally owned, retailing and manufacturing, small and large — have needs that are met by steady growth.

Growth cannot be so rapid or so haphazard as to cause instability, however. The city must be able to absorb new population or else it will be faced with serious problems of displacement and unemployment, increasing welfare costs, and rising vice and crime rates. The need for stable growth, has enticed business away from its early antiplanning stance: planning is no longer seen by most businessmen as a form of creeping socialism, but as a tool for assuring orderliness and stability in growth. But even planning cannot nullify some of the negative effects of growth. Growth has helped create the zone-in-transition with its low-income, "problem" residents; so there are some inconsistencies in a policy of "more is better." Unqualified pursuit of growth is an unrealistic goal.

When the problem groups come to be the dominant population in the central city, businessmen often modify their call for growth by encouraging selective growth — that is, more "desirable" people and land uses. Speaking particularly of downtown department store owners, Banfield and Wilson explain, "This means that they want to encourage good customers to come there and discourage "undesirable" ones, that is, people with little money to spend whose presence would make the shopping district less attractive to the good customers."[20] Thus many business people give enthusiastic support to urban renewal projects that aim to replace low-income residents (often black) with middle-income (often white) residents.

Even the absentee-owned business, say, the research laboratories of an oil company, while showing little interest in the growth pattern of the central city often wants a growing pool of professionals and a good nearby university, and realizes that continuing general growth of the area will tend to vent pressures for higher taxes on its property and operations. In short, the absentee-owned businesses want different "desirables" from those sought by the downtown stores. That fact embodies the potential for either cooperation or conflict between the two parties.

Keeping Taxes low

All businesses have a common interest in keeping their taxes low. Tax reform designed to increase business' share of revenues understandably will be resisted. Business' hesitancy to rework the tax base has been a major reason that cities have stayed heavily dependent on the property tax. In 1968-1969, 34.5 percent of local revenues came from the property tax even though that tax base is widely acknowledged to be regressive (it taxes low-income people more heavily than the rich). Besides that, the property tax is difficult to administer and does not accurately reflect the income-producing value of the property.[21]

In some cities, particularly the smaller cities which are anxious to grow, it is not uncommon for industry to be given tax advantages as an inducement to locate in the city or to expand facilities already there. The state of Mississippi pioneered in 1936 in such property tax exemptions to local industry by authorizing its cities to build and buy factories which could, in turn, be rented at low rates to newly arrived industries or to retain industry which might otherwise have moved.[22] This practice, however, is not always popular with business already located within the city and paying a share of the revenues, especially if they may be subsidizing a competing business. In general, local businesses seem content to work with the property tax base, operating on the assumption — whether accurate or not — that they are doing well with it.

The goal is to prevent tax reforms which would result in higher taxes to business and industry. However, support of low taxes is not a universal posture of local business. Williams and Adrian, for example, found in their four-city study that "business and industrial leaders were frequently the most vocal in favoring increases in tax-supported amenities."[23] This business position, however, does not call for a new tax structure, but supports higher tax rates to pay for a particularly deserving project.

Business resources and strategies

Business has a wider array of resources available to them than most other urban political participants: they command a supply of money; they are generally well respected as people who can "get things done"; they have a good public image, especially among the politically important middle class. All these resources provide ready access to the media and public officials.[24] Business is usually well organized and known locally. The Chamber of Commerce and the Junior Chamber of Commerce are the most prominent business organizations, and they are quite often politically active and influential. However, Chambers of Commerce are particularly susceptible to internal division when their membership is drawn from both absentee-owned corporations and local businesses. Often the Chamber becomes so divided that it cannot act. It is not difficult to understand how the owner of a local men's clothing store can have very strong feelings about zoning and planning decisions that encourage large shopping centers to be built. A businessman who wants to build a big new store in that shopping center sees the matter quite differently. Chambers of Commerce have fought to a deadlock over such internal differences. Service clubs like Kiwanis, Lions, and Rotary are also primarily businessmen's organizations. Their major goals are generally not explicitly political. However, it is not unusual for these organizations to be tapped for support of particular causes. In addition, they provide an easy meeting place for exchange of political information and some lobbying. In certain (usually small) cities, a service club can become the key political organization, but more often they are politically inactive.

How effectively have businessmen translated their resources into political power in American cities? Of course, the situation varies from city to city, but in general, three overall characterizations can be made: (1) businessmen constitute a power elite that dominates the city; (2) businessmen are ratifiers, not initiators of policies; and (3) businessmen exercise great control but largely through their veto power.

Business as Power Structure

A number of case studies of particular cities — Atlanta, Seattle, Yp-silanti, Baton Rouge, Wichita, and San Diego, for example — conclude that businessmen are substantially in control of the cities' politics. They do not exercise that control directly, by holding public office themselves, but covertly by pressuring officials and by supporting for office candidates favorable to their cause. Much more will be said about the details of these findings in Chapter 11, where we shall learn that many political scientists contest these findings; some, particularly the pluralists, feel that such conclusions are more a result of the techniques of study than a fact.

Business as Ratifier

Some of the most careful and systematic examinations of the role of businessmen in politics have been done by Peter B. Clark. He finds that business people are not initiators but are "front men" for policies which are initiated elsewhere. Usually, Clark says, civic associations or governmental agencies are the prime initiators of urban policies.[25] Others have suggested that certain kinds of public policy (particularly capital improvement projects) come from private consultants to local governments, but the one examination of that proposition found no evidence for it.[26] Clark finds that professional staff members of various community organizations usually generate new ideas but that the support of prominent business people is necessary to get a project adopted. Clark illustrates this point with the words of such a staff member.

> "I've got a project now. One of the greatest things we can do for the central area . . . . I am not doing it alone . . . . I am sitting with it until I can present it to the proper man to handle it as *his* idea. I think so much of it I've got to find the right guy to take credit for it . . . . The man I'm going to pick has to be president of his club . . . head of his business. That's 50, 70 percent of the success of the project."[27]

Business support is necessary for several reasons. First, businessmen can bestow their prestige on a proposal. Though some of us may doubt that businessmen are the "civic statesmen" they and others claim, still they are widely respected by public decision makers and middle-class citizens. Clark quotes a Chicago attorney: " 'By and large, those with strong business background command greater respect. . . . They transfer part of their business achievement into their public life.' "[28] Second, that prestige is a result of the feeling that businessmen are "conservative," and that if they approve a project it will not result in sweeping change or seriously disrupt established patterns. Third, business prestige is a result of its central connection to city-building forces. As Thomas Dye puts it, "The views of businessmen are respected in part because the communities' economic growth and continued prosperity are linked to business firms and the men who head them."[29] Business support offsets arguments that a particular change would damage the economic base of the city. Businessmen, in addition to prestige, also have some knowledge and skills which makes their support useful. Particularly if the project requires financial arrangements, as so many do (schools, streets, hospitals, urban renewal projects, for example), the businessman's knowledge of investment procedures will be valuable. Finally, businessmen often have technical information which most local governments do not have the staff to provide for themselves.

In general, Clark's view is that while business does not initiate policy, business support is essential for its success. This is considerable power, of course, although not the form of power commonly thought to be exercised by a self-conscious elite.

The Business Veto

"It is his capacity to withhold his approval and participation — even if participation means only his name on a letterhead — that constitutes the most significant basis of the big businessman's potential veto."[30] Reliance on the capacity to veto is often a quite rational, self-interested business orientation to local politics. Most established businesses do not need dramatic new programs in order to flourish. They are already central to the life of the city and are major recipients of the rewards of the well-established processes of urban development. This favored position seems to require a "maintaining" rather than an "initiating" orientation toward urban government and politics.[31]

Political diversity within urban business

It would be a mistake to leave the impression that business interests are always monolithic — organized, united, and equally engaged in all areas of urban government and politics. Business influence varies (1) in different cities, (2) with specific types of business connection to the city, and (3) with differing issues. The issue-to-issue variation of business participation in urban politics is a central concern of the pluralist school of community power study, which we shall take up in Chapter 10.

Power Variation by City

American cities have emerged at different times, developed at different rates; they have exploited a variety of resources and suffered differing setbacks. We should expect, then, that the level of business power varies from city to city.

Drawing from the several studies of particular cities done for the Harvard-MIT Joint Center for Urban Studies, Edward Banfield and James Wilson have described six types of influence structure which exist in America. Their classification, summarized in Table 5.1, is based on a comparison of two factors: (1) the degree of centralization in the economic and political spheres, and (2) the degree of influence each sphere is able to exercise consistently over the other.

Variations in the power of business from city to city is traceable in part to differences in business resources and the skill and experience business can use to mobilize them. However, we should also recognize that businessmen find it easier to use their resources effectively in relatively homogeneous, middle-class cities where governmental structure is "reformed" — that is, where there is a city-manager system, and where there are nonpartisan, at-large elections and other current innovations in government.

Power Variation Within the City

How organized and centralized business can be in any particular city depends in part on the degree of harmony of interests the various business interests feel. The potential for division among business interest is reasonably high. One basis of cleavage is size — the conflict of interests between large business and small business. Small, locally owned, financially marginal business is often an exception to the generalization that businessmen want growth: if the small businessman sees his gross income as fixed and his capacity to expand is poor, he is likely to oppose tax increases which would support community growth programs. The "Mom and Pop" grocery store owners, the small clothing retailer, the gas station owner are generally rigid low-tax advocates and often hold most firmly to a vision of classical capitalist ideology,[32] even while they are most subject to competitive disadvantages because of their economic marginality.

It is difficult to work analytically with the term "small business," since it is such a vague category. Is it intended to convey small profit, small dollar volume, few employees, or other operational characteristics? As a result of this ambiguity, different terms have often been used to underscore businessmen's different orientations to local politics — locally owned vs. absentee-owned businesses, for example. In a study of Ypsilanti, Michigan, it was found that the managers of large absentee-owned firms, like the General Motors plant there, were tending to withdraw from local participation. Absentee-owned firms usually stayed "neutral" on local issues except "in those rare instances in which local decisions conceivably could prove significant to their well-being. . . ."[33]

Table 5.1   Business Influence Structures in Selected Cities

Description of structure

1. High degree of centralization in both the business and political spheres, with both spheres controlled directly by the (business) elite.	Dallas
2. High degree of centralization in both spheres, with the business elite controlling the political sphere, not directly, but through control of a political boss.	Philadelphia (in an earlier era)
3. High degree of centralization in both spheres, with neither businessman nor politician able to impose his will on the other.	Pittsburgh
4. Moderate centralization in the business sphere but much centralization in the political one, with the (relatively many) controllers of business having little influence over the (few) controllers of politics.	Chicago
5. Much centralization in the business sphere but little in the political one, with the business controllers thus hampered in their efforts to effect political action.	Los Angeles
6. Decentralization in both political and economic spheres and, consequently, minimal influence of business.	Boston

Source: Assembled from Edward Banfield and James Q. Wilson, *City Politics* (Cambridge: Harvard University and MIT Presses, 1963), pp. 272-276.

A number of politically significant variations within the business sector are a direct result of the differing ways in which the business is connected to the city. A brief study of the political orientations of several important business groups will illustrate this point. Specifically, we shall examine the politics of banking and financial interests, professional organizations, real estate and contractors, the mass media, the public utilities and some of the business-related civic associations.

Banking and Financial Interests   Characteristically, reputational studies of power holding in cities name at least one banker as a prominent member of the power structure. Though we cannot simply assume that local bankers are politically prominent, still we must recognize that they are likely to have high stakes in both the economy and the politics of their city, and a variety of resources to protect them.

Bankers make important city-building and city-changing decisions as a result of their impact on money flow within the local economy. Banks often own or hold mortgages on downtown business property. They have, therefore, an interest in maintaining property values within the city. Banks also are involved in the decisions that lead to the growth both of individual businesses and of the city as a whole. By determining who may borrow money, how much, and for what purposes, the banks actually exercise a kind of city planning function. Whether a new housing development will be built is more often determined by a bank's decision than by the city planning officials. In making such decisions, banks subtly influence the attitudes and behavior of other businessmen. Further, banks provide financial backing to local governments. Bond issues for schools, public works and capital improvement programs all require the support of financial institutions. Finally, banks have a stake in protecting the interests of those to whom they have lent money. Consequently we can expect banks to be particularly attentive to government decisions regarding business, taxes, housing, zoning, and planning.

Professional Associations　　Many professional organizations have local chapters which have a stake in local politics: medical and dental organizations, engineering societies, associations of educators, and especially legal associations. Interestingly, however, medical and dental associations tend to focus their political interests at the state level and are, in most cities, attentive to only the issues most directly affecting them or where the profession is specifically called on to render a judgment — as it characteristically is when the fluoridation of the city water supply is at issue, for example. Engineering and educational associations are often, and surprisingly, inert in local politics. As a local civil engineer explained to me, "Most engineers — and especially those not directly involved with government — expect that politicians should come begging for the 'experts' help. No one comes and so the (local) SCE never gets involved."

By contrast, local bar associations and particular lawyers are often found at the vortex of local politics: ". . . no occupational group stands in more regular and intimate relation to American politics than the legal profession," Eulau and Sprague observed in their useful study of the involvements of lawyers at all levels of government.[34] This is so for a number of reasons: (1) like bankers, lawyers have a large economic stake in the local area; (2) law is a high-prestige occupation;[35] (3) lawyers monopolize major avenues leading to public office, e.g., law enforcement offices;[36] (4) law practice is an independent occupation; (5) lawyers possess the appropriate skills for a political career, the lawyers job "involves skill in interpersonal mediation and conciliation and facility in the use of words. Both of these skills are indispensable to the politician."[37] Eulau and Sprague suggest what they call a "convergence hypothesis" to explain the presence of lawyers in politics. That is, lawyers, more than other occupational groups, find opportunities in public life that make it easy for them to interchange "institutional positions, careers and professional roles."[38] In the San Francisco Bay area, lawyers and businessmen are more often recruited to city council posts than other occupational groups. The Stanford City Council Study suggests that the convergence hypothesis helps explain the lawyers and the businessmen's easy connection with active city politics: "There is a meshing of persons and of activities, a meshing which makes positions in the governmental sphere, the civic sphere and the business sphere practically interchangeable."[39]

Real Estate Brokers and Building Contractors   Both real estate and building contractor interests are directly connected with the physical growth of the city. Road building and repairing, construction of schools and other public buildings is generally done by private contractors for the city. Such companies characteristically recognize they have an important stake in local politics and can be counted on to donate to campaigns for public office of sympathetic candidates and to bring pressure when the city is making decisions that will lead to building.

Both builders and real estate brokers have other kinds of stakes in urban policy making as well. The city government, through its power of inspection and its increasingly elaborate building codes, establishes standards of plumbing, lighting, heating, maximum occupancy and the like which influence the uses to which buildings can be put and thus affects profit margins on any particular piece of property. On the decisions of the city in planning and zoning rides literally millions of dollars in potential profit for contractors and real estate brokers.

Again we must recognize that having a large economic stake in the city does not guarantee political power. In fact, the limited number of specific studies find real estate interests only occasionally effective. In Syracuse, New York, for example, it was found that real estate developers usually were successful only when supported by the local "influentials," who became involved in only those development matters which were "of fundamental importance to the community."[40]

The Mass Media   In explaining why his newspaper sponsored the building of McCormack Place, a convention center and exhibition hall in Chicago, editor Don Maxwell said:

You want to see your city continue to grow rather than to die. We have nowadays — what do they call it? — "urban movement" or something like that. The core of the city is being gutted. There are great investments at stake. You can't stand by and let it die. We thought we could prevent it from dying by bringing conventions here, on the front porch of the city.

We fought the NRA [National Recovery Act] for the people. We fight crime and vice. I don't know any paper that is strong and dominant that doesn't crusade for something.

Why did we put so much time into this? Because it's good for the city. But partly from selfish motives too. We want to build a bigger Chicago and a bigger *Tribune*. We want more circulation and more advertising. We want to keep growing, and we want the city to keep growing so that we can keep growing.

We think the community respects a newspaper that can do things like that. People will go by that hall and say, "See that? The *Tribune* did that singlehanded." That's good for us to have them say that.

If it hadn't come off — if those law-suits had turned out wrong — it would not have been good. It's good that people should think that their newspaper is powerful.

It's good that it be powerful.[41]

Not all newspapers are as influential as the conservative Chicago *Tribune*, but all struggle to balance the same elements that Editor Maxwell works with — civic responsibility, growth, and power. The tension between these three imperatives makes the newspaper's position in local affairs similar to that of any large business which is dependent on a local market. In fact, the cardinal principle for understanding the press as an urban political actor is that newspapers (like radio and television stations) are businesses. More than that, they are dependent on the other businesses of the city. Newspapers get two-thirds of their operating revenues from advertising and about three-fourths of that advertising is from local sources, especially department stores.[42] Only occasionally can most newspapers afford the luxury of taking political stands that will alienate advertisers. Moreover, as a business, newspapers find themselves in an increasingly precarious position for a variety of reasons: increased costs of newsprint and labor, growing competition from television and the decline of downtown business revenues due to the shift of the middle class to suburban areas. As a result of these shifts in the economic position of the metropolitan newspaper, very few cities now have two or more competitive daily papers. Ninety-one percent of the residents of metropolitan areas have at least two daily papers, but in many instances both papers are owned by the same publishing company. For example, in San

Diego the Copley Press owns both the morning paper, the *Union*, and the evening paper, the *Tribune*. Both, I can say without fear of contradiction, lean ideologically toward the Right and are imbued with the spirit of local boosterism.

The political positions of newspapers are broadly predictable. In metropolitan affairs, newspapers can be expected to support policies which maintain the central-city economy. This means probable support of mass transit, urban renewal, downtown parking, and other projects to keep the central city viable. Suburban daily and weekly papers are generally supported by businesses in the suburbs and can be expected to take a prosuburb (anticentral-city) stand on local issues.[43] The quality of these political positions varies widely: certainly it is clear that most newspaper editors do not restrict the expression of their values and opinions to the editorial page; rather, they "control" the news, especially local political news, through strategic placement of stories — burying news releases of some groups while seeking news from others, and failing to report items which might tarnish the image of the city (civil rights marches, civil disorders, crime and vice activities in certain areas of the city).

The quality of local political news coverage is also affected by the fact that few dailies assign more than one reporter to cover local government, and, as Banfield and Wilson delicately put it, "He is seldom the liveliest reporter on the paper."[44]

Unfortunately there has been little empirical study of the impact of newspapers on local politics. The scant literature suggests strongly that newspapers are more influential among middle-class than among working-class, black, or ethnic subpopulations. This is because newspapers are read more often and carefully by those with more formal education. Newspapers are a major political force in cities that: (1) are characterized by weak party organization, (2) are subject to long ballots, (3) hold nonpartisan elections, or (4) must cope with frequent and technically worded referenda.[45] In fact, any situation which muddies the local political situation contributes to the power of the newspaper since it becomes a primary dependable source of information and interpretation.

Thomas Dye concludes that newspapers have more influence on local politics than on state or national politics for three reasons: (1) the middle classes which read newspapers are likely to be relatively more important in local politics, (2) the relative obscurity of local politics to the voter results in his greater reliance on newspapers for information and viewpoint, and (3) party affiliations are relatively weak in their effect on local politics.[46]

There may be important differences in the political orientations of newspapers and those of the electronic media — radio and television. But these media are also primarily businesses and share many of the business dispositions of the press. One might suspect, because of the potential for instant communication to large audiences, that the electronic media could have a relatively greater influence on city politics than the newspapers, but that assumption has yet to be tested by political scientists.

Public Utilities   The political actors we have been describing so far have been essentially private interests which, because of their needs, become involved with public action. Public utilities are, obviously, public bodies created and regulated by state law specifically to operate for public purposes. Despite that seemingly great difference, public utilities in their mode of operation, in the orientations of their management, and in their concern with returning dividends to investors, often act like private businesses. Their political orientations and strategies parallel those of other business groups as well. Of course, most of the utilities' political action is directed at the state level, but they are characteristically active in the urban areas they service as well. Like other business groups, their basic orientation is in favor of growth: the more people, the more consumers. However, because of the large fixed costs of putting down and maintaining mains and power lines, they are especially anxious that growth be predictable and stable. A rapid shift of population from, say, the zone-in-transition to the suburbs could leave the company with excess capacity in the old area and not enough in the developing section. These strains can be severe when rapid, so public utilities executives often advocate comprehensive city planning and rigorous land-use control. Further, they are consistent advocates of a city policy aimed at attracting additional industry that would require power and water and that would employ additional home-owning consumers. Finally, public utility companies favor any political action that helps them stave off the occasional movements to make them fully public bodies under governmental ownership.

Civic Associations

The San Francisco Bay area study of city councilmen found that of the councilmen they interviewed only 28 percent named specific business groups (such as merchants, real estate brokers, or unions) as the most powerful interest groups that appear before them.[47] More often, the councilmen perceived that civic associations (like service clubs, ad hoc citizens groups, or improvement associations) were most influential. In fact, 94 percent of the councilmen who acknowledged group activity at the local level named civic associations as the most influential participants in city politics.[48] In addition, the San Francisco Bay area study revealed that civic associations were the most common training ground for the locally politically active. As Table 5.2 shows, 44 percent of those interviewed indicated that their involvement with a civic activity was their initial point of contact with city politics. In sum, "civic organizations and activities dominate the shaping of the politically active stratum."[49]

Does this mean that economic interests are less central than we have so far implied? Not really, because civic associations are characteristically, though not always, dominated by economic interests and are spokesmen for them. For example, I studied a movement in a Kansas town of about 45,000 which was launched by a group of ultraconservatives; its purpose was to pass by referendum an ordinance forbidding the city to undertake any urban renewal projects for a ten-year period. Most of the businessmen of the city opposed this ordinance. The Chamber of Commerce could have become the vehicle of organized opposition, its executive director told me; but, he said, "Too many people are wary of business, see us as mostly interested in making money for ourselves even if it hurts others." Instead, an ad hoc organization with an ambiguous title, "Stand Up for Midwest City," was formed. The executive director was direct about it: "I put it together," he acknowledged. Thomas Dye's observation is probably correct, that "civic associations are the predominant style of organized interest group activity at the local level, that businessmen, reform groups, taxpayer associations, merchants, service clubs, developers, and so on all organize themselves into civic associations for action at the local level."[50]

Not all civic associations have the same aims and characteristics. Let us briefly consider four kinds of civic associations: ad hoc groups, good-government groups, taxpayers groups, and neighborhood improvement groups.

Table 5.2   Experiences and Conditions Which Prompted Initial Political Activity of Individuals Later Elected to City Council, San Francisco Bay Area (N - 431)*

	%
Civic Activities	14
Partisan Involvements	13
Occupational Ties	26
Sense of Personal Investment in the Community	22
Communitywide Political Event	23

*Percentages total more than 100 because some councilmen reported more than one condition.

Source: Adapted from Kenneth Prewitt, *The Recruitment of Political Leaders* (Indianapolis: Bobbs-Merrill Co., 1970), p. 85.

Ad hoc groups

Like the "Stand Up for Midwest City" group in the preceding il-lustration, many civic associations form in response to a particular local issue or situation. Since unique situations call them into being, they often disappear after the issue cools.

The ad hoc organization has many advantages for local action; it can provide the grounds for a short-term coalition of usually differing groups. At the same time, the vagueness of the organizational name masks the fact that unaccustomed political bedfellows are getting together. No embarrassing public explanations have to be made if labor and management groups both support the ad hoc Citizens Committee to Fluoridate the Water. An ad hoc group can also assume a cloak of objectivity and neutrality, which permits it to court public support much more effectively than an established group with known biases.

Good-government groups

Here we have an example of a kind of interest group which develops as a response to the local political process itself. Good-government groups will be discussed more fully in connection with the reform movement (Chapter 8), because they usually aim to have the local government adopt one or all of the elements of the reform package — i.e. council-manager government, home rule, nonpartisan elections, civil service reforms, etc. Like the ad hoc groups, the good-government organization provides a ground for political coalition apart from established interests or parties and generally relies on a neutral-sounding, mother-and-apple pie name to convey a sense of their detached concern for the "public good." To illustrate, here is a list of some good-government groups in existence in American cities: The Citizens League of Pawtucket, The Richmond Civic Association, The Municipal League of Spokane, The Cleveland Citizens League, The Citizens Union of New York City, Citizens Action of Grand Rapids, The New Boston Committee, and The Hartford Citizens Charter Committee. While it is true that many of the active members of the good-government groups have no immediate self-interest to be served by the changes they advocate, it is also true that these groups generally promote the values of the middle class. In fact, the reform package, I shall contend in Chapter 8, is based on the middle-class conception of "good," and when implemented usually results in public policies more favorable to middle-class residents.

A few good-government groups are also involved in local elections. For example, the Citizens Association of Kansas City has virtually dominated the recruitment and elections of city councilmen since it was organized in 1941. The Citizens Association was founded in reaction to the Pendergast

Machine domination of the city and has, throughout its history, represented predominantly middle-class values even though in recent years it has actively sought to incorporate a broadened range of local interests.[51]

The League of Women Voters and the Parent-Teacher Association are special cases of good-government groups. The League of Women Voters commonly restricts itself to efforts to stimulate informed voting participation. One of the League's efforts, for example, is to prepare and distribute local candidates' responses to League-posed questions on local issues and government. Occasionally, after studying a particular local situation, the League of Women Voters will advocate a policy. It is not uncommon for the League to publicly support charter changes which fit the reform package. The PTA, of course, tends to specialize its interests in the area of education; but it often becomes involved in both city council deliberations and referenda elections which affect the level of financial support the city affords education.

Taxpayers groups

Quite like the good-government groups in basic aims are a number of taxpayers associations. As their name makes explicit, however, these groups specialize in matters of government taxation and expenditure. They generally keep pressure on city government to spend less and to spend more efficiently. To say that taxpayers associations are simply low-tax advocates would be a slight distortion, however, since often taxpayer groups can be found advocating government expenditures that will lead to the same kind of growth that business needs. A growing tax base, after all, relieves pressure on the taxpayers. In fact, it is usually the case that local taxpayers associations do not really represent the total taxpaying public; rather, they are organized by, supported by, and therefore represent the large taxpayers — that is, the business interests that have large investments in industrial and commercial property in the city.

Neighborhood improvement associations

Again, in this case, a grandiose-sounding group name masks a group's essentially economic goals. The neighborhood association represents some residents of a particular area of the city who are interested in safeguarding their property values. Characteristically the neighborhood associations are composed of both local homeowners and area businessmen, both of whom have a substantial amount of their capital invested in the neighborhood. Homeowners are interested in assuring that the other homes in the area stay as valuable as, or more valuable than, their own. Zoning which permits cheaper housing, multiple-unit housing, or business uses in a residential neighborhood is anathema to the homeowner because he fears that such developments will reduce the resale value of his home. Most neighborhood improvement associations find themselves resisting the current modes of achieving racial and ethnic integration of neighborhoods, simply because the newcomers are likely to need cheaper houses than those already there. So homeowners associations often come forward with the formulation: "We are not opposed to blacks as neighbors. Some of our best friends are blacks. We welcome any minority group member who is willing and able to buy and maintain a house here." What is left unsaid is that the association has pressured into existence the prevailing zoning ordinance which stipulates that any new residences in the area must be single-family dwellings on 1-acre lots.

In addition to the protection of property values, neighborhood improvement associations are likely to lobby government for street repair and improvement as well as adequate lighting and police protection.

Area business people are also supporters of neighborhood associations. Like the homeowner, they are interested in keeping property tax levels down. Businessmen also may worry about changes in the social composition of the neighborhood. If they are retail merchants, for example, they must guard against allowing industrial uses in the area that might cause neighborhood customers to move out.

Organized Labor

In general, organized labor is less active and less influential in local politics than it is at either the state or national level. After all, the governmental decisions which most directly affect the bread and butter of the union are made at those levels: wage and hour laws, regulations affecting job benefits and tenure, laws affecting collective bargaining, and laws setting terms for strike settlement. To be sure, local politics can affect the status of the union: the city police can harass strikers at a local factory, for example. But except for specific issues or elections which affect the economic position of the union rather directly, unions tend to minimize their local political activities.[52]

As one union leader in Toledo put it,

> City government is not as important for us. We've got to think about state and national issues. The state is in many ways the most important, I think, since it handles workman's compensation, unemployment and such things.[53]

However, this generalization masks great diversity of union political activity in American cities: in certain cities (like Detroit) unions aspire to control the city government, in others (like San Diego) the union is content to be relatively uninvolved. For example, one study of six union locals in and near Chicago found that all the union leaders interviewed wanted friendly treatment by police, courts, and public officials. But beyond that, their goals diverge radically. One of the United Mine Worker locals in this study ignored city politics. At the same time, the local United Steelworkers and the locals of the United Auto Workers were sensitive to their need for support from the dominant local Democratic party.[54]

One explanation of the differing political orientations of unions from city to city is that the craft unions have different connections to the local community than do the industrial unions. Craft unions, composed as they are of skilled, well-paid workers, are generally tied closely to competitive local markets and are more likely to be concerned about access to the local bureaucracy, local wage and hour regulations, and local police policy. The industrial unions, by contrast, organize unskilled and semiskilled workers in nationally owned and operated industries. They are less directly involved with local regulations.[55]

Beyond this craft-industrial division there is also a strong tendency for unions to be unable to act as a local political force because of internal divisions on local issues. To illustrate, the question of whether rents should be decontrolled was a hotly contested topic in Chicago at one time. Most of the members of the local Steelworkers were renters, and the union could reasonably be expected to take a stand for rent controls. Yet the local made only weak and ineffective efforts to represent its members on this issue. The leadership made no effort to mobilize members in either the meetings or in the local's newspaper. When the local's president appeared before the city council to oppose the decontrol ordinance, he was decisively opposed by a large, well-organized landlord group. In the landlord group were a significant number of union members, including a few active shop stewards, who were themselves landlords.[56]

Even when a local chapter of a union is able to agree on a position, they are generally less effective than are business leaders. Leaders of organized labor usually are less highly regarded in the city than are business leaders.[57] As we have noted, business leaders often are "symbols of civic legitimacy"; but union leaders characteristically do not achieve that level of public confidence: they "must contend with whatever stigma attaches to being from a lower-class background and associated with a special interest group."[58]

Public employees

City governments employ about 4½ million people. These employees of the city government share with other groups the need to protect and promote their interests.[59] In common with employees everywhere they form groups, sometimes union affiliated and sometimes not, to press for wage and salary increases, job benefits, and job security. City employees exert their influence through either unions or professional associations. Some of the professional associations are affiliated with international unions and, even when they are not, have increasingly come to function like unions in local politics. The American Federation of State, County and Municipal Employees (AFSCME), The International Association of Firefighters (IAFF), and the American Federation of Teachers (AFT) are all affiliated with AFL-CIO. Other groups, which strictly speaking are not unions, act like them — associations like the Fraternal Order of Police, the Uniformed Firemen's Association, and the National Education Association.

City employees have some bargaining advantages. They are more knowledgeable about city government than most citizens and have more inside information. They are in the position to be effective lobbyists if they so choose. City officials characteristically respect that potential power of the city employees and give special consideration to their wage and salary requests. City employees groups, nonetheless, have a major disadvantage in actualizing their political power: American law prohibits them from striking. Even so, work slowdowns and disruptions have a similar effect and are increasingly common. The reform movement has pressed further restrictions on political participation by city employees. When the first city manager of Skokie, Illinois, took office, he published a checklist of acceptable and unacceptable political activities (see Table 5.3). If seriously enforced, such regulations would go a long distance toward making city employees political "neuters." As you might expect, it is difficult to enforce these regulations.

Ethnic and Black Participants

"You can always tell who has no power," I was once told by a successful politician, "They yell a lot." Ethnics and blacks have been highly visible participants in urban politics because they yelled — and more. Their agitation has produced differential results thus far. The ethnic minorities seem well along the path of assimilation while the more recently arrived blacks and Spanish-speaking people remain ghettoized, and relatively powerless, in what are essentially internal colonies.

The assimilation pattern

America is rightly described as a nation of nations. New York City, for example, has more Italians than has Naples, more Greeks than Sparta, and more Puerto Ricans than San Juan. Most have been assimilated, that is, brought within the basic habits, attitudes, and mode of life of the national culture. Assimilation may occur in a single generation or more, or not at all. According to a number of scholars, most of the European immigrants (Italians, Irish, Greek, Polish, etc.) have become so thoroughly socialized in

Table 5.3   Regulation of Political Activities by Village of Skokie Employees

Type of Activity	Whether Permitted or Not			
	Partisan Elections	Nonpartisan Elections	On Village Time	On Employee's Time
Membership in a political party, club, or organization	Yes	— —	No	Yes
Officer or committee chairman for a political party or organization	No	— —	No	No
Attendance at political rallies or meetings, as spectator only.*	Yes	Yes	No	Yes
Speak at political meetings, make endorsements or appear on behalf of any candidate or proposal	No	Yes	No	Yes
Circulate petitions, distribute printed matter or badges, or sell tickets for any candidate or party	No	No	No	No
Sign a petition	Yes	Yes	Yes	Yes
Solicit or accept money from any person for any political purpose	No	No	No	No
Serve as precinct captain or party worker for any political organization	No	No	No	No
Assist in getting voters to polls on election day	No	No	No	No
Act as poll watcher for a political party	No	— —	No	No
Make contributions to political party or organization	No	No	No	No
Be a candidate for public office**	Yes	— —	No	Yes
Use or threaten to use influence of position to coerce or persuade vote	No	No	No	No
Participate in nonpartisan voter registration campaigns	— —	Yes	No	Yes
Participate in partisan voter registration campaigns	Yes	— —	No	Yes
Be a delegate to a political convention	No	No	No	No
Cast a vote	Yes	Yes	Yes	Yes

*Not permitted in uniform.

**Must take leave of absence during campaign and term of office.

Source: Bernard L. Marsh, "Regulating Political Activity of Employees," *Public Management*, 42 (October 1960): 229.

the culture of middle-class America that "their political attitudes and behavior are scarcely distinguishable from those of direct descendants of arrivals on the *Mayflower*."[60] Most American cities still have a "Little Italy" or "Germantown" but a substantial proportion of the descendants of those ethnic residents own homes in the suburbs. In 1960 there were as many ethnics living outside central cities as in them.

Robert Dahl suggests that the assimilation pattern creates three distinct stages of ethnic politics.[61] In the first stage there is relative economic and social homogeneity within the group. There are few indigenous leaders. The result is great similarity in voting habits. In the second stage group members begin to achieve different social and economic statuses. Some members attain professional positions. Even so, there remains a high degree of ethnic consciousness among the upwardly mobile. At this stage the pattern of voting similarity remains. In the third stage, considerable heterogeneity results from large numbers of the group being assimilated into the nonproletarian classes. Ethnic identity in the third stage becomes a source of personal embarrassment rather than pride. Thus, voting solidarity breaks down.

It would be premature to conclude that most of our ethnic populations have evolved to that third stage. Nineteen percent of our population still consists of first- or second-generation immigrants. In addition to this large number of unassimilated immigrants, several studies point to a persistence of ethnic politics in most cities. Polish-American voters in Illinois have been found to still cross party lines to vote for Polish names.[62] An ethnic name on the ballot takes on even greater significance in a nonpartisan election because it is one of a few available cues for voters in a relatively low-interest campaign.[63]

Some scholars seem to contradict even the basic assumptions of the assimilationists. Raymond Wolfinger, for example, re-examined ethnic politics in New Haven and found that: "The importance of ethnicity in voting decisions does not steadily diminish from an initial peak but instead increases during at least the first two generations."[64] That observation leads Wolfinger to formulate an alternative conception of ethnic politics — a "mobilization theory." The mobilization theory is based on the assumption that ethnic voting will be greatest when the ethnic group has produced a middle class, which occurs in the second and third generations, not in the first. The emergence of the ethnic middle class is important because it produces: (1) the capability for intense ethnic identification and (2) higher levels of ethnic relevance in an election. According to Wolfinger, "The most powerful and visible sign of ethnic political relevance is a fellow ethnic's name at the head of the ticket, evident to everyone who enters the voting booth. Middle-class status is a virtual prerequisite for candidacy for mayor's office; an ethnic groups' development of sufficient political skill and influence to secure such a nomination also requires the development of a middle class."[65]

The mobilization theory emphasizes the fact that ethnic groups cultivate political resources over time. Particularly important are access to political parties and emergence of leadership which produces greater public visibility of the ethnic candidate. In addition, middle-class ethnics have more money and more time, as well as more skill, to devote to political concerns.

The colonial pattern

A number of scholars, mostly white, see the blacks as simply standing further back in the assimilation line. Those scholars presume that, given time, the black urban dweller will follow the ethnic minorities to middle-class status.

The alternative formulation has been advanced that the condition of the black in urban America is different in kind, not just in degree, from that of the ethnic minorities. Militant blacks such as Malcolm X, Eldridge Cleaver, and Stokley Carmichael pronounced American life fundamentally racist and declared that racism had created and conditioned the structure of American society. They saw the relation of white to black in America as a relation of oppressors to oppressed, colonizers to colonized. William Tabb, an economist, finds the colonial analogy analytically useful. Tabb contends that the economic relations of the ghetto to white America closely parallel those between Third World nations and the industrially advanced countries. Specifically he finds the following similarities: (1) The ghetto has a relatively low per capita income and a high birth rate. (2) Its residents are for the most part unskilled. (3) Businesses lack capital and managerial know-how. (4) Local markets are limited. (5) The incidence of credit default in the ghetto is high. (6) Little saving takes place and what is saved usually is not invested locally. (7) Goods and services tend to be "imported"; only the simplest and most labor-intensive goods and services are produced locally. (8) The ghetto is dependent on one basic export, its unskilled labor power. (9) Aggregate demand for this export does not increase to match the growth of the ghetto labor force, and unemployment is prevalent. (10) Consumer goods are advertised 24 hours a day on radio and television, constantly reminding ghetto residents of the availability of goods and services which they cannot afford to buy. (11) Welfare payments and other governmental payments-in-kind are needed to support the needs of the ghetto. (12) Local businesses are owned in large numbers by nonresidents, many of whom are white. (13) Important jobs in the local public economy (teachers, policemen, postmen) are held by white outsiders.[66]

Colonialism rests, then, on two key relationships; both necessitate separation and inferior status. One involves economic control and exploitation, and the second involves political dependence and subjugation. As regards economic control and exploitation, we have already spent considerable time (Chapter 3) indicating that economic development is a major determinant of the physical character and the patterns of social segregation that occur in American cities. It should of course be underscored that such social differentiation is a consequence of the division of labor, *not* the product of a "conspiracy" to segregate any group. Irrespective of intent, the fact is that blacks are ghettoized and that ghetto economies are integrated into, or (if you will) exploited by, the economic institutions of the larger society. Richard Hatcher, the black mayor of Gary, Indiana, put the matter somewhat despairingly: "There is much talk about black control of the ghetto," he said. "What does that mean? I am mayor of a city of roughly 90 thousand black people, but we do not control the possibility of jobs for them, of money for their schools or state funded social services. These things are in the hands of the United States Steel Corporation and the County Department of Welfare of the state of Indiana. Will the poor in Gary's worst slums be helped because the pawn shop owner is black, not white?"[67]

If blacks were being assimilated, we should expect that fact to show in the desegregation of urban housing, for example. Yet the literature on residential segregation is virtually unanimous in finding a high degree of black segregation in metropolitan areas, and there has been a remarkable stability of this segregated pattern since the 1930s.[68] Several statistical studies have also concluded that residential segregation is not just a result of being poor.[69] It has been found that segregation of blacks results not so much from low income as from the working of "the exclusionary interests"; these can be defined as "real estate boards, suburban governments — that establish and maintain vast sanctuaries from Negroes and poor people."[70] There appears to be a great variety of available suburban housing. As one study put it, "The existing suburban housing supply, in terms of housing cost, provides ample opportunity for desegregation now."[71] Local government policy which could hasten desegregation often in effect subsidizes slumlords through lax or non-existent housing code enforcement. The result is that owning slum properties produces greater economic reward than it might.

In sum, there is considerable evidence that the black ghetto is economically an internal colony. Is it also politically dependent and subjugated? To answer that question, let us turn to an examination of the resources and strategies of contemporary black politics.

Black resources and strategies

We have been believers, believing in our burdens and our demigods too long. Now the needy no longer weep and pray; the longsuffering arise, and our fists bleed against the bars with a strange insistency.[72]

It is difficult to say when that "strange insistency" began to take a political form. The historic school desegregation decision in 1954 was

Marshall Henrichs

Bringing to everyone the best that urban living offers is a formidable task.

followed by a succession of civil rights acts, public accommodation laws, and open housing laws. These were undeniably significant changes, putting the law of the land at least clearly on the side of racial equality. But from the standpoint of the individual black, they were insufficient. Looking around, they saw the same deteriorated housing, the same problems of feeding and clothing themselves. Many came to the cities to seek the brighter tomorrow (see Table 5.4).

Black action in the fifties, sixties, and seventies has taken a variety of forms. In general the stance has moved from a conciliatory and nonviolent one in the beginning to confrontation and violence, and back again. There has been great variety in the specific strategies and resource bases which black Americans have utilized to present their conflict. In the pages that follow we shall discuss several: the voting strategy, the cultivation of black leadership,

Table 5.4   **Black Population of Nation's Largest Cities**
(Figures are percentages of city's total population)

	1940	1950	1960	1970 est.
New York	6	9	14	19
Chicago	8	14	23	32
Los Angeles	4	9	14	23
Philadelphia	13	14	26	32
Detroit	9	16	29	47
Houston	22	21	23	27
Baltimore	19	24	35	47
Cleveland	10	16	29	38
Washington, D.C.	28	38	54	68
Milwaukee	2	3	9	18
Dallas	17	13	19	25
San Francisco	1	6	10	17
St. Louis	13	18	29	46
Boston	3	5	9	13
New Orleans	30	32	37	45
San Antonio	7	7	7	10
San Diego	2	4	6	10
Pittsburgh	9	12	17	21
Seattle	1	3	5	9
Memphis	41	37	37	39
Buffalo	3	6	13	22
Phoenix	6	5	5	10

the strategies of disruption and violence, and the movement for neighborhood control.

Black Voting Participation

It has already been suggested that the urban poor participate less in politics than do those with higher social and economic status. There are of course some exceptions in particular cities and on particular issues to that overall pattern. But in general it is true that black voting participation rates are lower than those of whites.[73]

In signing the voting rights act of 1965, Lyndon B. Johnson asserted that the right to vote was "the most powerful instrument ever devised by man for breaking down injustice.... "[74] Blacks express great skepticism of that perspective and there is much in the political science literature to support such skepticism. For example, a very careful analysis of voting as a political resource in Durham, North Carolina, concludes that "the vote is a far more

	1940	1950	1960	1970 est.
Atlanta	38	37	38	39
Denver	2	4	6	10
Columbus, Ohio	12	13	16	32
Indianapolis	13	15	21	29
K.C., Mo.	11	12	17	24
Cincinnati	12	15	22	31
Minneapolis	1	1	2	5
Newark, N.J.	11	17	34	46
Forth Worth	14	13	16	20
Louisville	15	16	18	24
Long Beach	1	2	3	7
Portland, Ore.	1	3	4	7
Oklahoma City	9	9	12	18
Oakland, Calif.	3	12	23	39
Birmingham	41	40	40	40
Norfolk, Va.	32	29	26	23
Miami, Fla.	22	16	22	28
Omaha	5	6	8	12

Source: The National Advisory Commission on Civil Disorders, *Report* (Washington, D.C. U.S. Government Printing Office, 1968).

important instrument for achieving legal justice than social justice."[75] In other words, the study found that the vote aided blacks to achieve equal treatment by the government, but that in discrimination of the more important kind — including such things as comparable income, comparable jobs, opportunity for economic advancement and courteous and equal treatment by fellow citizens — the vote proved ineffective: "the really striking gains of Durham's Negro minority have come through resources other than votes."[76]

Black Leadership

Leadership is a crucial resource for any group. Skillful and effective leaders can mobilize a variety of resources: They can attract money and attention. They can select appropriate goals and dramatize them effectively. They can choose strategies appropriate to their goals. They can inspire the loyalty and action of their followers. And they can negotiate with both allies and opponents. These are obviously divergent and demanding skills. Black leaders have, over time, cultivated them in strikingly different ways. A number of blacks, as Table 5.5 shows, have achieved elective office, which is itself a political resource. Interestingly, the Southern states distinguish themselves in these figures, having many blacks in local offices.

There has been a traditional style of leadership in evidence throughout most of the history of the country. In addition, black political leadership has taken a moderate course and a militant course. We shall consider all three forms in the following pages.

Traditional Style   The old order among blacks has been led by a group of persons of prestige and personal achievement in the city. Such men are usually those who have achieved middle-class status in their occupational and social positions.[77] Black ministers are particularly important as leaders, since in the pursuit of their occupations they embody attributes that many blacks regard as central to leadership. They have a mass following, a dignified calling, and are accustomed to pronouncing the "truth" with authority. Prominent black doctors, lawyers, businessmen, and politicians are also often included among traditional black leaders. Such leaders are generally volunteers rather than professionals, working through voluntary associations such as the NAACP which are small in total membership, have no paid staff, and have little influence. They are also generalists, speaking for the blacks on all issues. The fact that traditional leaders are both generalists and volunteers inhibits their effectiveness. Volunteer generalists do not have the time or the knowledge to speak to all the needs of their constituents.

Traditional black leaders typically seek "welfare goals." This is a crucial point of distinction between the traditional leader and the more modern black leader. The modern black leader tends to seek status rather than welfare goals. The traditional, welfare orientation lays stress on individual

Table 5.5   Black Elected Officials in United States

		U.S.	State			County			City			Law Enforcement				
	Total	U.S. Congress	Senators	Representatives	Others	Commissioners, Supervisors	Election Commissioners	Others	Mayors	Councilmen, Aldermen	Others	Judges, Magistrates	Constables, Marshals	Justices of Peace	Others	School Board
Alabama	89			1		4		4	4	35	2		9	19		8
Alaska	1															1
Arizona	7		1	2												4
Arkansas	56								4	9	1			4		38
California	109	2	1	5		1			3	27	1	14				55
Colorado	7		1	2						2		1				1
Connecticut	46		1	4						23	1		5			11
Delaware	9		1	2		1				4						1
District of Columbia	8															8
Florida	38			1		1			2	30	1		2			1
Georgia	39		2	12		3			1	14		1				6
Hawaii	1									1						
Illinois	77	1	4	14					1	21	2	9				25
Indiana	31			3		2		1	1	8	2	2		1		11
Iowa	5			1								2				2
Kansas	6			3		1			1							1
Kentucky	41		1	2		1			1	22		4	4			6
Louisiana	66			1		5			3	29			13	7		8
Maryland	44		2	9					5	24		4				
Massachusetts	8	1*		2						2						3
Michigan	110	2	3	10		25		2	2	22		11	1			32
Minnesota	8			1								1	2			4
Mississippi	84			1		4	16	1	3	33			8	10	1	5
Missouri	65	1	2	13					2	23	4	5	1		1	13
Nebraska	2															2
Nevada	3			1						1		1				
New Jersey	79			4		3		1	4	38	1					28
New Mexico	3			1						2						
New York	121	2	3	9		4				10	2	20				71
North Carolina	68			1		1			5	47	1					13
Ohio	89	1	3	10		1			4	40	3	11	1			15
Oklahoma	36		1	4					2	10						19
Pennsylvania	57	1	2	9				1		13	1	17	4			9
Rhode Island	2			1						1						
South Carolina	42					2			2	29	1	4				4
Tennessee	39		2	6						9		12	3	1	2	4
Texas	30		1	2					1	15						11
Virginia	45		1	2		4		1		31				6		
Washington	4			1						1		2				
West Virginia	1															1
Wisconsin	10			1		2				6						1
Wyoming	1															1
Totals	1581	11	32	141	0	65	16	11	51	585	23	123	47	57	4	423

*U.S. Senator

Note: As of June 19, 1970, nine states had no black elected officials: Idaho, Maine, Montana, New Hampshire, North Dakota, Oregon, South Dakota, Utah and Vermont.

The MARC Corporation, 1819 H St., N.W., Washington, D.C. 20006

Source: A. J. Adams and Joan M. Burke, *Civil Rights* (New York: R. R. Bowker, 1970), p. 171.

material advances — higher welfare payments, better jobs, better working conditions, better housing conditions. In other words, welfare goals are aimed at ameliorative action within a segregated system.[78] By distinction, status orientations emphasize class advancement for blacks as a group. Status goals include ultimate desegregation and the abolition of legal, political, and social inequalities.

In the period in which traditional black leadership was the predominant style, black politicians usually proceeded by attaching themselves to and drawing their power from ties with the Democratic or Republican machines. This older style of machine leadership is illustrated by the career of the late Congressman William L. Dawson. Beginning in 1939, Dawson joined the Democratic party, was appointed to the position of committeeman of Chicago's second ward, and proceeded to create a network of obligations and loyalties which brought under his control the organizations of five or six black wards in central Chicago. Dawson's power was initially closely tied to the power of the city-wide Democratic machine under Mayor Edward Kelley; he continued that close association with the Daley machine. Like most machines, Dawson's tended to be nonideological. His leadership clearly fits the traditional style.

> The Dawson machine, like all machines, is an organization whose purpose is the election of men to office and which is sustained mainly through the distribution of tangible incentives to its members. To a greater extent than any other Negro organization which acts in the public or civic areas, it is "issue free."[79]

The Moderate Style   Moderates, as you might expect, tend to be in the middle. Typically, the goals sought by moderates are not "frontier area" status goals; but neither are they purely welfare objectives. The moderate leadership in Winston-Salem, North Carolina, for example, worked in 1962 and 1963 in the following areas: (1) They sought extension of full city services to blacks — that is, trying to get streets paved in black neighborhoods, trying to improve recreational facilities, and seeking increased expenditures for black pupils in the schools. (2) They sought to place more black employees in city government jobs. (3) They pressed for greater representation of blacks on city boards and commissions. (4) They worked for better employment opportunities for blacks.[80]

> These goals are not the kind that maximize race consciousness. They are not of the variety that can mobilize masses of people. At the same time, they are generally more "visible" than the goals of Conservatives and draw racial lines more sharply.[81]

By contrast to traditional leaders, the moderate leader tends to be a full-time civil rights worker; he is more likely to engage in continuous and overt strategies. The moderate tends to rely heavily on the vote as his major political resource and on legal attacks on segregation; he avoids the disruptive tactics of the militants.

People in the middle tend to get shot at from both sides. Moderate leaders in Northern cities found themselves increasingly uncomfortable during the urban riots of the late sixties. An incident which occurred during the 1965 Watts riot illustrates the point: Mervyn Dymally, a popular black assemblyman from south central Los Angeles, was walking the riot-torn streets when he was approached by a young rioter who asked, "Who you with?" "I'm with you, man," the assemblyman replied. "Then here's a rock, baby — throw it," the youth ordered. Dymally, quite upset by the incident, refused.[82] Dymally's quandary would be understood by all moderate black leaders who are personally and professionally committed to nonviolence, to orderly social change, and to maintenance of the existing institutional structure. In fact, most moderates work hard to confine protests to nonviolent responses.[83]

The Militant Style   When asked to define the militant political style, most white Americans immediately sieze on the militant's willingness to use violence as an instrument of social change as the basic point of distinction. It is true that H. Rap Brown has proclaimed violence "as American as cherry pie" and that most militant black leaders have refused to renounce violence as a strategy. But it is a severe distortion to discuss the militant style as if its central tenet were a belief in violence as an end in itself. The perspective of militant black leaders is considerably more elaborate and more sophisticated than such a formulation would suggest.

"Black power advocates," as militant leaders are often styled, are not in universal agreement. However, certain central tenets seem widely shared among militant leaders. The position usually expounds an admonition to blacks to *affirm their race*. It is not bad to be black; "black is beautiful." The black man has a history of accomplishment in America and is a descendant of a high African culture. It is assumed that the achievement of a prideful black identity is a necessary first step for self-help. This position necessitates *separatism* from the white society. In the short run, at least, this means the renunciation of the goal of black assimilation into white society. "The goal of black people must *not* be to assimilate into middle class America, for that class — as a whole — is without a viable consciousness as regards humanity. . . . The values of that class are based on material aggrandizement, not the expansion of humanity. The values of that class ultimately support cloistered little closed societies, tucked away neatly in tree-lined suburbia."[84]

Thus, *middle-class white institutions are seen as the central problem.* White institutions created the colonial ghetto situation and they perpetuate it. To explain, Stokley Carmichael and Charles Hamilton distinguished between institutional racism and individual racism. *Individual racism* is manifested for example, when white terrorists bomb an occupied black church. Individual racists can be singled out and held responsible; their acts are overt. *Institutional racism* is covert, indirect, and collective; thus personal responsibility for it is difficult to assign. "It is institutional racism that keeps black people locked in dilapidated slum tenements, subject to the daily prey of exploitative slumlords, merchants, loan sharks, and discriminatory real estate agents."[85] Those discriminatory white institutions do not yield either to the efforts of an individual black or to abstract moral argument. The most pervasive form of racial discrimination, then, is institutional racism. White institutions yield only to power. Only when blacks are sufficiently powerful as a group will they be able to achieve the necessary changes in recalcitrant white institutions.

Black solidarity and organization is the key to such power. "As Carmichael and Hamilton put it the 'fundamental premise' of black power is that 'before a group can enter the open society, it must first close ranks.' "[86] White support, in the form of coalitions with other groups, is still possible, but not while the movement is forming: "Enter coalitions only after you are able to stand on your own."[87] Put in this way, the assumptions of the black power movement fit perfectly with what we have called pluralist democracy.

Racial Rioting: Strategy or Outburst?

In the decade of the sixties, race riots occurred in American cities on an unprecedented scale. Watts, the L.A. ghetto, was the scene of major rioting in 1965. Violence again flared in the west side of Chicago and in the Hough section of Cleveland in the summer of 1966. But the summer of 1967 was by far the longest, hottest summer of the decade. Nearly 150 cities reported disorders in black — and in some instances Puerto Rican — neighborhoods that summer.[88] The most violent of these disorders erupted first in Newark, then in Detroit, and each set off chain reactions in neighboring cities. Were these disturbances the wages of black power? A substantial number of white Americans think so; a Harris Poll taken in August 1967 showed that 45 percent of the whites in his sample thought the violence was provoked by "communist backing," "outside agitators," or a "minority of radicals." The best evidence is contradictory. The rioters had a broadly political orientation but were clearly not being led by militant leaders, or indeed by any other leaders. That same Harris Poll found only a small percentage of blacks (7 percent) who formulated the rioting in terms of radicals, agitators, or communists. Most blacks cited social and economic conditions and police maltreatment as the cause.

In addition, we must put the rioting of the sixties in historical perspective. Serious racial disorders occurred in our cities long before the conception of black power was formulated. In fact, some 76 major racial disorders occurred in this country between 1913 and 1963.[89] There were major race riots in Chicago in 1919, and the East St. Louis riots of 1917 resulted in the deaths of at least 39 blacks and the destruction of about a million dollars' worth of property.[90]

More decisively, however, the view that the typical rioter is either a part of the "criminal element" or a "radical" is unsubstantiated. Much empirical work, in fact, flatly contradicts this so-called riffraff theory. Broadly, the riffraff theory makes three assumptions about riots: (1) that only a small proportion (1 or 2 percent) of the ghetto residents participate in the riots; (2) that most of the rioters are "riffraff," — that is, unattached youths, people with criminal records, the unemployed, disoriented migrants from the rural South, self-conscious radicals, and the like; and (3) that the majority of blacks deplore the violence, seeing it as pointless and unhelpful. [91] However comforting the riffraff theory may be to those who would choose to believe that there is really nothing wrong in the ghetto, the best evidence is contradictory. First there was a much larger percentage of ghetto dwellers involved in the rioting of the sixties than the riffraff theory assumes; a study of the Watts riot found that upwards of 15% were active riot participants and that between 34% and 50% expressed a sympathetic understanding of the rioters' goals.[92] In the 1967 Detroit riot, approximately 11% acknowledged active participation in the riot while another 20% to 25% said they were bystanders.[93] More important, the typical rioter has not proved to be much different from his fellow ghetto residents. A study for the Kerner Commission found that the "typical" rioter: (1) was slightly better educated than his fellow ghetto dwellers, (2) was likely to have been born in the area in which the riot occurred, (3) was employed, although usually at a job requiring less education than he possessed, (4) had an income about equal to that of other ghetto dwellers, and (5) was no more likely than anyone else in the area to possess a "record."[94] In sum, participation in and support of the rioting was by no means the position of a tiny minority of misfits.

Finally, it must be recognized that a large portion of the rioters think they are engaged in a lifetime protest against the actions of whites and expect that the outcome will produce an improvement in the lot of blacks and in their relations with whites.[95] For example, in the Watts riot:

> Of the 56% who claim the riot had a purpose, each cited one or another of the following goals of the riot: (a) to call attention to Negro problems, (b) to express Negro hostility to Whites, or (c) to serve an instrumental purpose of improving conditions, ending discrimination, or communicating with the "power structure."[96]

To disqualify the riffraff theory is not to invalidate the view that the riots were directly inspired by the black power movement. It seems that a large number of rioters, while not consciously black power advocates nor responding to specific commands of militant leaders, nonetheless broadly shared that political perspective. Particularly they shared a sense of grievance and persecution as well as a belief that only drastic measures could redress their grievances. This is not to say of course that rioting was selected as a rational strategy, chosen to dramatize their plight. The riots seem more accurately characterized as outbursts of righteous indignation.

In addition, it must be recognized that a number of rioters were involved out of other motives. Edward Banfield has emphasized some of these other motives (see Table 5.6).[97] He found rioters to be engaged in (1) rampage, (2) a foray for pillage, (3) an outburst of righteous indignation, or (4) a demonstration.

Banfield uses the Detroit riot of 1967 as an example of a foray for pillage. He quotes then: Governor Romney's statement that the Detroit riot was "not primarily a civil rights disturbance, but rather lawlessness and

Table 5.6   Banfield's Typology of Riots, Based on the Motives of the Rioters

Type	Hypothetical Situation	Example
Rampage	Two thousand juveniles break windows after an amusement park closes early, leaving them without transportation.	White youths rampage in Hampton Beach, N.H., and Seaside, Oregon, in 1964.
Foray for Pillage	A gang of hoodlums rob a clothing store and smash the display windows of three other stores, stealing watches, cameras, and rings.	Detroit, 1967.
Outburst	A young man has been shot and killed by the police during a burglary, and a crowd, shouting, "This is for Willie," pelts the police with rocks, bottles, and fire bombs.	Boston Riot of 1837, involving "a native American working class attack on Irish Immigrants." Beginning of 1964 Harlem riot.
Demonstration	Following an inflammatory speech by a racist politician, a mob overturns automobiles and assaults motorists.	1961 Black Muslim demonstration.

Compiled from materials in Edward Banfield, *The Unheavenly City* (Boston: Little, Brown, 1968), Chap. 9 especially pp. 187-192.

hoodlumism by Negroes and Whites."[98] Banfield noted that the major targets of looting were stores that had items that could be consumed directly — liquor, cigarettes, drugs, clothing, television sets, furniture — no matter whether black or whites owned them. Buildings symbolic of the white power structure were usually left untouched. Banfield concluded that the major goal of the rioters was pillage. He quotes a child explaining why the school was not burned: "There was nothing to steal in the school. Who wants a book or a desk?"[99] It would be foolish to deny that some of the rioters were motivated by the quest for fun and profit, but it is an overstatement to ascribe such motives to the majority of rioters — especially in view of the empirical work which disputes that conclusion.[100]

Whatever the intent of the black rioters, subsequent response has been relatively unsympathetic to the pleas many blacks thought they were making for social, economic, and political change. In fact, many whites ascribed the riots to black power advocates, looters, and undesirables. Some retaliatory events subsequent to the rioting have commonly been described as white backlash. The law and order movement has not been uniformly successful, but in a number of cities it has been responsible for the election of mayors and city councilmen. For example, Philadelphia in 1971 elected as mayor the hard-line former police chief, Frank Rizzo, after he campaigned on one of the most blatant antiminority platforms in recent history.

In sum, a number of the riots that broke out in the urban ghettos in the 1960s are best understood as outbursts of righteous indignation against the colonial status of ghetto life.[101] The best evidence indicates that the rioters, though not led by black power advocates in any specific way, had expected their actions to dramatize their plight to the white society. This proved to be a miscalculation.

Neighborhood Control

One of the more controversial proposals which gained currency as racial tensions mounted in the 1960s was that blacks should be given control of the ghetto. Particularly, militant leaders argued that since separation was a fact, blacks should at the very least have control over the local governmental and business institutions. In other words they argued for "colonial independence." This alternative to either integration or assimilation typically involves an agenda of reforms including the following: (1) devolution of as much authority as possible to "neighborhood governments," (2) direct representation of neighborhoods on city councils, boards of education, police commissions, and other significant city government bodies, (3) greater black representation at all levels of public service, (4) similar representation among organized labor groups, and (5) the vigorous application of public resources to develop black control of business within the neighborhood.[102] The implementation of such a reform program would add to the power-poor ghetto dwellers' political resources. Neighborhood control might also provide the means of achieving genuine black community — if, as the militants argue, the taproot of the racial problem in America is that the black man lacks a clear identity. It is debatable whether the black man can achieve such an identity in the current situation in which "he is confronted on all sides by white school teachers, white social workers, and white policemen. Even the stores in the ghetto are owned and operated by white shopkeepers."[103]

The opponents of separatism are many and influential. City officials often oppose it, seeing the movement as a threat to their own control over city

Table 5.7   Black Attitudes Toward Separatism and Toward the Use of Violence, and Black Perceptions of White Attitudes

Present Age	Age 16-19*	Age 20-39		
Highest Educational Level Achieved		8th Grade or less	Grades 9-11	Grade 12
Separatism				
Believe stores in "a black neighborhood should be owned and run by blacks"	22	19	18	18
Believe that schools with mostly black children should have mostly black teachers	16	8	11	10
Use of violence				
Blacks should be ready to use violence to gain rights	22	19	16	17
Would probably participate in a riot	13	11	10	8
Perceptions of white attitudes				
Believe few white people dislike blacks	38	28	36	33
Believe many dislike blacks	47	42	45	51
Believe almost all dislike blacks	12	22	11	12

*Combines all educational categories.

Source: Adapted from Angus Campbell and Howard Schuman, "Racial Attitudes in Fifteen American Cities," in National Advisory Commission on Civil Disorders, *Supplemental Studies* (Washington, D.C.: U.S. Government Printing Office, 1968), pp. 19, 26, 57.

decisions. Municipal bureaucracies, including teachers, policemen, and welfare workers, tend to oppose neighborhood control because they fear that increased black employment would mean that many current employes would lose their jobs.[104] Opposition to the community control movement is not limited to whites. Many moderate black leaders also oppose it. Bayard Rustin, for example, has argued that "black community control is as futile a program as black capitalism. . . . [105] In general these leaders feel that integration is the more hopeful direction and that community control would retard integration. Moreover, it appears that large percentages of blacks are skeptical of separatism. As Table 5.7 shows, a survey of black attitudes in 15 American

		Age 40-69				
Some College	College Graduate	8th Grade or Less	Grades 9-11	Grade 12	Some College	College Graduate
20	30	16	13	13	17	13
10	20	10	4	5	5	3
24	24	9	11	7	14	1
8	9	7	6	3	4	6
36	38	39	39	38	49	60
48	53	40	45	47	42	34
9	6	11	9	8	4	5

Marshall Henrichs

Neighborhood associations attempt to express the needs of their inhabitants.

cities finds that between 83% and 87% of blacks between the ages of 40 and 69 do not believe that a black neighborhood should be owned and run by blacks. Still it is interesting to note in that same table that the younger and more highly educated blacks show more support for separatism. This suggests that the subject of community control of ghetto institutions will be a policy question of increasing importance over the years.

SUMMARY

In this chapter we have surveyed the common political orientations of a number of urban political actors, ranging from some of the more powerful business interests to the relatively powerless minorities of the ghetto. These generalizations, of course, do not apply equally well to all American cities (or to All-American cities). But these materials can provide the starting place for those who are moving toward involvement in the politics of a particular city. For those more interested in the systematic analysis of city politics, this chapter has specified the processes of differentiation which were broadly sketched in Part One. The group theory of politics suggests that it is the interaction of these groups which results in public policy. Distribution of political resources and skill in using resources accounts for who wins and who loses.

Particular emphasis was given to the plight of the black in American city politics. The situation of the black has its parallel for a number of other power-poor minorities as well. Poor whites, youth, Chicanos, Indians, women — all give evidence of rising consciousness of their underrepresented status. Insofar as those groups have begun to formulate a program and articulate a position, they have tended to follow the patterns established by the blacks. As this last section indicates, black strategies and black attempts to cultivate their political resources have continued to meet with severe opposition. The vote has been an ineffective instrument in obtaining social justice: black leadership has divided; violence in the ghettos has stimulated both gains and losses for the black cause; and neighborhood control seems not to be in the immediate offing. Established political forces still shape the basic policies for black Americans.

NOTES

1. V. O. Key, *Politics, Parties and Pressure Groups* (New York: Thomas Y. Crowell Co., 1942).
2. David B. Truman, *The Governmental Process* (New York: Alfred A. Knopf, 1955), p. 29.
3. Betty Zisk, Heinz Eulau, and Kenneth Prewitt, "City Councilmen and The Group Struggle," *Journal of Politics* 27 (August 1965): 633.
4. Robert Salisbury, "An Exchange Theory of Interest Groups," *Midwest Journal of Political Science* 8 (February 1969): 1-32.
5. Ibid.; also Mancur Olson, *The Logic of Collective Action: Public Goods and The Theory of Groups* (Cambridge: Harvard University Press, 1965).
6. Ibid., p. 132.
7. Salisbury, "Exchange Theory of Interest Groups."
8. Earl Latham, "The Group Basis of Politics: Notes for a Theory," *American Political Science Review* 46 (June 1952): 376-397.
9. Ibid., p. 390.
10. Ibid., p. 391.
11. See especially on this point David G. Smith, "Pragmatism and the Group Theory of Politics," *American Political Science Review* 58 (December 1964): 1036-1048.
12. Bertrand Russell, *Power: A New Social Analysis* (London: G. Allen and Unwin, Ltd., 1962), p. 25.

13. Nelson Poslby, *Community Power and Political Theory* (New Haven: Yale University Press, 1963), p. 3.

14. This list borrows heavily from Robert A. Dahl, "The Analysis of Influence on Local Communities," in *Social Science and Community Action*, ed. Charles R. Adrian (East Lansing: Michigan State University, 1960), p. 32.

15. Michael Lipsky, *Protest in City Politics* (Chicago: Rand, McNally, 1960), p. 2.

16. Marion K. Saunders, *The Professional Radical: Conversations with Saul Alinsky* (New York: Harper and Row, 1965).

17. I would add this: actual disruption of an established procedure.

18. Lipsky, *Protest in City Politics* p. 2.

19. Dahl, "Analysis of Influence," p. 33.

20. Edward Banfield and James Q. Wilson, *City Politics* (Cambridge: Harvard-MIT Press, 1963); p. 262.

21. See on these points: Diel S. Wright and Robert W. Marker, "A Half Century of Local Finances," *National Tax Journal* 3 (September 1964): 274-291; and George A. Bishop, "Tax Burden By Income Class: 1958," *National Tax Journal* 14 (March 1961): 41-58.

22. Most taxing authorities think this unwise practice for cities to follow. For a supportive view, see W. E. Barkesdale, "Mississippi's BAWI Program," *State Government* 25 (July 1952): 151-152.

23. Oliver Williams and Charles Adrian, *Four Cities* (Philadelphia: University of Pennsylvania Press, 1963), p. 199.

24. In a study of 24 areas in Philadelphia it was found that lower-income people thought of politicians as local leaders while upper-income people named business and professional leaders; I. D. Reid and E. L. Ehle, "Leadership Selection in Urban Locality Areas," *Public Opinion Quarterly* 14 (Summer 1950): 262-284.

25. Peter B. Clark, *The Businessman as a Civic Leader* (Glencoe: The Free Press, 1964). See also "Civic Leadership: The Symbols of Legitimacy" (Paper delivered to the American Political Science Association, New York, September 1960).

26. Herbert M. Kagi, "The Role of Private Consultants in Urban Governing," *Urban Affairs Quarterly* 5 (September 1969): 51-52.

27. Clark, "Civic Leadership," p. 4.

28. Ibid., p. 6.

29. Thomas Dye, *Politics In States and Communities* (Englewood Cliffs, N.J.: Prentice-Hall, 1969), p. 327.

30. Clark, "Civic Leadership," p. 10.

31. Ibid., p. 11.

32. On this point cf. John H. Bunzell, *The American Small Businessman* (New York: Alfred A. Knopf, 1962); also Arthur Vidich and Joseph Bensman, *Small Town in Mass Society* (Princeton: Princeton University Press, 1958), Chap. 5.

33. Robert O. Schulze, "The Bifurcation of Power in a Satellite City," in *Community Political Systems*, ed. Morris Janowitz (Glencoe: The Free Press, 1961), p. 68.

34. Heinz Eulau and John D. Sprague, *Lawyers in Politics* (Indianapolis: Bobbs-Merrill Co., 1964).

35. See Ibid., pp. 32-39.

36. Cf. Joseph Schelsinger, "Lawyers and American Politics: A Clarified View,"

Midwest Journal of Political Science (May 1957): 26-39.

37. Donald Matthews, *The Social Background of Political Decision-makers* (Garden City, N.Y.: Doubleday, 1954), p. 30.

38. Eulau and Sprague, *Lawyers in Politics*, p. 132.

39. Kenneth Prewitt, *The Recruitment of Political Leaders: A Study of Citizen Politicians* (Indianapolis: Bobbs-Merrill Co., 1970), p. 164.

40. Herbert M. Kagi, in *Decisions In Syracuse*, ed. Roscoe Martin et al. (Bloomington: Indiana University Press, 1961), p. 260. For some specific examples of development politics see the case studies in Chapter 11, "Real Estate Development: Five Case Studies."

41. From an interview with W. Don Maxwell, editor of the Chicago *Tribune*, in Edward C. Banfield, *Political Influence* (New York: The Free Press of Glencoe, 1961), pp. 230-231.

42. These figures are adapted from the excellent discussion of the politics of the press in Banfield and Wilson, *City Politics*, Chap. 21. Original source is *Editor and Publisher* (April 20, 1957), p. 18.

43. It has been suggested that the weekly press in the U.S. facilitates the development of a sense of community; cf. A. S. Edelstein and O. N. Larson, "The Weekly Press Contribution to a Sense of Urban Community," *Journalism Quarterly* 37 (Fall 1970): 489-498.

44. Banfield and Wilson, *City Politics*, p. 316.

45. Cf. Reo M. Christenson, "The Power of the Press: The Case of the Toledo Blade," *Midwest Journal of Political Science* 3 (August 1959): 227-240.

46. Dye, *Politics in States and Communities*, p. 254.

47. Betty Zisk, Heinz Eulau, and Kenneth Prewitt, "City Councilmen and the Group Struggle," *Journal of Politics* 27 (August 1965): 633.

48. Ibid.

49. Prewitt, *Recruitment of Political Leaders*, p. 86 (original is italicized).

50. Dye, *Politics In States and Communities*, p. 249.

51. Cf. Stanley Gabis, "Leadership In A Large Manager City: The Case of Kansas City," *The Annals of the American Academy of Political and Social Sciences* 353 (May 1964): 52-63.

52. For documentation of this perspective, see particularly Joel Seidman et al., *The Worker Views His Union* (Chicago: University of Chicago Press, 1958).

53. From Jean L. Stinchcombe, *Reform and Reaction* (Belmont, Calif.: Wadsworth, 1968), p. 156.

54. Seidman, et al.; *Worker Views His Union.*

55. From Banfield and Wilson, *City Politics*, p. 278. Original source is Richard Baisden, "Labor Unions in Los Angeles Politics," (Ph.D. diss., University of Chicago, 1958).

56. Seidman, et al., *Worker Views His Union*, pp. 225-226.

57. When lists are compiled of reputed civic leaders, union men are not frequently named. See William Form and Delbert Miller, *Industry, Labor, and Community* (New York: Harper & Row, 1960). Also William Form, "Organized Labor's Place in the Community Power Structure," *Industrial Labor Relations Review* 12 (July 1959): 32-43.

58. Banfield and Wilson, *City Politics*, p. 283.

59. The American Assembly, *Public Workers and Public Unions* (Englewood Cliffs, N.J.: Prentice-Hall, 1972).

60. Cf. Robert L. Lineberry and Ira Sharkansky, *Urban Politics and Public Policy* (New York: Harper and Row, 1971), p. 69.

61. Robert Dahl, *Who Governs?* (New Haven: Yale University Press, 1961), pp. 34-36.

62. Robert A. Lorinskas, et al., "The Persistence of Ethnic Voting in Rural and Urban Areas," *Social Science Quarterly* 49 (March 1969): 871-899.

63. Gerald Pomper, "Ethnic and Group Voting in Non-Partisan Elections," *Public Opinion Quarterly* 30 (Spring 1960): 79-97.

64. Raymond Wolfinger, "The Development and Persistence of Ethnic Voting," *American Political Science Review* 1959, 59 (December 1965): 896-908, 906.

65. Ibid., p. 905.

66. William K. Tabb, *The Political Economy of the Black Ghetto* (New York: W. W. Norton, 1970), pp. 22-23.

67. Quoted by Robert L. Allen, *Black Awakening in Capitalist America: An Analytic History* (Garden City, N. Y.: Doubleday, 1969), p. 117.

68. Ibid., p. 12. See also Karl E. Tauber and Alma F. Tauber, *Negroes in Cities* (Chicago: Aldine Publishing Co., 1965), pp. 78-79.

69. Cf. A. H. Pascal, *The Economics of Housing Segregation* (Santa Monica, Calif.: Rand Corp., 1967).

70. Alvin L. Schorr, *Explorations in Social Policy* (New York: Basic Books, 1968), p. 208. Also see Chester Rapkin, "Price Discrimination Against Negroes in the Rental Market," in *Essays in Urban Land Economics* (Los Angeles Real Estate Research Program, University of California, 1966).

71. Richard Langendorf, "Residential Desegregation Potential," *Journal of the American Institute of Planners* 35 (March 1969): 90-95.

72. From a poem by Margaret Walker, "We Have Been Believers," in *Soulscript*, ed. June Jordon (Garden City, N. Y.: Doubleday, 1970), p. 131.

73. For example it was found that 61% of the black citizens of St. Louis voted in certain municipal elections. John C. Bollens, et al., *Exploring the Metropolitan Community* (Berkeley: University of California Press, 1961), p. 86.

74. Quoted in *Newsweek* (August 16, 1965), p. 15.

75. William R. Keech, *The Impact of Negro Voting* (Skokie, Ill.: Rand, McNally, 1968), p. 105.

76. Ibid.

77. This section draws heavily on James Q. Wilson, *Negro Politics: The Search for Leadership* (New York: The Free Press of Glencoe, 1960), Chap. 12.

78. Ibid., pp. 218-221.

79. Ibid., p. 53.

80. This description is from Everett C. Ladd, Jr., *Negro Political Leadership in the South* (New York: Atheneum Books, 1969), pp. 205-206.

81. Ibid., p. 206.

82. From Jerry Cohen and William Murphy, *Burn, Baby, Burn! The Los Angeles Race Riot, August 1965* (New York: Dutton, 1966), p. 119.

83. Among the moderates who worked to cool things off during the Watts riot were Wendell Collins, vice chairman of L.A. CORE, the Rev. Hartford H. Brookins,

of the United Civil Rights Committee, John A. Buggs of the L.A. County Human Relations Commission, and Congressman Augustus F. Hawkins. When the rioting erupted in August, these leaders called public meetings, spoke on radio and television, negotiated with police officials and youth leaders, and otherwise implored the residents to stay off the streets. Often their appeals were a great personal risk. For more detail see Robert Conot, *Rivers of Blood, Years of Darkness* (New York: Bantam, 1967), pp. 144-145. For other examples of the role played by moderates in the urban rioting of the middle and late sixties, see Robert M. Fogelson, *Violence as Protest* (Garden City, N.Y.: Doubleday, 1971), Chap. 6.

84. Stokley Carmichael and Charles V. Hamilton, *Black Power* (New York: Vintage Books, 1967), p. 40.
85. Ibid., p. 4.
86. Ibid., p. 44.
87. Ibid., p. 81.
88. See *Report of the National Advisory Commission of Civil Disorders* (Washington, D.C.: U.S. Government Printing Office, 1968), pp. 2-14.
89. Stanley Lieberson and Arnold R. Silverman, "The Precipitants and Underlying Conditions of Race Riots," *American Sociological Review* 30 (December 1965): 887-898.
90. Fogelson, *Violence as Protest*, pp. 6-7.
91. This discussion draws heavily on Robert M. Fogelson and Robert B. Hill, "Who Riots?" *National Advisory Commission on Civil Disorders, Supplementary Studies* (Washington, D.C.: Government Printing Office, 1968), Chap. 3.
92. T. M. Tomlinson, "The Development of a Riot Ideology Among Urban Negroes," *American Behavioral Scientist* 11 (April 1968): 28.
93. See *Report of the National Advisory Commission on Civil Disorders*, Chap. 2.
94. Fogelson and Hill, "Who Riots?"; also see Nathan S. Kaplan and Jeffrey M. Paige, "A Study of Ghetto Rioters," *Scientific American* 219 (August 1968): 19.
95. T. M. Tomlinson, "Development of a Riot Ideology," p. 26.
96. Ibid. For similar findings in connection with the 1967 rioting, see Angus Campbell and David Schuman, "Racial Attitudes in Fifteen American Cities" in National Advisory Commission on Civil Disorders, *Supplemental Studies* (Washington, D.C.: U. S. Government Printing Office, 1968).
97. Edward C. Banfield, *The Unheavenly City* (Boston: Little, Brown, 1968), Chap. 9.
98. Quoted from the New York *Times* (July 24, 1967).
99. Originally quoted in *Education News* (October 16, 1967), p. 16.
100. In addition to the materials already cited in this section, also see Joel D. Aberbach and Jack L. Walker, "The Meanings of Black Power: A Comparison of White and Black Interpretations of a Political Slogan," *American Political Science Review* 64 (June 1970): 367-388.
101. For a more detailed discussion of the "righteous indignation theory" of rioting, see Peter A. Lupsha, "On Theories of Urban Violence," *Urban Affairs Quarterly* 4 (March 1969): 273-296; also see Peter A. Lupsha, "Explanation of Political Violence: Some Psychological Theories Versus Indignation," *Politics and Society* 2 (Fall 1971): 89-104.
102. Alan A. Altshuler, *Community Control: The Black Demand for Participation in*

Large American Cities (New York, Western Publishing Co., 1970), p. 14.
103. Helen I. Safa, "The Case for Negro Separatism: The Crisis of Identity in the Black Community," *Urban Affairs Quarterly* 4 (September 1968): 45-63.
104. Altshuler, *Community Control*, Chap. 3. This chapter contains a much more elaborate and detailed description of the imposing array of interests.
105. Bayard Rustin, "The Failure of Black Separatism," *Harper's* (January 1970), p. 28.

Chapter 6

Patterns of Conflict
and Coalition

Urban politics is not the proverbial Hobbsian war of each against all; there are a number of integrative forces also at work. No one of the political actors described in the preceding chapter is able to dominate all the others. As a result, to get something done in the city, actors must make bargains, accommodations, and concessions to others. The grounds of potential division are many: rich against poor; nonwhite against white; men against women; rural against urban. No wonder "up against the wall" became such a common lament! But most of these factions, as well as the possibilities for compromise among them, are discussed in other contexts in this book. My aim in this chapter is to develop some broader grounds of political coalition — grounds which approach being ideologies, rather than conveniences, because they are elaborated belief systems which also prescribe some major rules for action. We shall discuss four such grounds of political coalition: mutual interests, shared ethos, similar connection to the city, and shared images of the city government.

MUTUAL INTEREST AS THE MOTHER OF COALITION

Pursuit of self-interest in city politics, as in all politics, is moderated by the realization that we need each other's support to accomplish our goals. Each actor's needs constrain him to moderate the demands he makes on others. Before an urban renewal project can be started, for example, administrators and politicians of the city must be persuaded to approve a specific plan; business interests, neighborhood associations, newspapers, and civic associations will have to cooperate. Many of those interests will come together out of a sense of shared interest; that is, participants will compare their costs of endorsing the proposal to the benefits they expect to receive from it. If they find the benefits substantially outweigh the costs they will support the proposal.

> A political decision is often (though not always) an exchange decision. One has to balance what he can get against what he had to forgo in order to get it.[1]

Often groups engage in a bargaining process with other potential supporters. The term "bargaining" does not imply the "back room deal." Far from being illegitimate, agreements between potential participants in politics help in many cases to moderate the severity of conflict.[2]

The political integration of the city does not, however, result exclusively from this kind of rational explicit bargaining process. Nor does it always rest on simple identification of mutual interests between the parties. To some extent political actors band together because they share certain attachments to the city itself. As Banfield and Wilson point out, "The city is among other things a set of values, habits, sentiments, myths, and understandings which are (more or less) shared by the people who live in it. . . . "[3] It could be expected, then, that those who share values, sentiments, etc. might find it easier to coalesce on any particular urban policy question, or even in some cases, to support political positions which do not materially serve their immediate interests.

ETHOS: UNITARISTS AND INDIVIDUALISTS

Edward Banfield and James Wilson have contended that broad differences in "ethos" characterize participants in urban politics. (Ethos can be briefly defined as the characteristic spirit which is expressed in the customs and actions of a people.) Specifically, they say that the native middle-class Protestants inherited from their Anglo-Saxon ancestors a very different political ethos from the one brought to our central cities by the more recently arrived immigrants from the Old World. In general, the Yankee Protestant political ethos is based on middle-class life. It demands the constant, disinterested activity of citizens in political affairs and demands a life run in conformance with general principles and abstract laws. The neutrality of law, then, is placed apart from and superior to personal needs of individual citizens or interests. The Yankee Protestant ethos presumes that government should aim to moralize the lives of individuals, while economic life should be relied on to stimulate the development of individual character. By contrast, the old world political ethos was

founded upon the European background of the immigrants, upon their un-
familiarity with independent political action, their familiarity with hierarchy
and authority, and upon the urgent needs that so often grew out of their migration, took for granted that the political life of the individual would arise out of
family needs, interpreted political and civic relations chiefly in terms of personal obligations, and placed strong personal loyalties above allegiance to
abstract codes of law or morals.[4]

The possessors of these differing orientations wanted divergent institutional arrangements. The WASP ethos moves toward at-large representation systems, nonpartisanship, the council-manager form of government,
master planning, and "strict and impartial enforcement of laws."[5] The institutional forms that expressed the Old World political style were the
machine, the boss, and ward politics.

Ethos as a Value Premise in Voting Behavior

The first empirical test of ethos theory, designed to determine
whether each ethos has its effect on voting behavior, operationalized the
Anglo-Saxon Protestant ethic as "public regarding," while the Old World
political ethos was seen as "private regarding." The public-regarding voter
was assumed to have a conception of the public interest which inspired him to
support measures that benefit the whole community whether or not they
produce specific rewards for himself.[6]

The white middle class was expected to vote for public expenditures
out of the sense of public regardingness on such referenda as veteran's
bonuses, urban renewal, and schools. The private-regarding groups — Irish,
Italian, Polish, and lower-income working class — were expected to vote
against public expenditures on these referenda. Study of a number of referenda elections in seven cities, illustrated in Table 6.1, confirms that white Anglo-
Saxon Protestants, blacks, and Jews tended to support public expenditures
more than Irish, Polish, Italian, or other Eastern European ethnic voters did.
Ethos assumptions then lead us to discover some coalitions which might not
have been expected. Particularly, the finding that Anglo-Saxon Protestants
and blacks join in their support of public expenditures. That alliance, of
course, breaks down on a number of other public questions, particularly election of officials.

A number of criticisms of this way of testing the impact of ethos on
voting behavior have led Wilson and Banfield to reformulate it.[7] Two objections were most influential: First, objections were raised that the use of the
phrase "private regarding" improperly implied selfishness, when in fact such
voters may simply be defining "public" differently, thinking of it as their im-

Table 6.1   Percentage of Various "Ethnic" Precincts Voting "Yes" on Selected Expenditures in Cleveland and Cuyahoga County

Ethnic Group and Number of Precincts	Percent Voting "Yes" on:				
	Co. Hosp. (11/59)	Court House (11/59)	Parks (11/59)	Welfare Levy (5/60)	Vet's Bonus (11/56)
	(%)	(%)	(%)	(%)	(%)
*Low-Income Renters**					
Black (16)	78.6	67.3	52.6	85.9	89.9
Italian (10)	68.8	53.3	43.5	49.9	74.8
Polish (6)	54.9	39.9	28.1	33.7	71.6
Middle-Income Home-Owners†					
Black (8)	68.1	54.0	39.6	73.2	79.2
Italian (7)	59.3	49.7	41.1	56.8	66.8
Polish (12)	52.9	35.8	34.3	46.4	61.7
Upper-Income Home-Owners‡					
Anglo-Saxon (11)	70.6	51.4	57.2	64.8	53.7
Jewish (7)	71.7	47.1	48.4	64.5	56.8

*Average median family income less than $6,000 per year; at least two-thirds of all dwelling units renter-occupied.

†Average median family income between $7,000 and $9,000 a year for whites; over $6,000 a year for blacks. At least 75 percent of all dwelling units owner-occupied.

‡Average median family income over $10,000 per year; over 85 percent of all dwelling units owner-occupied.

Source: Adapted from James Q. Wilson and Edward Banfield "Public Regardingness As A Value Premise In Voting Behavior," *The American Political Science Review* 58 (December 1964): 884.

mediate neighborhood or their own ethnic or occupational group. Second, the initial research imputed an immigrant ethos to those who may have been second or third generation. While not conceding these criticisms, Banfield and Wilson nonetheless "to avoid confusion on these matters" chose in subsequent studies to use the terms "unitary" ethos (formerly "middle-class Protestant Anglo-Saxon ethos" or "public regardingness") and "individualist" ethos (formerly the "immigrant" or "private-regardingness" ethos). In this reformulation the unitarist is presumed to: (1) think in terms of the interest of the whole, (2) place strong emphasis on the need to contribute to the welfare of unspecifiable individuals or of a "social organism," and (3) be willing to make some sacrifice for good-government virtues. The individualist is contrasting on all three dimensions, being: (1) a localist, (2) disposed to confer benefits on more or less specifiable individuals and groups, and (3) willing to sacrifice some of the good-government virtues in order to assure those benefits. Table 6.2 contains a summary of the two orientations.

Relying on a sample of 1059 predominately male Boston homeowners, Wilson and Banfield found that about one-fifth of those interviewed displayed one or the other ethos. As they expected, they also found unitarists to be much more likely to be Yankee or Jewish and to have higher incomes and more formal education than were either the individualists or the other persons interviewed who displayed no consistent orientation toward either ethos.[8]

One-fifth is of course not a large percentage of a sample to exhibit a trait. Banfield and Wilson acknowledge that it is weaker than they expected.[9] Also, contrary to what the ethos theory would lead us to expect, Banfield and Wilson report that those having a strong good-government orientation were not primarily unitarists. Neither was being "benefit minded" closely associated with the individualist orientation. They explain that these anomalies resulted from the fact that, unexpectedly, Jewish respondents were more likely to be benefit minded than good-government minded while Irish and Polish Catholic respondents with relatively low incomes and little schooling were more likely to be good-government minded than benefit minded.[10]

Wilson and Banfield do not claim that ethos theory has been entirely proved but they do believe that the data they gathered in Boston show a "strain toward consistency" — that the upper-income Yankees are closer to the unitarist ethos while Irish and Polish residents hold political orientations that seem more characteristic of the individualist mode. In interpreting these

Table 6.2   Comparison of Components of the Unitarist and Individualist Political Ethos

Unitarist	*Individualist*
1. Holist: disposed to think in terms of the "interest of the whole"	1. Localist: disposed to think in terms of competition among particular (usually local) interests
2. Community serving: feeling an obligation to contribute to the welfare of unspecifiable individuals or of a "social organism"	2. People helping: disposed to confer benefits (favor) on more or less specifiable individuals and groups
3. Good-government minded: willing to make some sacrifice for good-government virtues like honesty, impartiality and efficiency; rule oriented.	3. Benefit minded: willing to accept some sacrifice of good government to assure individual benefits; request oriented.

Source: Compiled from James Q. Wilson and Edward C. Banfield "Political Ethos Revisited;" *American Political Science Review* 65 (December 1971): 1048-1062.

findings, Wilson and Banfield acknowledge that their subjects show a weaker commitment to either ethos than might have been found when American city government was being organized into the forms we have today, that is, in the late nineteenth and early twentieth centuries. At that point the conflict between old stock Americans and the "newer races" was more intense. They also suggest that the unitarists in the sample "although a tiny part of the whole Boston electorate, do have an importance in the city's affairs far out of proportion to their numbers."[11]

Ethos and the Structure of City Government

The other empirical work which has been done using ethos as the guiding conception aims at discovering whether there is a correlation between the presence of "ethnics" and the state of reform of the city's government. It is assumed that a city with a large proportion of persons of foreign stock would be more likely to have an unreformed city government than a city with a large proportion of Anglo-Saxon Protestants. But Wolfinger and Field found that when they used statistical controls to account for regional variation, the differences between reformed and unreformed cities disappeared.[12]

Wilson and Banfield have argued that the contemporary period is the wrong time to be looking for the impact of immigrants on governmental structures. Daniel Gordon's examination of the 1930 and 1940 census characteristics, they note, is more supportive of ethos theory. Gordon discovered that in cities of 30,000 population or more, a strong relationship existed between the percentage of foreign born in the population and the incidence of unreformed institutions. By contrast to the Wolfinger and Field study, the 1930 data revealed that a statistical relationship remained even when controlled for region, for economic base, and for population size.[13]

The preliminary empirical work to assess the incidents and significance of Anglo-Saxon Protestant ethos and of Old World political ethos so far suggests that ethos affects voting behavior although probably less now than earlier in the history of the American city. Other studies suggest that a great many urban political battles can be understood as contests between Anglo-Saxon Protestants and urban ethnics. As yet, we have no studies which address other questions about the importance of ethos. One thing it would be useful to know is whether the behavior of city officials and political activists is importantly influenced by this ethos.

CONNECTION WITH THE CITY: LOCALS AND COSMOPOLITANS

A second way to look at the clustering and division among urban political actors has been suggested by the sociologist Robert K. Merton.[14] His study of a New Jersey city, which he called Revere, distinguished between two types of "influentials" — the "local" and the "cosmopolitan." These differing orientations toward the city result from the fact that political actors are attached to the city in distinctively different ways.

Locals focus their interests primarily on the city of their residence; the larger society hardly exists for them at all. Their orientation is parochial. Locals are mostly homegrown products, having been reared in the particular city; and their ability to affect local politics depends on the elaborate network of personal relationships they have developed over their years of residence. In other words their effectiveness depends on whom they know rather than what they know and on the respect they have earned from their fellow citizens. The locals' attachments to the city are personal and they maintain their contacts by becoming active in organizations that are designed especially for such purposes — particularly the Elks, Rotary, and Masons. Locals become economically and sentimentally rooted in the city in this way. Attitudes and public policies of boosterism attend the local orientation. Merton quotes one local as saying, " 'Revere is the greatest town in the world. It has something that is nowhere else in the world, though I can't say quite what is is.' "[15]

The "cosmopolitan" is oriented toward the larger world outside the particular city. He sees that the city is becoming integrated into a more elaborate system of organizations, not only politically but also economically and socially. The "cosmopolitan" was not born or reared in the local area; he is *in* but not *of* the city. He is connected to the city primarily because his position has brought him there. He may think that Revere is a pleasant enough place, but only one of many; and he is aware that in order to advance his career he may have to move on. The manager of the local branch of a chain store makes a particularly good example of a cosmopolitan. Cosmopolitans like these rely for their influence not on their local connections but on the status which is commonly ascribed to people of their position. They have little need to be associated with local service organizations but instead move toward membership in professional societies and leisure-activity clubs, ranging from country clubs to hobby groups. Merton describes the cosmopolitan as less interested in local boosterism than in public policies which recognize and ratify the integration of the city with the broad social, economic, and political systems of which it is becoming a part.

Thomas Dye used the local-cosmopolitan distinction in studying 16 Philadelphia suburban cities.[16] Dye developed a scale to discriminate between local and cosmopolitan political orientations which he administered to 340 residents and 105 elected public officials. As expected, those who exhibited cosmopolitan attitudes tended to come from the municipalities of upper social rank, while locals came from the cities of lower social and economic status.[17] Dye's study further suggests that in the conflict between local and

Table 6.3   "Do You Favor Using Zoning Laws to Keep Out of Your Community
the Type of People Who Usually Build Cheaper Houses on Smaller Lots?"

| | Social Rank Grouping of Municipality | | | | | |
| | Upper | | Middle | | Lower | |
	Percent Favor	Percent Oppose	Percent Favor	Percent Oppose	Percent Favor	Percent Oppose
Residents (N=123)*	91.5	8.5	75.8	24.2	82.0	18.0
Locals (N=31)	100.0	0	100.0	0	100.0	0
Cosmopolitans (N=31)	84.5	15.5	44.5	55.5	75.0	25.0

*Residents were persons questioned who could not be classified as either local or cosmopolitan in their orientation.

Source: Thomas R. Dye, "The Local — Cosmopolitan Dimension and the Study of Urban Politics" *Social Forces* 41 (March 1963): 245.

cosmopolitan perspectives, the locals tend to win. Political leaders (in this case, meaning elected public officials) were found to be even more localistic in their outlook than their constituents.

The study also verified the assumption that cosmopolitans and locals differ significantly in their responses to widely experienced urban problems. Cosmopolitans were significantly more likely than locals to favor proposals for improving mass transit systems in their area, for example, and also favored the creation of an area-wide government. On the subject of racial segregation, however, there is less contrast between locals and cosmopolitans — both support a kind of segregation. When asked, "Do you favor using zoning laws to keep out of your community the type of people who usually build cheaper houses on smaller lots?" Dye found that both the locals and the cosmopolitans overwhelmingly favored exclusionary zoning. (See Table 6.3). Even so, the locals show that tendency more than the cosmopolitans: over 71 percent of the opposition to discriminatory zoning came from the cosmopolitans.[18]

It is apparent that the proportion of the two types of influentials in a city and the manner in which they are distributed (as between official and unofficial leadership roles) will profoundly affect the style and outcome of a city's politics. Circumstances which affect the supply of the two types will clearly have important long-run effects on the governing of the city. Suburbanization, for example, has meant the desertion of cosmopolitans from the central city. It could be reasonably expected, then, that upper-income suburbs would be governed more in a cosmopolitan style while central cities would move toward localism. However we are unable to check out the reality of that expectation because, by the time a city has grown large enough to have its population broken down as upper-income suburbia and central city, there are such diverse influences at work on the populations that they cannot be characterized solely in such terms. The local-cosmopolitan cleavage seems most useful as it applies to medium-sized and smaller cities. This finding suggests that there are some other orientations at work not accounted for by the local-cosmopolitan dichotomy.

IMAGES OF CITY GOVERNMENT

Oliver Williams and Charles Adrian have suggested still another and more elaborate basis for coalition among urban political actors. They supply a typology based on four divergent images of the proper role of government which are held by citizens and officials in middle-sized cities. These four differing roles for local government include: (1) promoting economic growth, (2) providing or securing life's amenities, (3) maintaining (only) traditional services, (4) arbitrating among conflicting interests.[19] As the summary contained in Table 6.4 indicates, the typology not only describes the general expectation of each type but also its common adherents and some of the public policy preferences that attend the image.

As instrument of community growth

Those who see the city government as an *instrument of community growth* are centrally concerned to promote the expansion of the economy and the population of the city. From this viewpoint, politics and government are intended to serve production. This "boosterism" perspective assumes that growth is necessary and good, for the city must expand or die. This perspective is common among local merchants but is by no means confined to them. As we observed in Chapter 5, the most powerful interests of the city are often growth advocates: bankers, newspapermen, utility executives, city planners, and large property owners are likely to share this view. Growth advocates expect public policy to mirror their concerns. Typically, the booster wants the rezoning of land for industrial use and for housing developments, the extension of sewer and water lines to these building sites, and annexation policies designed to bring potential industrial areas into the city. He will often, though not always, embrace a policy of low taxation on new plants and on vacant land which is zoned for industrial use. He may also want the city to expend monies advertising the advantages of the city as a potential industrial or residential development site.

Table 6.4   The Williams - Adrian Typology of Images of City Government

Image	General Exploitation	Common Adherents	Typical Preferred Public Policies
1. Instrument of City Growth	1. Central priority is that city's population and economy should grow.	1. Bankers, local businessmen, newspapers, utilities, city bureaucracy.	1. Rezoning land for industrial use; extension of sewer & water lines to potential factory sites; low taxes on land zoned industrial and on new plants.
2. Provider of Life's Amenities	2. Central priority is that city should be a desirable residence.	2. Homeowner's associations, residential real estate brokers.	2. Exclusionary zoning; land-use control; industrial parks with light industry; heavy investment in parks, recreation & educational facilities.
3. Caretaker	3. Central priority is that city should provide only essential services. Low tax advocate.	3. Philosophical, conservative, retired, marginal homeowners.	3. Opposition to most proposals requiring additional taxes or bond issues.
4. Arbiter of Conflicting interests	4. No substantive central priority. Governments exist to settle disputes in accordance with principles of equity and justice.	4. Minority groups, others that have relinquished desire to govern in terms of their preferred image.	4. Open housing, equal job opportunity.

Source: Prepared from Oliver P. Williams and Charles R. Adrian, *Four Cities* (Philadelphia: University of Pennsylvania Press, 1963), especially pp. 23-26.

As provider of life's amenities

A number of small cities are dominated by those who assume that the central function of local government is to provide the amenities of life. With these political actors, the primary goal is to keep the city a desirable place to live. The amenities seeker's primary emphasis is on "the home environment rather than on the working environment — the citizen as consumer rather than producer."[20] Interested in the good life, the amenities seeker may actively oppose the goals of the city growth advocates if he is forced to choose how to spend scarce public monies. The amenities seeker prefers them to be spent on improvement of streets, expansion of parks and recreation sites, improvement of educational facilities, and other policies designed to make the city a good living environment. Exclusive zoning ordinances designed to keep out "undesirables" are commonly embraced. Business and industrial development are not opposed entirely, but the amenities seeker prefers light industry which produces no smog and does not require a large labor pool of low-income workers. The ideal strategy of economic development for the amenities advocate seems to be the industrial park which is located well away from most residential areas, is well landscaped, and hires mostly white-collar workers — for example, research centers of major corporations, and small electronics firms. The suburb of the stereotype — that is, of middle- and upper-middle-income residents — is the obvious model for the amenities-seeking type. One of the four middle-sized Michigan cities that Williams and Adrian studied was strongly affected by the amenities-seeking perspective. In this case, the

Marshall Henrichs

Unexpected coalitions occur in urban areas; who would have anticipated a few years ago the construction of Confucius Plaza on the Bowery?

amenities seekers were found to have come into power after the city had annexed its upper-class suburbs.[21]

As caretaker

The caretaker image is held by two kinds of people. They share the same image but for distinctively different reasons. What they share is the assumption that the city government should expend monies only to support those functions that are, from each one's viewpoint, essential. Those endorsing the caretaker image take seriously the credo "that government is best which governs least"; they demand little government intervention and low taxes: they may acknowledge it is proper for city governments to have streets patrolled, to purify the water supply, and to provide fire protection; but extension of city activities beyond these essentials is generally unwarrantable. One proponent of the caretaker role is, of course, the traditional philosophical conservative, the individual who is committed to the minimization of governmental activity at all levels. Another type of proponent embraces the caretaker image more out of personal economic necessity than out of philosophical commitment. Marginal homeowners and those living on a small fixed income, for example, oppose any program which will expand city expenditures — simply because they cannot afford the impact of a tax increase on their budget: if adoption of a school bond issue threatens a tax increase which results in less bread on the table, it should hardly be surprising that these people will vote no. The economically marginal then, may seem to prefer gravel to paved streets, open ditches to curb and gutter, septic tanks to sewers, and crowded schools to educational parks. In their case, it is more a matter of necessity than preference. We should recognize that the growing ranks of the retired elderly may well result in growth of the number of the caretaker oriented. Many small towns are dominated by the caretaker image. In rural areas, for example, where small towns have little prospect for immediate economic growth and there is a large proportion of elderly retired farmers we might expect the population's image of government to be dominated by the caretaker concept.[22]

As arbiter

Finally there are those who see the city government as that of an arbiter whose task is primarily to *manage conflicts arising among competing interests.* Instead of embodying one single image, the city government should simply function as an umpire among conflicting interests. The proponent of the arbiter role believes that government should find the least common denominator on the basis of which some settlement of disputes can be worked out. Often this image is held by the minority groups who see no prospect for controlling the local government but who are looking for a way to get a fair share of favorable public policy. To some degree, the traditional political boss also shared the arbiter conception. His power depended in part on satisfying the major demands of the various ethnic and minority groups in the central city. Many large central cities seem to be characterizable as arbiter cities. Most groups have long since given up any effort to control the operation of New York City, for example; and the style of Chicago under Mayor Daley seems an equally good illustration of city government functioning in the arbiter image.[23]

These images are not mutually exclusive. The growth advocates and the amenity-seeking residents could find a workable compromise; the growth advocates, the amenity seekers and the caretaker proponents could settle their differences by endorsing the image of the arbiter of conflicting interests. In fact, as Williams and Adrian point out, all these images as well as some of others probably exist in any city simultaneously. This overlapping of the types could be a weakness, depending on the use to which the typology is to be put. To a political researcher who must definitively place cities in a single category to satisfy a research design, the typology presents severe problems. Williams and Adrian recognize this potential deficiency and explain that it results from the fact that the types are "empirically, not logically, derived. . . . "[24] Another potential difficulty in the use of the typology for research purposes lies in the fact that Williams and Adrian provide no quantitative measures to be used as classificatory criteria. Still, the typology would seem to have a number of uses and stimulates a number of yet-unanswered questions for the scholar student of urban political life. For example, it could be argued that the Williams-Adrian typology embraces the other bases of political coalition discussed in this chapter. Merton's cosmopolitan comes close to Williams and Adrian's amenity seeker. The Old World political style is essentially the arbiter orientation.

More than just applying to middle-sized cities, the typology also seems to suggest a pattern of development from small town to large metropolis. Consider, for instance, the following pattern: A small town with a reasonably stable population and little prospect of growth is likely to be dominated by the *caretaker* image. In reaction to the relatively dim prospects of the city, there may emerge a group of civil boosters urging a program of expansion and plying the assumptions of the *growth* image. As the economic base develops — and particularly as white-collar jobs are created — a large proportion of residents may come to emphasize the need to make the city a good place in which to live, thus affirming the image of the city as a *provider of life's amenities*. In the final stage, as the city becomes so large and diverse as to defy control by the advocates of any single image, the city government may finally be asked to perform only the role of *arbiter of conflicting interests*.

Marshall Henrichs

In this dismal location, the graffiti message is unambiguous.

SUMMARY

There are a number of bases of political coalitions: Overlapping and mutuality of interests accounts for a number of political coalitions which result from explicit and tacit bargaining. Other groups and individuals come to share political positions because of common value and interest orientations to the city. Wilson and Banfield find substantial differences in voting behavior between those who hold what they call a unitary ethos and those who share an individualist ethos. Robert Merton has theorized, and Thomas Dye found promising initial evidence for it, that civil leaders who are locals in their connection with the city share views substantially different from those with a more cosmopolitan perspective. And finally, Williams and Adrian characterize four differing bases of political coalition resulting from differing images of the proper role of city government — instrument of community growth, provider of life's amenities, caretaker, and arbiter of conflicting interests. Urban political parties also provide a basis of coalition for the specialized purpose of electing officials. The urban party as a ground of political coalition will be discussed in the next chapter.

NOTES

1. R. L. Curry, Jr., and L. L. Wade, *A Theory of Political Exchange* (Englewood Cliffs, N.J.: Prentice-Hall, 1968), p. 2.
2. In fact, in a paper which recommends a bargaining paradigm for the study of urban politics this conflict-managing feature is made the core of the definition of

bargaining. "We define bargaining as transactions undertaken to manage conflict through the identification and promotion of mutual interests." Harvey Boulay, Betty Zisk, and Edward Berger, "A Bargaining Paradigm for the Study of Urban Politics: Theoretical Imperatives and Conceptual Clarifications" (Paper presented at the annual meeting of the American Political Science Association, Los Angeles, Calif., September 1970), p. 12.

3. Edward Banfield and James Q. Wilson, *City Politics* (Cambridge: Harvard-MIT Press, 1963), p. 47.

4. Richard Hofstadter, *The Age of Reform* (New York: Alfred A. Knopf, 1955), p. 9; as quoted and discussed in Banfield and Wilson, *City Politics*, pp. 38-44.

5. James Q. Wilson and Edward Banfield, "Political Ethos Revised," *The American Political Science Review* 65 (December 1971): 1048.

6. James Q. Wilson and Edward C. Banfield, "Public-Regardingness as a Value Premise in Voting Behavior," *The American Political Science Review* 58 (December 1964): 876-887.

7. Criticism may be found in Raymond E. Wolfinger and John Osgood Field, "Political Ethos and the Structure of City Government," *The American Political Science Review* 60 (June 1966): 306-326.

8. Wilson and Banfield, "Political Ethos Revised," p. 1062.

9. In fact, depending on how one interprets the data, it could be considered smaller than 21%. The simple correlation coefficient between the respondent's position on the holism index and whether or not they were community servers is plus .135, significant at the .01 level; the correlation between holism and stressing good government is plus .058, which is not significant at the .05 level. In other words, of the 268 voters who were found to be community servers, 151 or 56% were also holistic; and of those, 97 or 64% are good-government minded rather than benefit minded. Ibid.

10. Ibid.

11. Ibid.

12. Wolfinger and Field, "Political Ethos and Structure of City Government."

13. Daniel N. Gordon, "Immigrants and Urban Governmental Form in American Cities, 1933-60," *American Journal of Sociology* 74 (September 1968): 158-171.

14. Robert K. Merton, "Patterns of Influence: Locals and Cosmopolitans," in *Social Theory and Social Structure*, rev. ed. (Glencoe, Ill. The Free Press, 1957).

15. Ibid., p. 146.

16. Thomas R. Dye, "The Local-Cosmopolitan Dimension and the Study of Urban Politics," *Social Forces* 41 (March 1963): 239-246.

17. Ibid., p. 242.

18. Ibid., p. 245.

19. Oliver Williams and Charles Adrian, *Four Cities* (Philadelphia: University of Pennsylvania Press, 1963), especially pp. 23-32. The typology was originally contained in Oliver Williams, "A Typology for Comparative Local Government," *Midwest Journal of Political Science* 5 (May 1961): 150-164.

20. Williams and Adrian, *Four Cities*, p. 25.

21. Ibid., see especially pp. 198-221.

22. See Arthur Vidich and Joseph Bensman, *Small Town in Mass Society*

(Princeton, N. J.: Princeton University Press, 1958); and Warner E. Mills, Jr., and Harry R. Davis, *Small City Government* (New York: Random House, 1962).

23. See for example Wallace Sayre and Herbert Kaufman, *Governing New York City,* (New York: Russell Sage Foundation, 1960.)

24. Williams and Adrian, *Four Cities*, p. 35.

Chapter 7

Urban Political Parties
as a Basis of Conflict and Coalition

When most Americans think of urban political parties, they think of corruption. Whether or not parties are corrupt is a complicated problem; corruption, like obscenity, exists to a large extent in the eye of the beholder. In this and the next chapter we review the evolution of city politics — from the old-style, boss-dominated city machines through the government systems of the reform and postreform eras. The review may well prompt the thought that the reform movement, instead of curing the urban party, has come very close to killing it. Perhaps we are confronted with one of those classical situations in which the cure is worse than the disease.

After a brief description of the formal aspects of party organization, this chapter proceeds to a descriptive evaluation of the old-style urban machine and its decline, then takes up a discussion and assessment of the current status of party politics in our cities.

LOCAL PARTY ORGANIZATION

Organization charts and their verbal equivalents are always too clear. Like numbers, they can provide an illusory sense of clarity. With that caution in mind, let us briefly consider the typical hierarchical pattern of committees connecting the national party committee to the precinct.

The *precinct* (some places called "election district") is the smallest unit of a party organization, containing from 200 to 2000 voters. There are approximately 130,000 precincts in the U.S.; several of the largest cities contain as many as 3000.

Internal precinct organization varies widely throughout the country; however, there are two common features. One is that the affairs of the party

in the precinct are guided by two coequal officers, a committeeman and a com-
mitteewoman. (Unfortunately that is often the end of female equality in urban
politics.) Secondly, there is a precinct committee of three or more members. In
most states, the precinct committeeman and woman are elected in primary
elections. However, in a number of cities these offices are appointed by ward
leaders or, in other cases, elected at party caucuses. A major function of the
precinct officers is, of course, to get out as big a vote as possible for the party's
candidate. Precinct leadership is necessary to see to it that the party faithful
are registered, to maintain lists of persons who have not yet voted on election
day, to call and if necessary to transport voters to and from the polls, to
provide babysitters to allow mothers to vote, and similar functions. Good
precinct workers obviously are crucial concerns to a political party. Even so,
there is commonly little competition for the precinct offices, and surveys
reveal that one-third to one-half the precincts will be without party officers at
any given time. In many cities, party work offers few tangible rewards;
nevertheless, thousands of men and women seem to achieve some of the symbolic and status rewards promised by the passage from a Democratic National
Committee brochure:

> Being a Precinct Worker is a hard job, but it has its own rewards. You're help-
> ing people to understand the issues that affect us all. You're making the
> machinery of government work. You're doing your job as a citizen in a work-
> ing democracy. You're working to keep America free through the ballot box.
> You're proud to be a Precinct Worker. You're stepping up as a Party Leader.[1]

In American cities the next rung in the ladder of party hierarchy is
usually the *ward*. Characteristically, the ward embraces several precincts and
is governed by a ward committee or leader. The ward committee is normally
composed of the committeemen and women from its constituent precincts. In
a formal sense, the ward committee selects a chairman, directs the actions, and
decides the policies of the ward. The ward leader (chairman) often, however,
actually *appoints* the precinct officers in his area; as a result, he is in a
relatively strong position to influence the policies and activities of his ward, if
he chooses to do so.

The ward is intermediate between the precinct, on the one side, and
the *city or county level* of organization on the other. The city and county
organizations are generally acknowledged to be crucial and powerful links in
the chain of party organization. The ward committeemen (who are usually the
precinct committeemen) usually serve as the city committee; but, in a minority
of states, the city committee members are elected at the primary election.
County committees are constituted in one of three ways: (1) some are made up
of all the precinct committeemen in the county; (2) others are elected in party
primaries; and (3) in some areas, they are chosen in county party conventions.

The chairmen of both city and county committees are characteristically chosen by the committee they serve and are normally — at least in the formal sense — the most powerful single local party leaders.[2] Obviously, contests for power can develop between city and county committees. In general, the county committees will dominate the party committees of their small and middle-sized cities, but be unable to dominate the political affairs of the larger cities. City and county committees generally raise funds to be expended in local campaigns. Where there is national or state patronage to be dispensed, these organizations may play a central role.

Local Informal Variations

Local variations from the general organizational pattern are many and great. The impact of individual personalities and styles transforms sterile organization charts into living patterns. Most of us learn these patterns through trial and error. Samuel Eldersveld has done what most people do not; he has set down that informal party structure of Detroit in good academic form in Table 7.1. The Detroit pattern is not "typical"; instead it is illustrative of the adaptation of formal organization to local conditions and personalities. From that table we learn that the county chairman performs a "moderator" function, that district chairmen (a district being an intermediate level between the ward and the county organization) are the most powerful components of the Detroit party (i.e., the "top executive power elite"), that ward chairmen function as intermediate administrators and coordinators, and that precinct delegates are charged with direction of grassroots activity.

THE URBAN POLITICAL PARTY: OLD STYLE

A great many middle-class Americans reserve a special lofty scorn for urban parties. The "shame of the cities" is to them that the city fell prey to "bossism," that is, control by a "machine" dominated by "grafters and crooks" who were presumably lining their own pockets from their connections with criminal operations and by expropriating public tax money. Good cathartic fits of civic-virtuous indignation can still be aroused by invoking the shadowy hand of bossism. "Get rid of the bosses in city hall," is still an all-purpose campaign slogan in many American cities. Since my intention here is more analytical than carthartic, I invite you to join me in leaving behind such tempting invective. I do so for two important reasons: (1) Careful examination of the several political machines which operated in America from the post-Civil War period until the middle of the twentieth century finds that some of them were scrupulously honest, and in some instances even puritanical, in their mode of operation. In retrospect, we can see that the fault found with many of the machines resulted as much from antiurbanism and an antipolitics bias as from a clear-headed analysis of what the machines did. (2) When one begins to examine carefully the actual function of the urban machines of the era, one finds that the machines served a number of purposes which have been no better served by other political forms. In fact, the best interpretation of the boss era is that the *urban political machine was a conservative response to rapid social change.*[3] That point of view may be unfamiliar to you; it will be clarified as we examine the functions of the machine in more detail.

Table 7.1   Description of Wayne County Organizational Roles and Relationships

Hierarchy Positions	Organizational Conditions and Practices	"Functions" or "Roles"
Delegates to national convention	Technically picked in district caucus of district delegates to state convention; ratified by convention.	
Delegates to state convention	Elected by district conventions, directly before each state convention.	"Ambassadors" of the district organization at the national and state levels.
State central committee representatives	Two-year term. Two men and two women from each congressional district. Formally selected by state convention, in the spring of odd years. Actually picked by district caucus or convention.	
County chairman	Selected by county committee.	"Moderator" of district organization; coordinator of election campaigns.
County committee	State statutes and party rules define composition of county committee. District executive board members and others may sit on it. District chairmen *always* sit on it. Primary nominees entitled to seats by statute.	Countywide policy makers; candidate selection; patronage (i.e. appointment to office of friends and supporters).
District chairman	Interim selection of chairmen by executive board. Ordinarily by district convention (statute).	"Top executive power elite."
District	18 statutory members of boards — but usually larger by district party rule.	Secondary consultative, managerial, and representative cadre; leadership reservoir.

Source: Samuel Eldersveld, *Political Parties: A Behavioral Analysis* (Chicago: Rand, McNally, 1964), p. 37.

Functions of the Machine

One gets a sense of the excitement of the paleontologist in searching through the fossils of American party machines. Interesting and colorful creatures like Little Ed and Brother Bill Vare can be found in a Philadelphia dig; the Hague machine can be uncovered in Jersey City, Tom Pendergast's influence can be assessed in Kansas City, and Ed Crump's in Memphis. Some think that Chicago's mayor, Richard Daley, is an untransformed lineal descendant of the Chicago machines of "Hinky Dink" Kenna, "Bathhouse John" Coughlin, and "Big Bill" Thompson. In fact, there are those researchers who believe that these creatures are not dead but simply transmogrified; as one commentator has put it, "Exit the boss, enter the 'leader' ".[4] If true, that should be cause for neither surprise or alarm.

We are interested in old-style urban politics for more reasons than curiosity about ancient forms. In seeking to understand the function of the machine, we are attempting to gain insight into the character of contemporary urban parties and, more broadly, urban politics. To learn about form and function of the old urban machine, it is most useful to begin with an account of the conditions which facilitated its rise. Social and political forms are not brought by the stork: they are adaptations to human needs, and the machine is no exception.

The nineteenth century spawned five conditions which were direct determinants of the form that urban party organization took. *Massive urban expansion* occurred as a result of industrial and commercial growth.[5] Between 1860 and 1920, the urban population rose from 6.2 million to 54.2 million. Such rapid urban growth, of course, places a heavy strain on urban facilities. New demands were suddenly placed on governments which had previously operated with a minimum of effort and activity. Urban governmental forms at the time were generally *disorganized,* having numerous elected officials, weak executives, and large and unwieldy councils and boards. Further, there were an increasing number of *businessmen who needed the cooperation of city government* and in many cases were willing to pay directly for it. Some of these businessmen simply wanted to operate unrestrained by municipal authority while others sought contracts with the city to build the streets, sewers, and bridges that an expanding urban population needed. Further, the new city dwellers were predominately *dependent populations with great needs.* Most of the 25 million immigrants who came to the United States between the Civil War and the First World War were poor; they found jobs in the city, often at low wages with long hours and tedious, hazardous working conditions. The American tradition of *unrestricted suffrage* for males was one of the few major resources of these dependent populations. Their use of the vote was simple and direct: the ward captain provided for the needs of his people — favors, jobs, material rewards; in exchange, the poor of the city gave the boss their vote. The political organization which emerged to facilitate this "equilibrium of incentives," as it is sometimes called, had the following characteristics:

> 1. There was a disciplined party hierarchy led by a single executive or a unified board of directors.
>
> 2. The party exercised effective control over nomination to public office and, through this, it controlled the public officials of the municipality.
>
> 3. The party leadership — which quite often was of lower class social origins — usually did not hold public office and sometimes did not even hold formal party office. At any rate, official position was not the primary source of the leadership's strength.
>
> 4. Rather, a cadre of loyal party officials and workers, as well as a core of voters, was maintained by a mixture of material rewards and *nonideological* psychic rewards — such as personal and ethnic recognition, camaraderie, and the like.[6]

Overall, the urban political machine was essentially a large brokerage organization. It was not in the service of particular ideologies or devoted to specific issues. It was a business, the primary goal of which was to get votes and control elections. In the process, it enabled the city to assimilate a large number of new residents, businesses, and industries, and to grow and develop without major upheaval. Machine politics, then, was a conservative response to change in urban America because it opened alternatives to violence in managing the explosive conflicts of the rapidly changing urban environment of the post-Civil War period. It did this by increasing the legitimacy of the city government for transitional populations, providing them a route to integration and even upward mobility. It met the immediate needs of the dependent population. And finally, because the votes of all groups were equally valuable to the machine, it minimized class issues and fostered interclass cooperation.[7]

The socializing function of the machine cannot be taken lightly. The machine performed certain social functions more effectively, perhaps, than have the more modern alternatives.[8] It is not going too far to say that the machine performed the functions of the welfare agency, provided individual attention and recognition to its supporters, personalized government for its constituents, acted as an employment agency and as a street-level educational unit, teaching immigrants the norms of American life.

A patronizing attitude toward the poor seems implicit in most efforts at providing welfare.

The machine as welfare agency

One of the most colorful characters of the machine era was George Washington Plunkitt of New York City's Tammany Hall. Plunkitt has occasionally been called the philosopher king of old-style machine politics. He is the source of that cynical quotation which is a favorite of reformers, "I seen my opportunities and I took 'em." Plunkitt's homey insights are worth quoting at length, as, for example, in explaining how he would help people in need:

> "What tells in holdin' your grip on your district is to go right down among the poor families and help them in the different ways they need help. I've got a regular system for this. If there's a fire in the Ninth, Tenth or Eleventh Avenue, for example, any hour of the day or night, I'm usually there with some of my election district captains as soon as the fire engines. If a family is burned out, I don't ask whether they are Republicans or Democrats, and I don't refer them to the Charity Organization Society, which would investigate their case a month or two and decide they were worthy of help about the time they were dead from starvation. I just get quarters for them, buy clothes for them if their clothes were burned up, and fix them up 'til they can get things

runnin again. It's philanthropy, but it's politics too — mighty good politics. Who can tell how many votes one of these fires bring me? The poor are the most grateful people in the world, and let me tell you, they have more friends in their neighborhoods than the rich have in theirs."[9]

Welfare in this form is perhaps more easily accepted, and less damaging to the recipient than when it is given by a neutral "case worker" and a remote and seemingly judging welfare bureaucracy.

The machine as personalizer of government

The urban machine recognized a voter as a human being with specific personal problems and needs. A person in need does not want a sermon or a discussion of abstract moral principles or ideologies, or an investigation of his "financial status." The machine gave him none. Lincoln Steffans once quoted a Boston ward leader to the same effect:

> "I think that there's got to be in every ward somebody that any bloke can come to — no matter what he's done — and get help. Help, you understand; none of your law and justice, but help."[10]

George Washington Plunkitt knew just how to provide that help, by giving personal and individual attention.

> "I know every man, woman, and child in the 15th district, except them that's been born this summer — and I know some of them too. I know what they like and what they don't like, what they are strong at and what they are weak in, and I reach them by approachin' at the right side. For instance, here's how I gather in the young men. I hear of a young feller that's proud of his voice, thinks he can sing fine. I ask him to come around to Washington Hall and join our Glee Club. Then there's the feller that likes rowin' on the river, the young feller that makes a name as a waltzer on his block, the young feller that's handy with his dukes — I rope them all in by giving them opportunities to show themselves off. I don't trouble them with political arguments. I just study human nature and act accordin'."[11]

The machine as employment agency

The urban machine operated prior to the time of government unemployment insurance or a federal employment service. The machine served those functions by providing opportunities in city government — a service derogatorily called *patronage* — or in business where they had a number of contacts.

> "Another thing, I can always get a job for a deservin' man. I make it a point to keep on the track of jobs, and it seldom happens that I don't have a few up my

sleeve ready for use. I know every big employer in the district and in the whole city, for that matter, and they ain't in the habit of sayin' no to me when I ask them for a job."[12]

This may all sound like cynical manipulation of gullible masses, but the historical record seems to indicate that many bosses believed the kinds of things that George Washington Plunkitt so eloquently expressed. In addition, it also seems clear, in retrospect, that the petty favors and patronage dispensed by the machine won the votes of the city dwellers partly because of the sense of friendship and human concern that characterized machine efforts. A bushel of coal during a hard winter, the ten-spot lent in time of sore need, the donated new suit to help get a job were seen as tokens of friendship. Even Jane Addams, founder of the famous Hull House and vigorous opponent of the Chicago machine in the last decade of the nineteenth century, recognized this: "On the whole, the gifts and favors were taken quite simply as evidence of genuine loving kindness. The alderman is really elected because he is a good friend and neighbor. He is corrupt, of course, but he is not elected because he is corrupt, but rather in spite of it. His standard suits his constituents. He exemplifies and exaggerates the popular type of good man, he has attained what his constituents secretly long for."[13]

The machine as educator

Local ward leaders sometimes met immigrants at dockside and led them through naturalization and voter registration processes. Beyond that, the machines were equal opportunity employers. They did not discriminate by national origin, but instead saw to it that the ballot was strewn with funny-sounding names. As a result, politics became an American activity which the bright sons of Irish and Italian immigrants could learn and come to excel at. The ancestors of President John F. Kennedy, for example, rose to prominence in the Boston machine: Kennedy's grandfather, John "Honey Fitz" Fitzgerald, had been mayor.

The Decline of the Machine

The bosses did not pass quickly or easily. Their staying power is legendary and is illustrated by the attempts of Jane Addams and her associates to defeat the boss of Chicago's nineteenth ward, Johnny Powers. Addams and her reformist allies tried the powers of Powers in the city elections of 1895, 1896, and 1898. They lost. Following the second unsuccessful attempt, Powers gave a city job to nearly everyone who had campaigned against him. He appointed a printer who was also an opposition leader to a clerkship at City Hall; a driver opponent went to the police barns at a high salary; and the

Table 7.2   **Reasons For Choosing Candidates**

		Supporters of				
Reasons Given for Choice	Total	*Curley*	*Kerrigan*	*Reilly*	*Sawtelle*	*Lee*
Reasons of Efficiency	39%	51%	37%	28%	27%	13%
Past experience	20	15	28	27	7	—
Past accomplishments	11	18	7	1	14	5
Gives more for money	2	4	2	—	—	5
Will build up Boston	3	8	—	—	3	3
Will provide housing	1	1	—	—	3	—
Will provide jobs	2	5	—	—	—	—
Reasons of Ideology	27	22	22	33	46	78
Honesty	15	3	15	32	37	68
Progressive	2	2	3	—	3	5
Helps little man	7	14	—	1	—	—
Will help veterans	*	—	1	—	3	—
Will help needy	1	1	—	—	3	—
Will help young	2	2	3	—	—	5
Political Reasons	4	1	7	3	7	5
Not machine candidate	2	1	1	2	7	5
Party affiliation	*	*	—	—	—	—
Good backers	*	—	1	—	—	—
	2	—	5	1	—	—
Personal Characteristics	36	26	47	41	31	26
Good background	6	4	2	11	—	26
Young	6	—	18	2	—	—
Veteran	2	—	7	—	—	—
Better known	3	4	2	7	3	—
Good fellow	8	8	6	14	—	—
Know him personally	10	10	11	7	14	—
Nationality	1	*	1	—	14	—
Lesser of Evils	5	6	6	14	6	—
Miscellaneous	7	2	17	9	3	—
Best chance to win	*	1	1	—	—	—
Runs clean campaign	*	1	—	—	—	—
Deserves chance at office	7	*	16	9	3	—
Number of Cases	550	253	159	87	29	19

*Less than 0.5%.

Percentages total more than 100 since some respondents gave more than one reason for choosing candidate.

Source: Adapted from Jerome S. Bruner and Sheldon H. Korchin, "The Boss and the Vote: Case Study in City Politics," *Public Opinion Quarterly* 10 (Spring 1946): 14.

opposing candidate himself found a comfortable position in the construction department of the city. They can't lick you if they join you.

One of the most interesting explanations for the staying power of the boss emerged from survey research done in Boston just prior to the 1945 election for mayor. That race was won by Boss Curley, at 71 a thoroughly identified machine man who had had a long and stormy career "marked by indictments, feuds, charges and countercharges."[14] Though under indictment for fraud, Curley received approximately 46 percent of the vote in a six-man field; his nearest opponent mustered only 25 percent. As Table 7.2 shows, very few of those who voted for Curley did so because they were ignorant of the charges against him. An extraordinary number of those interviewed named Curley as their worst candidate and made remarks like, "He's a lousy crook," and "You can never be quite sure of the man's motives."[15] Boston voters, Table 7.2 makes clear, continued to support Curley because they perceived him to be efficient.[16] This seems to imply that to a great many Americans, efficiency and ability to "get the job done" are more important than honesty. The attitudes toward Curley seemed remarkably well diffused among Bostonians. He achieved the support of youth and women, and (as Table 7.3 shows) his appeal to the several ethnic groups remained high.

It is difficult to document the decline of the urban machine with any precision. Gradual changing social and economic conditions conspired to undercut the political resources on which the machine was built. The most important developments undermining the old-style machine were: a decline in

Table 7.3   Votes of Four Nationality Groups For Major Candidates*

Candidates	Percent Irish Vote	Percent Italian Vote	Percent Jewish Vote	Percent Yankee Vote
Curley	59	59	37	33
Kerrigan	26	25	17	36
Reilly	14	5	23	22
Others	1	11	23	9
Total	100%	100%	100%	100%
Number	173	53	34	87

*Irish is defined as a person with parent or grandparent born in Ireland. It includes as well, of course, those of Irish nativity. A comparable criterion is used for defining "Italian." "Jewish" is defined as any person who gives as his religious preference the Jewish religion. "Yankee" is used to describe those people whose American ancestry runs back four generations or more.

Source: Adapted from Jerome S. Bruner and Sheldon J. Korchin, "The Boss and the Vote: Case Study in City Politics," *Public Opinion Quarterly* 10 (Spring 1946): 10.

the availability of patronage, the many measures connected with the New Deal, the growth of the middle class, and the development of a reform "movement." The reform movement will be discussed in some detail in the next chapter, but the other factors need brief explanation.

Beginning with the Pendleton Act, the federal government began to abandon patronage as the major means of appointing government personnel. In a good many states and cities, jobs which formerly could be promised to party faithful were no longer available. Under such circumstances, the most a loyal party worker might be able to do is hope for some minor advantage. The local political organization could guarantee him nothing. The growth of civil service, of course, also corresponds with the development of technical requirements for many appointive positions. Many government jobs require specialized knowledge in matters like public finance, hospital administration, engineering, traffic control problems, and the like which the untrained though loyal party worker did not have.

The New Deal was also an important source of developments that undermined the urban machine. It is ironic, of course, that the Democratic President Franklin Delano Roosevelt's initiatives did so much to undermine the power of so many urban Democratic machines in American cities. The depression had created more poverty and personal misery than the machines were able to cope with. The New Deal, which aimed at providing massive relief for the distresses of the depression, increased government preoccupation with citizen welfare. Specifically, the governmental bureaucracy began to take over many of the functions formerly performed by the machine. The welfare and employment functions were taken from the machines. Ward leaders (heelers) were replaced by professional welfare workers and job counselors. Eventually the depression led to large programs — federally organized, financed, and supervised — of old-age insurance, unemployment compensation, and public assistance in a variety of forms which, though they lacked the personal touch, provided a level and consistency of benefits that machines could not match. Thus it was that, as the machine lost its function, it soon lost its following.

We should also note that the long-term growth of affluence in twentieth-century America played its role in laying the old-style boss to rest. In many ways it can be said that the urban machine served the very rich and the very poor. As the middle class in this country grew — and today white-collar workers are more numerous than blue-collar — the opposition to the urban machines grew in proportion. In fact, a number of political scientists characterize the reform movement as a reassertion of the values of the white Anglo-Saxon Protestant against the Old World political style which provided the value base of the urban machine.

Despite the long-term decline of big city machines, we must still recognize that certain strong party organizations continue to thrive and that a number of the functions performed by machines continue to be served, although in a modified form. For example, a study conducted in 1957 of the activities of party leaders in eight New Jersey counties found none of them conforming to the stereotype of the boss, yet they performed a wide range of traditional party services. For instance, 72% of the New Jersey party leaders reported that they "often" helped "deserving people get public jobs," 62% reported "helping citizens who are in difficulty with the law," and 54% of the county party workers interviewed indicated that they often showed people "how to get their social security benefits, welfare, unemployment compensation, etc."[17]

The Urban Machine and Democracy

The rise of the old style boss amounted to a conservative response to the kinds of changes that built our cities in the post-Civil War period. The boss met some of the pressing needs of an immigrant population for the token cost of the newcomer's vote. The boss himself operated primarily as a broker. To say only this much is to leave the impression that the boss system was in conformity with the premises of pluralist democracy. Recall we said in Chapter 2 that, in the pluralist democratic mode, the public decision maker's principal rule of decision is that he should be guided by the coalition of the most powerful actors which are attentive to the specific issue. In describing the activities of traditional bosses, we find that they tended to balance power on particular issues and were essentially nonideological. While it is probably correct that the machine style of politics comes much closer to the precepts of pluralist democracy than we might think at first glance, we should note at least one significant departure: pluralist democracy expects to operate within a rule of law; the machines provided specific material benefits to needy citizens, while *not* operating within the rule of law.

Whatever the merits and demerits of the machine, its decline is very real. As machines have departed, they have usually left extremely weak urban political parties as a legacy. As we shall see in the following chapter, undermining the power of the urban party was one of the chief aims of the reform movement. What is the remaining effectiveness of the political party in the city?

THE URBAN POLITICAL PARTY: CURRENT STYLE

Party membership figures generally tell us little about voting in local elections. San Diego, California, with its nominally nonpartisan election system has a majority of registered Democrats. Yet in the 1971 city council election, there were more Republicans elected than Democrats; and the largest votegetter was the Republican mayor, Pete Wilson. Party registration figures are especially unhelpful as a predictor of election outcome in cities in which one party has substantial control of government; under such circumstances, the voter may feel it is to his advantage to be registered in the dominant party but to in fact vote more consistently for the minority party candidate. It has been observed of New York City that party membership is "nominal and, at bottom, ephemeral," and as a result is "only loosely related to voting behavior."[18]

This is not to say that urban political parties have no impact on elections. The power to nominate is a substantial one, although even that power is compromised in the cities which have "nonpartisan" elections (which includes about 60 percent of our cities over 5000). Still, the ability to nominate can place power in the hands of local party leadership — as, for example, in New Haven, Connecticut, where "the whole paraphernalia of democratic procedures is employed not so much to insure control from below as to give legitimacy and acceptability to the candidates selected by the (party) leaders."[19]

In those cities in which party organization is strong and precinct workers are active, party influence on voting behavior increases.[20] Minority parties apparently gain even more from organization efforts than the majority party.[21] Yet the particular issues of the election may be more important than the organizational effectiveness of the parties.[22]

One of the interesting paradoxes of the urban political party is that, while it has declined in power, it has come closer to the assumptions of individualist democracy. Eldersveld's elaborate study of the political parties of Detroit found that party leadership is exercised through a "stratarchy" rather than by a unified hierarchy as it was in the urban machine.[23] That is, in a stratarchy, political power is diffused throughout the party structure; people of diverse social and economic backgrounds find their way into the leadership of the party; the parties become ideologically more distinct; and party leaders tend to be less power oriented than were their counterparts in the big-city machines of the past. Let us examine the evidence that forms the basis for the conclusion that urban parties tend toward stratarchy.

Backgrounds of Party Leaders

In 1959 and 1960, a survey was taken of the committeemen and women in New York City. Among other things, the scholars conducting that survey wanted to find out how the social background of Manhattan committeemen compared with that of the people who had dominated the parties during the machine era.[24] Their findings make an almost total contrast to the image of the party "hack." A party official of the machine had little education, a blue-collar occupation, tended to be in public employment, Catholic, a recent immigrant of European ancestry, and a male. The Manhattan study found that fully two-thirds of their committeemen had gone to college or beyond; one-fourth were professional people with incomes greater than the national average, and only 5% of their sample were on the public payroll. Protestants held one-quarter, and Jews occupied two-fifths, of the party leadership positions. Only 8% of the party leaders in Manhattan were born outside the United States. Very few were Irish (9%), and representatives of the other European origin groups were relatively evenly divided within the sample. Forty-four percent of the Manhattan committeemen were women.

Table 7.4   Occupations of Party Activists (in percent)

Occupation	St. Louis	New York[a]	Chicago, 1928[b]	Chicago, 1936[b]
Housewife	19.5[c]			
Blue collar	19.5[c]	32	17[d]	13
White collar and small business	33	37[e]	14	28
Government	14[f]	3	59	48
Professional	11	19[e]	10	11
Other and no answer	4	8		
Total	101	99	100	100

[a]Figures are taken from Robert S. Hirschfield et al., "A Profile of Political Activists in Manhattan," *Western Political Quarterly* 15 (1962): 489-507.

[b]Data are drawn from Harold F. Gosnell, *Machine Politics: Chicago Model* (Chicago: University of Chicago Press, 1937).

[c]If St. Louis respondents are classified according to the occupation of the head of household, the proportion in the blue-collar category increases to 33 percent, mostly at the expense of the housewife group.

[d]Gosnell labeled this group, "clerical, sales and blue collar," so it probably overstates the number of blue-collar members.

[e]Hirschfield et al., label one category "sales, clerical and small business," while the other is headed "business and professional." There may thus be some differences in classification, since in the St. Louis data all businessmen are small and are classed with white-collar workers.

[f]At various times, some 43 percent of the St. Louis group have held government jobs. Some, like election judges, were temporary and others, while full-time, lasted only a year or two. Still, the 14 percent figure may understate the number of government workers compared with the Chicago data.

Source: Robert H. Salisbury, "The Urban Party Organization Member," *Public Opinion Quarterly* (Winter 1965-66): 554.

Equally interesting, it was found that blacks, despite their numbers and long residence in the city, held only 11% of the committee seats; and Puerto Ricans were unrepresented.[25]

Studies of the social backgrounds of party leaders in other cities are insufficient to enable us to put the Manhattan findings in comparative perspective. However, the other studies do convey less contrast between the personnel of the machine era and of the contemporary urban party. For example, a study of party leadership in St. Louis at least partially contradicts the New York City findings that today's party workers are mainly "amateurs."[26] Table 7.4 shows that the St. Louis party members were more nearly like the profile of Chicago machine politicians than the Manhattan party leaders.[27]

The Ideology of Party Leaders

Machines were generally free of ideology. Several studies of new party leaders, however, have found a strain toward ideological consistency within the party — Republicans toward a "conservative ideology," the Democrats toward a more liberal position. The data in Table 7.5 show that strain for ideological consistency. Manhattan's Democratic and Liberal Party leaders are more likely to favor a variety of governmentally sponsored social programs — welfare, medical care, civil rights and the like — than are its Republicans.

The study of Detroit leadership reveals much the same pattern. There were striking differences in the ideologies of the top leadership of the two parties and also significant ideological differences at the precinct level as well. In Detroit, however, there was a sizable dissenting group in each party — from 10 to 25 percent of the leadership were ideologically nonconforming.[28] So while the party leadership moves toward ideological consistency, dissent is reasonably common. As Eldersveld says:

> The party machine is no monolith, co-opting and coercing a homogeneous and unique ideological leadership. Pressure to conform exists. But the party gladly embraces, and freely associates with a most ideologically conglomerate set of potential supporters and activists. From the bottom to the top, the party welcomes, and rewards, the ideological deviant.[29]

Power Orientations

To assess political motivations is tricky at best, but the empirical work done so far suggests that the new-style politicians are attracted to and maintained in their party work more by psychic rewards, such as devotion to a cause, than by a desire to wield power. The Detroit study, for example, found a large minority, mostly at the lower two echelons of the party structure, who were not conscious of the party as a "power group." Eldersveld

Table 7.5   Political Party Attitudes of the County Committeemen* of New York, 1960 (in percentage)

Policy Statement	Strongly Agree			Agree			Disagree			Strongly Disagree		
	D	R	L	D	R	L	D	R	L	D	R	L
1. The government ought to see to it that everyone who wants to work can find a job.	43	36	52	31	26	37	13	10	9	13	28	2
2. The government ought to help people get low-cost doctors and hospital care.	68	36	83	16	28	11	8	11	6	9	25	0
3. If Negroes are not getting fair treatment in jobs and housing, the government should see to it that they do.	65	43	85	18	22	9	8	16	2	9	19	4
4. The government ought to see to it that big U.S. corporations don't have much say about how the government is run.	51	32	53	25	27	27	9	20	15	14	21	4
5. If cities and towns around the country need help to build more schools, the government ought to give more money.	58	36	64	22	20	27	10	20	2	10	24	7
6. The government should leave things like electric power and housing for private business concerns to build.	22	35	14	19	28	12	21	18	21	38	18	52
7. The government should stay out of the question of whether white and colored children go to the same school.	14	20	7	6	8	4	12	12	5	67	61	83

*Number responding: D (Democrats) — 216; R (Republicans) — 118; L (Liberals) — 46.

Source: Robert S. Hirschfield, Burt E. Swanson, and Blarce P. Blank, "A Profile of Political Activists in Manhattan," *Western Political Quarterly* 15 (1962): 501.

labeled this 20 to 45 percent of his sample as either "idealists" or persons unable to articulate a goal for the party.[30] A similar pattern appears in the study of party activists in Massachusetts and North Carolina. Other situational factors have an impact on the power orientation of the party leaders. In Detroit, Eldersveld found that 77 percent of the precinct leaders from highly contested precincts had a strong power orientation: it seems that when you have to fight, you value power more.[31] Minority party leaders show a stronger tendency to minimize the power goal of the party: perhaps if you know you cannot get power, you may as well minimize its importance.

Suburban Contrasts?

Party leaders in the middle-class residential suburbs operate in the new style of urban politics. In fact, if the limited literature available on this subject is accurate, such suburbs have provided the model on which the new urban political style is based.

When Robert Wood wrote about suburban politics in the 1950s, he emphasized the contrast between the suburban style and the urban style by emphasizing the machine-like character of city politics.[32] The suburban party leader, Wood found, was a man "more interested in the fortunes of the organization than in personal prerogatives and power."[33] The suburban party leader's job is relatively easier than that of his urban or rural counterpart because the vote he is expected to deliver for the party usually delivers itself. This is the result of the tending social and political homogeneity of such areas. Since he can generally count on a good turnout of voters in his party, the leader in a suburban area does not need to expend most of his efforts on exhorting party members to go to the polls; instead, he is more likely to talk issues as a way of evoking additional party support. At the same time, the suburban party leader is expected to be covert politically. "Political workers of both parties in [suburbs] assert that the electorate resents the slightest attempt to encourage a citizen to avail himself of the right to vote, much less to induce him to support a particular party. The voters' adherence to political independence compels party activity of an oblique nature, quite different from that associated with party organization."[34] The middle-class suburban party leader, then, is rarely a partisan in the accepted sense of the word; he is much more the political amateur than is the urban politician.

These tendencies are borne out in a more recent study of party leadership in Nassau County, a suburb of New York City, where persons of relatively high social and economic status made up the party leadership. Within each party, leaders embraced common ideological perspectives, and there existed important ideological differences between the two parties. There were also distinguishable party positions on issues. As regards the motives of the Nassau party leaders, it was found that "the substance of politics rather than . . . politics as a mere channel for personal gain" characterized Nassau parties.[35] Interestingly, the leadership of the Democratic party of Nassau resembled the amateur mode, while among Republican leaders there was evidence of more professionally oriented perspectives.[36]

In a number of ways, the new style of urban politics amounts to the suburbanization of city politics. Far from being trivial, then, the development of suburban parties might well be a harbinger of things to come in our metropolitan areas.

New-Style Parties and Democracy: "Nonurban Nonparties"

As the new style of urban party moves back toward what we have called assumptions of individualist democracy, it is paradoxical that the party's impact on the total urban process has at the same time weakened. Where the party is dominated by political amateurs, it has tended to lose support. Where the new-style party has had more professional leadership, coherence has often been purchased at the cost of limiting amateur and popular involvement in the party hierarchy. On this latter point, for example, Robert Dahl finds in New Haven that rank-and-file party members are unable to control nominations by democratic means because of three patterns: (1) the enrolled adherents of each party are only a minority of the party following; (2) the members who are active in the caucuses and primaries are a minority of all the members; and (3) the semblance of democratic procedure used by the party is more to lend legitimacy and acceptability to the candidates chosen than to achieve rank-and-file control of those nominations.[37] However, Dahl concludes that while the party membership has no direct influence on the process, "their indirect influence was very great indeed, since the party leaders were anxious to present the candidate who had the greatest electoral appeal."[38]

As the overall effectiveness of the urban party has declined, some of its functions have been siphoned off and are served in other ways. For example, the proliferation of public referenda in our cities provides a means for dealing with public issues without the party's certifying one or another position on the referenda. A number of cities have developed organizations other than parties which function to nominate candidates for city office. These "nonurban nonparties" take a variety of forms, but their existence serves to dilute party effectiveness still further. It is difficult to say at this stage whether what we have called the new style of urban parties should be (1) celebrated as a democratization of the machine; (2) lamented as a stage in the death of an effective democratic instrument in our cities; or (3) welcomed as a necessary transitional stage to a more effective though proliferated democratic form.

If what we are seeing is the transformation of the urban party, there may be several developments which foreshadow these new forms; particularly interesting are two developments: (1) the seemingly nonpartisan slating committees; and (2) the political club. The slating committee is illustrated by the Kansas City experience. As the machine of Jim Pendergast decayed in the late 1930s, there formed a factional alliance consisting mostly of reform-seeking groups which called themselves the Citizens Association. It was composed of independent antimachine Democrats, a black editor and his following, the Republican party organization, an AFL-CIO interest grouping, the Republican Kansas City *Star*, and several civic organizations. Functioning as a candidate-screening and slating organization, the Citizens Association won six consecutive elections before it was finally defeated by a reformed Democratic party. Citizens associations of this kind are an ideal vehicle through which to express a party type of spirit without having to deny accusations of partisanship.

The formation of the so-called political club offers much the same advantage. The club, as James Q. Wilson describes it, is an element of the party that is held together simply by the satisfactions people find in being members of it.[39] Such clubs first existed when political machines were in their heyday. For example, Tammany Hall — when it was the Democratic party in New York — had clubs as its basic component.[40] Originally many of these clubs were centers for the distribution of patronage and other specific material benefits to their members. As these rewards atrophied, the clubs came to offer instead sociability and zeal in pursuit of one's personal political goals. The club, in other words, became the vehicle for the amateur, issue-oriented Democrat.

If the slating committees and political clubs are the emerging forms of urban political organization, their development seems to deserve the title of nonurban nonparty. "Nonparty" for obvious reasons — they represent specifically antiparty responses and operate *in the place of* regular party organization. "Nonurban" because, as channels for the representation of interest, they seem much better attuned to middle-class and upper-middle-class interests than to the representation of the relatively poor voters who lack the time, the commitment, and perhaps the access to them to express themselves in this way.

The relative weakness of the urban political party should be kept in mind as we turn our attention next to elections. Whereas national electoral behavior has been closely associated with party affiliation, it is not clear that the parties are similarly important in local elections. Weak parties that are sporadically or only selectively active leave voters looking elsewhere to find information to guide their voting decisions.

GENERAL CHARACTERISTICS OF LOCAL ELECTIONS

Fewer voters turn out at local elections than at state and national contests. When we look at Table 7.6, we see that in half the city elections held concurrently with state or national elections, 50 percent of the adults went to the polls; when there were no concurrent state and national elections, the turnout figure dropped to only 20 percent. That figure, as it pertained to

Table 7.6   Percent of Adults (in Cities over 25,000) Who Vote in City Elections

Election for Mayor[1]

	No. of Cities Reporting	Lower Quartile[3]	Median	Upper Quartile
Form of Election				
Partisan	42	28	43	55
Nonpartisan	105	21	32	44
Form of Government				
Mayor-Council	59	38	47	57
Commission	25	28	38	47
Council-Manager	63	19	26	33
Population Group				
Over 500,000	3	18	20	34
250,000 to 500,000	12	20	38	41
100,000 to 250,000	17	24	31	45
50,000 to 100,000	30	22	43	52
25,000 to 50,000	85	24	35	47
All cities over 25,000	147	23	35	47

Election for Council Only[2]

	No. of Cities Reporting	Lower Quartile	Median	Upper Quartile
Form of Election				
Partisan	14	22	37	50
Nonpartisan	140	17	23	32
Form of Government				
Mayor-Council	18	24	38	51
Commission	7	27	38	51
Council-Manager	130	17	23	31
Population Group				
Over 500,000	2	20	--	43
250,000 to 500,000	4	14	19	20
100,000 to 250,000	19	17	27	47
50,000 to 100,000	52	18	23	35
25,000 to 50,000	78	17	25	32
All cities over 25,000	155	17	24	34

[1]"Election for Mayor" includes cities which also elected councilmen at same election.
[2]"Election for Council Only" includes several cities which elected only officers other than mayor or councilmen.
[3]"Lower Quartile" of cities in terms of voting participation.

Table 7.6 continued

	No. of Cities Reporting	*All City Elections*		
		Lower Quartile	*Median*	*Upper Quartile*
Form of Election				
Partisan	109	37	50	57
Nonpartisan	350	21	30	43
Form of Government				
Mayor-Council	137	38	50	57
Commission	41	29	38	47
Council-Manager	281	20	27	39
Population Group				
Over 500,000	15	26	39	47
250,000 to 500,000	25	21	37	48
100,000 to 250,000	54	24	32	50
50,000 to 100,000	124	21	33	51
25,000 to 50,000	243	23	33	47
All cities over 25,000	461	22	33	48

	No. of Cities Reporting	*Held Concurrently with Other Local Elections*[4]		
		Lower Quartile	*Median*	*Upper Quartile*
Form of Election				
Partisan	22	48	53	58
Nonpartisan	65	27	35	47
Form of Government				
Mayor-Council	28	40	50	55
Commission	5	28	57	71
Council-Manager	54	26	35	47
Population Group				
Over 500,000	7	33	39	50
250,000 to 500,000	5	24	35	54
100,000 to 250,000	9	31	46	50
50,000 to 100,000	24	30	51	55
25,000 to 50,000	42	28	41	50
All cities over 25,000	87	29	44	51

[4]Excluding cities also holding election concurrently with state or national election.

Table 7.6 continued

		Held Concurrently With State or National Elections		
	No. of Cities Reporting	Lower Quartile	Median	Upper Quartile
Form of Election				
Partisan	31	47	51	65
Nonpartisan	32	31	43	59
Form of Government				
Mayor-Council	31	47	51	65
Commission	3	28	33	61
Council-Manager	29	29	43	60
Population Group				
Over 500,000	2	46	--	47
250,000 to 500,000	4	45	56	76
100,000 to 250,000	9	30	50	55
50,000 to 100,000	17	20	51	62
25,000 to 50,000	31	35	47	64
All cities over 25,000	63	35	50	62

		Held Independently of Any Other Election		
	No. of Cities Reporting	Lower Quartile	Median	Upper Quartile
Form of Election				
Partisan	56	26	41	53
Nonpartisan	246	19	27	39
Form of Government				
Mayor-Council	78	34	44	56
Commission	32	28	38	47
Council-Manager	193	18	23	32
Population Group				
Over 500,000	5	19	20	39
250,000 to 500,000	16	18	34	41
100,000 to 250,000	36	21	29	46
50,000 to 100,000	82	20	29	44
25,000 to 50,000	164	20	29	41
All cities over 25,000	303	20	29	41

Source: Adapted from Eugene C. Lee, "City Elections: A Statistical Profile," *The Municipal Yearbook, 1963* (Washington, D.C.: International City Managers Association, 1963), p. 81.

election of councilmen, increased when there were other city officials on the ballot. As Table 7.6 shows, these tendencies are more pronounced in council-manager and nonpartisan cities. ". . . the record of partisan cities — regardless of whether the municipal election is held concurrently with other partisan races or not — is substantially higher than that of nonpartisan cities."[41] Council-manager cities rank at the bottom of all forms in voter participation.

It is possible that the lower turnout rate in local elections makes no significant difference. If, for example, the voting nonparticipation rate were proportionate among all social groupings, then the local electorate is merely "the national electorate in miniature."[42] But, as we have already explained, the power-poor drop out in disproportionate numbers. Besides noting the tendency of reformed cities to turn out fewer minority voters, we can make a number of other generalizations about local elections which have considerable supporting evidence.

1. *The socioeconomic divisions that are important in national politics also operate in local partisan elections.* A study of voting behavior in Philadelphia and its suburbs, for example, found that the partisan vote in both central city and suburbs correlates with income, occupation, and educational levels. In the central city, race also correlates with party choice.[43] However, the association between these social and economic factors and party voting seems to vary with the size of the city. In smaller cities and towns, a "politics of acquaintance" seems to replace partisanship as a determinant of the vote. But in large cities, the voters more readily identify local candidates with parties.[44] In Michigan, for example, laborers in small cities were found to be less likely to vote Democratic than were laborers in large cities.[45] Similarly, materials collected by the University of Michigan's Survey Research Center, indicate that in large metropolitan areas blue-collar workers differ more from white-collar workers than in smaller cities.

The tendency for ethnic groups to manifest a degree of solidarity in larger cities is often enough noted that we need not dwell on it here. However, the assumption that Irish, Italian, or Polish citizens vote as a solid block is a hangover from the machine era which becomes increasingly dubious. If a candidate plays too heavily on his ethnic background, it can result in the loss of votes from the ethnic districts: ethnic voters have come to prefer candidates who represent the ethnic group but at the same time "display the attributes of the generally admired Anglo-Saxon model."

> The perfect candidate, then, is of Jewish, Polish, Italian, or Irish extraction and has the speech, dress, manner and the public virtues — honesty, impartiality, and devotion to the public interest — of the upper class Anglo-Saxon.[46]

2. *There is a tendency for one party to have a consistent majority in local elections.* In part, this tendency is a function of size — the smaller the

unit of government, the greater the likelihood that it will contain sufficient numbers of like-minded people to provide a consistent edge to one party. As a result, the larger cities tend toward greater competition between the parties while the small rural and suburban cities are more likely to elect their officials consistently from a single party.[47] This does not necessarily mean that the dominant party actively controls the city. Local parties in particular cities are often so disorganized and weak that they have little impact on elections and on the subsequent processes of governing. In addition, one-party dominance does not necessarily foreclose minority success in particular elections, especially where councils are chosen by districts. But one-party dominance over long periods of time does hamper the ability of a minority party to mobilize its potential vote.[48]

3. One-party dominance also generally follows the pattern wherein *large cities tend to be Democratic while suburbs and small rural cities are Republican*. This long-term trend is well illustrated by the materials in Table 7.7, which show that, at all educational levels, there are about ten percent more Republicans in the suburbs than in the central cities. To cite Democratic cities and Republican suburbs seems to invite construction of stereotypes. The party alignments suggest that the Democratic party coalition includes the low-income voters, ethnic groups, labor, and racial constituencies while the Republican party represents white, middle-class, educated, and managerial components. It has been projected that there is an "emerging Republican majority" which results from the growth of suburban areas.[49] Such a development depends on the growing affluence of the low-income voter, resulting in his purchase of the great American dream home in a suburb and his subse-

Table 7.7   Percentage of Metropolitan Voters, by Locale and Education, Who Identified With Republican Party, 1968

	% All Voters Interviewed		% White Voters Interviewed	
	in city	in suburbs	in city	in suburbs
Less than H.S. grad.	18.0	28.3	25.0	30.7
H.S. grad.	28.2	38.5	34.4	39.5
Some college +	40.1	41.0	45.6	57.6
Of all respondents identifying selves as D, R, or Ind., the % who claimed R were	28.0	41.0	35.4	42.9

Source: Adapted from Fredrick M. Wirt et al., *On the City's Rim: Politics and Policy in Suburbia* (Lexington, Mass.: D. C. Heath, 1972), p. 107.

quent conversion to Republican politics. The rate of that growth of Republicans, however, has thus far been offset by the constantly diminishing number of Republicans in small towns and rural areas. It has also been urged that growing antipathy between blacks and other urban poor will enable Republicans to win the support of the white "backlash" elements. However, backlash voting so far has not produced a solid basis for long-term Republican resurgence in the central cities. In fact, many of the candidates articulating backlash sentiment are Democratic — possibly because, in some cities, there's no point in running on the Republican ticket, so the entire spectrum of feelings about blacks will be expressed by Democratic candidates. Despite the sense of turmoil and change that has characterized American politics in the sixties and seventies, the identification of the Democratic party with the central city is remarkably intact.

4. Finally, in local elections, *unique situations have a relatively greater impact* than in other elections. A wide variety of factors peculiar to a city often determine election outcomes. Local situations — the closing of a large industry, the building of a new freeway — can stir controversies which have decisive impact on election day. A strong personality may invite the voters' reaction to him. Particular issues may themselves appear in referendum elections. When city elections focus on such issues, they provide an excellent opportunity for us to examine the urban voters' thinking. Recognizing that political parties seldom play a role in referenda elections and passing over theories that would emphasize the importance of "opinion leaders" and other small-group forces, James Wilson and Edward Banfield theorize that a voter in a local referendum aims to maximize his family income. They assume the referendum voter engages in a kind of cost-benefit analysis — that is, he weighs the benefits he expects to come to him from a bond issue against the amount of tax that he will have to pay to receive these benefits. These assumptions of voter rationality in pursuit of self-interest have a number of implications and limitations: rationality depends on knowledge, and knowledge is often limited in referenda elections. Unless a voter undertakes some independent research prior to the election, he is not likely to know whether the bonds he is about to vote on will benefit him or not. As a general rule, the ballot seldom specifies precisely which streets will be paved or which schools will be improved. Still, the assumption that the voter acts rationally within his own knowledge seems a plausible explanation. To test that assumption, Banfield and Wilson examined returns on 35 expenditure proposals voted in 7 cities in 20 separate elections. They found that voters in districts with few homeowners almost invariably supported all expenditure proposals. Support for additional expenditures consistently declined as home ownership increased in an area. Obviously, this goes some distance in verify-

ing what has been referred to as the revolt of the property taxpayer.[50] The same study also found that the higher-income families gave relatively greater support to public expenditure referenda. Urban residents with higher incomes and with more valuable property supported public expenditures. There emerges, then, in a great many referenda elections what might be thought of as a peculiar coalition wherein the relatively poor and the wealthy join to support public expenditure proposals which are opposed by middle-income homeowners.

There are a number of potential explanations for these findings. The increase in taxes represents a smaller sacrifice for the wealthy than for the middle-income taxpayer. Homeowners who are less well-to-do may come to share what we earlier called the caretaker image of a city government because they simply cannot afford tax increases.

SUMMARY

The effectiveness of the Old Style of urban parties has been significantly undercut by contemporary developments, especially the reform movement which will be discussed more fully in the following chapter. Before we celebrate the passing of the "machine," however, some revision of our understanding of what the old style was like is in order. The machine was in many respects a *conservative reaction* to rapid social and economic changes in our cities. The machine performed many functions which a dependent population required.

The more contemporary parties are the products of reform, reflecting the efforts of the white, middle class to increase their political power in the cities. The parties have tended to become more ideological, that is, more like the assumptions of Individualist Democracy — but at the cost of becoming, at the same time, less central actors in the political processes of most cities. They have tended to become "nonurban nonparties."

NOTES

1. Woman's Division, Democratic National Committee, *The Key to Democratic Victory, A Guide Book for County and Precinct Workers* (Washington, D.C.: The Committee, 1952). As quoted in George S. Blair, *American Local Government* (New York: Harper & Row, 1964), p. 129.
2. For both fun and enlightenment see James A. Michener, *Report of the County Chairman* (New York: Random House, 1961).
3. This perspective is developed by James G. Scott in "Corruption, Machine Politics and Political Change," *The American Political Science Review* 63 (December

1969): 1154-1156. He finds that machine politics develops in other countries in periods of rapid social change.

4. Warren Moscow, "Exit the Boss, Enter the Leader," *New York Times Magazine* (June 22, 1947), pp. 16, 17, 47, 48.

5. This discussion draws heavily on Fred I. Greenstein, "The Changing Pattern of Urban Party Politics," *Annals of the American Academy of Political and Social Sciences* 353 (May 1964): 2-13.

6. Ibid., p. 3.

7. Summarized from Scott, "Corruption, Machine Politics, and Political Change," p. 1154.

8. For a similar perspective, see Theodore J. Lowi, "Machine Politics: Old and New," *Public Interest* 9 (Fall 1967): 83-92. Much of the material that follows is from Robert K. Merton, "The Latent Function of the Machine," in *Social Theory and Social Structure*, ed. Robert K. Merton (New York: Free Press of Glencoe, 1957), pp. 71-81.

9. Quoted in William L. Reardon, *Plunkitt of Tammany Hall* (New York: McClure, Phillips, 1905), p. 52.

10. Lincoln Steffans, *Autobiography* (New York: Harcourt, Brace and World, 1931), p. 618.

11. Quoted in Reardon, *Plunkitt of Tammany Hall*, p. 46.

12. Quoted in Ibid., p. 53.

13. Jane Addams, *Democracy and Social Ethics* (Cambridge: Belknap Press of Harvard University Press, 1964), p. 254.

14. Jerome S. Bruner and Sheldon J. Korchin, "The Boss and the Vote: Case Study in City Politics," *Public Opinion Quarterly* 10 (Spring 1946): 2.

15. Ibid., p. 18.

16. This perception is a striking parallel to the observations of journalists in connection with the re-election of Mayor Richard Daley of Chicago in 1971. Daley had been widely splashed as an old-style boss and had been subjected to strong adverse national publicity for his handling of the rioting at the 1968 Democratic National Convention. He had also been criticized in the so-called Walker Commission Report, which held Daley responsible for what it called the "police-riot" that had occurred at that convention. Still, Daley won his most overwhelming victory in that election. It was apparently common for voters to say, "Of course he's an old-style boss, but he gets things done. New York City is disorganized though democratic. We prefer organization, even if it *is* in the hands of a boss."

17. Richard T. Frost, "Stability and Change in Local Politics," *Public Opinion Quarterly* 25 (Summer 1961): 231-232.

18. Wallace S. Sayre and Herbert Kaufman, *Governing New York City* (New York: Russell Sage Foundation, 1960), p. 129.

19. Robert Dahl, *Who Governs?* (New Haven: Yale University Press, 1961), p. 105.

20. Cf. Raymond E. Wolfinger, "The Influence of Precinct Work on Voting Behavior," *Public Opinion Quarterly* 27 (Fall 1963): 387-393.

21. Daniel J. Katz and Samuel J. Eldersveld, "The Impact of Local Party Activity Upon the Electorate," *Public Opinion Quarterly* 25 (Spring 1961): 1, 24.

22. As Wolfinger suggests in "Influence of Precinct Work" (p. 398), the impact of precinct work "will vary in inverse ratio to the salience of the election to the voters."

23. Samuel Eldersveld, *Political Parties: A Behavioral Analysis* (Chicago: Rand, McNally 1964), pp. 9-11, Chap. 5.

24. Robert S. Hirshfield, Burt E. Swanson, and Blanche D. Blank, "Profile of Political Activists in Manhattan," *Western Political Quarterly* 15 (1962): 489-507.

25. Ibid., pp. 492-494.

26. The term amateur is used here in a nonevaluative way, simply to mean those people who are not professional party workers. The use was suggested by the work of James Q. Wilson, *The Amateur Democrat* (Chicago: University of Chicago Press, 1962).

27. Robert H. Salisbury, "The Urban Party Organization Member," *Public Opinion Quarterly* 29 (Winter 1965-66): 550-564. The St. Louis sample is of members of the Democratic ward and township organizations.

28. Eldersveld, *Political Parties: A Behavioral Analysis*, p. 216.

29. Ibid., p. 219.

30. Ibid., p. 242; and cf. Lewis Bowman, Dennis Ippolito, and William Donaldson, "Incentives for the Maintenance of Grass Roots Political Activism," *Midwest Journal of Political Science* 13 (February 1969): 126-139.

31. Eldersveld, *Political Parties: A Behavioral Analysis*, pp. 242-243.

32. See Robert C. Wood, *Suburbia, Its People and Their Politics* (Boston: Houghton Mifflin, 1958), especially the section titled, "The Suburban Boss," pp. 166-175.

33. Ibid., p. 170.

34. G. E. Janosik, "The New Suburbia," *Current History* (August 1956), p. 87.

35. Dennis S. Ippolito, "Political Perspectives of Suburban Party Leaders," *Social Science Quarterly* 49 (March 1969): 800-815, 814.

36. Ibid.

37. Dahl, *Who Governs?*

38. Ibid., p. 106.

39. "Political machines, when they collapse, often break into factions, and clubs are a common form that the factionalism takes." Edward Banfield and James Q. Wilson, *City Politics* (Cambridge: Harvard University Press, 1963), p. 132.

40. See Roy V. Peel, *The Political Clubs of New York City* (New York: G. P. Putnam's Sons, 1935).

41. Eugene C. Lee, "City Elections: A Statistical Profile," *The Municipal Yearbook, 1963* (Washington, D.C.: International City Managers Association, 1963, p. 83.

42. That statement and the following discussion draw heavily on Robert L. Lineberry and Ira Sharkansky, *Urban Politics and Public Policy* (New York: Harper & Row, 1971), pp. 89-92.

43. Oliver P. Williams et al., *Suburban Differences in Metropolitan Policies* (Philadelphia: University of Pennsylvania Press, 1964).

44. See Alvin Boskoff and Harmon Zeigler, *Voting Patterns in a Local Election* (Philadelphia: J. B. Lippincott, 1964), p. 23.

45. Nickolas A. Masters and Deil S. Wright, "Trends and Variations in the Two-Party Vote: The Case of Michigan," *American Political Science Review* 53 (December 1958): 1078-90.

46. Banfield and Wilson, *City Politics*, p. 43.

47. Cf. Charles E. Gilbert and Christopher Clague, "Electoral Competition and Electoral Systems in Large Cities," *Journal of Politics* 24 (May 1962): 323-349. Also see Charles Gilbert, "National Political Alignments and the Politics of Large Cities," *Political Science Quarterly* 79 (March 1964): 35-51, which analyzes elections in large partisan cities of the northern states and finds that national party affiliations are closely associated with local partisan choice. However, in a study using 1960 Presidential election data, it was found that party competition does not necessarily increase with urbanization [Charles M. Bonjean and Robert L. Lineberry, "The Urbanization-Party Competition Hypothesis: A Comparison of All United States Counties," *Journal of Politics* 32 (May 1970): 305-321].

48. Cf. Warren Miller, "One Party Politics and the Voter," *American Political Science Review* 50 (1956): 707-725.

49. Kevin Phillips, *The Emerging Republican Majority* (Garden City: Doubleday, 1969).

50. James Q. Wilson and Edward C. Banfield, "Public Regardingness as a Value Premise in Voting Behavior," *American Political Science Review* 58 (December 1964): 876-887.

Chapter 8

The Reform Movement: Its Impact on Patterns of Conflict and Coalition

After the beginning of this century, the indigenous Yankees and the growing middle class of all nationalities, displaying luck and pluck like Horatio Alger's, gradually asserted substantial control over urban government. This chapter deals with the politics of governmental reform, that is, with the attempt to alter the form of government. Such attempts were undertaken not as ends in themselves but in order to change the dominant political patterns, which had become relatively stable in the machine era. That perspective on reform, as well as some exceptions to it, will be developed as we discuss in this chapter the history of urban reform, reform as an ideology, the elements of the reform package, the consequences of reformed government, and, finally, some evidence of an emerging postreform period.

A BRIEF HISTORY OF REFORM

An adequate history of the reform movement has yet to be writtten; but, when it is, a probable finding will be that reform is importantly shaped by a number of ideas, developments, and individuals. The ideas of the *progressive era*, for example, included a general sense of pragmatic reform and a call for specific governmental change at all levels. Frederick W. Taylor's *scientific management* also emerged from the incubator of practical reform and remained a part of the good-government ethos of the twenties and thirties. The *muckraking journalists* articulated and focused discontent with the machine: for example, Lincoln Steffans wrote a number of articles in *McClure's Magazine*, exposing urban corruption. A collection of his exposés, *The Shame of the Cities*, is a classic of muckraking journalism and one of the first studies of urban power structure. Steffans said in his preface that the "moral weakness" of both citizens and politicians had corrupted our cities: "St. Louis exemplified boodle; Minneapolis, police graft; Pittsburgh, a political and industrial machine; and Philadelphia, a general civic corruption; so Chicago was an illustration of reform and New York of good government."[1] Beginning in 1869, the influential New York *Times* began to editorialize against its local machine, "Tammany Hall," and the *Times* political cartoonist, Thomas Nast, began to build a national reputation for his cartoons decrying the excesses of boss William Tweed and his organization.

Reform has a radical image. It picked up that image in the early stages of the movement, not only because it called for change but also because so many of the protest writers of the period were socialists. Upton Sinclair, for example, who exposed in *The Jungle* the extraordinarily unsanitary practices of the meatpacking industry, thought of his work as primarily a protest of the excesses of capitalism. And though his book gave impetus to the movement for regulation and inspection of the meatpacking industry, he was unhappy about its overall impact. Sinclair had intended "to frighten the country by a picture of what its industrial masters were doing to their victims." He had aimed at the public's heart and lamented that "by accident I hit it in the stomach."[2] A number of progressive scholars shared Sinclair's distrust of the business world — Charles Beard and Thorstein Veblen, for instance. And socialism had a greater impact on municipal elections than is commonly assumed. In fact, in 1911, some seventy-four cities and towns elected socialists either as mayor or to other major municipal offices. While most of these cities were small and located in Midwestern states, they included Berkeley and Watts in California; Schenectady, New York; and Milwaukee, Wisconsin.[3] However, 1911 was the highwater mark. By 1920, only two cities — Davenport, Iowa, and Milwaukee, Wisconsin — retained their socialist municipal officers. Even these socialist mayors, however, were not an indication of overwhelming socialist sentiment in their cities. Many of them came into office as a result of more generalized discontent. When Woodrow Wilson met the socialist mayor of a small Nebraska town, he asked, "Does this mean that this town is socialist?" "No sir," replied the mayor, "I have not deceived myself; the vote by which I was elected was about 20% socialist and 80% protest."[4]

Reform retained its radical image for many voters even into the sixties and seventies. Consider, for example, the following exchange between a college professor and an objector on the subject of a council-manager plan which the professor had been asked to discuss at a meeting of a veterans organization.

> Objector: This looks to me like overthrow of the government.
> Professor: Well, I think that's a bit too strong; this is a change, yes, but hardly an overthrow of the government.

While reform need not always be radical, it may be. This political participant rejects the usual channels for what he feels will be more effective.

> Objector: You're throwing out the mayor and the alderman; if that isn't overthrow, I don't know what is.
>
> Professor: May I remind you, sir, that the state's statutes provide that the people . . . .
>
> Objector: Sure, the people, but what people? A minority brought this whole thing up, and if a minority overthrows the government, that's overthrow in anybody's book.
>
> Professor: As I was saying, the statutes provide for an orderly transition from one form of government to another. I would like to refer you to Chapter 24, Article 20 of the Revised Statutes, which read . . . .
>
> Objector: Looks like overthrow of the government to me.[5]

The Organization of Reform

Though much of the early critique off city politics was aimed at the abuses of capitalism, the reform movement evolved so as to serve middle-class and business interests. How this change occurred can be understood only by looking into the specific organizations that pressed for reforms. The first organized efforts at changing the direction of municipal government began at least as early as the 1870s but tended to be highly localized, sporadic, and amateurish. The efforts of the Rev. Charles H. Parkhurst, for example, who put on his sporty black and white checkered trousers and strode off to gather intelligence on New York's saloons and brothels in behalf of the City Vigilance League, were colorful but provided little of the organizational foundation for a national reform movement. Those foundations were laid with the creation of organizations like the National Municipal League in 1894, the American Proportional Representation League in 1893, and the National Short Ballot Organization in 1909.

Richard Childs: The father of the reform movement

The major formulator of reform ideology and specific reform programs was Richard S. Childs. It is difficult to overstate Child's importance to the reform movement. He was the original founder of the National Short Ballot Association and the prime mover of the National Municipal League throughout most of its history.

Childs spent most of his boyhood in New York City, the son of a highly successful financier and businessman. Childs' father had been a reformer himself. Graduating from Yale in 1904, Childs began a long business career. He started this career as an advertising executive, moved on to become general manager of the Bon Ami Company (founded by his father) and at different times served as executive vice president of Lederle Laboratories and as a director of the American Cyanamid Corporation. Childs' involvement with municipal reform was an avocation until 1947, at which time he became a full-time reformer.

As his background suggests, Childs was importantly different from the more visible figures of urban reform. He disagreed often with Lincoln Steffans, even though attracted to his moral ardor: "There was another prophet of doom, Lincoln Steffans! As a reporter of municipal corruption, superb; as diagnostician, all wet! For he sneeringly belittled our original Model Charter and our efforts to simplify the complex and preposterous mechanism of the democratic process, and took the line that, whatever happens, the people were to blame."[6] Childs seems to have found particularly abhorrent the progressive conception that big business was the ultimate enemy. He rejected much of what he found in the writing of Charles Beard and Thorstein Veblen. When asked if he had agreed with Upton Sinclair's and Lincoln Steffans' proposals for public ownership of municipal utilities, Childs replied, "No. After all, I was the son of a capitalist."[7] It is tempting to think of Childs as the Samuel Gompers of the urban reform movement.

The success of the reform movement is partly related to long-term social, economic, and political change for which it was not directly responsible and could take little credit. But the effectiveness of reform is also a result of the successful national articulation of the cause by Richard Childs and the

National Municipal League. As an advertising man, Childs knew the importance of stating an abstract program in concrete terms. We, too, as students of politics, know that a well-formed ideology can be an important political resource.

THE IDEOLOGY OF REFORM

The ideology of reform contains three leading assumptions.

1. *Stunt and eliminate the boss and machine.* The reformer's distinctive cry is "Corruption!" Movements characteristically begin by defining an enemy, an easy job for the urban reformer. The political organization providing direct material benefits to large numbers of working-class citizens was an easy target for the charge of corruption. Many of the reformer's efforts were aimed at undermining the organization of the dominant party, usually the Democratic party. One of the major implementing principles of this element of the reform ideology, then, required the separation of politics from administration: politics should be minimized and dealt with by elected officials, while administration should be conducted by experts.

2. *Make local government neutral, efficient, and economical.* Reform ideology posits this as the route to "progress." Neutral, efficient, and economical city government, it is presumed, will be created through "administrative integration" and also by the "professionalization" of the city bureaucracy.

Because working out the details of the mechanics of reformed government was a major emphasis of the reform movement, reform ideology soon settled on a series of principles to guide the integration of city administration. In general, the reform movement agreed that administrative integration was achieved by: (1) concentration of authority in the hands of a single or a few top executives who are responsible for the overall operation; (2) grouping of the activities of city administration by function — a process sometimes called "departmentalization"; (3) the elimination of appointed boards when possible; (4) central coordination of staff services such as purchasing, typing, etc.; and (5) provision for an independent audit of city accounts.[8] Professionalizing the bureaucracy was to be accomplished through an extension of civil service, that is, through appointment of nonelective officials on the basis of competitive examination; competence, rather than patronage, was the key.

Many of these elements in reform ideology are so ingrained in Americans that they sound more like "truth" than an element of a particular ideology. That is itself a monument to the success of the reform movement. Without entering into a full-scale critique, I should probably at least mention

here that a great deal of practical experience with reformed governmental institutions leaves many political scientists skeptical about the viability of
attempting to separate politics and administration: "A strong implication of
recent studies is that politics and administration are so heavily interwoven
that the distinction, while analytically useful, may be practically uninstructive
and no guide for the creation of governmental forms."[9]

 3. *Eliminate politics.* This is, of course, poetic overstatement. The
real aim of the reformer is to circumscribe politics very carefully by limiting it
to settings in which policy alternatives are being discussed and selected. But
they choose more dramatic language to emphasize their hostility to political
parties. Parties were seen as the vehicle of boss control and the reformers' vision of democracy required stunting the party. They feared no loss: "obviously there could not, properly, be a Republican or a (Democratic) way of
running (local government)."[10] They felt that partisanship leads to a confusion of federal and state concerns with local decisions and that city government becomes "nine-tenths business, with ordinance-making as a mere
sideline."[11]

 Implementation of the reform vision of democracy also required
revision of the electoral machinery of the city: nonpartisanship, short ballots
without party identification of the candidates, and at-large elections were
meant to replace the ward-based politics of the machine. The reformed election machinery was expected to improve the quality of officeholders. Childs
and subsequent reformers expected that competition for public office in cities
would be between candidates running without organization support on a
man-to-man basis, "on their simple merits," and assumed that under such circumstances, the "one best man" would triumph.[12]

 In many ways, the vision of democracy which inspired reform
ideology was similar to the concept of individualist democracy. Reform
emphasized the primacy of the vote as a political act and the need for independence in the exercise of the franchise. Under such circumstances, the
voters of the city should behave rationally. However, the movement, because
of its hostility to urban machines, avoided the "responsible party" position of
the individualist assumption and moved instead to a faith in neutral administration.

 Another parallel has probably already struck you too: government
was seen as analogous to the corporation. Of course, not every institutional
remedy in the reform tradition has a direct analogy in business enterprise, but
it is clear that the success of the corporate form had a marked influence on the
reform package. This congruence of reform and business values is recognized
by a number of social scientists.

"The ideology of the reform movement rested upon assumptions congenial to the business interests who were a main resource of reform campaigns . . . those accepting the ideology were committed to concern with the city not as a pluralistic universe of interests and power, but as a corporation."[13]

If the desire to make government a business is implicit in reform ideology, it is often explicit in campaigns for reform. For example, in 1930 in Dallas, when the city manager plan was under consideration, a newspaper asked

"Why not run Dallas itself on a business schedule by business methods under businessmen? . . . The city manager plan is, after all, only a business management plan. . . . The city manager is the executive of a corporation under a board of directors. Dallas is the corporation. It is as simple as that."[14]

And a study of reform in New Jersey cities in 1964 found the prevailing theme in these campaigns to be "efficiency and economy," which local leaders of the reform effort thought of as businesslike.[15]

Illustration 8.1 gives us a wry look at reform politicians from the point of view of "Mr. Dooley," the vehicle for the humor and homespun philosophy of F. P. Dunne, a turn-of-the-century American humorist.

THE REFORM PACKAGE

Childs and other reformers recognized the advantage of presenting reform not as an ideology or an abstract set of principles but as a package of concrete proposals which embody those principles. In creating a "reform package," the role of the National Municipal League has been central.[16] The League has made the reform movement national in scope. It acts as a research center and a conference organizer for municipal officials; it disseminates its viewpoint widely by providing appropriate lecturers and by publication of the *National Civic Review* (formerly *National Municipal Review*). The League prepares and keeps up to date a "Model City Charter" which has become widely respected and often used.

The three central elements of the reform package have come to be: (1) The council-manager form of government; (2) nonpartisan elections; and (3) at-large elections. In Chapter 9, we shall discuss intergovernmental reforms — reform of the relations between levels of government.

The Council - Manager Form

Reformers were initially attracted to the commission form of local government. The distinguishing feature of the commission form is that it

Illustration 8.1   Mr. Dooley on Why Rayformers Fail.

"Whin a rayformer is ilicted he promises ye a business administhration. Some people want that but I don't. Th' American business man is too fly. He's all right, d'ye mind, I don't say annything again' him. He is what Hogan calls th' boolwarks iv progress, an' we cudden't get on without him even if his scales are a little too quick on th' dhrop. But he ought to be left to dale with his akels. 'Tis a shame to give him a place where he can put th' comether on millions iv people that has had no business thrainin' beyond occasionally handin' a piece iv debased money to a car conductor on a cold day. A reg'lar pollytician can't give away an alley without blushin', but a business man who is in pollytics jus' to see that th' civil sarvice law gets thurly enfoorced, will give Lincoln Park an' th' public libr'y to th' beef thrust, charge an admission price to th' lake front an' make it a felony f'r annywan to buy stove polish outside iv his store, an' have it all put down to public improvemints with a pitcher iv him in th' corner stone.

"Fortchnitly, Hinnissy, a rayformer is seldom a business man. He thinks he is, but business men know diff'rent. They know what he is. He thinks business an' honesty is th' same thing. He does, indeed. He's got them mixed because they dhress alike. His idee is that all he has to do to make a business administhration is to have hones men arround him. Wrong. I'm not sayin', mind ye, that a man can't do good work an' be honest at th' same time. But whin I'm hirin' a la-ad I find out first whether he is onto his job, an' afther a few years I begin to suspect that he is honest, too. Manny a dishonest man can lay brick sthraight an' manny a man that wudden't steal ye'er spoons will break ye'er furniture. I don't want Father Kelly to hear me, but I'd rather have a . . . competint man who wud steal if I give him a chanst, but I won't, do me plumbin' thin a person that wud scorn to help himsilf but didn't know how to wipe a joint. Ivry man ought to be honest to start with, but to give a man an office jus' because he's honest is like ilictin' him to Congress because he's a pathrite, because he don't bate his wife or because he always wears a right boot on th' right foot. A man ought to be honest to start with an' afther that he ought to be crafty. A pollytician who's on'y honest is jus' th' same as bein' out in a winther storm without anny clothes on."

provides for a small group of elected commissioners, each heading an administrative department (parks, public works, public safety, for example). The commissioners sitting collectively also function as the local policy-making body. The commission plan gained support of reformers after the city of Galveston used it as an emergency government in 1900 to rebuild after a hurricane. By 1910, one hundred and eight cities — without benefit of hurricane — had followed Galveston's example. But the commission form just as quickly lost the support of reformers, primarily because it violates the reform principle requiring separation of politics and administration: the com-

"Another thing about rayform administhrations is they always think th' on'y man that ought to hold a job is a lawyer. Th' raison is that in th' coorse iv his thrainin' a lawyer larns enough about ivrything to make a good front on anny subject to annybody who doesn't know about it. So whin th' rayform administhration comes in th' mayor says: 'Who'll we make chief iv polis in place iv th' misguided ruffyan who has held th' job f'r twinty years?' 'Th' man f'r th' place,' says th' mayor's adviser, 'is Arthur Lightout,' he says. 'He's an ixcillent lawyer, Yale, '95, an' is well up on polis matthers. Las' year he read a paper on "The fine polis foorce iv London" befure th' annyal meetin' iv th' S'ciety f'r Ladin' th' Mulligan Fam'ly to a Betther an' Harder Life. Besides,' he says, 'he's been in th' milishy an' th' foorce needs a man who'll be afraid not to shoot in case iv public disturbance.' So Arthur takes hold iv th' constabulary an' in a year th' polis can all read Emerson an' th' burglars begin puttin' up laddhers an' block an' tackles befure eight A.M. An' so it is on ivry side. A lawyer has charge iv the city horseshoein,' another wan is clanin' th' sthreets, th' author iv 'Gasamagoo on torts' is thryin' to dispose iv th' ashes be throwin' thim in th' air on a windy day, an' th' bright boy that took th' silver ware f'r th' essay on ne exeats an' their relation to life is plannin' a uniform that will be sarviceable an' constitchoochinal f'r th' brave men that wurruks on th' city dumps. An' wan day th' main rayformer goes out expictin' to rayceive th' thanks iv th' community an' th' public that has jus' got out iv jail f'r lettin' th' wather run too long in th' bath tub rises up an' cries: 'Back to th' Univarsity Settlemint.' Th' man with th' di'mon' in his shirt front comes home an' pushes th' honest lawyers down th' steps, an' a dishonest horse shoer shoes th' city's horses well, an' a crooked plumber does th' city' plumbin' securely, an' a rascally polisman that may not be avarse to pickin' up a bet but will always find out whin Pathrolman Scanlan slept on his beat, takes hold iv th' polis foorce, an' we raysume our nachral condition iv illagal merriment. An' th' rayformer spinds th' rest iv his life tellin' us where we are wrong. He's good at that. On'y he don't undherstand that people wud rather be wrong an' comfortable thin right in jail."

"I don't like a rayformer," said Mr. Hennessy.

"Or anny other raypublican," said Mr. Dooley.

Source: F. P. Dunne, *Observations by Mr. Dooley* (New York: Harper and Brothers, 1906), pp. 167-170.

missioners were both administrators and policy makers. The commission was said to foster vote trading and a "you stay out of my department and I'll stay out of yours" assumption among commissioners. As Childs said, "When each commissioner had his pet department, log rolling for appropriations was a logical result . . . with nobody taking responsibility for the whole bill."[17]

A more perfect embodiment of reform ideology was found to be a council-manager government. The distinctive feature of this form is that it provides for an elected council which has responsibility for only two things: policy making and the appointment of a professional administrative officer or city manager, who serves as long as the council keeps him and who is singly responsible for the conduct of city administration. Staunton, Virginia, appointed a manager as early as 1908. Through Childs' efforts primarily, the adoption of the council-manager form got fully under way with the 1912 adoption in Sumter, South Carolina. By the end of 1913, ten other cities had followed Sumter and, as Childs put it, the plan was off "like a bunch of firecrackers."[18] In the early stages of reform, proponents made extraordinary claims for the council-manager experiment. For example, Childs claimed "politics went out the window when Dayton's first city manager blew in. . . ."[19]

By 1941, there were 315 cities with a population of over 5000 (or 15.5%) which had adopted the council-manager plan. That number was 1245 or 40.3% by 1966. Within this overall pattern of growing popularity, certain characteristics began to become noticeable. For one, as Table 8.1 makes apparent, larger cities have preferred to stay with a mayor-council form: only 19.2% of cities over 500,000 have reformed. However, among cities of smaller population, the plan seems much more popular. There is also some variation by state; as of 1961, only six states accounted for 48% of the city manager adoptions.[20]

Nonpartisan Elections

The reform package also includes a nonpartisan election system. Nonpartisan elections are those in which candidates are not identified on the ballot by party affiliation. Nonpartisanship is the most widely adopted feature of the reform package — 61% of our cities over 5000 population have adopted nonpartisan election systems. Of course, a nonpartisan election system does not guarantee that urban parties are uninvolved. In many of the cities in which party affiliations are not indicated on the ballot, parties are visibly active anyway. Chicago, for example, elects its aldermen (city councilors) on a nonpartisan ballot; nevertheless, party affiliations are generally widely publicized and it is widely acknowledged that it is practically impossible to be elected to the city council unless affiliated with a party. It has been remarked that the Chicago city council is composed of 47 nonpartisan Democrats and 3 nonpartisan Republicans.

Nonpartisan elections are closely associated with the council-manager form. Of the 1756 council-manager cities, 84% are nonpartisan, while only 44% of the mayor-council cities are nonpartisan. There is some regional variation in the adoption of the nonpartisan election system which, in general, indicates that the reformers took Horace Greeley's advice. Only about 24% of the cities in the Middle Atlantic states are nonpartisan; that figure is

Table 8.1   Form of Government in Cities over 5000 Population

Population of City	Cities in U.S.A.	Cities in this Study	Mayor - Council		Commission		Council - Manager	
			No.	%	No.	%	No.	%
Over 500,000	27	26	20	76.9	1	3.8	5	19.2
250,000 to 500,000	27	27	11	40.7	3	11.1	13	48.1
100,000 to 250,000	96	96	34	35.4	12	12.5	50	52.0
50,000 to 100,000	232	227	84	37.0	22	9.7	121	53.3
25,000 to 50,000	476	462	167	36.1	50	10.8	244	25.8
10,000 to 25,000	1,165	1,105	538	48.7	99	9.0	468	42.4
5000 to 10,000	1,171	1,146	746	65.1	58	4.9	344	30.0
All cities over 5000	3,189	3,089[1]	1,600	51.8	243	7.9	1,245	40.3

Source: International City Managers' Association, *Municipal Yearbook, 1967* (Chicago: The Association, 1967), p. 103. Reproduced with adaptations by permission of the International City Management Association.

[1]Not included in this table are: Washington, D.C.; 40 cities with town meeting government; 26 with representative town meeting government; and 33 other cities for which no information was received.

about 74% in the Border states and the South, 98% in the Plains states, 83% in the Mountain states, and 96% in the West.[21]

At-Large Elections

Where there is a mayor and a council and partisan elections, it is also usual for election of councilmen to be from districts. In the district election, of course, councilmen are elected from and represent the district. The "reformed" city elects its councilmen at large. The central feature of the at-large system is that it gives all councilmen the same constituency: the whole city. Reformers claim that since the councilman in an at-large system must look to the city as a whole for votes, he must necessarily take a broad, citywide view and address himself to the public interest. The at-large system is designed to minimize the effect of neighborhood and ethnic bloc voting and to undermine machine politics. As with some of the other devices in the reform package, the at-large election sounds ideal but in fact has some inherent problems. It often prevents candidates of the minority neighborhoods from being elected. Also, at-large elections are costly and therefore give the advantage to candidates with money or those who attract the support of monied interests. As can be seen from Table 8.2, a majority of our large cities have adopted at-large election systems, or some combination of the at-large and district system.

For a time, in the first decades of the century, reformers championed a modification of the at-large system known as "proportional representation." About twenty-five cities tried that form and all but one — Cambridge, Massachusetts — have abandoned it. Cincinnati used proportional representation between 1924 and 1957 and New York, from 1936 until 1949. In the particular form of proportional representation used in New York and Cincinnati, the candidates ran at large, and each voter ranked them on the ballot by marking 1 for the first choice, 2 for the second, 3, etc. by the candidates' names. A candidate had to receive a "quota" to be elected, which was determined by dividing the total of ballots cast by the number of council seats to be filled plus one and adding one to the quotient. Ballots were then sorted according to first choices; any candidate receiving the quota is declared elected. His ballots in excess of those he needs to be elected are then distributed according to the second choices marked on them. If no one reaches the quota as a result of first choices, the candidate with the least number of first choices is eliminated and his ballots distributed according to the second choices marked on them. This process continues until as many candidates are elected as are required. It is, of course, quite possible under such a system that fourth, fifth or even sixth choices come to be counted.

Proportional representation served to increase the number of councilmen of minority parties and groups. In Cincinnati, for example, it usually resulted in the election of one or two blacks. In New York, proportional representation allowed the Republicans a sizable representation on a council that had been entirely Democratic; and it permitted over its history the election of five members of the American Labor Party, two Liberal Party members, and two Communists. Indeed, it was this feature of proportional representation that enabled its opponents to defeat it. In Cincinnati, it was claimed that proportional representation would eventually give the city a "Negro boss." And the election of Communists in the immediate-postwar period in New York proved the undoing of proportional representation there.

A number of other changes in governmental form are an outgrowth of reform principles. Comprehensive city planning is a response to reform principles, as is extension of civil service. It is also possible to see the connection between reform and the many efforts to consolidate the multiple local governmental units. And the development of "planning-programing-budgeting" (ppb) which subjects public policy choices to a careful cost-benefit analysis is a technologized refinement of the reform impulse to economy through efficiency.[22] Even those cities which have not adopted the reform package have been influenced. The desire for efficiency, economy, and neutral, expert administration is everywhere in evidence. Many mayors have administrative offices that operate suspiciously like those of city managers. Clearly, reform has been widely influential. What has been its impact?

THE IMPACT OF REFORM

Experience with reformed cities shows that the reformers have delivered much of what they promised, but as with every political program the blessings are mixed. In assessing the impact of reform, then, it is important to understand two seeming paradoxes: (1) the politics of antipolitics and (2) the high costs of efficiency.

The Politics of Antipolitics

Reformers promised an end to *politics*. After assessing nonpartisan elections in 48 cities, Richard Childs concluded that reform had delivered on

Table 8.2   Electoral Systems in Cities over 500,000 Population* 1960

	At-Large	District	Combination
Partisan Cities	Pittsburgh	Chicago Cleveland	Baltimore Buffalo New York New Orleans Philadelphia St. Louis
Nonpartisan Cities	Boston Cincinnati Dallas** Detroit San Antonio San Diego** San Francisco Seattle	Los Angeles Milwaukee	Houston

* Excluding Washington, D.C.
**In Dallas and San Diego, councilmen are nominated by districts but run at large.

Source: Compiled from materials in *Municipal Yearbook, 1967* (Chicago: International City Managers' Association, 1967), pp. 84-140.

that promise: "Testimony covering over 500 elections demonstrates that politics without politicians is actually with us."[23] What this really means is that *party* affairs and *party* politicians have been seriously undermined by the reform movement — a point underscored in the preceding chapter. However, to use the term politics as a synonym for *party* politics, which is so often done in popular usage, is misleading. The definition used in this book, you recall, holds that politics includes all those processes by which social conflicts are managed. Obviously, more than parties are involved in those processes. In fact, the pluralist model of democracy presumes that the prime presenters of conflict are groups and influential individuals. Reform does not eliminate politics in its broader sense, then, but simply transforms it; the specific result of transformation varies somewhat with local conditions. In general, it has benefited business, civic associations, newspapers, and other similar interests while neglecting the poor, the black, and the other power-poor minorities. That perspective can be illustrated, as can some contrary findings, as we review the politics of the three major elements of the reform package.

The impact of at-large elections

While, say, a black candidate might be able to win in a district which contained a large number of blacks, he is more likely to lose in an at-large contest. In San Diego, for example, where blacks make up approximately seven percent of the population and are located primarily in the southeastern section of the city, the election system calls for nomination from districts, but election is at large. Experience there has been that the southeastern district has nominated a number of minority candidates for city council, but that these nominees have lost in the at-large general election.[24] And San Diego is not atypical. In Boston, the old ward system gave minority interests better representation than the at-large system. Among the 110 councilmen elected in 25 years under the ward system, there were 12 Jews, 9 Yankees, 4 Italians, and 1 black. After the return to the at-large system, the numerically superior Irish and Italians made a clean sweep. The first 45 councilmen elected after that were Irish or Italian.[25]

The impact of nonpartisanship

Four political patterns have emerged in cities that have adopted the nonpartisan ballot.[26] The first form of politics within a nonpartisan election system finds the major parties intact and operating as central though informal participants. This pattern is not as common as is often supposed, but is clearly illustrated by the Chicago experience in which the Democratic party is the decisive force in city elections despite the nonpartisan ballot. A second pattern finds the majority party operating as an important force while the minority party has come to associate itself with some civic association to form an opposition coalition. This type is to be found in Hartford, and in Cincinnati in the late fifties. In other cities, a third pattern has appeared, in which both major parties are inactive, but local nonparty groups have sprung up to support candidates. Such groups vary in the extent to which they maintain continuity as organizations. Some of these organizations seem to be parties by another name. A study of a Massachusetts city, for example, found two such groups — "progressives" and "nonpartisans" — which consistently opposed one another. There was a high correlation between the stated objectives of progressives and Democrats and between those of nonpartisans and Republicans.[27] The fourth pattern of nonpartisan elections involves no continuous groups but, instead, a tendency for candidates to band together as a slate. The slate then runs a combined campaign.[28] And, finally, it may be presumed that there is a fifth pattern, that somewhere there are elections which run without either parties or other groups actively supporting candidates.

By weakening the traditional party structure, nonpartisanship has produced a number of consequences for urban politics. The nonpartisan ballot has cut the voter off from one source of knowledge of the candidates and has increased the financial cost of elections. It has also altered the structure of participation in local elections. When party labels are unavailable, voters are prevented from exercising their characteristic party loyalty — a motive which the voting studies find consistently strong. The result is that voters who have the time, interest, and other resources to develop their own information about candidates stay involved. Those who do not develop their own information tend to become confused and disengaged from participation. Needless to say, this pattern produces a greater responsiveness among the educated and professional. When parties are involved in elections, party workers and party propaganda efforts provide information on which voters can base a judgment. In the absence of party efforts, voters come to rely on other cues, some of them quite incidental to the merits of the candidate. But, in a study of Newark, it was found that ethnic identification was a persisting cue for voters in a nonpartisan race.[29]

Lower-income groups tend to stay away from nonpartisan elections in disproportionate numbers. These voters are most heavily reliant on party affiliation as a cue to voting; they are less likely than the middle class to have access to the substitute party organizations or to several alternative sources of political information. Reformers might rejoice at the lower turnout of party-dependent citizens, but recent evidence suggests that their presupposition that the result would be a more active, knowledgeable, attentive body of voters seems not to have developed. One study, in fact, finds "the more partisan cities seem to have a much more active local electorate, well-educated and with a fairly high interest in local affairs."[30] By contrast to nonpartisan cities, "Partisanship seems to be the concomitant of aware, issue-oriented voting rather than its antithesis."[31]

The politics of the council-manager form

The manager is a politician.[32] The reformer's demand for separation of politics and administration has not been realized, may not ever be, and perhaps should not be. In many council-manager cities, in fact, the manager assumes the central conflict-regulating role. There are a number of features of the council-manager plan which impel the manager toward politics. One is that the manager develops expertise beyond that of the council. He is able to do this because he has a virtual monopoly of technical and other information and, as a full-time professional, has more time to spend digesting and formulating responses to that information. All lines of communication converge in the manager's office. It is in the nature of organization that those who can control the flow of information become powerful. Since councilmen are amateurs, they come to depend on the manager for their information. Whether the individual manager likes it or not, this gives him a large measure of control over the council. Another feature of the council-manager plan that disposes toward a political manager results from the fact that it is risky for an elected official to sponsor a controversial measure. If public response to a public question is uncertain, the council can at least partially insulate itself from adverse public response by maneuvering the manager into taking or seeming to take responsibility. As Banfield and Wilson put it, "If the boat *must* be rocked, they want the public to think that the city manager's hand is on the tiller. If all goes well, they can take credit later with the electorate. If not, they can blame him and perhaps even make 'political capital' by firing him."[33] Even though a political role for the manager is a direct contradiction of reform ideology, it is probably indispensable to the successful working of the plan. The Code of Ethics of the International City Managers' Association has come to give tacit approval to a kind of political involvement of city managers: when managers first met in 1914, there was some criticism of the ineffectiveness of city councils and an expressed attraction to active rather than passive roles for the managers. Managers came to distinguish "policy" from "politics" as a way of maintaining their apolitical stance while engaging in matters related to "policy." The 1952 revision of the Code of Ethics dropped out the former repudiation of politics.

Varieties of Manager Adaptation to Politics

Experienced and effective managers are ones who have learned to live with and use the ambiguous distinction between their political and administrative roles. Whether they are able to be innovative and maintain themselves in office depends crucially on the overall character of the politics of their city. In general, the more factionalized the city's politics and the more intense the conflict, the greater will be the difficulty of the city manager in maintaining a neutral image. Banfield and Wilson suggest that there are five basic types of council-manager relationships which depend on the level of conflict in a city. First, in those cities where there is little conflict, the manager usually plays a strong role. He comes to be in full charge of the routine decisions which are the mainstay of local government activity in such areas. Many relatively homogeneous cities and suburbs illustrate this type; for example, Winnetka, Illinois. Second, in cities characterized by conflict between two factions with approximately equal power, the role of the manager may become unstable. If the manager is politically astute, he can play one faction against the other. This strong political role is potentially dangerous to the manager's tenure, however; if one faction gains control, it will likely make ridding itself of a strong manager one of its first priorities. Third, in a city in which there is approximately equal division of power between two or more factions, the manager may decide to do little. If he sees that he cannot accomplish much without antagonizing one side or the other, he may decide that it is best to occupy himself with minor housekeeping chores and to avoid identifying himself with any group or issue. The result of this strict construction of the neutral role of manager is stalemate. Fourth, in cities in which, though conflictful, there is nonetheless a stable majc ity or a consister tly dominant coalition, the manager may become the instrument (or in some cases, even the leader) of the dominant faction. In such circumstances, the manager is able to take initiatives without fear of being overridden by the council. Finally, in cities where there is considerable conflict but no dominanc coalition, the manager may once again withdraw into strict constructionism or he must put together a number of councilmen to help him win; needless to say, this is an extremely difficult position to be in while trying to maintain the image of neutrality. Managers in this kind of political setting usually do not last long. They are quickly accused of "favoritism" and "politics" by the losing side on any given issue and since losers change from issue to issue, it is not long before there is a large reservoir of groups and activists who feel the manager has played his role improperly.[34]

Though the mode of political involvement of the manager varies from city to city, the fact that he must be involved with politics in some way does not. The astute manager is able to use the formulation of his job as "purely administrative" — and therefore neutral — as a shield against the unwary. The competent players of the game of local politics are not fooled, and they develop the necessary resources to work with or on the city manager when their vital interests are at stake. The less knowledgeable — once again the poor, the minorities, the average inattentive citizen — are more likely to get lost in the ambiguity and be less successful.

The "Quality" of Managers and Councilmen

Richard Childs was fond of arguing that reformed city government would enable the "one best man" to win the contest for public office. Evidence to date suggests that if your definition of "best" is a Republican of the middle class, a veteran, a member of a civic club, a person engaged in business or professional pursuits and having little or no previous political experience, then you are likely to agree that reform has done its job.[35] This is, of course, a heavily middle-class conception of quality. Others would want to measure the quality of councilmen not so much by their attributes and backgrounds as by the effectiveness of the policy that they create. We shall have more to consider about the policies produced by reformed city governments in the next few paragraphs. The usual assumption is that a high-quality council is an active and powerful one. By that standard, reform is a failure. As we have already indicated, the norm is that reformed city governments tend to less active, amateur-dominated councils.

And what of the quality of the manager? Recall that the reformers assumed he would be a neutral professional. Several close observers of urban politics find that many managers, because of prevailing patterns of recruitment and training, tend to be pro business in their social values and conservative in their political outlook:

> Very many managers are engineers, and some are trained in the schools of business administration. This means that they receive much of their education in the most conservative colleges of our universities. They are likely to be personally conservative in political views. They are business oriented in their social values. Many of them have had experience in private business before becoming managers; others may hope to move into good positions in private business after serving a number of years in city government.[36]

There is not sufficient evidence to take this observation at face value. But, study of 26 incumbent managers in the state of Missouri tends to bear out these generalizations. Of the Missouri city managers, only 30% indicated that they were interested in a career in business, while 65% indicated a preference for "teaching, governmental service or politics."[37] The latter managers were also found to be more "liberal" in their attitudes toward free speech and the rights of blacks. But the remainder of the composite drawn in the quotation above was intact in the Missouri study: the "average" manager was found to be a Protestant, a Rotarian, a reader of technical journals related to his job rather than of publications which espouse liberal points of view. He accepted the existence of both labor unions and large corporations, but, on balance, "the views expressed were more favorable toward the business corporation."[38] Using a set of questions designed to test the liberalism-

Marshall Henrichs

The goal of efficiency can produce an austerity that is, at best, unpalatable.

conservatism of the managers, the study found that 73% of them could be classified conservative.

The Costs of Efficiency

No theme recurs more often in reform campaigns than the plea for "efficiency and economy." The substance of this appeal is based on a large, loose analogy to business, asserting that governmental organizations should be rationalized to maximize clearly stated goals. When a study group recommended to Livingston Township (New Jersey) citizens that they change their form of government, their report said, "We must analyze the existing government in absolute terms to see whether it is efficient and economical." And a similar study group in Orange, New Jersey, promised, "The use of improved managerial techniques will most certainly tighten the administrative structure and get more mileage from the tax dollar."[39] Moreover, efficiency has become the watchword of a culture increasingly affected by bureaucratic and technological assumptions. There are some severe problems in applying such assumptions to the operation of government at all levels, urban included. For one thing, clarity of goals is necessary to achieve efficiency. In a business, there is relative clarity and singularity — profit. The goals of government are not always so clear. Nor is it a simple matter to clarify them once the ambiguity has been found; the goals of government are formulated in response to diverse public needs and are the subject of continuing conflict. Governmental goals are the central concern of the political process. A public policy is a stated goal, and such policies are often studies in necessary unclarity because they result from compromise among competing interests whose goals are, in an absolute sense, incompatible. When clarity is demanded for the sake of efficiency, it is often at the cost of ignoring the desires of the less powerful political actors. In other words, when one group clearly wins the struggle for power, the result in policy is clear and efficiency is more easily served. But such efficiency must deny the compromise element of a pluralistic process. In sum, there is great tension between the value of representativeness and that of efficiency.

A limited number of empirical examinations of the impact of reform on the policies of cities illustrates the tensions between the efficiency-and-economy mode and the equal-representation mode. Robert Lineberry and Edmund Fowler have made a particularly important analysis of taxing and spending policies in 200 American cities having populations of 50,000 or more. They found that reformed city governments did, in fact, spend comparatively less money. They also found: (1) the more middle class the city (as measured by income, education, and occupation), the lower the general tax and spending levels; (2) the more home ownership in the city, the lower the tax and spending level; and (3) the larger the percentage of religious and ethnic minorities in the population, the more the city taxed and spent.[40] And what of the costs of that efficiency and economy? Lineberry and Fowler found that reformed cities appeared to be less responsive in tax and spending policies to differences in income, education, occupation, and religious and ethnic characteristics in their populations than were unreformed cities. Reform, in other words, produces policies less favorable to the interests of the already disadvantaged.

THE URBAN COUNTERREFORMATION

Many of the contemporary attempts to modify the form of city government are advanced by persons whose experiences and expectations are quite different from the traditional assumptions of the reform movement. While the San Diego charter was being reviewed in 1969, for example, most of the black leaders who testified before the charter study commission urged a return to the ward system of election. Many of their statements indicated that they wanted more neighborhood autonomy and power than the reform principles could accommodate. The urban decentralization movement in many ways runs counter to reform. The attempt to devolve power to what one political scientist calls new "civic units" has a variety of forms — neighborhood planning associations, Alinsky-style neighborhood groups, "little city halls," and urban communal movements.[41] The revitalization of participation in such new civic units is not *logically* incompatible with a rationalized hierarchy of governments like that envisioned by Robert Dahl:

> We begin to think about appropriate units of democracy as an ascending series, a set of Chinese boxes, each larger and more inclusive than the other, each in some sense democratic, though not always in quite the same sense, and each not inherently less nor inherently more legitimate than the others.[42]

In other words, it is possible that civic units could be integrated into citywide units which in turn could be integrated into regional units which in turn could be integrated into state administrative units. However, this organization chart neatness begs the central question: how is power distributed among the levels? Traditional reformers clearly opt for the right of the central power to make decisions which resolve the conflicts below. Counterreformers call for sufficient autonomy to enable them to say a decisive "No" to central authority on fundamental political questions. That difference between reformers and counterreformers seems crucial.

SUMMARY

Though it has a radical image, the reform movement developed an ideology and specific forms — council-manager, nonpartisanship, and at-large elections systems — which moved local governmental organization closer to the private corporate form. At the same time, reformed governments have proved more hospitable to the interests of white, middle-class residents and less responsive to the needs of urban minorities. While the reform movement has emphasized the need to be antipolitical and efficient, it is nonetheless apparent that there is a politics of antipolitics and that some high costs accompany this kind of efficiency. The reform movement is best understood as itself a political strategy, designed to wrest control from the hands of "bosses" and "machines" with lower-class clienteles and to invest power instead in the white, middle class. It is not surprising that there has begun to develop an urban counterreformation wherein many of the traditional elements of the reform package are being discarded.

NOTES

1. Lincoln Steffans, *The Shame of the Cities* (New York: Hill and Wang, 1957), pp. 10-11. The comment on moral weakness is to be found on page 7.

2. Upton Sinclair, "What Life Means to Me," *Cosmopolitan* 61 (October 1906): 591-601.

3. The other cities and towns are named as well as similar listings for the years 1912-1920 in James Weinstein, *The Decline of Socialism in America: 1912-1925* (New York: Random House, 1967), pp. 116-118.

4. Cited in ibid., p. 108. Original source is Woodrow Wilson, *The New Freedom* (New York: Doubleday, Page, 1913), p. 26.

5. William O. Winter, *The Urban Polity* (New York: Dodd, Mead, 1969), pp. 246-247.

6. Richard S. Childs, "Civic Victories in the United States," *National Municipal Review* 44 (September 1955): 398.

7. Quoted in John East, *Council Manager Government: The Political Thought of its Founder, Richard S. Childs* (Chapel Hill: University of North Carolina Press, 1965), p. 27.

8. From A. E. Buck, *The Reorganization of State Governments in the United States* (New York: Columbia University Press, 1938), pp. 14-15.

9. William A. Schultze, "On the Governor's Powers," in *New Perspectives in State and Local Politics*, ed. James A. Reidel (Waltham, Mass.: Xerox College Publishing Co., 1971), p. 250.

10. Richard S. Childs, "Politics Without Politicians," *The Saturday Evening Post* 182 (January 22, 1910): 5.

11. Richard S. Childs, "State Manager Plan," *National Municipal Review* 6 (November 1917): 660.

12. Richard S. Childs, "Civic Victories," p. 180.

13. Scott Greer, "Dilemmas of Action Research on the Internal 'Metropolitan Problem,'" in *Community Political Systems*, ed. Morris Janowitz (Glencoe, Ill.: Free Press, 1961), p. 187. For similar statements see also Robert C. Wood, *Suburbia: Its People and Their Politics* (Boston: Houghton Mifflin, 1958), pp. 46-53; and Charles R. Adrian, "Some General Characteristics of Non-Partisan Elections," *American Political Science Review* 66 (September 1952): 766.

14. Quoted in Harold Stone, Don Price, and Kathryn Stone, *City Manager Government in the United States* (Chicago: Public Administration Service, 1940), p. 27. Original source is given only as Dallas *News*.

15. William A. Schultze, "Public Leadership in Charter Revision: Case Studies in Four New Jersey Municipalities," (Ph.D. diss.; Rutgers University, 1967), pp. 118-130.

16. For a more complete discussion of that role, see Frank M. Stewart, *A Half Century of Municipal Reform: The History of the National Municipal League* (Berkeley: University of California Press, 1960)

17. Childs, "Civic Victories," p. 137.

18. Ibid., p. 147.

19. Ibid., p. 148.

20. Those states were Pennsylvania, Maine, Michigan, Florida, Texas, and California. Duane Lockard, "The City Manager, Administrative Theory and Political Power," *Political Science Quarterly* 77 (June 1962): 224-236.

21. Calculated from the *Municipal Yearbook*. See Charles R. Adrian, "Some General Characteristics of Non-Partisan Elections," *American Political Science Review* 46 (September 1952): 766-776.

22. There are several excellent discussions of the pro and con of ppb; cf. Steven B. Sweeney and James C. Charlesworth, eds., *Governing Urban Society: New Scientific Approaches* (Philadelphia: American Academy of Political and Social Sciences, 1967.

23. Childs, "Civic Victories," p. 303.

24. The one black city councilman, Leon Williams, was originally appointed and subsequently re-elected.

25. From Edward Banfield and James Q. Wilson, *City Politics* (Cambridge: Harvard University Press, 1963) p. 95.

26. Taken from Charles R. Adrian, "A Typology for Non-Partisan Elections," *Western Political Quarterly* 12 (June 1959): 449-458.

27. J. Lieper Freeman, "Local Party Systems: Theoretical Considerations and a Case Analysis," *American Journal of Sociology* 64 (1958): 282.

28. Wichita, Kansas is an example; cf. Marvin A. Harder, *Non-Partisan Election: A Political Illusion?* (New York: McGraw-Hill, 1958).

29. Gerald Pomper, "Ethnic and Group Voting in Non-Partisan Elections," *Public Opinion Quarterly* 30 (Spring 1966): 79-97.

30. Heywood T. Saunders, "Cities, Politics and Elections: Partisanship in Non-Partisan Elections," *Municipal Yearbook: 1971* (Washington, D.C.: International City Managers Association, 1971), p. 19.

31. Ibid., p. 20.

32. Carl Bosworth, "The Manager is a Politician," *Public Administration Review* 18 (Summer 1958): 216-222.

33. Banfield and Wilson, *City Politics*, p. 175. Originally quoted from Gladys M. Kammerer, *Florida City Managers, Profile in Tenure* (Gainesville: University of Florida Public Administration Clearing Service, Studies in Public Administration, No. 22, 1961), pp. 32-34.

34. These types are summarized from Banfield and Wilson, *City Politics*, pp. 177-180.

35. Eugene C. Lee, *The Politics of Non-Partisanship* (Berkeley: University of California Press, 1960), pp. 50-56.

36. Charles Adrian, *Governing Urban America* (New York: McGraw-Hill, 1961), p. 229.

37. Lloyd M. Wells, "Social Values and Political Orientations of City Managers: A Survey Report," *Social Science Quarterly* 48 (December 1967): 433-450.

38. Ibid., p. 442.

39. Many other similar examples from New Jersey charter revision efforts are to be found in Schultze, "Public Leadership in Charter Revision," Chap. 5.

40. Robert L. Lineberry and Edmund P. Fowler, "Reformism and Public Policy in American Cities," *American Political Science Review* 61 (September 1967): 201-216.

41. John Crittenden, "The Battle for Local Reform: An Advanced Outpost," in *New Perspectives in State and Local Politics*, ed. James A. Reidel (Waltham, Mass.: Xerox College Publishing Co., 1971), p. 33.

42. Robert Dahl, "The City and the Future of Democracy," *American Political Science Review* 61 (December 1, 1967): 959.

PART THREE

Urban Conflict
Management

Conflicts in urban America are many and profound. The most serious conflicts that we have as Americans have been discussed in the foregoing pages.

  The last road from the frontier ends in the city. It is not an overstatement to say that the city is the crucible in which it will be determined whether
we are after all a viable nation. Here we shall discover whether we can live
with our fellow man and ourselves in cooperation and creativity or whether
our differences will cause us to exhaust ourselves in endless, stultifying
struggle. In part — and only in part — the answer to that question hinges on
the effectiveness of our institutions which aim to manage those conflicts. It is
a common mistake to assume that good government, like good milk, comes
from a dispenser — that tinkering with the institutions of local government
will ensure good public policy. We already know too much about the power of
nongovernmental institutions, groups, and long-standing physical and
economic forces to believe that governmental institutions are the sole determinants of public policy.

  What processes and structures currently exist in American cities?
What patterns of behavior attend the operation of urban conflict-regulating
activities? And how effective are these processes? These are the central
questions of Part Three. The chapters in this section are arranged to permit
discussion of the processes by which urban policies are created. We shall examine processes of policy formulation and leadership and processes related to
the adoption and application of urban policies; we shall also briefly discuss

policy adjudication. We must begin, however, by reiterating that city governments are far from autonomous. The power to deal with local conflict is severely fractioned and must be understood if the activities of local governing are to be put in perspective.

Chapter 9

Intergovernmental Relationships and Politics

God must have loved local governments; He made so many of them. The fact of metropolitan fragmentation is indisputable. A recent calculation shows 20,000 units of local government in the 230 metropolitan areas. The larger the metropolitan area, the worse is the fragmentation; the ten largest cities in the United States average close to 500 separate governing bodies in each. (The average for all metropolitan areas is more like a modest 90, however.[1]) To illustrate the range of governmental units, for example, the people of Park Forest, a suburb of Chicago, find themselves well governed by the following units: Cook County, Will County, Cook County Forest Preserve District, the village of Park Forest, Rich Township, Bloom Township, Monee Township, Suburban Tuberculosis Sanitarium District, Bloom Township Sanitary District, Non-High School District 216, Non-High School District 213, Rich Township High School District 227, Elementary School District 163, and South Cook Mosquito Abatement District.[2]

CONSEQUENCES OF THE DIVIDED POWER TO GOVERN

Looking at the complex interrelationships of national, city, and state governmental units, polite academics have settled on the simile of the marble cake — meaning that governmental functions are not nicely separated and layered but are instead mixed and swirled.[3] Many privately think it would be more accurate to say, "It's a hell of a mess." They reason that this fracturing at the local level of the power to decide is at the core of the metropolitan "problem." They claim that often the scope of the problem is different from the scope of the relevant governmental unit. If, for example, a suburban dweller feels the need for additional lanes on the freeway he travels to work, his appeal to the government will probably result in his dealing not only with the city but also with the county and the state departments of roads, as well as other bureaucracies at different levels.

Though complexity is not bad, per se, the particular form it takes in contemporary metropolitan areas is difficult to rationalize. Some would argue that local governmental fragmentation is the price of local autonomy, or that it is *necessarily* complicated because of the specialized needs each unit serves. But such viewpoints are difficult for frustrated citizens to embrace. Most of us experience problems that are total, that don't divide neatly into components coinciding with relevant governmental units. To most citizens, fractionated local authority leaves us feeling we have been "taken" as victims of a kind of governmental shell game: the power to resolve our problem is never in the place we seek it. Besides citizen frustration and disorientation, there are other consequences of the fragmentation of metropolitan area government.

1. Lack of Coordination   The most obvious negative consequence of multiple local units of government is the need for constant efforts at coordination among those units to avoid duplication of effort and working at cross purposes. The expansion of a freeway may encourage automotive traffic, which creates additional policy problems for the air pollution control agency. The strictly enforced measures of New York City and the Port of New York Authority to keep the Hudson River clean are of no avail if the cities and industries upstream are unconcerned. These most obvious examples of needed coordination among local or regional units point up more than the necessity of the spirit of cooperation; they remind us that the cooperating units must be willing to bear some of the *costs* of regulation too. Needless to say, governmental units do not willingly increase costs when they cannot demonstrate clear benefits to the local taxpayers. Fractionation of local governments thus encourages evasion of political responsibility, cost shifting, and striking inequities between costs and services.

2. Evasion of Political Responsibility   When there are large numbers of governmental units, it is difficult for a citizen to decide where to take his problem. It is also tempting for those he confronts with his problem to tell him he has come to the wrong place. When asked to pass a resolution condemning a war, a city council can be counted on to claim that determination of national policy is not in their hands. Yet that same council shows no hesitancy to lobby the federal government for grants to purchase additional riot control equipment. Many are the strategic uses to which limited authority can be put.

3. Cost Shifting   The action of one local governmental unit often produces changes — sometimes unintended — elsewhere. These "spillover

Marshall Henrichs

The inequity of costs and services is apparent in these two photographs of educational facilities. The urban school, above, is a wretched contrast to the massive, modern complex of the Dobyns Bennett High School in Kingsport, Tenn. The high school itself is the complex of white-roofed buildings at the center. Adjacent are the swimming pool (lower left), the civic auditorium, parking facilities, and the sports field. Photograph courtesy of Eastman Chemical Corp., Kingsport, Tennessee.

effects" or "externalities," as economists call them, are often political strategies designed to shift costs. The use of planning and zoning policies in a number of suburban areas is a good example.[4] The suburban city can manipulate its zoning so as to ensure that only "clean" industry and commerce can locate there and that only middle-income residents are attracted. This has the effect of maximizing the benefit to the city while allowing the costs — that is, the less antiseptic businesses and the poor residents — to spill over into other cities.[5]

4. *Inequity of Costs and Services*   The result of proliferated semiautonomous local units is often that one area has great resources and few needs while the adjacent area has great needs but few resources. Examples are not difficult to find. In the early sixties, a New Jersey municipality had an assessed valuation of $5.5 million per school pupil while a neighboring municipality had a valuation of $33,000 per pupil.[6] The greatest inequities, of course, usually exist between central city and surrounding suburbs. In Detroit, for example, twenty-five suburban school districts spent up to $500 more per child per year in their public schools than did the central-city schools.[7]

COPING WITH THE DIVIDED POWER TO GOVERN

Despite the inefficiencies we know to exist, American intergovernmental relations are not absolutely chaotic. There are a number of forces at work which facilitate coordination of functions at the national, state, and local levels. The development of intergovernmental coordination has occurred for one of three major reasons: (1) as a result of intentional efforts, (2) as an unintended consequence of politics, or (3) as a result of professionalism.[8] To explain, much of the effort of local officials and of the court system aims to create a pattern of laws which permits a conscious sharing of functions among federal, state, and local authorities. Federal grant-in-aid programs, which we shall discuss more fully in the following pages, are also examples of sharing by design.

Secondly, some unintentional sharing of functions occurs as a result of the politics of federalism. Because the American party system has its roots within the states, congressional districts, counties, and municipalities, party needs create a modicum of coordination. A pattern of mutual obligation and mutual need connects the local leadership with the national leadership of the party: congressmen owe their political obligations to the leaders of state and local party organizations; financial support for candidates often comes along the same route. More purposeful use of politics to achieve coordination in the federal system can also be found: the rivers and harbors program, for example, was not designed primarily to aid cities; but because cities can wield some political influence over the process of allocation of funds in that program, the political processes of the cities' politics result in some coordination.

And third, much of the activity at the several governmental levels is coordinated as a result of the growing professionalization of those who administer the programs:

> The tendency of professional workers at each level of government to identify themselves with the function to be performed, rather than with the particular government served, has become more pronounced as the number of workers at the several levels who are products of the same professional training increases.[9]

In other words, the federal urban renewal administrator, the state planner, and the local administrator of an urban renewal project are increasingly likely to have a shared educational background, a shared fund of technical information, and similar expectations and evaluation criteria for projects under their supervision.

A full-scale review of the details of federal-state-local cooperation is a major study in itself. Here we shall consider only the major features of the attempts to cope with the divided power to govern: we shall examine federal initiatives, state efforts, and the attempts at self-healing which the cities have attempted by means of metropolitan reorganization.

Federal Aid to the Cities

For the city in distress, the federal government has, since the New Deal, come to appear as the hero. In 1968 the federal government budgeted $17 billion for direct federal-local aid; and the budget for 1971 included approximately $28 billion for state and local governments. In the early 1970s there were some seventy federal aid programs that directly supported urban area activities.[10] As Tables 9.1 and 9.2 indicate, federal aid is available in a large number of specific program areas.

Federal grants to meet urban needs are given under a great variety of conditions, but in general they follow a common broad pattern. First, each program has a specific purpose; until 1972 there was no "bloc grant" program in which a specified amount could be given to the city for whatever purposes the city's government determined. Second, recipient agencies must provide a matching amount of money to support the program. And finally, as has often been bemoaned, federal grants usually are accompanied by a description of program standards which the local agency must achieve.

Table 9.1   Some Important Federal Grant-in-Aid Programs for Cities

	Program	*Content*
1.	Workable Program for Community Improvement	Requirements for planning and coordination as a condition of receiving federal grants
2.	Urban Renewal	Individual projects to renew blighted areas
3.	Community Renewal	Planning for community-wide renewal
4.	Low-rent Public Housing	Inexpensive housing for the poor
5.	Rent Supplement Program	Grants for the difference between what the poor can afford for rent and the market rent for housing
6.	FHA Section 221 (d) (3)	Insurance for low interest loans for the construction of housing for those above the public housing level but too poor to afford regular housing
7.	Low-income Housing Demonstration Program	Experiments with rent supplements and purchase of homes by low-income families
8.	Housing for the Elderly and the Handicapped	Public housing, FHA insured loans for low-rent units, and federal loans to non-profit corporations
9.	Neighborhood Facilities Program	Youth centers, health centers, community buildings, etc., for large and medium-sized cities
10.	Urban Mass Transportation	Grants for demonstration projects and loans for equipment and facilities
11.	Open Space and Beautification	Grants for purchase of land and for improvements
12.	Metropolitan Planning	Grants for area-wide planning
13.	Urban Planning Assistance	Grants for individual city planning
14.	Public Facility Loans	Water and sewer systems, storm sewers, health clinics, municipal buildings, etc.; mostly used for small towns
15.	Basic Water and Sewer Grants	Provide up to half the cost of construction
16.	Advances for Public Works Planning	
17.	College Housing	Aid to education, but it relieves some burden on the housing market
18.	Housing for the General Market	FHA loan insurance for middle-income homes (Average: $17,000)
19.	Mortgage Credit, Federal National Mortgage Association	Purchase of federally insured loans to expand credit supply

Source: Department of Housing and Urban Development, "Summary: HUD: 1961-66," *The Federal Role in Urban Affairs*, Subcommittee on Executive Reorganization of the Committee on Government Operations of the U.S. Senate, vol. 1 (Washington, D.C.: The Department, 1966), pp. 229-234.

Table 9.2   Federal Aid Payments in Urban Areas, 1961, 1966, and 1968 (budget and trust accounts in millions of dollars) [a]

Function and Program	Actual	Estimate	
	1961	1966	1968
National defense (civil defense and national guard centers)	$ 10	$ 20	$ 26
Agriculture and agricultural resources	155	149	235
Natural resources	54	105	200
Commerce and transportation			
Highways	1,398	2,138	2,176
Economic development		2	36
Airports	36	30	33
Other	1	52	6
Housing and community development			
Public housing	105	169	208
Water and sewer facilities			61
Urban renewal	106	235	336
Model cities			132
Urban transportation		14	98
District of Columbia	25	44	71
Other	2	23	100
Health, labor, and welfare			
Office of Economic Opportunity		449	1,010
School lunches, special milk, food stamps	131	196	290
Hospital construction	48	75	95
Community health	33	127	450
Public assistance (including medical care)	1,170	1,905	2,243
Vocational rehabilitation	37	108	211
Employment security and manpower training	303	417	501
Other	21	47	101
Education			
Elementary and secondary	222	895	1,292
Higher	5	37	172
Vocational	28	90	160
Other	3	27	80
Other functions		— [b]	6
Total aids to urban areas	$3,893	$7,354	$10,329

[a]Excludes loans and repayable advances.

[b]Less than $0.05 million.

Source: Advisory Commission in Intergovernmental Relations, *Fiscal Balance in the American Federal System*, vol. 1 (Washington, D.C.: U.S. Government Printing Office, 1967), p. 295.

In addition to the grant-in-aid system, there are several other devices which enable the federal government to provide technical and financial assistance to state and local governments. There are direct federal benefits to urban residents, federal loans and loan guarantees, and tax credits; and in 1972, a revenue-sharing program was begun wherein a bloc of undesignated federal money was turned back to each city.

It is commonplace to argue that federal money can be the instrument through which federal control is exercised over the local governments. That objection, strong in the earliest days of the grant-in-aid, seems to have waned. Many of those active in local government view federal activities not as "the forceable intrusion of a distant central government but almost invariably, as the successful consequences of local efforts to secure federal benefits to serve local ends."[11] This is, of course, not to say that the federal governments and localities have worked out a smooth, hitch-free relationship. It is simply to say that most contemporary critics are looking for ways to streamline and expand the federal-local relationship rather than seeking the means to abolish existing grant programs. Among the complaints that persist, however, three are most common: (1) objections to planning requirements, (2) objections to policies and procedural requirements, and (3) objections to audits.[12]

Jerome P. Cavanagh, mayor of Detroit, sums up the ongoing objections of many administrators when he says:

> some of these programs appear to be wrapped in complex rules and regulations that at times at least to some of us seem to be designed more for the convenience and protection of some distant administrators than for flexibility. . . . [The] veritable crush of paperwork, the delays and lack of funding, the urban renewal program, for example, allows little local discretion.[13]

Federal urban policy

Even though local dependence on federal support has become one of those hard facts of life, the federal government has yet to develop a coherent set of urban policies. Specific grant programs have developed ad hoc to meet local problems as they have arisen; and as a result, the federal structure for making urban policy is "vague and hopelessly diffuse."[14] Among the efforts to create a structure at the federal level for coping with federal, state, and local relationships was the creation by the Congress in 1959 of the Advisory Commission on Intergovernmental Relations (ACIR). The commission functions as a research agency of the federal government, providing information and technical assistance to state and local governments as well as attempting to facilitate the administration of federal programs.[15]

The cabinet-level Department of Housing and Urban Development (HUD) seems the logical apparatus for creating a coherent federal-local policy, but as yet it has not lived up to such high expectations. Many federal urban programs still work at cross purposes with each other: for example, in its earlier form (until 1965, the Housing and Home Finance Agency) HUD presided over the flight of the middle class to the suburbs, subsidizing it with FHA mortgage insurance; at the same time, the urban renewal administration of HUD was trying to lure suburbanites back to the central city through renewal programs. In addition, "the public housing administration built low rent units for the poor while urban renewal was tearing them down."[16] The Nixon administration has created posts for special assistants to help deal

Marshall Henrichs

There is general agreement on the need to demolish substandard housing in urban areas. The optimal form of replacement is, however, hotly contended.

with the problems of coordinating urban relationships: the Council on Urban Affairs, originally chaired by Daniel P. Moynihan, and an Office of Intergovernmental Relations have been the two major efforts.

The urban lobby

We have already acknowledged that politics accounts for some of the coordination achieved between federal and local levels. The presence in Washington of a number of lobbyists speaking for various aspects of the needs of American cities contributes significantly to federal-city integration. The list of private organizations lobbying for federal urban policy is impressive, including the United States Council of Mayors (USCM), the National League of Cities (NLC), Urban America, Urban Coalition, The National Association of Housing and Redevelopment Officials (NAHRO), and the National Housing Conference (NHC). The lobbying groups appear as fractionated as the authority of the federal government is. But a more careful examination reveals that this cluster of lobbying groups are constantly in contact with one another, formally and informally, "on matters of mutual interest about which they bargain or exchange information in a continuous process of interaction."[17]

Suzanne Farkas, in a careful examination of this constellation of urban lobbyists, has found a number of reasons for the relative coherence of this "policy subsystem." Their goals are remarkably similar; all of these groups have agreed that, in their terminology, there exists an urban crisis which requires a national response of shifting priorities in the allocation of funds and there is an urgent need to create a national urban policy. All these groups have pressed for a reordering of priorities and have identified housing shortages for the poor as a primary problem. Further, all have criticized the size of the defense budget. In short, the urban lobby has not only developed common goals but has also come to use a common language to express those goals.[18]

In addition to confluence of goals, other reasons the urban lobby coheres are overlapping membership, overlapping leadership, formal consultation, overlap and exchange of staff, informal exchanges of services and joint prospects, and informal communications including general "touching base" on policies of general interest to the cities.

The urban lobby serves an important function in providing communication channels from cities to the national government. It provides a point at which urban interests can be brought together and made somewhat cohesive. It provides a point at which political strategy can be mapped and executed. In short, the urban lobby performs the functions of any political actor. In the process it helps to aggregate otherwise diffuse interests. As a result, when and if a federal urban policy emerges, urban lobbyists will have played a crucial part in the shape it takes.

The Reluctant State

If the federal government has often been cast as the hero in the drama of the urban crises, the state is usually the heavy. We've already made the point that legally the municipal corporation is a creature of the state, that it is created by the state and can be ultimately controlled by it. Since this rule was pronounced, it has been subject to judicial softening.[19] Still, a number of commentators presume that the basic power to deal with metropolitan areas is in the hands of the state and that the difficulties of the cities are, therefore, a result of the failure of the state. Because there is such variation from state to state, it will not be possible in this short space to examine all the data necessary to establish that conclusion firmly. Instead, let us summarize some of the most important characteristics of the state-local relationship.

States provide aid to their municipalities in a pattern much like that of federal aid. In general, however, state aid emphasizes tax sharing and bloc grants. *Tax sharing* involves a conscious policy of the state to tax certain activities (for example, gasoline sales) but to leave to the municipalities the right to tax others (for example, property). A *bloc grant* involves the granting of a sum of money to a city for general types of programs; the federal grant-in-aid pattern, you will recall, funds only specified projects. It is common for state law to provide that a fixed portion of taxes reverts to the local jurisdiction in which they were collected. So state aid may simply be designated for education or roads — and in some cases are not specified even that much. Again, by distinction from federal grants-in-aid, state aid generally requires no matching from local revenues. State aids, then, generally provide more flexibility to recipient cities than federal aid does.

When we look more closely at the variety of aid patterns, we get a stronger sense of how state aid facilitates intergovernmental cooperation. A variety of criteria are used for the allocation of state funds to local governmental units. Some, for example, use state aid to equalize resources as between "have" and "have not" jurisdictions; state aid for schools characteristically follows this pattern. Some states mechanically return to cities the proportion of state taxes that were collected there. A third criterion of aid which is commonly used makes state aid a reward for having made some effort to use the local unit's own resources in certain program areas. Some states award funds according to preordained criteria, such as population. And finally, some states rely on special considerations, like emergencies or specially negotiated agreements, as bases for determining the amount of aid given to their local governments.

There is wide variation in the role that state governments play in raising revenues for their local units. Overall, state governments raised slightly over 50% of the total state and local revenues in the late sixties and early seventies. But that nationwide average masks a range extending from 78.8% in Delaware to 37.5% in New Hampshire. In 1968 the states transferred approximately $22 billion to their local subdivisions. In 1960 that figure had been $9.3 billion.[20]

State aid to localities is primarily for education, highways, and public welfare — much the same pattern as that of federal aid. As the figures in Table 9.3 suggest, there is a tendency for low-income states to rely most heavily on state-raised revenues. Using public welfare expenditures by state and local governments as an example, we can see that low-income states like Louisiana, Arkansas, and Alabama provide a large state contribution; while the relatively well-to-do states of New Jersey, New York, and Massachusetts make localities more dependent on their own revenues.

City, Heal Thyself: Reform Again

By contrast to the success of the movement to reform the municipal charter, the attempts to reorganize and consolidate area-wide governmental units, to create "supergovernments" as they are sometimes called, have been a smashing failure. It has been accurately observed that

> through the second quarter of this century many political scientists were writing on why metropolitan areas needed to be politically integrated through local government consolidation. Thus far, in the third quarter, a major theme has been documented of how thoroughly this advice has been rejected by the American people.[21]

Advocacy of area-wide government has become one of those great commonplaces among political scientists. It is almost a knee-jerk response to the question, "How do we solve the 'urban problem'?" But, the fact that few local governmental consolidations have occurred is one of the more impressive monuments to the different perspectives of political scientists and people in general. Not that there have been no attempts to reorganize metropolitan government: a recent count disclosed that fifty referenda have been held in the U.S. on metropolitan reorganization proposals since World War II.[22] The successful reorganizations are easily named; there have been several city-county consolidations in Virginia, also in Baton Rouge, Nashville, and Jacksonville; a city-county consolidation of the federation type was accomplished in the Miami-Dade County area. Indianapolis-Marion County can be added to this short list of metropolitan governments, but in this case the consolidation was imposed by the state legislature and did not require a referendum of the people. Like most sermons, then, irrespective of whether they are delivered by ministers or political scientists, proposals for area-wide governments are much easier to deliver than to act on.

Table 9.3   Percentage of Total Public Welfare Expenditures by State and Local Governments, 1968 [a]

	State	Local		State	Local
Alaska	55.1	—	Ohio	43.9	5.2
Hawaii	54.3	—	Maryland	45.0	5.6
Rhode Island	50.2	—	South Dakota	26.2	5.9
Washington	49.0	—	Michigan	45.7	7.3
New Mexico	28.7	—	North Dakota	23.8	7.6
Louisiana	27.5	—	Maine	28.1	7.9
Arkansas	25.4	—	Nebraska	28.2	9.1
Utah	35.5	0.1	Oregon	36.3	9.3
Missouri	33.9	0.1	Nevada	30.4	10.5
Idaho	31.7	0.1	Delaware	30.8	11.3
Oklahoma	31.2	0.1	Iowa	31.7	11.4
Alabama	23.8	0.1	Colorado	35.4	11.5
Arizona	27.9	0.2	North Carolina	14.6	14.4
Connecticut	53.8	0.7	Virginia	19.2	16.1
South Carolina	25.4	0.7	California	33.1	16.9
Mississippi	20.6	0.8	Wyoming	26.8	19.1
Kentucky	23.8	0.8	Indiana	28.5	19.2
Texas	23.8	0.9	New Hampshire	23.8	19.4
West Virginia	24.9	1.4	Massachusetts	31.1	21.4
Vermont	31.3	1.6	Kansas	24.4	21.7
Florida	22.9	2.3	Wisconsin	23.0	22.3
Pennsylvania	47.4	2.6	Minnesota	18.6	27.5
Illinois	49.4	3.5	New York	31.7	27.9
Georgia	19.5	3.9	Montana	19.3	30.9
Tennessee	20.3	4.8	New Jersey	28.6	31.1

[a]Remaining percentage represents federal expenditure.

Source: Adapted from Advisory Commission on Intergovernmental Relations, State and Local Finances, 1966-1969 (Washington, D.C.: The Commission, 1969), p. 30.

The failure of the public to respond to the consolidation proposals cannot be attributed to the political scientists' failure to make specific recommendations. On the contrary, the literature is filled with detailed proposals of alternative modes of urban reorganization.

Modes of metropolitan reorganization

The Advisory Commission on Intergovernmental Relations (created by the Congress in 1959 to gather and disseminate information on intergovernmental problems in the U.S.) has distinguished ten alternative forms of metropolitan reorganization. Ranging from the least to the most far-reaching, they include:

1. Municipal extraterritorial regulation of real estate developments in the rural fringe outside municipal borders;
2. Intergovernmental agreements;
3. Voluntary metropolitan councils;
4. The urban county;
5. Transfer of functions to state governments;
6. Metropolitan special districts;
7. Annexation and intercity consolidation;
8. City-county separation, that is, separation of the urbanized and rural areas;
9. Consolidation of the city with the urbanized county surrounding it;
10. Federation of several municipalities.[23]

Without getting into excessive detail, let us consider the most commonly discussed plans for metropolitan reorganization: metropolitan federation; comprehensive urban counties; and a county-city contract service plan.

Federation

You might expect that the nation which pioneered the concept of federalism — dividing governmental power between a central unit and a series of local units — might apply that concept to the organization of its metropolitan areas. There has been considerable advocacy of local federation, particularly in the late nineteenth and twentieth centuries. To its many advocates, this reform method seems optimal because it meets the need for area-wide or metropolitan government while retaining more localized units. There have, in fact, been several attempts to create federated local governments in the United States. For example, Boston considered such a plan in 1896, Oakland (Alameda County) defeated a federated charter in 1921, as did Pittsburgh (Allegheny County) in 1929. St. Louis and San Francisco also discussed and then discarded federation plans.[24] The only example of a metropolitan federation plan functioning in North America is the one in Toronto, Canada.

Toronto confronted severe service crises and mounting local taxes as a result of population growth and suburbanization in the late forties and early fifties. As a result the Ontario Municipal Board drafted a series of recommendations which the Ontario parliament subsequently enacted, bringing into creation on January 1, 1954, the Municipality of Metropolitan Toronto, a federation composed of the city of Toronto, three villages, four towns, and five townships. The specific form of federation in metropolitan Toronto called for the creation of a strong metropolitan government, one empowered to deal with the most central functions of city government. The metropolitan government was empowered to assess property and to maintain the services of water supply, sewage disposal, arterial roads, transit, and health and welfare agencies; it was also to oversee the administration of justice, the maintenance of metropolitan parks, and public housing and redevelopment; and finally, it was given an overall planning capacity. Certain of these functions were to be exclusively area wide, while others, like water and sewage, were to be shared functions with the lesser units. In several instances, this sharing of functions was accomplished by making the metropolitan unit a financial overseer. For example, in education, the metropolitan government was to determine the amount of money to be approved for the purchase of school sites and construction of school buildings and to issue bonds for such purposes against its own credit. In this way, metropolitan government has been able to assure some degree of equalization of educational opportunity within the area since the metropolitan school board pays some of the debt charges for schools and makes uniform per-pupil payments to local school boards. The eleven locally elected school boards are charged with the operation of the public elementary and secondary schools in their municipalities.

The tendency since the creation of the metropolitan area government has been for the central governmental unit to grow in power. Still, the local governments retain a number of functions; in addition to the conduct of education, they are responsible also for libraries, fire protection, and most phases of public health. To an advocate of neighborhood control, this allocation of functions may seem inverted. The Toronto mode of federation is clearly more interested in area-wide coordination than it is in local autonomy. That emphasis is, of course, not inherent in metropolitan federation.

The central governing body of Metropolitan Toronto is the Metropolitan Council. The Metropolitan Council was initially composed of twenty-four members, twelve from the city of Toronto and one from each suburban entity. A twenty-fifth member of the council was to be a chairman, elected by the council. Subsequent growth of the Toronto area has necessitated reapportionment, so that in 1966 the Ontario parliament enacted legislation consolidating the original thirteen municipalities into six cities, ranging in size from 91,000 to 682,000. Each city was given one representative on the Metropolitan Council for approximately each 50,000 people. This increased the size of the council to thirty-two members.

Whether "Metro" has been successful or not, of course, depends on the values of the observer. For example, to the person who values local autonomy, Toronto might seem to be a failure. Most observers class Toronto a success, however, basing that conclusion on the fact that the new federated government has been able to achieve a large number of economies of scale. That is, Metro has enabled Toronto to increase dramatically its level of services to a growing population and at the same time maintain a favorable financial position. Because all borrowing is done by the metropolitan government, its bonds have acquired a "double A" rating, the highest classification a foreign corporation can receive on Wall Street. The resultant savings from lower interest rates have been estimated at $50 million since 1954.[25]

Specific improvements in services have also been noted. Area-wide traffic authority has made possible the coordination of traffic signals, accomplished by vehicle detectors buried beneath regional streets which feed traffic flow information to a central computer. Utilizing this information of traffic flow in far-out suburban feeder roads, the system can meter cars onto arterial highways more efficiently than had been previously possible. As a result it has been estimated that motorists stop only one-third as often for red lights as they did prior to centralized traffic programing. It has been estimated that a cross-Metro trip via public transportation requires only one-fourth the time consumed before routes, schedules, and fares of every bus, trolley, and subway car were integrated into a single interlocking system.

Metro has also made possible a large number of improvements in the area of public works. The water capacity of the metropolitan area has doubled; $60 million has been invested in sewage disposal facilities; 150 new schools have been constructed; and 259 additions have been made to old schools. The strong position of the metropolitan government has resulted in effective master planning as well. In the first half of the century, the city of Toronto had prepared seven master plans, all of which had been substantially ignored by city officials — a situation quite familiar in most American cities.[26] Improved capacity to plan has minimized urban sprawl, even while population has grown. Centralized control over basic services and finances allows Metro to decide when and where such basic city-building functions as water lines and roads will be extended and makes possible a framework to guide the zoning decisions made at local levels. Because Metro is able to enforce its plans, it has succeeded not only in preserving the parks system but in expanding park lands, despite the strong pressures of land developers.[27]

While Metro seems an ideal governmental form, permitting sound physical development and equally sound fiscal policy, it is not free from criticism. One student of Metro Toronto charges that the system has overemphasized the physical aspects of urban development and neglected social services. The first capital works program, for example, provided 76% of the total budget went for roads, sewers, and water supply; 21% of the budget went to educational expenses, leaving a meager 3% for all other services and facilities. This means that 3% of the budget had to be spread among programs for housing, welfare, conservation, parks, and the administration of justice. The second capital program doubled the allotment, but that was still only 6% of the budget for these services.[28]

Comprehensive Urban County Government

A second and quite similar mode of consolidating local governmental units proposes the creation of a comprehensive urban county. This plan calls for a simultaneous reallocation of various functions from all municipalities to a county; the county then becomes a metropolitan government. The county government assumes those functions which are considered area wide, while leaving to its constituent municipalities and other local governments the capacity to provide local services. A major difference from the federation plan is that the comprehensive urban county plan does not require the creation of an additional unit of government in an already fragmented system. This is considered especially advantageous if urbanization has occurred almost entirely within a single county.

Like the federation plans, the urban county plans have failed to be widely adopted. One version or another of the comprehensive urban county proposal has been considered and rejected in Cleveland, Pittsburgh, Houston, and Dayton, for example.[29]

When its charter went into effect in July 1957, Miami became the first city in the United States to try the comprehensive urban county plan. Voter acceptance of the plan did not come easily, however. The first attempt failed in 1947, and the 1953 proposal to abolish the city of Miami and transfer all its functions to Dade County had also lost at the polls. The closeness of the 1953 vote (it lost by less than 1000 votes) inspired a follow-up campaign which eventuated in 1957 in the narrow victory (44,404 to 42,620) of the new charter for Metropolitan Miami. The closeness of the victory in turn produced a number of counterattacks which for the most part have been successfully staved off.[30]

The new charter for Metropolitan Miami provided for a strong and integrated county government and for the continuance of the twenty-six existing constituent municipalities. Miami Metro was empowered to construct expressways, regulate traffic, own and operate mass transit systems and transportation terminals. It was also responsible for maintaining central record keeping, for training and communications within the fire and police departments, and for the provision of hospitals and uniform health and welfare programs. Miami Metro also acquired the power to designate and maintain parks and recreational areas; to establish and administer housing and urban renewal; to oversee flood control, beach erosion control, air pollution control, and drainage programs; to regulate or own various public utilities; and to engage in industrial promotion. Significantly, it was also authorized to prepare and enforce comprehensive plans for the development of the county, and it was permitted to adopt and enforce zoning and business regulations and uniform building codes throughout the county. With respect to the relationship of the Metro to the several local units, Metro was also empowered to set reasonable minimum standards for all governmental units in the county and to take over any activity in which a local unit failed to meet minimum standards.

The original plan reorganized the Board of County Commissioners to include five members elected at large, five more by county district, and one member elected for and by each city having a population of over 60,000. These members were to be chosen in nonpartisan elections. The Board of Commissioners served staggered terms of office and received a yearly salary of $6,000. The Board was authorized to elect its own chairman and vice chairman and to appoint a county manager, county attorney, judges, and clerk of the metro court. The Board serves as a policy-making body. In addition to its county responsibilities, the Board also serves as the Port Authority and appoints a Port Director. The county manager, who is appointed by the Board, is quite similar to a city manager in his form and function. He is responsible for the operation of all county departments, preparation of the budget, and execution of policies adopted by the Board.

The supporters of Miami Metro claim a number of accomplishments. A summary of the first four years of the Metro's operation noted the completion of a preliminary land-use plan, an economic base study, and a downtown redevelopment plan. Significant progress was also claimed in the areas of public transportation, seaport development, the planning of a water and sewer system, and new efforts at flood control.[31]

Metro's major difficulties have been of two kinds: political and financial. The continuation of the close political division that characterized the adoption of the charter made the job of county manager an extremely hazardous one. The first manager, O. W. Campbell, in trying to assert his leadership, provoked substantial opposition on the council which led finally in 1961 to his dismissal by the commission. After a number of disputes, mostly over assessment policy, Campbell's successor, Irving G. McNayr, was dismissed in 1964. In sum, "the Dade County experience raises serious doubts about the appropriateness of the [county] manager form of government for a metropolitan complex."[32]

The financial difficulties of the Metro seem to result from the financial structure created in the original charter. According to one careful examination of the operation of the Metro, these shortcomings are: (1) lack of sufficient revenue for the central governing unit, (2) inequity in the distribution of the tax burden, particularly as between incorporated and unincorporated areas, and (3) inefficient and inequitable utilization of those monies which are collected. This last situation is due primarily to the unwillingness of the cities to relinquish much of their previous autonomy in tax matters.[33] Even though the Metro has managed some savings, the fiscal decentralization required by the charter prevents Metro from undertaking programs of the magnitude successfully concluded in Toronto.[34] Then, too, the Metro's revenues are limited — as are those of all American cities — by the limitations of the real estate and personal property tax base.

County - City Contract Service

Even though there have been few area-wide comprehensive governments adopted in United States metropolitan areas, there have none-theless developed a series of techniques which facilitate cooperation. The county has often played an important role in achieving cooperation. As Bernard F. Hillenbrand, executive director of the National Association of County Officials, has claimed:

> Amid the clamor for an overall solution to the exploding metropolitan problem, many urban counties are quietly and unobtrusively meeting the challenge through formal and informal cc perative agreements. Petty jealousies are being cast aside as elected representatives of counties, cities, and states cooperate to bring more efficient and effective government to the people at the lowest possible cost.[35]

Such county-city cooperation can take a number of forms. But one of the most often discussed is that in which the county government provides services to municipalities by making contracts for specific services — police, fire, and water, for example. The "Lakewood Plan," pioneered in Los Angeles County, established the pattern for this mode of county-city cooperation. In response to annexation disputes, the Board of Supervisors of Los Angeles County announced a plan whereby they would provide services on a contract basis to incorporated areas within the county.[36] After defeating a move to annex Lakewood to Long Beach, Lakewood residents incorporated their city and became the first city to participate in the county's contract service program. By contracting with the county for basic public services, Lakewood was able to avoid bonded indebtedness which is usually forced on new municipalities when first they seek to finance such capital expenditures as fire and police protection and water and sewage facilities. By incorporating, the city also gained access to approximately $500,000 in the first year as their share from the gasoline tax, motor vehicle license fees, and liquor license fees collected by the state. As a result, the new municipality of Lakewood had only ten employees by the end of 1954 but was, nonetheless, obtaining a high level of services while its property tax rate stood at a low assessed valuation (29¢, 30¢, and 24¢ per $100) during its initial three years.[37]

The contract service plan has been accepted by nearly all the municipalities, irrespective of size, that have been incorporated since 1954 in

Los Angeles County. Not all the cities participating purchase the same package of services from the county; the common practice has been for the newly incorporated cities to purchase at the beginning virtually all the municipal services they need. As time goes on, cities have terminated particular service contracts when they have determined that they can provide those services more economically themselves. The contents of the service package varies according to a city's decisions as to what it needs from the county and what subsequent changes should be made in its original arrangements.

There are some shortcomings to the Lakewood Plan, even though it succeeds at organizing political fragmentation so as to ensure maintenance of basic service standards while meeting the diverse needs of new municipalities at reasonable cost. By emphasizing local autonomy, the contract plan leaves area-wide planning unemphasized. Further, equalization of the burden of taxation and of the quality of services does not occur where local control is this rigorously maintained. It has also been argued that the Lakewood Plan hastens political fractionation by encouraging new incorporations; the rapid incorporation of new cities since the advent of contract service seems to validate the charge. Because several of the newly incorporated cities have been estate-type, upper-middle-income residential communities, it has become clear that the contract plan enables those who can afford it to escape from areas of lower socioeconomic status. In other words, the plan seems to have facilitated suburban social segregation.

A number of other plans for dealing with the problems of multiple local governments are being experimented with — for example, metropolitan regional councils as in New York and Washington, D.C.; and councils of government (or COGs) as in the San Francisco Bay Area and central Oklahoma areas. All represent efforts to bring governmental harmony out of cacophony. But as even this brief review makes clear, most of the attempts at achieving such harmony have fallen short. The more comprehensive solutions like federated plans or supergovernment proposals have not been able to be passed in many American cities. Why have such beautiful and symmetrical and orderly plans excited so little approval? The answer to that question lies in the politics of metropolitan reorganization.

The politics of reorganization

The more comprehensive proposals — that is, the best laid plans — have generally run afoul of the requirement that a majority of voters in the affected region must approve. This should not be surprising in the light of what we have already said about the fate of comprehensive measures in a diverse and conflictful social setting. All that is required to ensure defeat is that the comprehensive package contain one element that is abhorrent to a group to assure that group's opposition. The more comprehensive the measure, the more likely it is that it contains something to alienate everybody. Another and quite different theory holds that reorganization plans fail because of citizen apathy. Political scientists are unable to provide a satisfactory empirically based explanation at this point, despite the accumulation of much explanatory material.[38]

First, it has been found that central-city public officials and power structures of the metropolitan area rarely initiate reform. More often it is a good-government group like the League of Women Voters, a newspaper, or a band of academics that initiate the move. Such political actors seldom have the capacity to ensure necessary public enthusiasm; and, perhaps more important, they have great difficulty generating public confidence in a far-reaching reform. Even though officials and notables often come around as the campaign proceeds, their endorsement seldom has the impact that their initial sponsorship would have had. If public officials appear relatively uninvolved with reorganization, voters are likely to sleep right through the campaign.

Second, voters are characteristically unengaged by the subject matter of metropolitan organization. They tend to place higher value on goals such as local autonomy than on reform. As a careful observer of the effort to consolidate metropolitan St. Louis put it,

> Standing back a little distance from the St. Louis campaign, one is struck by an essential absurdity in the performance. A few people. intensely involved, swam in a sea of concepts and phrases — notions about the good life, the good society, the concrete effects of changes in a charter, the means of persuasion, the Spirit of the Laws. . . . Yet the voters hardly knew who they were. They didn't recognize the face, and if they did they didn't know which side the leader was on or why he was there. Most of the voters didn't even know what the District Plan was.[39]

Survey evidence indicates that in one of the Miami-Dade County campaigns, less than a third of the electorate had heard of the reform proposal.[40] And even in the election in which Miami Metro was adopted, only about one-fourth of the county's registered voters took part in that special election, indicating a general lack of concern.

Third, suburban officials can be counted on to oppose reorganization. A major source of organized opposition in the St. Louis campaign was a citizens committee dominated by municipal officials and Republican party leaders from the county. Other political party leaders tended either to refrain from participation in the reorganization efforts or fell in with the opposition. Certain suburban officials may have opposed reorganization because they feared for their jobs. The reasons for the opposition of the Republican party leaders are less clear. Edward Banfield suggests that the Republican party would have benefited from consolidation:

> Even if the proportion of Republicans declined sharply in the suburbs, metropolitan government north of the Mason-Dixon line would almost everywhere be Republican government. In effect, advocates of consolidation schemes are asking the Democrats to give up their control of the central cities, or at least to place it in jeopardy.[41]

Local Republicans in St. Louis seemed more intent on protecting local autonomy from consolidation than on achieving such a long-run benefit to the Republican party.

Fourth, black leaders and labor leaders generally oppose reorganization. Black leaders have consistently opposed reorganization proposals. The most impressive evidence of that opposition was gathered in a study of voting in the Cleveland-Cuyahoga County referendum on reorganization which narrowly lost. Ten reorganization proposals were presented in that area over a twenty-five year period, and the study found that black support had declined with each election.[42] At the same time, black voting strength in the city during that period was generally increasing, leading to the 1967 election of the first black mayor of Cleveland, Carl Stokes. Blacks have opposed reorganization because they anticipate (usually correctly) that their voting power would be diluted in a larger area government. They also fear that area-wide government would come to be more concerned with large capital improvement programs, giving less attention and money to social issues related to the needs of ghetto residents.

Finally, the overall size and socioeconomic characteristics of the metropolitan area affect the likelihood of successful reform. In the largest cities with the most socially diverse populations, metropolitan integration confronts the most difficulty. It has been found that the sharper the socioeconomic differences between suburban and central-city areas, the smaller is the probability of reform. These observations have been documented in studies of school district mergers and municipal annexation. They have found that where the central city and suburban populations are homogeneous, annexation is more easily attained than when the two populations are socially and economically dissimilar.[43]

Reform, then, is opposed by a number of significant political actors: by suburbanites and suburban organizations who have left the central city and do not wish to be reunited with it and its "problems"; by officials, both in the city and outside it, who fear for their jobs; and by low-power central-city groups such as blacks who anticipate a loss of power in a larger metropolitan area government. That combination of forces has proven fatal to a great many of those best laid plans. There seems little reason to expect significant political actors to change their positions readily; and for that reason, metropolitan integration seems to have a dim future indeed. This leaves urban decision makers with the difficult task of coping with continuing fractionated authority.

SUMMARY

The multiplicity of local governmental units is an often lamented fact. But, like the weather, there is apparently not much that can be done about it. Though the fragmentation is costly both in terms of dollars and in terms of delay and lost authority, the political realities are such that efforts at consolidation characteristically fail. There are many models of local governmental consolidation and cooperation — federation, comprehensive county government, and city-county contract service, for example — but none has been widely adopted. What coordination does occur within the fragmented local governmental process results from some efforts at voluntary cooperation — through tax sharing, grant-in-aid programs, and some conducive political realities. It is remarkably hit or miss for a country that prides itself on its efficiency. A comprehensive national urban policy does not seem on the horizon either.

NOTES

1. Richard H. Leach, *American Federalism* (New York: W. W. Norton, 1970), p. 147.
2. Advisory Commission on Intergovernmental Relations, *Government Structure, Organization and Planning in Metropolitan Areas* (Washington, D.C.: U.S. Government Printing Office, 1961), p. 14.
3. Morton Grodzins is responsible for the widely used analogy. See his "The Federal Systems," in *The President's Commission on National Goals, Goals for Americans*, ed. Morton Grodzins (Englewood Cliffs, N.J.: Prentice-Hall, 1960).
4. This discussion draws heavily on Robert L. Lineberry, "Reforming Metropolitan Governments: Requiem or Reality?" *Georgetown Law Journal* 58 (March-May 1970): 675-718.
5. Seymour Sacks and Allen Campbell, "The Fiscal Zoning Game," *Municipal Finance* 35 (May 1964): 140-149.
6. For many other examples, see Robert C. Wood, *Fourteen Hundred Governments* (Garden City, N.Y.: Doubleday Anchor, 1961). This one is found on page 55.
7. *National Commission on Civil Disorders Report* (Washington, D.C.: U.S. Government Printing Office, 1968), p. 241.
8. Paraphrased from Morton Grodzins, *The American System* (Chicago: Rand, McNally, 1966), p. 11.

9. Ibid., p. 71.

10. See Advisory Commission on Intergovernmental Relations, *Metropolitan America* (Washington, D.C.: U.S. Government Printing Office, 1966), p. 8.

11. Daniel J. Elazar, "Local Government in Intergovernmental Perspective," *Illinois Local Government: University of Illinois Bulletin* Vol. 62, No. 92 (June 1965): 20.

12. Summarized from Roscoe C. Martin, *Cities and the Federal System* (New York: Atherton Press, 1965), pp. 151-162.

13. Quoted in United States Senate Subcommittee on Executive Reorganization of the Committee on Government Operations, *The Federal Role in Urban Affairs* (Washington, D.C.: U.S. Government Printing Office, 1966), Part III, pp. 619-620.

14. Frederic N. Cleaveland et al., *Congress and Urban Problems* (Washington, D.C.: The Brookings Institution, 1969), p. 375.

15. See Deil S. Wright, "The Advisory Committee on Intergovernmental Relations," *Public Administration Review* 25 (September 1965): 193-202.

16. James Q. Wilson, "The War on Cities," in *A Nation of Cities*, ed. Robert Goldwin (Skokie, Ill.: Rand, McNally, 1966), p. 19.

17. *Urban Lobbying: Mayors in the Federal Arena* (New York: New York University Press, 1971), p. 79. This section draws heavily upon Ms. Farkas' work.

18. Ibid., pp. 80-85.

19. For example, in the case of *Gomillion* v. *Lightfoot*, 364 US 339, 342-345 (1960). "The court has never acknowledged that the States have power to do so as they will with municipal corporations regardless of consequences. Legislative control of municipalities, no less than other state power, lies within the scope of relevant limitations imposed by the United States Constitution. . . ."

20. Daniel J. Elazar, *American Federalism: A View from the States* (New York: Thomas Y. Crowell, 1972), pp. 192-193.

21. Oliver Williams, "Life Style Values and Political Decentralization in Metropolitan Areas," *Southwestern Social Science Quarterly* 48 (December 1967): 299.

22. Lineberry, "Reforming Metropolitan Governments" p. 678.

23. Advisory Commission on Intergovernmental Relations, *Alternative Approaches to Governmental Reorganization in Metropolitan Areas* (Washington, D.C.: U.S. Government Printing Office, 1962).

24. Some discussion and additional bibliography related to each of these federation attempts is found in John C. Bollens and Henry J. Schmandt, *The Metropolis* (New York: Harper & Row, 1965), pp. 472-474. Much of the discussion of federation in this section is taken from Bollens and Schmandt and also from an unpublished paper, "Regional Government: City of the Future?" by Andrew Marcus, a graduate student at San Diego State University, 1972.

25. Bollens and Schmandt, *The Metropolis* p. 485.

26. The following discussion of planning is from Harold Kaplan, *The Regional City* (Toronto: Canadian Broadcasting Company, 1965).

27. Cf. "Where Home Rule Wings Are Clipped," *Business Week* (May 18, 1968), p. 65. For other evaluation of Metro, see Frank Smallwood, "Metro Toronto: A Decade Later," *Taming Megalopolis* Vol. 2 (New York: Frederick A. Praeger,

1967); or H. Wentworth Eldredge, ed., *How to Manage an Urbanized World* (Garden City, N.Y.: Anchor Books, 1967).

28. "Where Home Rule Wings Are Clipped," p. 69.

29. For a discussion and bibliography related to these unsuccessful attempts, see Bollens and Schmandt, *The Metropolis*, pp. 453-455.

30. See Edward Sofen, *The Miami Metropolitan Experiment* (Bloomington: Indiana University Press, 1963).

31. For more specifics on these accomplishments, see Government Research Council of the Miami-Dade County Chamber of Commerce, *Metropolitan Dade County . . . Its First Four Years, A Summary Report* (Miami: The Council, 1961).

32. Bollens and Schmandt, *The Metropolis*, p. 469.

33. Reinhold P. Wolff, *Miami Metro* (Coral Gables: Bureau of Business and Economic Research, University of Miami, 1960), pp. 133-148.

34. It is estimated that centralized county purchasing saves up to $50,000 a year; cf. John Berger, "How Miami's Metro Purchases," *American City* (October 1961): 125.

35. Bernard F. Hillenbrand, "Urban Counties, 1958," *Public Management* 41 (May 1959): 106.

36. For a good discussion of the history and characteristics of the Lakewood Plan, see Robert O. Warren, *Government in Metropolitan Regions: A Reappraisal of Fractionated Political Organization* (Davis: Institute of Governmental Affairs, University of California, 1966).

37. Ibid., pp. 157-159.

38. The following discussion leans heavily on the presentation of Robert L. Lineberry and Ira Sharkansky, *Urban Politics and Public Policy* (New York: Harper & Row, 1971), pp. 140-142.

39. Scott Greer, *Metropolitics: A Study of Political Culture* (New York: John Wiley and Sons, 1963), p. 191.

40. Sofen, *Miami Metropolitan Experiment*, p. 76.

41. Edward C. Banfield, "The Politics of Metropolitan Area Organization," *Midwest Journal of Political Science* 1 (May 1957): 77-91.

42. Richard A. Watson and John H. Romani, "Metropolitan Government for Metropolitan Cleveland," *Midwest Journal of Political Science* 5 (November 1961): 365-390.

43. See Thomas R. Dye, "Urban Political Integration: Conditions Associated with Annexation in American Cities," *Midwest Journal of Political Science* 8 (November 1964): 430-446.

Chapter 10

Policy Formulation and Leadership:
Is There a Power Structure?

It was suggested in the previous chapter that local decision makers are far from autonomous. They are guided by law and directives from county, state, and national governments. Even the political actors at the local level are often themselves components of large organizations that are national in scope. The demands and expectations of such actors are not always worked out in the local political arena; their eye is sometimes on other levels of government or on nongovernmental activities altogether. In sum, local decisions are made in a national, sometimes international, context.

How do policy alternatives get formulated in our cities? Who exercises leadership in this process? A common way to formulate this topic is to ask, "Is there a power structure?" Anyone who has been inside the city limits for more than twenty-four hours has an answer to that question. There is nearly always some readily available inside dope, which usually amounts to this: "The big boys run this town"; then the informant proceeds to name half a dozen or so big boys. Like most inside dope, it requires verification before the prudent inquirer attempts to act on it. Once committed to that verification, however, social scientists have found that such a seemingly simple question becomes extraordinarily complex and difficult to answer. From the vast literature on local decision making there has emerged a profound disagreement — not only as to whether there is a power structure, but even as to how to proceed to find out.

For the sake of simplicity and to be true to the natural history of the development of the subject matter, I have organized this chapter around the two major and contending sets of findings about power structures: (1) those studies which find that an elite actually governs a particular city, and (2) those studies which find that *several* elites govern, creating a pluralistic political process.

We shall identify each of these findings by its technique of inquiry rather than by its substance: those which have usually found an elite are the studies conducted by "reputationalists" and those which have found pluralism are the studies of "issue area analysts." In the next chapter we shall deal with a third mode of studying local leadership — the "formal positional" approach — and discuss local officeholders.

It is important to recognize from the outset that even the pluralist findings do not allow the conclusion that "the people" govern directly. The beliefs and hopes of populists can find little support in the studies of community power. The differences between the elitists and pluralists are not dramatic; they amount to saying that the difference is between a single, pyramidal structure of power and a more amorphous, plural elite structure. Both findings mean that a small number of people do the policy making and governing in America's cities.[1]

By staying true to the natural history of the study of community power, I shall be able to develop an additional subtheme in this chapter: that procedures — techniques and tools of analysis, definitions, units of analysis, and ideologies of researchers — can have a decisive impact on the findings of scientific research.

Broadly speaking, there has been a dialectical development of our knowledge of power structures. What began with single case studies of particular cities by individual researchers, with each researcher using his own definitions, assumptions, etc., has moved toward comparative analysis.

> After a power elitist stage inspired by Hunter and Mills, and a pluralist stage influenced by Dahl, a comparative stage now seems to be in the offing. This third stage does not just pose new questions but new types of questions: no longer content with "who governs?" The query is extended to "who governs, where, when, and with what effects?"[2]

Let us review each of the three stages of development in more detail, beginning with the elite studies, moving to the pluralist alternative, and culminating in a comparative stage of study.

AN ELITE GOVERNS: FLOYD HUNTER AND THE REPUTATIONALISTS

As earlier discussions have emphasized, a careful student of urban politics cannot simply assume that the formal officeholders are the real decision makers. Sociologist C. Wright Mills, who pronounced the existence of a national power elite, argued that, "the power to make decisions of national and international consequence is now so clearly seated in political, military, and economic institutions that other areas of society seem off to the side and, on occasion, readily subordinated to these."[3] Mills' counterpart on the local level was Floyd Hunter, also a sociologist. Hunter's study of Atlanta pioneered the use of the reputational technique and found an elite.[4] Hunter's work inspired a number of subsequent studies, and because of its seminal role we need to examine that study more carefully.

The reputational technique starts from the common sense assumption that if you want to know who is in charge of a city, you ask people who ought to know. The muckraking journalist, Lincoln Steffans, had taken this direct approach;[5] Hunter formalized it for his own research. First, he obtained four kinds of lists of leaders, which he had solicited from civic organizations: a list of community affairs leaders from the Community Council; a list of business and financial leaders from the Chamber of Commerce; a list of "local political leaders who had at least major governmental committee chairmanship status"[6] from the League of Women Voters; and lists of socially prominent and wealthy members of the city from newspaper editors and other civic leaders. These lists gave Hunter a total of more than 175 preliminary names. He then asked a panel of fourteen judges, chosen because of their long-standing acquaintance with activities in a variety of institutional sectors of the city, to say who were the top leaders on each of the four types of lists. Hunter reports that the fourteen judges "revealed a high degree of correlation in their choices," leaving him with a roster of forty people who were most mentioned.[7] The top twenty-seven of those nominated were interviewed and asked to pick the top ten community leaders from the list of forty names or to add others not on the list. In this way the listings gradually came to show the recurrence of certain names which Hunter concluded were the most influential decision makers in Atlanta.

Atlanta, as Hunter found it, was run by a small group of powerful men. As he describes them, they interacted socially and they determined the outlines of policy for Atlanta informally and behind the scenes. The Atlanta elite was not an equal opportunity organization: "The test for admission to this circle of decision-makers," according to Hunter, "is almost wholly a man's position in the business community in [Atlanta]."[8] As Table 10.1 shows, eighteen of the forty top leaders in Atlanta were engaged in commercial or financial activities. The domination of businessmen is a common finding among those using the reputational technique.

A second important characteristic of Atlanta's elite was that they operated covertly rather than overtly; they interacted socially, made policy determinations, and then passed those decisions along to the "understructure of power," the actual officeholders who implemented the policy. As Hunter puts it, "Organizational leaders are prone to get the publicity; the upper echelon economic leaders the power."[9] The major political figures of the city,

Table 10.1   Occupational Characteristics of Top Leaders in Atlanta

Occupation	Number of Leaders	Positions Held
Banking, finance, insurance	7	President, executive vice-president, etc.
Commercial	11	Board chairman, president, editor, etc.
Government	4	Mayor, superintendent of city or county schools, county treasurer
Labor	2	Local union president
Leisure	5	Social leader
Manufacturing, industry	5	Board chairman, president
Professional	6	Attorney, dentist
Total	40	

Source: Adapted from Floyd Hunter, *Community Power Structure* (Chapel Hill, N.C.: University of North Carolina Press, 1953). Table 4.

according to Hunter, were members of the understructure. Atlanta's power structure was not benevolent; rather, it ruled in its own self-interest. And since it held the upper hand, its major policy goal was simply to prevent drastic change. Again quoting Hunter, "When new policy is laid down it must be consistent with the general scheme of old policy and should not radically change basic alignments of settled policy . . . so that the basic equilibrium in the social systems of the community may undergo as little disruption as possible."[10]

The reputational technique has been used in a variety of cities with some minor variations but with the same fundamental finding — that an elite governs. For example, in Baton Rouge,[11] it was found that "the control of community affairs and policies resides in dominant interest groups which feel little incentive to disrupt the existing pattern of superordination and subordination."[12] The reputational technique was also used to study the northern cities of Ypsilanti, Michigan, and Seattle, Washington. Both cities were found to be substantially dominated by a small power group, although in Ypsilanti the power structure was called "bifurcated" — that is, shared between the economic leaders who monopolized a potential for determinative action and a new power group "of middle class business and professional men."[13]

In sum, Hunter and the many researchers who have followed him tend to find their case study cities dominated by a ruling elite composed primarily of businessmen. The elite functions conspiratorially, rather than openly, in that (1) they meet behind the scenes and decide the public policies they want; (2) they are not elected or otherwise responsible to the citizenry; and (3) they prescribe rules that sometimes promote, but more often protect, their own selfish interests.

If these studies could be proved to be reliable (their reliability is called into doubt in the following critique), they would be strong evidence of one of the major assumptions that runs through this book — that is, that local politics is directly tied to the economic system. Needless to say, these findings fit the ideological expectations of those on the political Left. The Left has long argued that the business system dominates American life. Marxism, for example, has held that those who dominate the means of production dominate the other institutions of the culture as well. This congruence of Hunter's findings with New Left analysis has not been lost on those who dispute the existence of an elite in our cities. Let us turn now to their alternative view.

Critique of the Reputational Technique

Despite the enthusiasm of many political scientists for Hunter's approach, there has also developed a strong body of negative criticism, especially among those who studied New Haven, Connecticut's public leadership: Robert Dahl, Nelson Polsby, and Raymond Wolfinger, in particular. Their rejection of reputational technique and its findings is total; Wolfinger calls the studies a "dry hole" and asks,

> What should be made of the reputational method? It requires a factual assumption that is obviously false; its findings are often invalidated and never confirmed; and its product conveys very little useful information about a local political system.[14]

This harsh conclusion is the necessary result of three major criticisms of the reputational technique. First, and most fundamentally, the critics argue that the reputation for power may not be equitable with actual power. If a man's life work has been banking, the critics insist, a researcher should presume that the banker will spend his time at the bank and not in manipulating community decisions, "until the banker's *activities* and *participations* indicate otherwise. . . . "[15] In other words, to accept the reputation for power is to accept hearsay evidence. Since the exercise of power requires action, the critics argue that one should observe some power-directed action before one proclaims a powerholder. (The gap between reputation and reality is a lesson many of us learned the first time we dated someone with a reputation.)

Some defenders of the reputational technique respond to this criticism of hearsay evidence by asserting that reputation may well disclose those with a high potential for power. The critics counter that this possible advantage is likely to be misleading, taking the researcher on a fruitless chase for phantom decision makers. As Dahl says,

> If the overt leaders of a community do not . . . constitute a ruling elite, then [a finding of elite control] can be saved by arguing that behind the overt leaders is a set of covert leaders who do. If subsequent evidence shows that this covert group does not make a ruling elite, then the theory can be saved by arguing that behind the first covert group there is another and so on.[16]

A second major objection to the reputational technique is that it contains the embedded assumption that the power structure is stable over time and does not change substantially from issue to issue. This assumption offends our common sense. There seems to be too much going on in a city for a power elite to dominate it all. In any case, the assumption takes as given what should be a hypothesis for ongoing investigation. As Polsby puts it, " . . . power may be tied to issues, and issues can be fleeting or persistent, provoking coalitions among interested groups and citizens ranging in their duration from momentary to semipermanent."[17] To make any other assumption, the critics urge, is to introduce systematic inaccuracies into the study.

Finally, the critics of the reputational technique attack the assumption that there is, in fact, an ordered system of power which has simply to be discovered. By asking the question, "Who rules this city?" the reputationalist researcher puts his interviewee in the position of answering a "have you stopped beating your wife yet?" kind of question. Virtually any response short of a total unwillingness to answer supplies the researcher with a power structure. This situation results from the fundamental assumption of the reputationalists that there is, in fact, structured power in any given city. The critics urge that nothing categorical should be assumed about power in any setting. "If anything there seems to be an unspoken notion among pluralist researchers that at bottom *nobody* dominates in a town, so that their first question is not likely to be 'Who runs this community?' but 'Does anyone at all run this community?' "[18]

These are by no means all the objections that have been raised to the work of Hunter and his followers. It does, however, reflect the seriousness and the high points of that criticism.[19] As the criticisms imply, the critics have an alternative technique of local leadership study in mind. Specifically, they recommend the analysis of the *actual behavior* of decision makers as they *participate in the resolution of specific issues.*

PLURAL ELITES GOVERN: ROBERT DAHL AND THE ISSUE AREA ANALYSTS

While they were honing their criticism of the reputational technique, a group of political scientists called issue area analysts were developing an alternative method of inquiry. The first and most influential formulation of the alternative approach to the study of local power holding was that of Robert Dahl and his associates, who examined New Haven.[20] The major steps of the procedure utilized in the study of New Haven were as follows:

1. Selecting Key Issues   Every city has experienced conflicts over questions of public policy. During such a conflict, political actors are required to act in behalf of their goal. The researcher's first task, then, is to determine which have been the key issues in the recent past of the city. It has proved a complicated task to choose key issues because it is unclear what is properly defined as a key issue. Is it an issue that is representative of other issues and disputes within the city? Or is it a unique issue that happens to be of great importance to the life of the city? Or is it something else?[21] The New Haven study selected the key issues to study for political actors' involvement by using "one or another, or a combination" of four criteria to judge each issue: (a) the number of people affected by the issue outcome; (b) how many different kinds of community resources were distributed by the outcome; (c) what amount of resources were distributed by the outcome; and (d) how drastically the outcome of the issue altered the distribution of community resources.[22] Accordingly, the New Haven study focused on three major types of issues: contests for political nominations, decisions regarding urban redevelopment, and a series of decisions on public education.

2. Designating the Stages in the Resolution of Each Issue   Public issues, especially complicated ones, are resolved in a variety of settings and at different times. Issue area analysts insist on the need to specify each major phase of decision making. Dahl, for example, designated eight such stages of decision making on the issue of redeveloment between 1950 and 1959 — including, for example, the creating of the redevelopment agency, the redeveloping of the Church Street area, and negotiations between a local merchant and the city over the proper price for his property.[23] Such a procedural choice, of course, leads the researcher to study public decision-making sessions among officials.

3. Observing Actual Decision-Making Behavior at Each Stage   Pluralists demand systematic observation of the actual behavior of those individuals participating in the resolution of the issue during the period in which the conflict is being resolved. The New Haven study attempted a quantitative expression of the influence of particular actors by observing "the number of successful initiations or vetoes by each participant and the number of failures."[24] In this way, a numerical score was compiled, changing from one decision-making stage to the next. Thus, according to Dahl, a particular participant should be considered influential if "the relative frequency of his successes out of all successes is higher, or the ratio of his successes to his total attempts is higher than other participants."[25] Dahl did not use this quantitative material without referring to the settings in which particular actors decided; in other words, Dahl used qualitative data to supplement these materials.

In this way, the issue area analysts gather the necessary materials to determine which of the actors who participate in the resolution of an issue are the most powerful. By proceeding in this way, it is possible to determine whether or not power is structured and exercised by a dominant few. If, say the issue area analysts, the same people are influential in all the issues studied, then it can be said that there exists a power structure. If, on the other hand, different people are influential from issue to issue, then another formulation is necessary. A summary figure for the issue area analysts, then, is the number of participants who *overlap* several issues; that is, the number of leaders who are active in more than one issue area.

Dahl's substantive findings in New Haven were a complete contrast to Hunter's in Atlanta. Hunter did not calculate an overlap figure, but presumably it is near 100 percent. By contrast Dahl found only a 6 percent overlap. Dahl found no ruling elite in New Haven, but instead coalitions and leaders which shifted from issue to issue. Within this pattern "only the Mayor was a member of all the major coalitions, and in each of them he was one of the two or three men of highest influence."[26] Dahl calls this pattern of local decision making the "executive-centered coalition." Also in contrast to the Atlanta study, it was concluded that New Haven economic and social leaders had "relatively little direct influence on government decisions."[27] Far from being ubiquitous, businessmen in New Haven were found to be relatively unimportant participants, specializing primarily in the issue which most directly affected their immediate interests, urban redevelopment. In connection with that issue, urban redevelopment, Mayor Lee had created a Citizens Action Commission (CAC) which included the heads of most of New Haven's largest business firms. But careful analysis of the activities of the CAC caused the

New Haven researchers to conclude that they acted as a rubber stamp for the mayor rather than as major formulators of policies; "we were able to uncover only a very few trivial instances in which modifications were made in the plans presented by city technicians."[28] Finally, by demonstrating the centrality of elected officials to the decision-making process, the study lends support to the conclusion that New Haven politics was characterized by a high degree of citizen control over the making of public policy. New Haven, in other words, was found to fit well the theoretical formulation of pluralist democracy.

Critique of the Issue Area Technique

While the issue area approach overcomes a number of the problems identified in the reputational technique, it contains some conceptual and methodological pitfalls of its own. Most importantly, the issue area approach, by focusing on the behavior of decision makers, may overlook more subtle influences on decision making. Peter Bachrach and Morton Baratz insist that an adequate conception of decision making must include study of what they call nondecision-making behavior — that is, behavior of those outside the actual decisional setting. They criticize the issue area technique because it "takes no account of the fact that power may be, and often is, exercised by confining the scope of decision-making to relatively 'safe' issues."[29]

> Of course power is exercised when A participates in the making of decisions that affect B. But power is also exercised when A devotes his energies to creating reinforcing social and political values and institutional practices that limit the scope of the political process to public consideration of only those issues which are comparatively innocuous to A.[30]

Nondecision making is a highly abstract conception. The best way I know to clarify the central concern of nondecision making is with an illustration — this one from my own experience in education: My first full-time teaching job was at a small liberal arts university. Shortly after arriving on campus, I sat in on a discussion in the faculty club among members of the drama department who were trying to select the plays to be produced in the upcoming year. They were considering plays which I personally considered unimaginative and uninteresting. Tactfully, I think, I raised that point. One committee member explained to me that most of them would prefer to work with avant-garde materials but that they thought it was useless to consider them because of the past actions of the university's president. The previous year, the president had canceled a controversial play while it was in rehearsal, only one week prior to its performance. The president had claimed that it would offend the university's constituency. In the decision-making session I was watching then, the president was a nondecision maker. He was not physically present and did not participate in the deliberations, yet his past actions influenced the active decision makers, causing them to anticipate that his behavior would be similar in the future; as a consequence, they limited themselves to the consideration of "safe" alternatives.

If patterns like this one occur in public decision making — and nearly everyone who has participated in it seems to recognize such situations intuitively, then it must be said that the issue area technique leaves them unconsidered. This illustration conveys but one form of nondecision making, "anticipated reactions," which simply stated means that decision makers will limit themselves if they anticipate hostility from persons they perceive to be important.

Bachrach and Baratz also suggest that those who seek control over active decision makers may achieve it as well through the manipulation of values, myths, political procedures, and rules of the game. They point out that organizations in general, by their very nature, perpetuate and organize particular sets of "biases" which predispose active decision makers to behave in particular ways and to refrain from acting in others. However provocative the hypothesis of nondecision making may be, the supposition that it operates in American political life is still unverified. There have been a few empirical studies using the concept, but recent criticism of the nondecision-making hypothesis makes clear how difficult research will be that might attempt verification.[31]

A second point to keep in mind in evaluating the issue area technique is more a caution than a criticism. Although the pluralists strain toward careful use of scientific method, and thus lay claim to "objectivity," pluralism has an ideological coloration of its own. Pluralist democracy, as it appears in the local decision-making studies, is reconstituted liberalism.[32] Neoliberals have a strong faith in certain procedures — elections, free speech, secret ballots, civil rights, party politics, for example. So long as these procedures are intact the neoliberal presumes operative democracy exists while at the same time he can recognize some uncomfortable realities: "the reality of mass emotion, self-interest, group egotism, and the prevalence of oligarchic and hierarchal social and economic organizations need no longer be denied in the name of democratic values."[33] More specifically, associating pluralists with neoliberalism, of course, does not invalidate their findings. It does, however, caution us in interpreting them. Even if pluralist findings are correct, they demonstrate only that procedural democracy is intact. That the *process* be democratic is a necessary condition of democracy, we can agree, but it is not a sufficient condition. Outcomes must be broadly acceptable as well.

Other objections have been raised to the issue area technique: (1) that it provides insufficiently detailed criteria for distinguishing "key" issues from trivial ones;[34] (2) that it ignores the cumulative impact of routine decisions;[35] (3) that it gives insufficient place to the impact of ideologies and particularly the shared ideological perspectives of leaders.[36]

ONGOING RESEARCH: THE COMPARATIVE PHASE

Thus far, our examination seems to show that the leading attempts to demonstrate or deny the existence of a power structure in American cities have fallen short. Moreover, there is no easy way to reconcile these strongly held diverging views. But one suspects, as in many disagreements, that the disputants are talking past each other on important questions. After trying several ways of reconciling the divergencies between Hunter's and Dahl's techniques and their findings, one observer concluded that "the disciplinary background of the investigator tends to determine the method of investigation he will adopt, which, in turn, tends to determine the image of the power structure that results from the investigation."[37]

The most important conditions precedent to reconciliation of those contending viewpoints in future power studies are five: (1) development of a framework to permit systematic comparative studies; (2) agreement on the meanings of the central terms used in the studies; (3) standardization of the

Table 10.2   Four Dimensions of Power Structure

"Pluralist" Structure	Dimension	"Monolithic" Structure
Leaders hold public or associational office	LEGITIMACY ←——→	Leaders do not hold public or associational office
Leaders are recognized by general public	VISIBILITY ←——→	Leaders are unknown to general public
Leaders do not form a cohesive, interacting group	COHESIVENESS ←——→	Leaders form a cohesive, interacting group
Leaders are specialized and exercise power in one or a few policy areas	SCOPE OF INFLUENCE ←——→	Leaders are general and exercise power in most or all policy areas

Source: Adapted from Charles M. Bonjean and David M. Olson, "Community Leadership: Directions of Research," *Administrative Science Quarterly* 8 (December 1964): 291-300.

Table 10.3   **Typology of Power**

Political Leadership's Ideology	Distribution of Political Power Among Citizens	
	Broad	*Narrow*
Convergent	Consensual Mass	Consensual Elite
Divergent	Competitive Mass	Competitive Elite

Source: Robert Agger, Daniel Goldrich, and Bert Swanson, *The Rulers and the Ruled,* Rev. Ed. (N. Scituate, Mass.: Duxbury Press, 1972), p. 38.

processes for choosing and justifying particular issues to be studied; (4) research strategies which will enable description of relationships between local leaders and leaders at other levels of government — county, state and national — government and (5) a satisfactory operationalization and testing of the nondecision-making hypothesis.

There have been a number of attempts to provide a comparative framework for the study of power structures. The most common formulation for comparative study presumes that there are two polar types of power structure — centralized (elitist) and decentralized (pluralistic). As Table 10.2 shows, the differences between the two poles involve the dimensions of legitimacy, visibility, cohesiveness, and scope of influence. It is, of course, doubtful that any particular city could be characterized as completely monolithic or completely decentralized. One can expect most cities to fall somewhere along a continuum between these two poles.

Other students of power structure have argued for a more complex set of categories. Agger, Goldrich, and Swanson suggest that there are at least four types of power structures.[38] As Table 10.3 shows, they believe that regimes should be classified in terms of these criteria: (1) whether there is a broad or a narrow distribution of power among citizens, and (2) whether the political leadership's ideologies are convergent or divergent. To illustrate, it may well be that there is a high level of agreement among a particular city's leadership on its ideology and that there is very little power exercised by the citizens. Using the criteria of Table 10.3, an observer would classify the power structure of such a city as "consensual elite." This classification scheme of

Agger, Goldrich, and Swanson seems a useful extension, but it has been little used since it was originally formulated.

What comparative study has been accomplished thus far has tended to use the twofold classification of decentralized vs. centralized structures of power. The comparative studies to date have found that a number of conditions within particular cities are associated with the structure of political power there. These propositions are tentative and not "laws of politics." Still, some of them can usefully be reviewed since they highlight the characteristics of the city which correspond to concentration and dispersal of political power. In general, the comparative studies have found that American cities are becoming more decentralized in their decision-making structure.[39] This fact seems at least partially related to the growth in size of American cities. The larger cities tend to exhibit power structures that are more pluralist in nature than those of small cities. However, the evidence for that proposition is mixed, and the most broadly based comparative study to date reveals only a moderate relationship between city size and decentralized decision-making structures.[40] It is more firmly established that the smaller communities tend toward elite domination.[41] Population size appears to be less important in shaping the power structure than is the social and economic heterogeneity that attends population growth. Clark has found pluralistic power structures in 'ties with a diversified economic system, with a more industrial economic base, with a larger proportion of absentee-owned enterprises, and where there are strong labor unions. In addition, decentralized decision making is likely to be found in cities in which there are larger numbers of groups (secondary associations). Finally, decentralized decision making is associated with certain governmental and political patterns: where local political leadership believes in and emphasizes widespread citizen participation and political equality, decision-making structures tend to reflect that.

Paradoxically, it has been found that the higher the level of reformism undertaken by a city, the more monolithic is its decision-making structure. As our earlier discussion of reformism indicated, reform is usually purchased at the expense of minorities, an assumption which this finding corroborates. Nonpartisanship, for example, is more commonly associated with monolithic structures of power. The propositions which these findings suggest are put for your further study and reflection in List 10.1.

SUMMARY

We have seen that studies of community power have moved through a case study phase and through a deadlock over techniques into a period in which comparative studies are generating a number of useful findings. That

List 10.1   Propositions Associating City Characteristics with Structure of Power

1. *The larger the number of inhabitants in a community, the more pluralistic is the power structure.*

2. *The more diversified the economic system within a community, the more pluralistic is the power structure.*

3. *The more industrialized the community, the more pluralistic is the power structure.*

4. *The stronger labor unions are in a community, the more pluralistic is the power structure.*

5. *The larger the proportion of absentee-owned enterprises in a community, the more pluralistic is the power structure.*

6. *The more socially heterogeneous the community, the more pluralistic is the power structure.*

7. *Pluralism is promoted by community and, particularly, elite attitudes emphasizing widespread participation and political equality.*

8. *The larger the number of secondary associations in the community, the greater is the probability of pluralism.*

9a. *Nonpartisanship is more commonly associated with monolithic structures of power.*

9b. *Competitive party politics is more commonly associated with pluralistic structures of power.*

10. *The higher the level of reformism of political institutions (form of government, type of elections, and type of constituencies), the more monolithic is the decision-making structure.*

11. *Competition among different elements of the power structure is a necessary condition for widespread citizen participation.*

Source: Adapted from Robert Lineberry and Ira Sharkansky, *Urban Politics and Public Policy* (New York: Harper & Row, 1971), pp. 159-161.

history and this discussion should make it clear that our early tendencies to generalize about all American cities were oversimple. Most American cities fall somewhere on a continuum between elite domination and decentralized decision making. We also have good reason to believe that social, economic, demographic, and governmental characteristics of the particular city heavily influence the shape of the power structure.[42] When we know the configuration of the exercise of power in a particular city, then we have taken a long step toward understanding how and in what terms public policy will be formulated there. If a consensual elite governs, we shall expect policy that serves those interests; where decision making is more decentralized, we can expect the political process to more nearly approximate the assumption of pluralist democracy.

Pluralism, we should recall, gives to the formal decision makers a central place in the formulation of policy and in the adoption and application of policy. Let us turn in Chapter 11 to a discussion of those public decision makers.

NOTES

1. Kenneth Prewitt and Alan Stone, *The Ruling Elites* (New York: Harper & Row, 1973).
2. Terry N. Clark, "Community Structure, Decision-Making, Budget Expenditures, and Urban Renewal in 51 American Communities," in *Community Politics: A Behavioral Approach*, eds. Charles M. Bonjean, Terry N. Clark, and Robert L. Lineberry (New York: Free Press of Glencoe, 1971), p. 311.
3. C. Wright Mills, *The Power Elite* (New York: Oxford University Press, 1956), p. 16.
4. Floyd Hunter, *Community Power Structure* (Chapel Hill: University of North Carolina Press, 1953).
5. See M. Kent Jennings, *Community Influentials* (New York: Free Press of Glencoe, 1964).
6. Ibid., p. 269.
7. Ibid.
8. Hunter, *Community Power Structure*, p. 79.
9. Ibid., pp. 86-87.
10. Ibid., p. 209.
11. Ronald J. Pellegrin and Charles H. Coates, "Absentee-Owned Corporations and Community Power Structure," *American Journal of Sociology* 61 (March 1956): 413-419.
12. Ibid., p. 413.
13. The study of Ypsilanti is by Robert O. Schulze, "The Bifurcation of Power in a Satellite Community," in *Community Political Systems*, ed. Morris Janowitz (New York: Free Press of Glencoe, 1961). And there have been several studies of Seattle. See, for example, Delbert C. Miller, "Industry and Community Power Structure," *American Sociological Review* 23 (February 1958): 9-15; and Ernest A. T. Barth and Baha Abu-Laban, "Power Structure and the Negro Subcommunity," *American Sociological Review* 24 (February 1959): 69-76. These studies are carefully critiqued by Nelson W. Polsby in *Community Power and Political Theory* (New Haven: Yale University Press, 1963), pp. 56-68. The only instances in which users of the reputational technique have not found an elite involve studies of cities in other countries. Cf. William H. Form and William V. D'Antonio, "Integration and Cleavage Among Community Influentials in Two Border Cities," *American Sociological Review* 24 (October 1959): 804-814; Delbert C. Miller, "Industry and Community Power Struc-

ture: A Comparative Study of an American and an English City," *American Sociological Review* 23 (February 1958): 9-15; and Orin E. Klapp and L. Vincent Padgett, "Power Structure and Decision-Making in a Mexican Border City," *American Journal of Sociology* 65 (January 1960): 400-406. For additional bibliography and discussion, there are a number of reviews of the literature. A useful book, though now becoming somewhat dated, is Wendell Bell, Richard J. Hill, and Charles R. Wright, *Public Leadership* (San Francisco: Chandler Publishing Co., 1961). Also see the bibliography compiled by Ronald J. Pellegrin, "Selected Bibliography on Community Power Structure," *Social Science Quarterly* 48 (December 1967): 451-465; and Michael T. Aiken and Paul Mott, *The Structure of Community Power* (New York: Random House, 1970).

14. Raymond E. Wolfinger, "A Plea for a Decent Burial," *American Sociological Review* 27 (December 1962): 845.

15. Nelson Polsby, "How to Study Community Power: The Pluralist Alternative," *Journal of Politics* 22 (August 1960): 481.

16. Robert A. Dahl, "Critique of the Ruling Elite Model," *American Political Science Review* 52 (June 1958): 463.

17. Polsby, "How to Study Community Power," p. 478.

18. Ibid.

19. For a more exhaustive discussion, see Nelson Polsby, *Community Power and Political Theory* (New Haven: Yale University Press, 1963), Chap. 3.

20. See Robert A. Dahl, *Who Governs? Democracy and Power in an American City* (New Haven: Yale University Press, 1961). Companion volumes were written by Dahl's associates in the New Haven study and include Nelson Polsby's *Community Power and Political Theory* and Raymond E. Wolfinger's *The Politics of Progress* (Englewood Cliffs, N.J.: Prentice-Hall, 1972).

21. This problem is discussed at greater length in Raymond E. Wolfinger, "Nondecisions and the Study of Local Politics," *American Political Science Review* 65 (December 1971): 1064-1065; and also by Frederick W. Frey, "Comment: On Issues and Nonissues in the Study of Power," in the same volume, pp. 1081-1088.

22. From Polsby, *Community Power and Political Theory*, p. 96.

23. See Dahl, *Who Governs?* pp. 333-334.

24. Ibid., p. 333.

25. Ibid.

26. Dahl, *Who Governs?* p. 200.

27. Ibid., p. 233.

28. Polsby, *Community Power and Political Theory*, p. 73.

29. Peter Bachrach and Morton Baratz, "Two Faces of Power," *American Political Science Review* 61 (December 1962): 948-949.

30. Ibid., p. 948.

31. Bachrach and Baratz have themselves used nondecision making in a study of the poverty program in Baltimore. See *Power and Poverty* (New York: Oxford University Press, 1970). Those who are skeptical of the nondecision-making hypothesis argue principally that it is not amenable to empirical testing, par-

ticularly, that is it nonfalsifiable (that is, that there is no way to put an empirically testable opposite hypothesis). In addition to the works by Raymond E. Wolfinger, "Nondecisions and the Study of Local Politics," and Frederick W. Frey, "Comment: On Issues and Nonissues in the Study of Power," previously cited, see also Richard Merelman, "On the Neo-Elitist Critique of Community Power," *American Political Science Review* 62 (June 1968): 451-460.

32. David M. Ricci, "Background to the Study of Community Power: Liberalism, Its Decline, Power Analysis, and After," in *Political Power, Community and Democracy*, eds. Edward Keynes and David M. Ricci (Chicago: Rand, McNally, 1970), pp. 3-24. Also see Ricci's *Community Power and Democratic Theory* (New York: Random House, 1971). A parallel argument is found in Peter Bachrach, *The Theory of Democratic Elitism: A Critique* (Boston: Little, Brown, 1967).

33. Lane Davis, "The Cost of Realism: Contemporary Restatements of Democracy," *Western Political Quarterly* 17 (March 1964): 39.

34. Wolfinger, in defending the issue area approach, argues only that the issues studied in New Haven were important. Wolfinger, "Nondecisions and the Study of Local Politics," pp. 1064-1065. Differing viewpoints are found in Andrew S. McFarland, *Power and Leadership in Pluralist Systems* (Stanford: Stanford University Press, 1969); and Frey, "Comment:", pp. 1086-1088.

35. Cf. Ira Sharkansky, *The Routines of Politics* (New York: Van Nostrand and Reinhold, 1970), especially Chap. 2.

36. See particularly Robert Agger, Daniel Goldrich, and Bert E. Swanson, *The Rulers and the Ruled* (New York: John Wiley and Sons, 1964), pp. 76-77.

37. John Walton, "Discipline, Method and Community Power: A Note on the Sociology of Knowledge," *American Sociological Review* 31 (October 1966): 688.

38. Agger, Goldrich, and Swanson, *Rulers and the Ruled*, pp. 73-78.

39. These materials are taken primarily from Terry N. Clark, "Community Structure and Decision-Making," in *Community Structure and Decision-Making: Comparative Analyses*, ed. Terry N. Clark (San Francisco: Chandler Publishing Co., 1968), pp. 91-126. Additional pertinent material is found in Clair W. Gilbert, "Community Power and Decision-Making: A Quantitative Examination of Previous Research," pp. 139-156 in the same volume, and also Robert Presthus, *Men at the Top* (New York: Oxford University Press, 1964), especially pp. 93-95.

40. Terry N. Clark, "Community Structure, Decision-Making, Budget Expenditures, and Urban Renewal in 51 American Communities," *American Sociological Review* 33 (August 1968): 576-593.

41. Cf. Gilbert, "Community Power and Decision Making"; also Arthur Vidich and Joseph Bensman, *Small Town in Mass Society* (Princeton: Princeton University Press, 1958).

42. See on this point, Edward T. Hayes, *Power Structure and Urban Policy: Who Rules In Oakland?* (New York: McGraw-Hill, 1972).

Chapter 11

Policy Adoption and Application: The Formal Decision Makers

As the last chapter made clear, we cannot simply assume that the official decision makers of the city are the sole conflict managers. Still, they are involved. In this chapter we shall examine the role of mayor, city manager, city council, and bureaucracies in coping with urban political conflict. We begin by considering the legal-institutional setting in which those decision makers operate.

FORMAL STRUCTURES OF LOCAL GOVERNMENT

The structure of government does have an effect on policy. It affects the access and influence of particular groups and it defines constraints on officeholders. It would, of course, be impossible to reproduce here the details of the governmental organization in specific cities; we must settle for a workable simplification. It is possible to classify cities as having governmental structures of three types: council and manager, mayor and council, or commission.

Council - Manager Form

There are certain features of the council-manager plan which occur consistently, distinguishing it from other forms of city government (see Figure 11.1).[1]
1. A popularly elected city council with legislative powers is created. There are some variations among council-manager cities as to the size and method of selection of the council; but in general, the number of councilmen is small, usually nine or less. The council is characteristically elected at large and on nonpartisan ballots.

2. A chief administrative officer or city manager is chosen by the council. As a general rule, the manager is chosen because he has specialized, professional training or experience in urban administration. He serves as long as the majority of the city council is satisfied with his work.

3. The other major administrative officers, department heads, and the like are appointed by the manager and serve at his pleasure.

4. There is often a presiding officer for the city council who is given the title of mayor. He is a regular voting member of the council but usually possesses no more administrative authority than any other council member; he simply presides at meetings. The only other functions of the mayor are ceremonial.

In terms of our previous discussion of reform, we would find that the council-manager form approximates the corporate form. By separating politics from administration, its proponents believe it promotes greater efficiency and economy than the alternative modes of urban governmental organization.

Mayor - Council Form

Slightly more than fifty percent of our cities are governed by the form of organization known as the mayor-council (see Figure 11.2). The usual characteristics of this plan are:

1. A mayor who is the chief executive of the city and who is popularly elected.

2. A city legislative body called either a council or a board of aldermen who are popularly elected. Most often the city councilmen are elected from districts or wards. This, however, need not be the case.

3. Additional administrative officers may either be popularly elected or appointed by the mayor. Where appointed by the mayor, these officials usually must be approved by the council. These administrative officers are responsible for the day-to-day operation of the city government.

4. In very small cities there may be one or more municipal courts with the mayor acting as judge; but in the larger cities, judges are either popularly elected or appointed by the mayor with council approval. As the oldest form of local government, the mayor-council form resembles the national government. The fact that the structures are more separated than they are in the council-manager form suggests a kind of "separation of powers" in it. Here, as elsewhere, the idea of "separation of powers" is more accurately thought of as a *sharing* of powers. The mayor has the veto power; he has the power to address the council and is often able to exercise a strong position of political leadership; and he is generally charged with the supervision of administration. On the other hand, the council controls the purse strings and ratifies appointments by the mayor. Many charters provide that the mayor

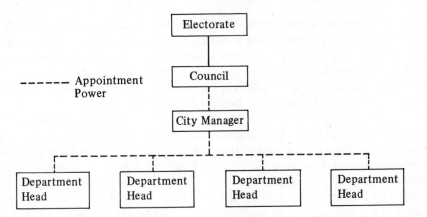

Figure 11.1. The council - manager form of government.

can be removed by the council before his regular term expires. The federal government analogy does not apply to council sessions, however, for these are administered by the mayor.

As mayor-council government has evolved over a long period of time, it has adapted to the particular environment of the city in which it is set and has been transformed by specific issues and controversies within that city. As a result there are important variations in the form from city to city. Two variations are most common: the weak mayor form and the strong mayor form. In essence, the weak mayor is one who has very little control over the several elements of the local administration. There may be a large

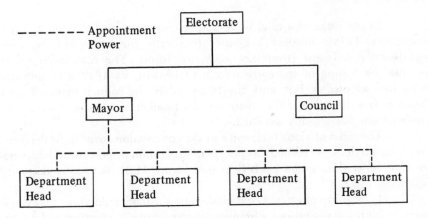

Figure 11.2. The mayor - council form of government.

number of elected administrators, and many boards and commissions which are only tentatively responsible to the mayor; in this situation, there is little possibility that the mayor can achieve administrative coherence and secure control. Because he can neither appoint nor remove key administrative officers, the mayor is unable to direct any of them to fit their statements and policies into a single pattern of broad policies of his design.

In the strong mayor version, there is considerably more administrative integration. The mayor is able to exercise control over other administrative departments and officers because they are appointed by him rather than elected. If they defy his will, he can remove them from office. However, the mayor appoints with the approval of the council and is also limited by the fact that not all municipal officers, even in the strongest mayor systems, are appointed. City treasurers, prosecuting officers, and comptrollers often are elective, even within a strong mayor system. In those cities in which the strong mayor has responsibility for preparation of the budget and also has a full-time professional administrative officer to aid him in his job, the strong mayor system comes to look very much like the reform ideal. The mayor resembles an elected manager.

We should not form the impression, however, that the leadership capacity of the mayor's office is determined by the structure of government. Strong personalities can make a strong mayor. Highly developed party organization can make a strong mayor. The city of Chicago would have to be classified organizationally as a weak mayor system. But the personality of Mayor Richard Daley has resulted in a mayor's office with considerable power; we shall turn to him again later in this chapter.

Commission Form

In the wake of a tidal wave that severely damaged the city in 1900, Galveston, Texas, adopted a charter that calls for a government form significantly different from the other two forms. The commission form became the darling of the early reform movement; by 1917, five hundred cities had adopted it. But since the 1920s, when the council-manager form began to fire the ardor of the reformers, the number of cities with governing commissions has steadily declined.

The most obvious difference in the commission form from the other two is that it does not embody a concept of separation of powers and does not provide for a chief executive officer (see Figure 11.3). It usually takes the following form:

1. A group of elected commissioners — usually from three to seven — exercise both legislative and administrative authority. Collectively, the commissioners act as a policy-making body, much as a city council does.

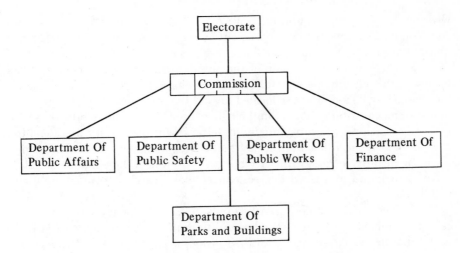

Figure 11.3. The commission form of government.

2. Often the commissioners appoint one of their number to act as mayor. He is regarded simply as the first among equals and seldom has any additional powers. He presides at commission meetings and performs ceremonial functions in the name of the city.

3. Each individual commissioner is elected to serve as head of one specific administrative department of the city, presumably because he is best qualified to administer that department. Acting in this capacity, he hires employees in his department, prepares estimates of his budgetary needs, decides matters of administrative policy, and, in general, functions as department head just as he would in any other form of government.

WHO ARE THE OFFICIAL DECISION MAKERS?

What kinds of people assume these official decision-making roles? Let us now discuss what we know about the kinds of people who become the leaders in the process of adopting and applying urban policy: councilmen, mayors, city managers, and city bureaucrats.

Councilmen

If anyone can become President, surely anyone can become a city councilman. That proposition is undoubtedly true, but we must reasonably deny that anyone can become President. In the same manner, we might well question the supposition that city councilmen can come from all social and economic stations; it is not borne out by realities. A number of careful inquiries have found that our elected leadership is not a mirror reflection of the social and economic composition of the population from which it comes. We have seen that elitism operates at all levels of American political decision making. "Some social strata, those located toward the upper end of the stratification system, contribute more than their share of offices. Other strata, those in the lower echelons, are substantially underrepresented in political leadership circles."[2] However, it has been found that city councilmen do not come from the most wealthy sectors of the city but instead "reflect the religious, ethnic, occupational, and to a lesser degree, educational diversity of a metropolitan middle class."[3]

There appears to be a range from which councilmen are recruited. In careful examination of city councilmen in the San Francisco Bay Area, it was found that this range shifted according to the social composition of the community. In cities with a large working-class population, the lower limit of the "ruling class" included union officials, public school teachers, craftsmen, and (from time to time) skilled laborers. In more middle-class cities, the lower limit was found to be set a bit higher: druggists, successful car salesmen, and realtors occasionally appeared on the councils, but union leaders, school teachers, and so forth fell below the social threshold. And, of course, in the upper-class city, even the middle-class entrepreneur discovers that his occupational status is more a liability than an asset in seeking public office.

Speaking in broadest terms, then, it is possible to discern a "typical" councilman. He is a white, middle-aged male, a businessman or professional; he is relatively well educated and most likely to have an upper-middle income; he is active in civic associations, and a Republican. Deviations from this pattern are associated with differences in the social rank and class composition of the city and the structure of city government. The cities with more well-educated and moneyed populations elect councilmen who come from higher status backgrounds, while working-class cities elect councilmen with working-class occupations.[4]

Of course social background and recruitment patterns of city councilmen are only one factor to consider in explaining the decisions these councilmen make in office. We cannot simply assume that a person makes decisions in behalf of the class or group from which he comes. It is possible for a rich man to make good policy for the poor.

A second factor which will have its impact on the decision-making behavior of a city councilman is whether or not he is politically ambitious — that is, whether he thinks of his present post as the end of his political career or whether he is preparing himself for higher or other political offices. There is a popular judgment, an outgrowth of typical antipolitical bias among

Americans, which condemns a politician with ambitions and extols the political amateur. Some of the empirical work on city councilmen provides grounds for reassessing that judgment. The San Francisco Bay Area studies found that the councilmen they classified as ambitious had a broader policy outlook than those who were not.[5] The ambitious councilman is more likely to recognize that problems and policies that affect the total Bay Area need to be considered by his local council. He is often favorable to attempts at the creation of regional governments. The politically ambitious councilman was found more likely to expand the powers of higher level governmental authorities. Finally, he was found to be more sensitive to the constituency which controls the office he aspires to than to other constituencies. Thus, we can expect that councils dominated by ambitious members will be more receptive to proposals for intergovernmental coordination than those dominated by political amateurs; perhaps the failure of regional government, then, is at least partially explained by the findings of the San Francisco Bay Area study — that 62 percent of the councilmen they interviewed were not politically ambitious and that only 17 percent were "clearly ambitious."[6]

Councilmen's roles

As with any formal position, there are a variety of ways that the formal office can be translated into action by the individual officeholder. For example, ward-based elections tend to produce councilmen who cast their role in terms of careful and literal representation of the immediate desires of their constituents. An extreme illustration is quoted in a study of a Michigan city that has a ward system. One councilman there is reported to have shouted to another at a meeting, "You bastard, you had three more blocks of blacktopping in your ward last year than I had. You'll not get another vote from me until I get three extra blocks."[7] This is, of course, an unattractive stance to a citizen who feels city councilmen ought to be cosmopolitan rather than localistic. However, if the citizen is convinced that his interests have been systematically neglected, he would probably cheer such a hard-hitting proponent of his cause.

Despite the persistence of the popular view that most councilmen think in terms of narrow representation of constituencies, studies of city councilmen consistently find the contrary.[8] To use the terminology of formal "role" study, most city councilmen perform in their representative role more as "trustees" than as "delegates."[9] By "delegate" role, we mean that the councilman feels bound to vote the interests and sentiments of his immediate constituents, even if they conflict with his own views. The "trustee" casts his role in terms of voting his own conscience and best judgment, even if it means contradicting the preferences of his constituents. Downes' study found that fully three-quarters of the St. Louis area city councilmen made decisions on the basis of their own judgment or principles — in other words, as trustees. The explanation for the tendency of city councilmen to vote their own consciences is important but unclear. Some scholars suggest that since councilmen are likely to be amateurs — part-time, and receiving low salaries — they feel free to ignore constituency pressures. Others suggest that city councilmen often have great difficulty in finding out what the public prefers. Since the electoral process and interest group activities convey unclear or conflicting pictures of constituency preferences, councilmen perhaps find it easier to use their own judgment than to find more accurate information.

Pluralist democratic assumptions would suggest that public decision makers are carefully attentive and responsive to the representatives of urban interests. However, it has been found that, congruent with the trustee orientation, most city councilmen are not as attentive to groups as we might expect. The San Francisco Bay Area study found that 43 percent of the councilmen they interviewed thought groups were useful; 44 percent were more neutral, indicating only that they thought groups had a right to be heard; while 13 percent felt a need to resist group pressures. One of the councilmen, who believed that group contact should be avoided, put it this way:

> I don't think groups should contact councilmen. They should take their problems directly to the city — to the staff or to the whole council. I don't trust points of view formed by small groups without open hearings and the other side being represented. I must be a little special in this.[10]

In general, then, most councilmen do not view interest group activities as indispensable to the political system; they do not share the assumptions of pluralist democracy. They find no reason to encourage group approaches and tend not to turn to groups for help. "It appears that the 'group struggle' in local political systems (at least in these 22 cities) takes place largely on a one-way street upon which relatively little traffic is noticed or invited by those who dwell at the upper end."[11] Exceptions to this pattern seem to occur in those cases in which groups are both recognized and valued by the city councilmen. These councilmen, who exhibit positive attitudes toward the group process, are pluralists; they were found to be not only receptive and accommodating toward community organization but also more likely to make legislative allies of such groups. However, they constitute only about one-quarter of the total sample of councilmen in the San Francisco Bay Area.

Councils as decision-making groups

How does a city council work? We all know that councils meet periodically, hear positions on public questions, debate, and decide on policy. If you ask a councilman on what basis they make those decisions he is likely to say, as one did to me, "We decide on the merits. The policy which is best for the city is the one we adopt." But if you need to know more fully why the council does what it does, you need to know much more than its formal mechanisms and that it engages in judicious consideration of the merits. Its decisions, its very conception of the good, emerges in part from the ongoing experience of relationships that develop among councilmen as they work together. Most councils, then, can be understood to be small groups in the social-psychological sense. That is, they develop a group identity and sometimes pride; they evolve informal rules prescribing appropriate and inappropriate behaviors; and they develop techniques for rewarding and punishing their members. The structure of the decision-making group and the outcome of its deliberations will be affected by its character as a small group. The group character of the city council needs to be emphasized because its importance is generally underestimated by most Americans. People do things in groups that they might not do as individuals. The group is indeed a powerful force in shaping behavior.[12] (See, for example, the treatment of groups in Chapter 4.) Group character is, of course, not peculiar to city councils. It occurs throughout American life.

Unfortunately, our research on the character of the council as a small group is still at the toddler stage. Even so, several studies indicate broad outlines. There is some evidence, for example, that city councilmen begin to learn group norms well before taking their seats; there is seldom a formal or informal crash socialization process for new councilmen.[13] From the study of the San Francisco Bay Area cities, Heinz Eulau, using sociometric analysis, found three types of council structures — unipolar, bipolar, and nonpolar.[14] A *unipolar* council is one in which all members tend to vote together, although there may be an occasional deviant. A *bipolar* council is one in which there is a relatively permanent division between two factions, although many such councils have swing voters who shift from time to time between factions. A *nonpolar* council is one which does not exhibit a recurrent voting pattern. Such a structure may contain a minority clique which votes together, but there is a sufficient degree of shifting around so that no consistent pattern emerges. Presumably, it is ideologies, friendships, constituency differences, and adaptation to group life, among other factors, which determine whether a particular council will become unipolar, bipolar, or nonpolar.

As study continues, several propositions seem to be emerging. A few of the more interesting are:

1. Councils characteristically have "opinion leaders" who function both as "catalyst of the mass mood and as transmitter of elite messages," thereby facilitating the integration of the council.[15]

2. Contrary to some expectations, swing voters, especially in bipolar councils, are not at all well respected.[16] The "swinger" is not revered for his

independence in bipolar councils but is, instead, more likely to be characterized as wishy-washy or undependable. In the bipolar councils of the San Francisco Bay Area, only 40 percent of the swingers were accorded respect by their fellow councilmen; while of the nonswingers, those who never crossed factional lines, 64 percent were named as respected.

3. It might be supposed that friendships are most characteristic of unipolar councils and least characteristic of bipolar structures. Such is not the case. The most conflictful city councils evidence the most declarations of friendship in the San Francisco Bay Area study.[17] Full explanation is not yet possible, but additional research has suggested that "the antagonistic atmosphere of the group as a whole seems to call out strong friendship relationships in the council's subgroups, but not across subgroup lines."[18]

4. Finally, there is apparently no impact of expertise on the decision-making structure of the council. Expertise as an attribute of the group may be present or absent, regardless of whether the decisional structure of the council is conflictful or harmonious, integrated or fragmented, permissive or constraining.[19]

What we now need to know more about is how different types of small-group structures affect the policies that each kind of council enacts. We might expect, for example, that bipolar councils would stalemate and produce very little public policy, and that decisions could be made only on trivial matters. We could expect unipolar councils to produce a volume of internally consistent policy in behalf of a unified position. And we could expect nonpolar councils either to be do-nothing councils or to reflect the diversity of the urban environment, in which case they would more properly be called multipolar. The multipolar council seems most compatible with a pluralist democratic process. But these policy implications are merely speculative; they are at the current frontier of our knowledge of the work of city councils.

Mayors

The role and effectiveness of American mayors varies with the structure of the city government, with the personality of the mayor, and with the political environment of the city. Before specifying the usual roles of urban mayors, we can observe the interplay of these forces on one of the most talked-about contemporary mayors, Richard J. Daley.

Profile of a mayor: Richard Daley of Chicago

Daley has served as mayor of Chicago since 1955. He remains, as of this writing, the captain of his old Eleventh Ward Democratic Committee and chairman of the Cook County Democratic Committee. The Committee is a powerful organization, which enables him to pick candidate slates, to distribute patronage, and to dominate nearly all of the fifty aldermen of Chicago's city council. Also, like the bosses of old, Daley wields influence that reaches beyond the city: a Democratic governor of Illinois must be responsive to his wishes; Chicago's nine-member delegation to the House of Representatives of the United States can usually be counted on to act promptly as Daley recommends; and the Cook County Democratic delegation to the Illinois legislature is firmly in his hands.[20]

Chicago has had a tradition of bosses. There was "Big Bill" Thompson, who was in control most of the time between 1915 and 1931. Thompson was a Republican boss, among other interesting activities. After his death, it was discovered that he had left a safe-deposit box stuffed with $1.5 million in cash. The machine of Democrat Ed Kelley succeeded Thompson, lasting about fifteen years (1933-1947). Kelley's most conspicuous activity was using his influence to provide his personal and political friend, contractor Pat Nash, with a great many lucrative public works projects. Then came reform. Democrat Martin Kennelley was elected in 1947, but as with so many reformers, his good intentions were not matched by an understanding of the politics of the situation into which he stepped. As a result, his popularity waned and he was unseated by Daley in 1955.

Daley's personal history is one of those great American stories of a boy born in the slums who made good with a little help from his friends. He was born in the poor Bridgeport district of Chicago near the stockyards. He worked in those same stockyards and sold newspapers on the street as a boy. Working his way up to clerk in a stockyards office, he went to night law school at DePaul University. At age twenty-five he was appointed secretary to the City Council. In 1936, upon the death of a state legislator from Daley's district, Democratic boss Ed Kelley and ward leader Jake Arvey gave the job to Daley. Daley moved up in the Kelley-Arvey machine; and when Adlai Stevenson became governor of Illinois in 1949, he repaid the support of the Chicago machine by making Daley the state director of revenues. But more important to Daley's political power, he was also made county clerk for Cook County. This put him in charge of all the voting machinery in the county and of a number of patronage positions as well. Unlike bosses of the past, and against the specific advice of Jake Arvey, Daley broke with the tradition that a boss should not run for public office himself but operate instead from behind the scenes. Winning the mayorship in 1955, Daley moved quickly to make himself the unchallenged leader of the Illinois Democrats. From that position Daley has since that time exercised considerable influence on even Presidential outcomes. Since Adlai Stevenson was not a machine Democrat, he and Daley remained somewhat cool toward one another; but Daley was a staunch supporter of John F. Kennedy. It was through Daley's efforts on election day in 1960 that Kennedy was able to carry the state of Illinois, thus turning the election tide in his favor as a result of a slim 9000-vote margin. Kennedy had lost the downstate vote badly but, thanks to the Daley machine, had piled up a 450,000-vote margin in Chicago. Daley easily weathered the later charges of voting irregularities in Chicago. At that time, Daley was considered the friend of liberal Democrats everywhere. He lost much of that goodwill in becoming the "villain" of the 1968 Democratic national convention by presiding over what was later called a police riot in suppressing antiwar demonstrations. A great many Daley critics lay the defeat of Hubert Humphrey to the violence at the convention and to the boss image Daley projected over national television. Many Americans still have a vivid recollection from television coverage — the mayor surrounded by people waving American flags and banners proclaiming "We love Mayor Daley," while he was shouting what seemed to be obscenities at Senator Abraham Ribicoff who was denouncing Daley from the rostrum.

It is Daley's personal style, in fact, which is often at issue when people decry him as a boss. Daley's personal appearance and his tangled grammar make him an easy target of middle-class whites and the liberal press. They also ensure his continued support among working Chicagoans. His rhetoric is often purple, as when he ran for mayor originally: "If I am elected," he said, "I will embrace mercy, love, charity, and walk humbly with my God." It is often unintentionally funny as well, as in the following exchange with attorney William Kunstler during the trial of the so-called Chicago Seven — the purported instigators of the demonstration at the Chicago convention:

> Kunstler: Mayor Daley, do you know a federal judge by the name of Judge Lynch?
>
> Witness: Do I know him?
>
> Kunstler: Yes.
>
> Witness: . . . We have been boyhood friends all our lives.[21]

And, "Together we must rise to ever higher and higher platitudes,"[22] and "Ladies and Gentlemen of the League of Women Voters."[23]

When we get down to what Daley has done in Chicago, however, his programs and his approach to them are not so different from what other contemporary, big-city mayors are doing. Like the mayors of other large cities, including the black mayors, Daley's most persistent problem has been race relations. Approximately one-third of the city's population is black, as are about half the public school pupils. Despite the fact that Daley has insisted "we have no ghettoes in Chicago,"[24] the slums of the south side and the west side are among the worst in the country. Further, his authorization to the police in the wake of the rioting that followed the assassination of Martin

Luther King made him many enemies in the civil rights movement: "shoot to kill any arsonist or anyone with a Molotov cocktail in his hand in Chicago because they're potential murderers, and . . . shoot to maim or cripple anyone looting any stores in our city."[25] Still Daley has been able to count on the support of a great many black leaders, especially the moderate ones. It is the militant blacks who have given Daley so much difficulty. The following description by the Chicago journalist, Mike Royko, which tells "how integration came home to Mayor Daley," illustrates why the Daley administration has received so much criticism.

> John Walsh, high school English teacher, civil rights worker, pacifist, amateur actor, and lawyer, had an idea.
>
> "I believed that it was only proper that a Negro should live on the same street near the home of the mayor of Chicago."
>
> Stated that way, simply and directly, there was nothing revolutionary about his idea. Why not a Negro on the same street near the mayor's home? It was 1964, the civil rights movement was sweeping across the land, all the way into the halls of Congress. First Kennedy, then Johnson, had placed themselves firmly on the side of fair play and integration. Daley, in his public utterances, was with them.
>
> That being the case, John Walsh set about proving that the mayor was right. If there was no segregation in Chicago, a Negro in his neighborhood should not attract attention. Walsh and a friend with money quietly bought a small frame house containing three apartments at 3309 Lowe, a block and a half from the mayor's pink bungalow. Their plan was to rent one of the flats to Negroes.
>
> Our biggest problem was finding somebody willing to move in. Bridgeport's reputation was well-known among Negroes. It was the kind of neighborhood they wouldn't walk through at night, and during the day it wasn't a good idea either. We finally found a young couple and they got as far as the front door. Then the key jammed and they panicked. They turned right around and left. We found two other couples, and each time they backed out at the last minute.
>
> Walsh kept looking, and he finally found two college students who said they would move in. On a Friday in October they arrived with their belongings. Integration had come to Bridgeport for the first time in its one hundred year history.
>
> The old Daley neighbors did not take kindly to the new Daley neighbors, and over the week-end angry crowds drifted up and down Lowe Avenue. They tried to talk to Daley, but the police kept them away from his house, so they went back to the three-flat and chanted hate messages at the two nervous, young black men. Rocks crashed through the windows and bottles broke against the door.

By Monday night it was a junior-sized riot, with at least four hundred people from the neighborhood fighting with the police, trying to storm the building, a dozen getting arrested, and four policemen being injured.

Through it all Daley stayed out of sight. He did not poke his nose out of his house once and did not say anything about the battle being fought 350 feet away. The news media cooperated by virtually ignoring the incident.

Behind the scenes, however, the Eleventh Ward Regular Democratic Organization was working out a way to settle the matter.

While the two students were at school, the police went into the flat and carried their belongings to the corner police station. People from the neighborhood rushed in and threw the place up for grabs, smearing excrement on the walls.

The real estate man who handled the move-in was summoned by the ward organization and told what to do. He listened because real estate licenses are under the control of the mayor of the city of Chicago. They told him that the two black youths were no longer tenants in the building, that two white men from the neighborhood were going to move in and were going to be given a long, unbreakable lease for the apartment, and that it was all going to happen immediately. The lease was drawn up, signed, and the two white tenants moved in. The jubilant crowd joined them in the apartment for a celebration and to help clean up the mess.

When the black students got back to Bridgeport that night, they were taken to the police station, given their belongings, and told that they no longer lived in Bridgeport. When John Walsh got home that night, he found that he owned a three-flat with white tenants, and all of them had unbreakable leases. Walsh soon sold the building. If he had not, he would have gone broke trying to meet the city building department's demands for improvement. Chicago has one of the nation's strictest building codes. Although rarely enforced, it provides City Hall with a powerful club over property owners.

"I proved that Daley was guilty of passive hypocrisy," Walsh said. "He could have prevented all the trouble. He could have controlled his own people. And he knew what we were doing. Weeks before we moved everybody in, I told the city's Human Relations Commission about my plan. I promised them that we would rent only one apartment to Negroes and that all the income from the property would be used for improving it. Instead, they let it happen, they let the people in the neighborhood drive us out. And Daley didn't lift a finger."[26]

In fairness, even Royko's account would suggest that, in the area of race relations, Daley is more culpable for the leadership he has *failed* to exercise than for his sins of commission. On questions of race relations, Daley has acted much as he has in connection with other issues facing Chicago — that is, he has acted in the classic style of the *political broker*: he does not actively seek to thwart the interests of black residents; instead, he usually seeks to arrange compromises aimed at winning support from both blacks and whites. If the balance of the compromises generally favor whites, it is probably because Daley expects that the whites can deliver more political power than the blacks on most questions.

Daley has acted as a political broker on most other public questions too. As a result, a number of commentators on Chicago politics think of Daley's accomplishments as largely progressive. Much of his record looks as if it could have been compiled by a reform mayor. Despite some well-publicized contrary examples, Daley has not tolerated much corruption in office; and compared to earlier eras, he has kept a relatively tight rein on gambling, prostitution, and organized crime. When a scandal involving the Chicago police department broke out in 1960, Daley moved quickly to clean it up. He brought in the nation's leading criminologist, a University of California professor, Orlando W. Wilson, whom Daley gave a free hand to clean up and revitalize the force. It is widely acknowledged that Wilson succeeded, although the solution to that problem led to some of the rather strict enforcement policies that black residents so deplore.

Daley has compromised the operating power of his organization in a number of ways that any reform mayor would be proud of: he instituted an executive budget for the city; he extended the merit system; he initiated new zoning and housing codes, for example. In undertaking these kinds of reforms, Daley has been clearly responsive to prominent businessmen whose support he has often sought and received for city projects. Daley has often had support from the major Chicago newspapers and even, on occasion, of good-government associations. Despite his public image, then, Mayor Daley is not the reincarnation of the pure nineteenth-century boss. Daley's is probably the most effective big-city organization still operating in the seventies.

Daley, of course, is in no sense a typical American mayor. An interesting contrast to Daley was his contemporary, Mayor John Lindsay of New York. Lindsay is an affluent, white Anglo-Saxon Protestant, who ran first as a Republican with the support of the Liberal party of the city; he was denied renomination in 1969 for a second term and was forced to create his own Urban Party to narrowly win re-election. Lindsay is generally regarded as having excellent rapport with the many ethnic groups of the city, especially with the blacks. Even the most superficial consideration of these two men shows us the difficulties in making generalizations about American mayors.

The following generalizations, though not easily derived, will deal with the recruitment of mayors, their roles and resources, and the changing character of the big-city mayor.

Recruitment of the mayor

Broadly speaking, American mayors are likely to be recruited from the same social and economic backgrounds as are city councilmen. Although we recognize immediately that John Lindsay was an exception — a white Anglo-Saxon mayor of a highly ethnic city — still the greatest likelihood is that there will be coherence between the social and economic composition of the city and the background of the mayor.

If we take a historical view of the social and occupational backgrounds of the mayors of particular cities, we can discern yet another pattern. For example, Robert Dahl's studies of New Haven showed that the mayors of that city fell into three main groupings: (1) The "patricians" were well-educated, legally trained, members of well-established New Haven families. The patricians dominated that city from 1784 to 1842. (2) The "entrepreneurs" were heads of the largest and most prominent New Haven industrial and commercial firms. Even though some of them did not have high social standing, they consistently were elected to the office of mayor between 1842 and 1899. (3) The "ex-plebes" were men from working-class, ethnic backgrounds who were able to capitalize on the large ethnic population's support and, thereby, to become the major political figures in New Haven from 1899 almost until the present. Dahl characterized Mayor Richard Lee (elected 1953) as possibly the first of the "new men." The "new man" is one who builds on an ethnic base but who also has a wider support as a result of his advocacy of reform programs — particularly urban redevelopment, in the case of Lee.[27]

An examination of the backgrounds of the mayors of Chicago reveals somewhat similar groupings, but instead of "new men," the dominant type of mayor since 1931 has been the "political administrator."[28] None of the four mayors of Chicago since 1931 (Cermak, Kelley, Kennelly, and Daley) could be counted among the top leaders in the industrial, commercial, financial, or social affairs of the city. They had demonstrated administrative and managerial abilities, however. Like Mayor Lee and Mayor Lindsay, then, Mayor Daley approaches the reform style more than is popularly imagined.

> Given this transformation of the urban setting, the present mayor of Chicago, like those in Philadelphia, New Haven and Detroit, must represent the process of collective betterment and not the process of machine greed. A new ethos of "the good of the community" becomes dominant and shapes the administration of the mayor.[29]

Roles of the mayor

There is considerable variation in the political resources available to mayors in particular cities. We have already noted the difference between strong mayors and weak mayors, one which depends on the legal setting in which they take office. Those resources can also vary in consequence of the method of selecting the mayor, his term of office, and whether or not he has a veto power. A mayor without a veto who is selected by the council for a one- to two-year term is likely to have much less freedom of action than one who is directly elected for a three-year or longer term, during which he has a veto power.[30] Individual mayors can convert limited political resources into considerable power, while others with more generous resources can fritter them away. What will be the level of effectiveness of the mayor, of course, depends on his own concept of appropriate conduct in the role.

Mayors are in a tough spot. We Americans have a vision of chief executives as men of courageous action and bold vision and considerable administrative skill. Small wonder we cannot think of any mayors who live up to that idealization.

> The nature of the urban political environment makes intense demands on the mayor for special leadership skills of a high order if the need for social change is to be met; at the same time, however, the realities of urban political life make it difficult for him to perform these role requirements effectively and consistently. The root of this paradox lies in the considerable fragmentation of authority and dispersal of power characteristic of the formal governmental structure of American urban areas.[31]

Fragmented governmental authority, then, often undermines the ability of the mayor to be a strong leader. Such incapacity is particularly clear in large cities with many problems.

We have no studies of the formal role concepts of American mayors based on interview schedules similar to the ones administered to the city councilmen in the San Francisco Bay Area. Still we can piece together a number of functions which are performed by urban mayors. This will give us some sense of the variations in role which are likely to emerge when those studies are undertaken.

The Mayor as Party Leader   There are very few mayors who show strong leadership as head of the urban party; Daley of Chicago is an impressive exception. In those cities in which the reform movement has been able to change the form of government, it has, often at the same time, inhibited mayors from exercising strong party leadership. Such reform mayors as Richardson Dilworth and Joseph Clark of Philadelphia were able to have only a minimal impact on the life of their city, in part because they lacked a political organization necessary to effect changes.[32] A great many contemporary mayors are caught in this dilemma: the articulate constituency is divided between the influence of an old-style ward leader and that of good-government groups. Effective administration in this situation usually proves so difficult a balancing act that party organization becomes either diluted or deadlocked; and "where the party has become debilitated, as it has in most . . . cities today, an important means of political leverage is thereby lost to the mayor."[33]

The Mayor as Legislative Leader   Strong political executives are assumed to be able to take the lead in formulating policy and mobilizing support for its adoption. The weak mayor, of course, can rarely become a major legislative leader since he tends to function at the periphery of the actual policy formulation process and lacks the resources to bring those processes under his control. Former Mayor Henry Maier of Milwaukee suggests that the key to strong legislative and executive roles for the mayor is that he must dominate budget making. Mayor Maier explained how Milwaukee failed to permit this necessity:

> The mayor does not prepare an executive budget as is done in cities of the "strong mayor" type. Instead, a number of cooks are involved in the making of the budget pie. The Budget Department goes over requests with individual department heads, usually paring their requests sharply. The formal budget is prepared at hearings conducted by the Budget Examining Committee of the Board of Estimates, on which the mayor serves as chairman, together with the council's Finance Committee, the Comptroller and the Budget Supervisor as secretary.[34]

Reform, especially when it has been piecemeal, has occasionally had the effect of undermining the legislative capacities of the mayor. For example, New York City's Board of Estimate was formerly a representative body that did indeed provide a forum in which conflicts among the representatives of the boroughs could be managed. The mayor presided over the Board of Estimate, which dealt with such important functions as the location of public improvements, changes in zoning, special assessments for sewer installation, franchises granted by the city, and leases and contracts entered into. The last New York City charter revisionists, however, were horrified by the amount of detail on the Board of Estimate calendar and endeavored to turn many of its decisions over to professionalized, nonpolitical boards. The result has been that the changes removed the most important bargaining chips from the political game and have made political accommodation more difficult.

> Today, the Board of Estimate frequently resembles a penny ante poker game among men who have been accustomed to playing for table stakes; their wives have reformed them, and the game has lost its savor. It no longer fulfills its deepest psychological purposes — the provision of an atmosphere of real risk or danger, real costs and benefits, which makes possible the resolution of conflict by honorable compromise.[35]

With the diminution of power and effectiveness of the Board of Estimate, so too, the power of a mayor system that was already weak is further diminished.

The Mayor as Chief Executive   A strong political executive should be able to exercise ongoing supervision over the several administrative agencies of the city. He can ensure conformity to his will, in part through budgetary controls and in part through the ability to hire and fire. The mayor's hand is considerably strengthened in cities that provide for a city administrative officer to aid the mayor in the exercise of these functions. But most American cities are far from implementing the conception of strong executive leadership. The mayor of Los Angeles, for example, has relatively little formal responsibility for personnel policies. In Los Angeles, "mayoral control of departmental programs and policies, to the extent it exists, has been accomplished by informal methods, outside the limits of the 1924 charter."[36]

The executive capacities of the mayor are potentially challenged, too, by the existence of unions among city employees. If the mayor sees himself as opponent of the union, he is quite likely to dissipate much of his energy simply in holding his own against them. A mayor must cultivate the good will and loyalty of his city hall constituency in order to ensure their support at crucial times.[37] The mayor is also important to the union leaders in that he establishes the conditions under which the employees work. A mayor can use this resource to establish closer relationships with union leaders, as a means of securing needed cooperation. Mayor Robert F. Wagner, who preceded John Lindsay in New York, is reputed to have been a master at cultivating his relationships with city unions. Mayor Lindsay was less successful.

The Mayor as Lobbyist for the City   Since the federal government has taken on the job of providing funds and programs to alleviate some of the most pressing problems of the cities, mayors have assumed the role of chief lobbyist for the city. Major cities keep lobbying staffs on hand in Washington and, as we have already noted, the United States Council of Mayors articulates the collective will of the member mayors in association with other members of the urban lobby. The lobbying function of the mayor's office has grown dramatically since World War II, but its importance is not generally recognized. In many of our larger cities, however, the best perspective is that the lobbyist role is the one most important to a strong mayor. Starr has asserted that "Congress is *the most significant* legislature through which the mayor of New York City can affect policies in his city."[38]

The mayor must also play lobbyist before the state legislature. This body determines what share from state revenue sources will be reallocated to the city's several functions. The level of organization of the city's lobby at the state varies, of course. Again looking at New York City as an example, we find that the mayor is treated with respect in Albany; he is acknowledged as the representative of a very large lobby, and his recommendations are not treated lightly. Cooperation between the city and state often goes on despite mutual recriminations between the mayor and governor.

The Mayor as Umpire   In those cities in which formal structure and political realities make it impossible for the mayor to be a strong leader, the mayor may opt for the role of umpire. In other words, he may see himself in the role we earlier described as "arbiter of conflicting interests." Doing so, the mayor casts his role as one who is partial to the cause of no particular interest or group but is instead a peacemaker, equally devoted to all the objectives of the contestants. This is no easy position: it requires painstaking familiarity with the language and strategic goals of the city's constituents. Nor is it a very popular role: who loves the neutral? Discussion of the city is currently framed in the language not of moderation but of crisis. "In a period when every hack editorial writer cries for 'commitment' and 'innovative responses,' the umpire with his dark blue suit and pocket whisk broom seems . . . irrelevant. . . . "[39] The current feeling about the city, even among those who oppose change, is that mere neutrality will fail to head off disaster. This situation produces a clear dilemma for the mayor who has read a great deal of political science and fancies himself a pluralist. The umpire role is quite congruent with pluralist democracy — the public decision maker (mayor) acting as neutral balancing point of the forces articulated by groups and powerful individuals who pull at him. But such a pluralist may find himself uncelebrated and unre-elected.

The Mayor as Myth Maker   The mayor is also a myth maker. He personifies, projects, and even exaggerates the qualities of a city — just as we expect a symbol to do. In choosing a mayor the voters are often selecting the image of themselves they would like projected. San Diego, for example, calls itself the City in Motion; in 1971, San Diego voters elected Mayor Pete Wilson who personified the "young, dynamic, aggressive" image. Lindsay, according to Starr, embodies New Yorkers' idea that New York is "the richest city in the world, that it consists of cloud-shrouded skyscrapers inhabited by glamorous creatures from the world of theater and arts, waited on by bankers and powerful businessmen,"[40] Fiorello H. LaGuardia, however, personified the other New York City self-concept, the myth of the happy polyglot. LaGuardia was busy and ever present, squeaking excitedly while reading the funnies over the radio. Part Italian, part Jewish, part Catholic, part Protestant, he was living evidence of the effectiveness of the melting pot. This mythic quality "won him support from among New Yorkers who had not the faintest

In Quincy, Mass., Mayor Walter J. Hannon has rejected the umpire role in favor of a commitment to, among other things, improving life for the elderly. Photograph Courtesy of Office of the Mayor, Quincy, Massachusetts.

idea of what he really accomplished as mayor, most of which amounted to giving Mr. Robert Moses a free hand. They loved LaGuardia and rejected Moses simultaneously."[41]

Transformation of the big-city mayor

If the pluralist assumptions were being realized in contemporary urban America, the emerging role of the mayor would be that of umpire. That does seem to be the case. But James Q. Wilson argues that a more important and potentially far-reaching transformation is occurring which may well usher in a new era in city politics. That new era, he argues, will be unlike either the era of the political machine or the era of conventional political reform. This change results primarily from the fact that for many contemporary mayors their audience is increasingly different from their constituency.[42] By *audience* he means those persons who are most interested in and attentive to the mayor's actions, "those persons from whom he receives his most welcome applause and his most needed resources and opportunities."[43] By *constituency* he means those people who can vote for or against him in an election. In the machine era the mayor's audience and his constituency were largely the same people; the mayor looked to the political party and the city's voters and they looked to and elected him. So, too, in the reform era, the mayor's constituents were those voters who were disgusted by scandal or bored by sameness. In both eras the audiences were *local people.*

Federal involvement in the life of the city has resulted in a new, significant, nonlocal audience for the mayor. This new audience consists principally of various federal agencies, and especially those that give grants directly to the cities.

> The large foundations, and in particular the Ford Foundation, that can favor the mayor with grants, advice, and future prospects; the mass media, or at least that part of the media — national news magazines and network television — that can give the mayor access to the suburbs, the state, and the nation as a whole; and the affluent (and often liberal) suburban voters who will pass on the mayor's fitness for higher office.[44]

The new audience emerged as urban social issues, like poverty and racial unrest, came to the fore. As they grew within most cities, programs like the Model Cities Program, the War on Poverty, programs for civil rights and aid to education, as well as a whole series of projects and experiments sponsored by the federal government and private foundations — all these brought into the city a large number of people associated with implementing them. These people became the mayor's audience, though they were not among his constituents. Needing to look good to his audience, the mayor tried to project a "progressive" image and demonstrate that he understands and can supply leadership in coping with the forces that underlie such social issues. Wilson suggests among other things that this set of changes helps explain why so few mayors, in the wake of the racial and Vietnam war disturbances, took hard "law and order" stances. Their new audiences would not have approved.

There are a good many implications of Wilson's view, the most obvious and far reaching of which is that the mayor and the city are becoming nationalized, that is, the most crucial policy making for coping with urban problems is increasingly done under constraints imposed by nonlocal decision makers.[45]

City Managers

The formal responsibilities of the manager usually include: (1) seeing to it that the policies made by the council are implemented, (2) preparing and submitting a budget to the council, (3) appointing and removing the principal department heads, and (4) making recommendations on policy to the council. By requiring the manager to make recommendations on policy the stage is set for the manager to become — depending on how he interprets his role — a political leader.

Managers' roles

The behavior of city managers can be "fully and exhaustively characterized by three role categories: managerial, policy, and political."[46] The *managerial* role is, of course, involved with the relationship of the manager to his municipal bureaucracy, including supervision and control of personnel and policy administration. By *policy* role, we mean the manager's relationships with the city council, particularly as he is the source of policy recommendations. The *political* role includes efforts as a community leader and as a representative of community needs and interests before the council, the community at large, and other governmental units. Different managers emphasize different roles and perform the roles in a variety of ways, depending on their own personal characteristics and their adaptation to the specific urban environment in which they find themselves.

A prime difficulty in the managerial role is to control the bureaucracy. We have already indicated that mayors, especially weak mayors, generally fail. One study finds that the successful manager is one who is able to develop sufficient resources, particularly information, and has relative freedom to use his resources.[47] In his administrative role, the manager is able to use his professional staff and his control of the budget, as well as his power to appoint and remove department heads, as effective resources. Effective managers usually guard carefully their autonomy in appointment and removal, lest their control of the city bureaucracy slip.

There is some variation and ambiguity in the manner in which the policy role is played. Deil Wright has found that in most council-manager cities the manager is the dominant policy initiator. This dominance is established in a variety of ways. Most importantly, managers set the agenda of the city council; Wright found that two-thirds of the managers he surveyed decisively controlled the agendas of their city councils.[48] This is no small power, since control of the agenda allows the manager to control which questions will be heard and which will not. The same proportion, two-thirds of the city managers, report that most items considered by the council are on the agenda because they chose to put them there. Besides controlling the agenda, the manager is also able to exercise an important policy role because he is the major source of information for the city council. Even in those cities in which he is called on to present both sides of the question, the formulation of the alternatives is inevitably done on his terms. The manager, then, is in a very good position to determine which policies will be adopted and which will not.

In the exercise of his political role, managers like mayors are often called on to deal with state or federal bureaucrats. But the manager often feels constrained to present information rather than to serve as a spokesman, as the mayor does. Within the city, the manager plays an important role in representing and explaining policies to the public at large. When addressing

the local audience the tendency of managers is to present technical information rather than to make statements which would excite local political interests. In essence, he keeps things cool by talking over the heads of his
listeners.

Managers are most at home in their administrative role. They devote
most of their time to it and report that they obtain more personal and job
satisfaction from those activities.[49] Their specific administrative commitments
are found to be greatest in matters of capital improvements and in the conduct
and supervision of established programs. They generally are less enthusiastic
in assuming responsibility for the formulation of social policy. Social policies
are controversial, and it is particularly difficult to appear the "neutral administrator" in working with them. It has long been pointed out that "the
manager is a politician."[50] While it is true that there are many inescapable
political elements in the job of manager, Wright's findings make us realize
that most managers cast their own role primarily as administrators and
become uncomfortable as they move toward the exercise of political responsibilities. Where the manager fails to exercise such responsibilities and the
mayor has been reduced to a figurehead and the council has become
dependent on the manager, difficult political questions may never be faced by
a city.

The Bureaucrats

When the term "bureaucrat" is used, most of us think of graft, corruption, laziness, incompetence, red tape — a long list of undesirable
associations. Without denying that on occasion those epithets are deserved,
we should not allow such images to prevent our understanding the vital role
of the bureaucracy in city politics — for a good policy poorly implemented is
bad policy. In addition to efficient administration of government policy,
bureaucracy can perform some other desirable functions. The bureaucracy is
one of the few places in governmental structure for common people; it is more
"democratically" composed than the other conflict-managing structures.
Equally important, individual bureaucracies often have more direct and personal contact with the people affected by a particular policy than do urban
policy makers at the higher levels.

However we judge bureaucracy, the one conclusion we cannot reach
is that it is politically neutral. We have already discussed bureaucracy as an
interest group (see pages 131-132). Organized as professional associations
and occasionally as unions, the organizations of a bureaucracy can and do
present conflict, not just regulate the conflict of other parties as their job roles
require them to do. We should keep in mind that the common motives of
groups representing elements of the bureaucracy are two: (1) maintenance of

THIS IS *Your*
POOL AND PLAYGROUND
LET'S KEEP IT CLEAN
THIS POOL IS PROVIDED THROUGH THE COOPERATION
OF YOUR NEIGHBORHOOD ASSOCIATION WITH
THE CITY OF BOSTON HON. KEVIN H. WHITE, MAYOR
THE BOSTON REDEVELOPMENT AUTHORITY, AND THE
DEPARTMENT OF HOUSING AND URBAN DEVELOPMENT

Marshall Henrichs

As this park sign makes clear, it is both possible and necessary for bureaucratic goals to converge.

their autonomy, job security, and freedom from interference from outside sources, and (2) expansion of their program. The bureaucracy, then, is rather often in the seemingly contradictory position of being resistant to change that affects their autonomy while pressing for change that leads to the extension of public policy into new areas.

More specific patterns of bureaucratic operation vary widely from agency to agency within a city as well as from city to city. This is not the place to attempt to characterize those patterns fully. However, one central point is well established and provides an important preliminary insight for understanding the work of city bureaucracies — that is, that city bureaucrats exercise broad discretion.

Broad scope of bureaucratic discretion

A popular image of the bureaucrat depicts him as a neutral automaton, a mere cog in the machinery of government. This image fosters the assumption that bureaucrats simply shuffle paper, exercising little discretion in the manner and outcome of their work. This image is mistaken. The considerable collective power of the bureaucracy stems directly from the fact that individual bureaucrats exercise considerable discretion in the way in which they execute policy. In their massive study of New York City, Sayre and Kaufman document bureaucratic discretion in a number of ways.

> It is in execution that the bureaucrats have their most nearly complete monopoly and their greatest autonomy in effecting policy. They give shape and meaning to the official decisions and they do so under conditions favorable to them. Here the initiative and discretion lie in their hands; others must influence them.[51]

For example, police departments in almost every city have great breadth in the manner in which they apply the law. The result can be some extreme variations from city to city. One study reports, for instance, that while Boston and Dallas have about the same population size, in one year Dallas policemen wrote twenty-four times as many traffic tickets as did Boston policemen.[52] It could be that Dallas residents are relatively more lawless than Bostonians, but that seems an unlikely explanation. The attitude of the police leadership seems to be the most determinative: "in general, the rate of enforcement of traffic laws reflects the organizational norms of the police department — the extent to which superior officers expect and encourage particular policies regarding ticket writing."[53]

We are not saying, of course, that bureaucrats at any level have complete discretion. If nothing else, each member of the bureaucracy is involved in a situation in which he must anticipate the expectations of his superiors.

We should also recognize that the latitude of discretion varies widely from one position to another. Partly because it must be flexible enough to deal with a wide variety of contingencies, the police department may have more latitude than other local agencies. In those governmental activities in which policies are likely to be applied over and over in the same way, the resultant routinization of administration diminishes the discretion of the officeholders in the agency.

Transformation of the bureaucracy

In opposition to those who argue that the mayor is leading us to a new era of urban politics, Theodore Lowi feels that the bureaucracy is the more transforming force.[54] Lowi sees the legacy of the reform movement to be a highly decentralized and weak urban decision-making process. As a result, he feels that centralized leadership is unlikely to emerge even when a public official wants to take charge. One effect of this dispersion is that the greatest single combination of organized resources now resides in public bureaucracies. The "new machine" of city politics, then, is the urban bureaucracy. The new machines are different from the old machines because they are efficient and free from "corruption." But the urban bureaucrats are not bound to their local constituency. So the new machines become "relatively irresponsible structures of power. That is, each agency shapes important public policies, yet the leadership of each is relatively self-perpetuating and not readily subject to the controls of any higher authority."[55] The outcome, in Lowi's view, is not a happy one, for the new machine means the arrival of the "bureaucratic city state" in which cities "become well run but ungoverned."[56]

RATIONALITY AS A STANDARD FOR CONFLICT MANAGEMENT

As I hope this chapter has made clear, the roles and structures which function to manage urban conflict are complex and, therefore, not amenable to any pat characterization. A city government not only seeks to resolve conflicts which are pressed upon it by factions of the urban environment, but also generates its own conflicts. There is no simple rule of decision making which enables public decision makers to resolve all conflicts. The standard most often demanded of public decision makers is that the process be "rational." Rationality, as we suggested earlier, is a distinguishing feature of an urban culture. We identified conceptions of a rational political actor and rational political decision makers as two components in the pluralist democracy. Certainly, the desire to produce a rationalized (more usually put, "organized") governmental structure was the fundamental aim of Richard Childs and the reform movement, which has so importantly transformed city governments. Individual decision makers, too, are expected to observe the canons of rationality. More than that, rationality is widely respected in our social system; and it becomes our favorite parlor game to condemn the political process for its irrationality. The feeling seems to run that if politics cannot be rational, there must be something inherently wrong with it. But even rationality has its limits. Despite the progress of the reform movement, we know that urban governments do not operate as fully rationalized organizations. We know, too, that urban decision makers often deviate from the canons of rationality.

There are a few commentators on the urban political scene who argue that the process not only is not rational but cannot, and should not, be so. Speaking of the total urban process, Richard Sennett has found much to praise in disorder.[57] Sennett chides the public decision maker, especially the city planner, who seeks to impose his own vision of the good (meaning well-ordered) city as a person who possesses a "purified identity." A purified identity uses rationality as a means of screening out conflict, diversity, and ambiguity — not as a means of problem solving but as a defense for a shaky and inflexible personality.

This is not the place to attempt to resolve this political debate on the value of rationality. I raise it here simply because its importance is fundamental. Before leaving the topic, however, we can clarify the nature of rationality in urban decision making by reviewing the criteria of rational decision making and then by assessing some of the limitations on rationality as it relates to public decisions.

According to Charles E. Lindblom, a rational policy maker: (1) identifies his problem; (2) clarifies his goals; (3) ranks his goals according to relative importance; (4) lists all possible means, or policies, for achieving each of the goals; (5) assesses all the costs of each set of alternatives and the benefits of each set of alternatives which seem likely to follow; and (6) selects the package of goals and associated policies that would bring the most benefits and fewest relative disadvantages.[58]

There are a number of reasons why pure rationality is impossible as a standard for urban political decision makers, even if we desired it. First, there is a problem of time. Critics and academics have an unlimited amount of time in which to contemplate alternatives to any given problem, but public decision makers are usually constrained by a particular time period. To specify, say, all the costs and all the benefits of all the policy alternatives for any important issue sounds more like a lifetime's work than a realistic goal for a city council. In addition, it must be recognized that decision makers do not have, nor can they easily get, all the information necessary to even understand the alternatives. Information takes time, effort, and sometimes money to obtain and to comprehend. Though these limitations are severe, two others seem more important. The first stems from the fact that certain policy alternatives in a city simply cannot be compared; they are "incommensurable." In considering the budget, for example, how can a city decision maker know whether another dollar invested in school integration programs will produce greater benefit than putting that same money into a program to promote industrial development? Second, a rationally selected policy alternative may not be *politically* feasible. In the last analysis, the selection of a particular public policy is made on the basis of what the electorate and attentive groups and "political influentials" want, not necessarily on the most rational alternative. Public attitudes toward taxation, for example, are likely to be a major constraint to any purely rational approach to problem solving.

In short, urban policy making is, and perhaps can be, only partially rational. Lindblom provides a more accurate conception of the process by which public policy is made when he suggests that government involves the creation and maintenance of procedures for accommodating tensions that arise within the body politic because of dissatisfaction with current programs and policies. These tensions are managed more by a process of "mutual adjustment" than by a process that is starkly rational. Lindblom calls it "muddling through."[59] Muddling through is a political expression of the "hang loose" ethic: decision makers are required to recognize that they cannot make permanent solutions; their choices are likely to be minor adjustments which accommodate for a certain amount of time some of the conflicting demands made on them. In other words, their decisions are more incremental than they are comprehensive. Muddling through, as you might suspect, often involves a strategy of avoiding conflict when that is possible.[60]

Muddling through suggests (1) that only those conflicts which are most severe will be dealt with by the political process, and (2) that those groups and individuals with the most political resources effectively mobilized on the particular question will get what they want. Less powerful interests may either lose or be put off. These assumptions make the concept of "muddling through" quite compatible with pluralist democracy.

SUMMARY

The making of authoritative policy to regulate urban conflict is institutionalized in a wide array of patterns described by the actions of city councils, mayors and managers, and bureaucrats. Each of these important political actors is involved at various stages in the formulation, adoption, and application of policy. Separation of powers is a relatively meaningless concept in urban governance.

We have also seen suggestions that urban government is moving beyond the machine era and the reform era to a time in which the mayor and the bureaucracy are coming to exercise relatively great power — often without direct accountability to the constituency of the city — as they bring urban policy in line with federal programs and initiatives.

Finally, in this chapter, we have suggested that urban decision makers are not, perhaps should not be, purely rational as they approach their decisions; instead, they tend to give central place to the need to adjust tensions arising in the city.

NOTES

1. The following description relies heavily on the summary of Carl A. McCandless, *Urban Government and Politics* (New York: McGraw-Hill, 1970), pp. 173-175.
2. From Kenneth Prewitt, *The Recruitment of Political Leaders: A Study of Citizen-Politicians* (Indianapolis: Bobbs-Merrill Co., 1970), p. 47.
3. Ibid.
4. These findings were made in two separate studies, one in St. Louis the other in Philadelphia. Cf. Brian T. Downes, "Municipal Social Rank and the Characteristics of Local Political Leaders," *Midwest Journal of Political Science*

12 (November 1968): 514-537; and Oliver Williams et al., *Suburban Differences and Metropolitan Politics* (Philadelphia: University of Pennsylvania Press, 1965), p. 228.

5. See particularly Kenneth Prewitt and William Nowlin, "Political Ambitions and the Behavior of Incumbent Politicians," *Western Political Quarterly* 22 (June 1969): 302; also Kenneth Prewitt, "Political Ambitions, Volunteerism, and Electoral Accountability," *American Political Science Review* 64 (March 1970): 5-17.

6. Prewitt and Nowlin, "Political Ambitions," p. 307.

7. Oliver Williams and Charles Adrian, *Four Cities* (Philadelphia: University of Pennsylvania Press, 1963), p. 264.

8. Cf. Downes, "Municipal Social Rank," pp. 534-537.

9. This terminology is defined and explained first in John Wahlke et al., *The Legislative System* (New York: John Wiley and Sons, 1962), Chap. 1.

10. From Betty Zisk, Heinz Eulau, and Kenneth Prewitt, "City Councilmen and the Group Struggle: A Typology of Role Orientations," *Journal of Politics* 27 (August 1965): 618-646.

11. Ibid., p. 644.

12. For a discussion of the relevance of small-group findings to the study of political science, see two major reviews of that literature: Sidney Verba, *Small Groups and Political Behavior — A Study of Leadership* (Princeton: Princeton University Press, 1961); and Robert T. Golembiewski, *The Small Group: An Analysis of Concepts and Operations* (Chicago: University of Chicago Press, 1962).

13. Cf. Prewitt and Nowlin, "Political Ambitions," p. 300.

14. Heinz Eulau, "The Informal Organization of Decisional Structures in Small Legislative Bodies," *Midwest Journal of Political Science* 13 (August 1969): 341-366.

15. Ibid., p. 353. Also see James Barber, *Power in Committees: An Experiment in the Governmental Process* (Chicago: Rand, McNally, 1966), pp. 153-154.

16. Peter Lupsha, *Swingers, Isolates and Coalitions: Interpersonal Relations in Small Political Decision-Making Groups,* (Ph.D. diss., Stanford University, 1967).

17. Eulau, "Decisional Structures," pp. 355-356.

18. Ibid., p. 356.

19. Ibid., p. 357.

20. The following discussion of the political organization of Mayor Daley rests primarily on three sources: Edward C. Banfield, *Political Influence* (New York: Free Press of Glencoe, 1961); Thomas R. Dye, *Politics in States and Communities* (Englewood Cliffs, N. J.: Prentice-Hall, 1969), pp. 260-262; and Mike Royko, *Boss: Richard J. Daley of Chicago* (New York: New American Library, 1971).

21. Quoted by Royko, *Boss: Richard J. Daley*, p. 30.

22. Quoted in *Newsweek* (March 13, 1967), p. 63.

23. Quoted in *Holiday* (December 1963), p. 42.

24. Chicago *Tribune* (July 9, 1963), p. 1.

25. Press conference reported in the Chicago *Daily News* (April 17, 1968).

26. From Royko, *Boss: Richard J. Daley*, pp. 133-136.
27. Robert A. Dahl, *Who Governs?* (New Haven: Yale University Press, 1961), pp. 1-81.
28. Donald S. Bradley and Mayer N. Zald, "From Commercial Elite to Political Administrator: The Recruitment of the Mayors of Chicago," *American Journal of Sociology* 70 (September 1965): 153-167.
29. Ibid., p. 167.
30. For figures on the distribution of these attributes among the mayors of cities with populations of 5000 or more in 1960, see The International City Managers' Association, *Municipal Yearbook: 1967* (Chicago: The Association, 1967), pp. 104-105.
31. Alexander L. George, "Political Leadership and Social Change in American Cities," *Daedalus* 97 (Fall 1968): 1196.
32. See James Reichley, *The Art of Government* (New York: Fund for the Republic, 1959), especially pp. 107-115 and 122-125.
33. Leonard I. Ruchelman, *Big City Mayors: The Crisis in Urban Politics* (Bloomington: Indiana University Press, 1969), p. 230.
34. Henry W. Maier, *Challenge to the Cities* (New York: Random House, 1966), p. 114.
35. R. Starr, "The Mayor's Dilemmas: Power and Powerlessness in a Regional City," *Public Interest* 16 (Summer 1969): 17.
36. Winston W. Crouch and Beatrice Dinerman, *Southern California Metropolis* (Berkeley: University of California Press, 1963), p. 170.
37. The notion of "professional reputation" is as important to a mayor as it is to a governor or a president; cf. Richard Neustadt, *Presidential Power* (New York: John Wiley and Sons, 1960), pp. 58-59.
38. Starr, "Mayor's Dilemmas," p. 15 (emphasis supplied).
39. Ibid., p. 23.
40. Ibid., p. 11.
41. Ibid., p. 12.
42. James Q. Wilson, "The Mayor vs. the Cities," *Public Interest* 16 (Summer 1969): 25-40, p. 28.
43. Ibid.
44. Ibid., p. 29.
45. For a similar point of view, see Robert H. Salisbury, "Urban Politics: The New Convergence of Power," *Journal of Politics* 26 (November 1964): 775-797.
46. Deil S. Wright, "The City Manager as a Development Administrator," in *Comparative Urban Research*, ed. Robert T. Daland (Beverly Hills: Sage Publications, 1969), p. 218. See also Gladys M. Kammerer, "Role Diversity of City Managers," *Administrative Sciences Quarterly* 8 (March 1964): 421-442.
47. Wright, "City Manager as a Development Administrator," p. 219.
48. Ibid.
49. Ibid., p. 236.
50. Carl Bosworth, "The Manager Is a Politician," *Public Administration Review* 18 (Summer 1958): 216-222.
51. Wallace Sayre and Herbert Kaufman, *Governing New York City* (New York:

Russell Sage Foundation, 1960), p. 421. See also David Rogers, *The Management of Big Cities: Interest Groups and Social Change Strategies* (Beverly Hills: Sage Publications, 1971), especially pp. 25-74.

52. John A. Gardiner, "Police Enforcement of Traffic Laws: A Comparative Analysis," in *City Politics and Public Policy*, ed. James Q. Wilson (New York: John Wiley and Sons, 1968), pp. 151-172.

53. Ibid., p. 161.

54. See Theodore J. Lowi, "Machine Politics — Old and New," *Public Interest* 4 (Fall 1967): 86. Also see Eugene Lewis, *The Urban Political System* (Hinsdale, Ill.: Dryden Press, 1973).

55. Ibid., p. 87.

56. Ibid., p. 86.

57. Richard Sennett, *The Uses of Disorder* (New York: Alfred A. Knopf, 1970).

58. Adapted from Charles E. Lindblom, *The Policy-Making Process* (Englewood Cliffs, N.J.: Prentice-Hall, 1968), p. 13.

59. Charles E. Lindblom, "The Science of Muddling Through," *Public Administration Review* 19 (Spring 1959): 79-88.

60. William L. C. Wheaton, "Integration at the Urban Level: Political Influence in the Decision Process," in *The Integration of Political Communities*, ed. Philip Jacob and James V. Toscano (Philadelphia: J. B. Lippincott, 1964).

Chapter 12

Urban Justice:
The Courts of First Resort

Everyone has his favorite story of crime rampant in the city. Consider the following story of the hazards of living in an apartment house on East 78th Street in Manhattan:

> Burglars attacking the [apartment house] go at it like commandos dropped behind enemy lines. Mostly heroin addicts and often black, they are after whatever can be quickly converted into cash. Escape routes are prepared, barbed wire cut, bricks pulled from building walls to give footholds to the roof. Inside, the tenants hear noises and wait for the sounds of chisels, the face at the window. A teacher in 4D has been burglarized once, and many other times has seen prowlers on the fire escape. One night her window opened and two hands came through and parted the curtains. She says, "I screamed, and called the police a lot." A stewardess in 3D no longer opens her door to anyone whose voice she cannot recognize. While she was away on a flight, burglars picked her lock and emptied the apartment, clothes and all. The man in 5C had a fake burglar alarm sign on his door. It was stolen —along with the door mat. The tenants . . . try to help each other. The man in 4A, himself burglarized once, ran to a neighbor's aid with a steel bar, and on another occasion chased away lock pickers with a butcher knife. Once he had a German Shepherd for protection. Someone stole it.[1]

When that story appeared, along with a number of equally fear-inducing details and pictures, readers were asked to respond to a questionnaire published along with it. Of the 43,000 readers who responded, 78% reported that they sometimes feel unsafe in their own homes; 80% of those who lived in cities of over a half a million said they were afraid in the streets at night; 41% reported feeling that police protection was inadequate; and 30% said they kept a gun for their own self-protection.[2] A fear of crime has led to unprecedented pressure on the police and other law enforcement officials to

303

take strong measures to assure "law and order." But zealous police often become part of the problem, as the following situation illustrates:

[Dollree Mapp] lived alone with her 15-year-old daughter in the second-floor flat of a duplex in Cleveland. At about 1:30 in the afternoon of May 23, 1957, three policemen arrived at this house. They rang the bell, and the appellant, appearing at her window, asked them what they wanted. According to their later testimony, the policemen had come to the house on information from "a confidential source that there was a person holding out in the home, who was wanted for questioning in connection with a recent bombing." (This "confidential source" told the police, in the same breath, that "there was a large amount of policy paraphernalia [numbers slips] being hidden in the home.") To the appellant's question, however, they replied only that they wanted to question her and would not state the subject about which they wanted to talk.

The appellant, who had retained an attorney in connection with a pending civil matter, told the police she would call him to ask if she should let them in. On her attorney's advice, she told them she would let them in only when they produced a valid search warrant. For the next two and a half hours, the police laid siege to the house. At four o'clock, their number was increased to at least seven. Appellant's lawyer appeared on the scene; and one of the policemen told him that they now had a search warrant, but the officer refused to show it. Instead, going to the back door, the officer tried to kick it in and, when that proved unsuccessful, he broke the glass in the front door and opened it from the inside.

The appellant, who was on the steps going up to her flat, demanded to see the search warrant; but the officer refused to let her see it although he waved a paper in front of her face. She grabbed it and thrust it down the front of her dress. The policemen seized her, took the paper from her, and had her handcuffed to another officer. She was taken upstairs, thus bound, and into the larger of the two bedrooms in the apartment; there she was forced to sit on the bed. Meanwhile, the officers entered the house and made a complete search of the four rooms of her flat and of the basement of the house.

The testimony concerning the search is largely nonconflicting. The approach of the officers; their long wait outside the home, watching all its doors; the arrival of reinforcements armed with a paper; breaking into the house; putting their hands on appellant and handcuffing her; numerous officers ransacking through every room and piece of furniture, while the appellant sat, a prisoner in her own bedroom. . . .

The purported warrant . . . disappeared from the case. The State made no attempt to prove its existence. . . .

This presentation of the facts is not the report of an angry partisan in the fray; it is, rather, the reconstruction of events by Justice of the Supreme

Court William O. Douglas, which he pieced together from testimony.[3] Not finding what they were looking for, the police finally seized some allegedly pornographic books and pictures they found in the home. In this instance, the court felt that the violation of constitutional protections against unreasonable searches and seizures was so blatant, and was becoming so dangerously widespread, that they ruled that illegally seized evidence would no longer be admissible in state criminal trials.[4]

These two situations point up the dilemma of law enforcement in an increasingly urbanized society. The city becomes an intolerable place to live if its residents cannot feel free to walk its streets and enjoy its diversity. But as Louis Brandeis said, "If the government becomes a lawbreaker, it breeds contempt for the law. . . . " The dilemma becomes more complex when we acknowledge that large numbers of city dwellers are technically criminals for engaging in both public demonstrations and private unlawful behavior — such as homosexuality, lesbianism, smoking marijuana, "loitering," and drunkenness. These acts are technically crimes in some jurisdictions, though crimes without victims.

Arrests and prosecutions have become so numerous in the process of urbanizing America that our courts, particularly our city courts, find it nearly impossible to handle the load. It has often been pointed out that "justice

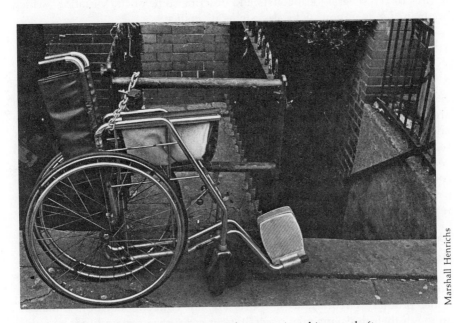

Marshall Henrichs

Many urban residents feel that anything they own is subject to theft.

deferred is justice denied." Yet the case load statistics indicate that deferred justice is what we are getting. The President's Crime Commission estimated that in 1962 four million misdemeanor cases (a misdemeanor is a relatively minor offense, precise meaning varies) were brought before the lower courts of the United States. The number of felony defendants (a felony is a serious crime, precise meaning varies also) in 1965 reached more than 314,000.[5] Also in 1965, there were five million reports of the most frequent criminal offenses — drunkenness, disorderly conduct, larceny, driving under the influence of alcohol, simple assault, burglary, violation of liquor laws, vagrancy, gambling, and motor vehicle theft. In New York City alone in 1967, the average load of traffic cases for each judge was 50,000. That same year, each judge had an average load of 740 felony cases to try.[6]

It should be clear, then, that the cities are critically involved in major legal matters. Many of the epoch-making decisions originate in the urban environment, and cities often provide the courts of first resort. In addition, the situations we have just reviewed should make it clear that there is no clear distinction between law and justice on the one hand and politics on the other. Indeed, the courts are engaged in the management of conflict because they must deal with differences between contending parties over the proper application of the law. Such a conflict-managing stance is by definition political. In the discussion that follows, we shall examine the structure and powers of the several local courts and describe some of the variations which occur in the operation of local systems of justice.

THE STRUCTURE, FUNCTION, AND PERSONNEL OF THE URBAN JUDICIARY

There is no simple and neat judicial hierarchy in most American cities. There are a large number of courts sitting in cities, but very few of them are purely municipal courts; many are created by state and federal law. The law applied in each of these courts may originate as city ordinances, as state or federal statutes, or as interpretations of city charters or of state and federal constitutions. In addition, courts sitting in cities make rulings based on the common law and on other bodies of law evolved within the Anglo-Saxon legal tradition.[7] As a study of the New York City courts concluded, "In a strict sense, there is no such thing as a wholly local court. . . . "[8] The great majority of courts operating in cities are part of the state court system; their organization, personnel, jurisdiction, and methods of procedure are determined by the state rather than by city charter or ordinance.

The unique role of the courts in the management of urban conflict is probably grounded in the nature of the judicial process itself. For one thing, under ordinary circumstances, courts are not conventional policy makers, although their decisions may necessitate or encourage certain kinds of policy change. The courts are passive; they must wait for some other person or group to bring a specific question to them for decision. The question must be a real "case or controversy" arising from a real rather than a hypothetical set of facts.[9] There must be adversary parties in order to have such a case brought before a court. The court's decision is not general public policy, but is binding only upon the parties to the dispute.

In reaching their decision, the courts may have to resolve conflicts over what are the facts of a particular situation. Facts are seldom self-evident, and the disagreement about what actually happened is often the very basis of the dispute. Once the facts have been established, the courts must decide what law is to be applied to the established set of facts. Since there are multiple and sometimes conflicting laws, there is a large measure of discretion involved in deciding which law is applicable.

Finally, the courts determine what judicial sanction or remedy is applicable to each case. In assigning such remedies there is also a measure of discretion in the hands of the court.

This brief discussion obviously does not equip anyone to become a practicing lawyer. It does make sufficiently clear, however, that the judicial function involves much more than a mechanical process in which the court lays out the facts alongside the law and justice results automatically. To the contrary, there is great latitude in which the judge must exercise and apply his own values, attitudes, experiences, and judicial philosophy in reaching a decision. Why else would we call them judges? Since these judgments resolve conflicts, we must call them political personnel as well.

Local Court Organization

There are a few courts that are purely municipal. Most cases, even though they concern local subject matter and parties, find their way into state courts. There are also a number of federal courts sitting in our cities, but they will not be discussed here.

Municipal courts

A municipal court is one specially authorized by the city charter or by permissive state legislation to hear cases arising under the city charter and ordinances. For example, a city enacts its own dog control ordinances and presumably a suit against an uncontrolled dog could be brought in a municipal court, as could suits concerned with violation of gambling ordinances, of traffic ordinances, and of massage parlor regulations. The police department may be required to serve as marshall for the municipal court, charged with enforcing its orders and decrees. The city attorney's office is responsible for the assignment of a lawyer to serve as prosecutor of those cases which involve violation of the charter ordinances of the city. The number of municipal courts depends on the size of the city. In some large cities there are many municipal courts operating on both night and day shifts to handle the case load.

For the most part, the legal business arising in the cities is handled in state courts. The structure of state courts varies from one state to another, of course, but it is possible to discern a simplified generalized pattern. Most states have the following kinds of courts: (1) minor courts, (2) regular trial courts, (3) intermediate courts of appeals, (4) high courts, and (5) specialized courts.[10]

Minor courts

Many states have created small local courts that are limited both in the geographical area of their jurisdiction and in the gravity of the offenses with which they can deal. These courts are most commonly called justice of the peace courts or magistrate courts. It is not uncommon for the justice of the peace to be without legal training and to pay little attention to the niceties of judicial administration. As a general rule, minor courts are able to handle both civil and criminal cases, but usually only those criminal cases in which the defendant is accused of a misdemeanor, not a felony. Civil cases, which are usually suits for money damages, may be heard in minor courts only if the damages do not exceed an amount stated in state law; $1000 is a common limit.

Justice of the peace courts are notorious. They are often criticized and have been eliminated in many states. Criticism usually focuses on the lack of legal training of justices of the peace and on the fact that the JP's salary often comes from the fines he collects. Everyone has his favorite story of judicial abuse at the hands of a justice of the peace (my own is of a friend who was fined $50 for using live bait while fishing in a North Carolina river).

Regular trial courts

The decision of a minor court can be appealed into a trial court for a full hearing. This is the level of the judicial hierarchy on which the jury trial occurs. Juries are selected, witnesses are called, and the full-scale judicial drama is acted out. There are usually no limits on the jurisdiction of these courts regarding either seriousness of crime or amount of damages that may be sought. The only limitations on the jurisdiction of the regular trial courts are territorial: states are usually divided into judicial districts, with one trial court in each district. The number of judges in each judicial district is determined by the size of the case load normally handled there. Large cities, which usually constitute a single district, may have as many as fifty judges.

Regardless of the number of judges serving a district, only one judge presides at a trial.

In an urban district, one of the judges may preside over what is often called the "assignment division," meaning that he is responsible for assigning cases on the docket to a particular division where they will be tried. City courts often specialize in particular subject matters. There may, for example, be a criminal division presided over by specified judges. There may be other specialized courts within the regular trial court system — for example, it is common to find a juvenile division, a civil division, a domestic relations division, and an equity division (courts hearing cases that arise under the body of rules known as "equity law"). Judges may be assigned to these courts on either a permanent or a rotational basis.

Intermediate courts of appeals

Appeals from unfavorable decisions in the regular trial courts may be taken to an intermediate court of appeals. These courts are also usually assigned on the basis of territorial jurisdiction. Most often, appellate courts are multi-judge courts.

Jurisdiction of the appeals courts is not perfectly clear nor is it the same in each state. Certain states, by statute, limit the subjects which can be dealt with in the appellate courts. It should be underscored that appellate courts do not decide cases in the same sense as do trial courts: their primary function is to determine whether or not mistakes in judgment or in application of the law have occurred in the original trial. If so, reversal of the decision or retrial may be ordered. Such judgments are made only after review of the proceedings below, sometimes supplemented by the presentation of additional arguments.

The supreme court

All states have a high court, usually called the State Supreme Court. It is also an appeals court, making the final determination as to whether or not the law and judgment below has been legally correct. The number of judges in state supreme courts varies, but seven is a common number. Trials do not occur here either, although hearings are often held. The decisions of this court either uphold the record and decision of a lower court or, if they find substantial error, send the case back to the lower court with instructions for rehearing.

Specialized courts

States may create courts to deal with very specialized types of legal problems. One such court is the probate court, which is limited to handling

Marshall Henrichs

Signs like this one are seen more and more on vehicles in urban areas.

wills and legal problems that result from settling the various claims on the estates of deceased persons. Probate courts are usually located in each of the counties of the state. Often, juvenile courts are organized as special courts. And several states have created what are called small claims courts, which exist to allow a citizen to recover a small amount of money in a situation where use of the regular civil court would cost more than the damages he is seeking to recover.

Personnel of the Courts: Judges

The judge is the central figure in the judicial process. Except for judges of the minor courts, judges must be qualified for the practice of law in the state. Membership in the state bar assures that the judge will, to some degree, feel constrained to act within the canons of his profession.[11] It is virtually assured, then, that judges will have been subjected to the kind of socialization process which occurs in three years of study at a law school. It also means that those men and women who can afford to go to law school will be recruited. That is not to say that the available pool of judges is better or worse than the total population, only that it is likely to recruit the upper end of the economic and social categories.

There are two general methods of selection of judges from the pool of available lawyers: some judges are appointed by the chief executive, usually with some kind of legislative approval and often with consultation from the local bar association. Once in office they remain there, during good behavior, for life. The popularly elected judge comes into office via the usual election process, sometimes on a partisan ballot, and must stand for re-election when his term expires. There is some evidence that the two systems select judges who are somewhat different from each other. Popular election is a self-selection process (people *choose* to run), while the appointed judge owes his appointment either to political connections or to a reputation within the bar association. These differences may have some impact on the decisions a judge makes. We might assume, although we have no concrete evidence to cite, that the popularly elected judge will be more sensitive in his decision making to public attitudes than an appointed judge will be. The appointed judge may feel inclined to let his own personal attitudes, values, and prejudices dominate his decisions.[12]

The Missouri nonpartisan plan is a reform alternative to both the elective and appointive techniques of judge selection. Initiated by the state of Missouri in 1940, this procedure has been widely imitated. The plan provides that when a vacancy occurs, an appellate judicial commission selects the names of three properly qualified persons as candidates for the vacant position. The governor chooses one from among those three. After the newly appointed judge has served for a stated time period (one year in Missouri), the Secretary of State is required to prepare a ballot to be given to all the voters at the next regular election asking them to either approve or reject the newly appointed judge. In other words, the judge runs against his record, not against another candidate for the office. Designed to separate law and politics, the Missouri plan stipulates that no political party affiliation can appear on the ballot; if paper ballots are used in the regular elections, the judicial ballot must be separate from the regular ballot.

Other officers of the court

There are other important roles in the process of local judicial politics. In criminal cases in which the government acts as protector for the public by initiating court procedure to punish a person accused of violating the criminal law, the *prosecutor* represents the government. The prosecutor performs the important function of determining what situations deserve to be brought to trial. We can view the judicial process as a filter through which cases are screened: some are advanced to the next level of decision making while others are either rejected or the conditions under which they are processed are changed; the prosecutor's office occupies a key role in that screening process.

On the basis of limited available statistics, it appears that approximately one-half of those arrested are dismissed by the police, prosecutor, or magistrate at an early stage in the case.[13] This statistic suggests broad discretion in the hands of the prosecutor. "A prosecutor plays a central role since he decides most of the strategic moves: he recommends bail, selects the charges, chooses the judges, and determines if a lesser plea will be accepted."[14] A study of the King County (Seattle) prosecutor's office found, for example, that as a matter of course, charges were never filed when a case involved fornication or attempted suicide. The prosecutor in effect was saying that these were crimes which, in his view, ought not be punished. In other cases the prosecutor was compelled by public reaction to prosecute to the fullest. One King County deputy prosecutor alluded to a case involving the murder and molestation of a six-year-old girl: "In that case there was nothing we could do. As you know, the press was on our back and every parent was concerned."[15] In addition, the exercise of the discretionary power in the hands of the prosecuting attorney is limited by the close relationship which characteristically exists between the prosecutor and the police; although the prosecutor's office may have criminal investigators of its own, the prosecutor is usually dependent on the police for evidence and testimony. While it is difficult for the prosecuting attorney's office to disregard a case built by the police, still the prosecutor must choose what specific charges to press. In the case of the six-year-old girl's molestation and murder, many would think commitment to a mental institution a more intelligent charge than first degree murder. Plea bargaining is an increasingly common practice which gives the prosecuting attorney's office discretionary power.

The *grand jury*, where it exists, performs an additional screening function in the judicial process. When the prosecutor determines that he has sufficient evidence to prosecute a case against a person, he is often required to submit his case to a grand jury for their approval or disapproval. The prosecutor submits the evidence that he has against an accused person and asks the jury to vote a true bill of indictment. Evidence is presented in a secret session; there are witnesses and defense for the accused, and all jurors are sworn not to divulge information discussed in the grand jury session.

Grand juries are also used as investigative bodies. Regular state trial courts may empanel grand juries and have them investigate the conduct of public officers, the activities of departments of government, or the actions of private persons or corporations where violations of the law are suspected. Grand juries are held in secret in these instances also — as a way of protecting reputations should allegations prove false.

In summary, the machinery of local justice appears to be capable of handling a moderate case load. However, owing to what has been called the "law explosion," the local courts — like all American courts — find themselves burdened beyond their capacities. As a result, the President's Commission on

Our stately courtrooms of yesteryear have been partitioned into smaller ones to accommodate the far greater caseloads of present times.

Law Enforcement and Administration of Justice expressed shock at the conditions it found in the lower courts:

> It has seen cramped and noisy courtrooms, undignified and perfunctory procedures, and badly trained personnel. It has seen dedicated people who are frustrated by huge case loads, by the lack of opportunity to examine cases carefully, and by the impossibility of devising constructive solutions to the problems of offenders. It has seen assembly line justice.[16]

But whether or not justice is served in our cities depends on much more than the machinery of justice and its workload. Let us turn, then, to an examination of the products of the American judicial process at the lower level.

HOW JUST IS LOCAL JUSTICE?

This is not the place to update Plato's *Republic* on the meaning of "justice"; instead, we shall assume what much of the recent literature on judicial process assumes — that justice means equality of treatment before the law.[17] This somewhat narrow conception of justice provides both a normative and an empirical referent. The ideal of such a conception of justice is that all persons accused or found guilty of committing one type of crime shall receive identical treatment. By this standard of justice, variations in treatment that are attributable to socioeconomic status, judicial procedures, or local prejudice will be called "unjust."

What do we know about variations from equal treatment before the local bar of justice? Examinations of local practices suggest that there is quite a range of variation depending on (1) the particular city, (2) the socioeconomic status of the accused, and (3) the attitudes and actions of local judicial personnel.

Variation by City

The patterns of conflict adjudication in a particular city are adapted to the overall pattern of conflict management of that city. For example, if a city is dominated by an elite, it would be reasonable to suppose that the elite would be able to impress its will on the judicial process. It has been suggested that there are three types of legal adaptation to the urban environment: the exchange type, the elite-bar type, and the communal type.[18] Each type, you will notice, involves some variation from equality of treatment.

The exchange type

This model of legal adaptation is characterized by a series of mutual dependencies as a basis for exchange among political leaders, professional criminals, and other legal personnel. The essence of an exchange system is benefit conferred for cost paid, so those who can pay the fee will receive the appropriate treatment.

In one respect, the exchange type of city is a tidy example of equality at work in the judicial system: a black numbers man, for example, will in all probability receive the same treatment as a white "bookie"; and any motorist, irrespective of political ideology, who can raise the money can have his traffic ticket fixed.

A number of conditions are usually found to be associated with such a system. There is much criticism. The press is critical but probably ineffectual. The police are likely to be badly trained and "on the take." The local bar association is likely to be divided. The cosmopolitan bar association members are consistently critical of the operation of the exchange judicial process, while the locals participate in the division of the spoils. The judges themselves are fully committed players, sharing the rewards of the process.

Though corrupt, the exchange type operates on a kind of equality — the equality of the marketplace in which each person's dollars count equally.

Inequality, of course, results between those who are able to pay and those who are not.

The elite - bar type

In contrast to the overt inequities of the exchange type, the elite-bar type of legal adaptation seems outwardly, at least, an orderly and equitable system. It induces a close alliance between a highly professional local bar association and the local socioeconomic elite. The courts function smoothly, pay-offs are infrequent, the police force is well trained, and the local lawyers and judges express belief in the "fundamental fairness" of the local legal system. In general, there is a fairly high level of satisfaction with the system and its operation in the city at large. With its emphasis on nonpartisanship and professionalism and its loathing of "corruption," the elite-bar type of legal adaptation is the darling of the reformer.

Nonetheless, such systems will harbor major inequities. First, "in all probability, the outputs of the system will be biased against those of low status, e.g., Negroes and those with minimal incomes."[19] A one-time law enforcement official in an elite-bar type of city in Oregon explained that prejudice against blacks was a widely shared disposition at the upper elite levels of the city.

> The prejudice diffused itself downward into public and private agencies in the community. The police department was no exception. There were no Negroes on the force. One Negro who did qualify was spied upon continuously by officers on the force organized by the chief and his lieutenants for that purpose. The hope was to get "something on him." Apparently they succeeded. Members of the establishment let it be known that they wanted no Negroes — police officers or otherwise — moving about in the better parts of town. We patrolled the Negro sections of town much more closely. I'm sure the parties of the white young people and older white folks in their private clubs were every bit as boisterous as those held in the Negro subcommunity. But the better and well to do have built in immunity against close police surveillance. Not so with Negroes. You wouldn't think — because you've been conditioned not to — of keeping white neighborhoods under the close scrutiny that you maintain in Negro neighborhoods. We lean a little harder on Negroes. They don't have the defenses possessed by whites.[20]

In the elite-bar type city, the legal profession is not overly concerned with the plight of the poor and disadvantaged. Policemen, district attorneys, prosecutors, even judges, may express both public and private disagreement with Supreme Court decisions protecting the rights of defendants. And the dominant atmosphere of the city constrains lawyers "from straying too far from safe, middle-class practice and clientele, either directly through pressure or indirectly through the bar's internalization of the norms."[21]

The communal type

This style of judicial adaptation to the local environment makes few pretenses of being professional. The police are likely to lack training, and the bar is likely to be poorly organized and composed almost exclusively of locals. The political system and the legal system are closely identified, the values promoted by the political process being those enforced by the legal process. The product of the communal type of legal system is biased, but the basis of the bias is membership in the community, not social class.[22] The law serves the purpose of protecting residents of the locality while dealing in a hostile and even punitive way with outsiders. An outsider may either be someone living outside the area or someone living in the city who is deviant (for example, an immigrant or, in some cities, a black). By contrast to the exchange type of judicial adaptation, membership in the communal privileged class is ascriptive rather than purchasable. Further, the biases in the communal system are conscious and justified in terms of "local traditions" of long standing, whereas in the elite-bar type, biases are likely to be unconscious and justified in terms of legal tradition.[23]

In each of the three types of local judicial systems, there are major inequities. Particularly, the scales of justice are tipped against the poor, members of minorities, and outsiders.

Influence of Socioeconomic Factors on the Delivery of Justice

The kind of justice you get at the local level depends in part on who you are. We have known for some time that differences in wealth can make a difference in the outcome of a judicial proceeding. The impact of money can have both obvious and subtle manifestations. The better lawyers command higher fees; a man of wealth and power who belongs to the same "cosmopolitan" club of which the judge is a member has an advantage. Other manifestations are more subtle. The Manhattan Bail Project, for example, after analyzing bail procedures in New York, disclosed that an accused person who had the ability to post bail (a sum of money put up as collateral by an accused to ensure his appearance at a future date) was much less likely to be convicted than one who could not obtain the money to post bail.[24]

A more concrete illustration of the unjust distribution of justice is the method of determining which persons are to have preliminary hearings. The *preliminary hearing* allows the judge to decide whether there is enough evidence against an accused to justify a trial. The judge decides whether a preliminary hearing is justified. The preliminary hearing is an advantage for the accused for a number of reasons: it deters the use of high-pressure interrogation; it allows counsel to appear and plead for the accused, particularly with regard to bail; it opens the door to the assertion of other rights, for example, the right to a copy of the complaint; and it makes it possible for counsel to secure other guarantees as well. In short, the preliminary hearing is a safeguard for the rights of the accused; and its denial is a limitation to those rights. A study using an elaborate data base found that 34 percent of the poor accused of felonious assault in the state courts did not get preliminary hearings, while only 21 percent of those with money were denied hearings.[25]

Race

Many blacks are poor and many poor people are black, so figures on poverty and race must overlap. But the figures are not identical and the differences are important. In general, the poor suffer even more discrimination than blacks in criminal justice. For example, a black is more likely to get a preliminary hearing than a poor man. The black person is not as likely as the white defendant to be released on bail, but much more likely to be released than the poor defendant. Important black-white differences show up at crucial stages in the judicial process. For example, the lawyer of a black is more likely to be court appointed than is the lawyer of a white defendant. In federal larceny cases in one year, for example, 52 percent of the blacks did not have their own lawyers as contrasted to 25 percent of the whites.[26] Blacks are particularly discriminated against when it comes to probation or suspended sentences. This is true in assault convictions, but the figures are even more dramatic for larceny: 74 percent of guilty blacks were imprisoned in state larceny cases against only 49 percent of guilty whites. Even with previous record of the defendant held constant, the disparity still holds up.[27]

Age

Younger defendants are less likely to receive the procedural safeguards than are older defendants. However, they are more likely to get light sentences. There may be several reasons for this: younger people usually have short prior records; but the main reason is probably the widespread belief that the young are not as responsible, are more easily rehabilitated, and suffer from hardships while in prison.

Evidence from different cities suggests that there is considerable variation in the treatment of youth at the prearrest and arrest stage. A number of police departments mark youth, particularly hippie-type youth, as among the problem population deserving of extraordinary surveillance. As a result, young people with long hair, beards, and unconventional dress are disproportionately the subjects of police field interrogations. One study suggests that different attitudes toward the handling of the young at the prearrest and arrest stage varies with the type of city. Cities composed of more middle- and upper-class residents show a tendency to use law enforcement agencies as a means for resolving relatively petty disputes in which youths are involved.[28] In such cities, public machinery is expected to deal with matters which in an earlier era or in other cities would be considered pranks or personal problems rather than crimes. Stealing from the neighbor's melon patch, for example, may be treated in the small town with a parental reprimand; but in some cities stepping on a neighbor's prize flower or cutting across the corner of his lawn may result in a police call.

Sex

Women, too, receive differential treatment in criminal proceedings. Like juveniles, women are the recipients of "paternalized" justice. It is especially true that women receive lighter sentences. Women are much more likely to be released on a bail that they can afford than are men. In trial, women are more likely to be found innocent and, if found guilty, are more likely to be put on probation or be given suspended sentences. In explaining these sex differentials, Stuart S. Nagel says, "Studies in women's prisons have shown that women develop fewer defenses against the pains of incarceration than men and perhaps suffer more, and it is possible that judges and juries know or sense this. Or perhaps they simply find the idea of women in prison, away from their families, offensive."[29]

The discriminatory patterns in American justice at the local level follow expected lines. The poor and the minorities, particularly black, are most consistently denied access to the full array of judicial protections. It is small wonder, then, that the poor man looks on the law more as an enemy than as a friend. As Nicholas Katzenbach, former U.S. attorney general, put it,

> Most of us have little contact with welfare laws or housing codes aimed at rat infestations or with minimum wage laws or with protections against usurious loans or installment purchase contracts. And even if we did have the contact, we are equipped as articulate, educated citizens, to deal with such matters. To us, laws and regulations are protections and guides, established for our benefit, and for us to use. But to the poor, they are a hostile means, established as harrassment, at all costs to be avoided.

Discrimination affects juveniles and women in a manner different from the way it affects the black and poor before local courts. The former are the recipients of a paternalized justice — a different kind of inequality, but inequality nonetheless.

THE POLICE AS CONFLICT MANAGERS

The police also play an important role in assuring justice while managing conflict. In contemporary America, they have played that role in a most controversial way. The importance of the police system is undeniable. The individual policemen is, in effect, the court of first resort: he is in a position to administer justice without trial. As with most important roles, it is a difficult one to perform wisely. The policeman is frequently in a situation in which he must implement all the guarantees of the system of justice which demand equal treatment and defense of the rights of individual citizens; but if he does take great care to implement these guarantees, it may result in his being hurt or killed.

The tensions and incidents in the late 1960s served to crystallize long-held opposing views of the role of policemen. Polarization proceeded to the point at which some citizens viewed policemen as heroes while others thought of them as monsters. The policeman in his uniform is a kind of "Rorschach Test" for each of us. As he walks his beat with his nightstick, gun, helmet, mace can, and summons book, he stimulates fantasy and projection in us all.

> Children identify with him in the perennial game of "cops and robbers." Teen-agers in autos stiffen with compulsive rage or anxiety at the sight of the patrol car. To people in trouble the police officer is a savior. In another metamorphosis the patrolman becomes the fierce ogre that mothers conjure up to frighten their disobedient youngsters.[30]

Praise or blame for the policeman, as with every judgment based on a stereotype, is often misconceived. We find it easy to blame the individual policeman for enforcing laws that we do not like, especially if he seems to relish it.

A sound understanding of the policeman must go beyond stereotypes. Perhaps the most fundamental insight to start with is that the policeman is not fundamentally a policy maker, but is instead a bureaucrat. As with all urban bureaucrats, he has a range of personal discretion open to him as a result of the ambiguities of the law and directives under which he operates. Beyond that assumption, we can sharpen our understanding of the role of policemen in urban America by discussing (1) what kind of people become policemen, (2) the sense in which there is a common "working personality" of a policeman, and (3) what important variations in police behavior occur from city to city.

Police Recruitment

In the post-World War II years, during a cycle of relative prosperity, the bulk of candidates for policemen's jobs has come from the working class with a sprinkling from the lower-middle class. For example, an examination of the backgrounds of recruits graduating from the New York Police Academy in the 1950s showed that 85% of the recruits came from working-class family backgrounds. Only about 3% came from professional or semiprofessional families.[31] Records on educational background showed that 95% of the recruits had no college training.

Policemen, in other words, are recruited from those segments of the population which are most inclined toward overt racial prejudice, most intolerant of dissent, and most likely to exhibit that cluster of personality traits social scientists call "authoritarianism." Police recruits have also been found likely to exhibit dispositions common to those with similar backgrounds: in particular, impatience with intellectual and social explanation; also, a predisposition toward toughness and masculinity in dealing with conflict; and a tendency to uncritical obedience to established authority.[32]

Two other conditions affecting police recruitment deserve mention. For one, the pay of a policeman has declined in recent years relative to other occupations for persons with comparable backgrounds. As a result, the prestige of the occupation has fallen and there has been a decline in the quality and quantity of new recruits. In the 1930s top-grade patrolmen in New York City earned enough to enable them to afford the luxuries that were the envy of the middle class. In the postwar period, police pay has lagged badly. "Patrolmen's pay in major cities [in 1968] averages about $7,500 per year — 33% less than is needed to sustain a family of four in moderate circumstances in a large city, according to the U.S. Bureau of Labor Statistics."[33] As a result, new police recruits are being taken from a pool of undereducated people. In many urban departments today, the older policemen are better educated and qualified than are the young policemen, reversal of the trend operating in most every other occupation in America.[34]

Paradoxically, a second factor accounting for a decline in the qualifications of police recruits has been the drive toward professionalism. A number of cities, in their efforts to improve the quality of recruits, have made the screening process more rigorous. Most cities first require a written examination which has become a modified intelligence test. Those who pass the minimum standards set by the particular city are then subjected to an elaborate character investigation. These investigations are often quite thorough and based on the guiding principle that "any and every doubt must be resolved in favor of the department." As a New York City police commissioner, reviewing the screening procedures, observed, "We investigate candidates from the time they were in kindergarten to their entrance in the department. The report on everyone of them runs from 60 to 75 pages of material."[35] Beyond this, many departments also subject applicants to psychiatric examinations, and in a number of cities, lie detector tests are also required.[36] The lie detector test, as one police captain describes its use, is to enable the detection of attempts at "deception and to uncover a multitude of undetected crimes such as thievery, homosexuality, emotional instability, and

The public relations staff of an urban police department has a full-time job.

attempts to hide physical disabilities or ailments and any omissions and false statements made on the official police questionnaire."[37] As has often been pointed out, the result of such screening processes is that a number of people who might be sensitive to social problems but who might have had say, adolescent homosexual contact or some experience smoking marijuana, are disqualified as poor risks. As Arthur Neiderhoffer sums it up, "The end result of the process of elimination is to accentuate the medium and mediocre at the expense of the independent and exceptional."[38]

Police Role and Personality

Joe Fink of New York City's Ninth Precinct enumerates three functions that the police perform in urban society: "One is law enforcement. Another is keeping the peace. The third is furnishing services."[39] Radio, television, and movie imagery would lead us to believe that the law enforcement role occupies the greatest part of the policeman's attention. This is not the case, however.

A study of Syracuse, New York, for example, shows that only about 10 percent of police calls required exercise of the law enforcement function — that is, to interrupt a burglary in progress, to check a car, or arrest a prowler[40] (See Table 12.1). Providing services occupies much more police time than is commonly assumed. In Syracuse it was found that about 38 percent of citizen complaints required the police to perform such services as attending at accidents or illnesses, escorting a vehicle, aiding at a fire or at a downed power line or tree, or helping recover a lost person or lost property.

Beyond these services, a number of police departments expend time and resources on community relations programs which they consider to be services. The Nassau County Police Department, for example, stands ready to provide speakers for civic or school affairs and maintains a full-time staff of twenty-four officers to operate a boys' club program.

The "keeping of the peace" role involves maintenance of order. Characteristically, peacekeeping situations result from breaches of public serenity. Such situations usually involve at least two parties in disputes in which the "fault" is not self-evident and is perhaps equally shared. Specifically, a breach of the peace may involve husband and wife fights, feuding neighbors, or a group of juveniles gathered at a streetcorner. These situations involve a great deal of ambiguity and, therefore, provide a great range of discretion to the officer. According to James Q. Wilson, the peacekeeping activity is distinguished by the fact that the policeman approaches these incidents with an eye toward enforcing the law, but more in terms of "handling the situation."[41]

Table 12.1   Citizen Complaints Radioed to Patrol Vehicles, Syracuse Police
Department, June 3-9, 1966
(based on a one-fifth sample of a week's calls)*

	Calls	Number in Sample	Full Count (sample multiplied by 5)	Percent
Information Gathering		69	345	22.1
Book and check	2			
Get a report	67			
Service		117	585	37.5
Accidents, illnesses, ambu-lance calls	42			
Animals	8			
Assist a person	1			
Drunk person	8			
Escort vehicle	3			
Fire, power line or tree down	26			
Lost or found person or property	23			
Property damage	6			
Order Maintenance		94	470	30.1
Gang disturbance	50			
Family trouble	23			
Assault, fight	9			
Investigation	8			
Neighbor trouble	4			
Law Enforcement		32	160	10.3
Burglary in progress	9			
Check a car	5			
Open door, window	8			
Prowler	6			
Make an arrest	4			
Totals		312	1,560	100.0

*Not included are internal calls — that is, those originating with another police officer (as, for example, when an officer requests a check on the status of a person or vehicle or requests the wagon, and so forth) — or purely administrative calls.

Source: James Q. Wilson, *Varieties of Police Behavior* (Cambridge: Harvard University Press, 1968), p. 18.

The discretion inherent in the peacekeeping role provides the individual policeman his greatest opportunity to impose his personal dispositions on the processes of law enforcement. In doing so, the personal idiosyncrasies, emotions, and occasionally prejudices of the officer are exercised. How do policemen use this discretion? A number of other studies have attempted to describe the "working personality" of the policeman, a research effort somewhat parallel to the search for the "military mind" — and with similar limitations. What these studies suggest is that policemen are highly conventional people. As one observer of the New York City police force put it, "All a cop can swing in a milieu of marijuana smokers, interracial dates, and homosexuals is the nightstick. A policeman who passed a lower East side art gallery filled with paintings of what appeared to be female genitalia could think of doing only one thing — step in and make an arrest."[42] Jerome Skolnick suggests that there is a set of philosophical underpinnings to the police personality and action which are quite widely shared among policemen. He says that the policeman's working assumption about humanity can best be described as the "rotten apple" view of man. By this, Skolnick means that the policeman, like so many Americans, believes that crime and disorder are attributable mainly to the intentions of evil individuals. It presumes that a person's behavior transcends his past experience, culture, and society, and should be understood "in terms of wrong choices, deliberately made."[43] In contradiction to the assumptions of all the behavioral sciences, then, the policeman's analysis of a given situation usually excludes social factors such as poverty, inadequate housing, and discrimination. Skolnick quotes one policeman's simple summary, "Poverty doesn't cause crime; people do."[44]

The rotten apple view of man carries with it a rather thoroughgoing cynicism about individual men and society; but, more specific to the work of the individual policeman, it helps him justify his need to sort out a certain category of people against whom he must always be on guard. Because a policeman's work requires him to be occupied continually with potential violence, he develops a perceptual shorthand to identify certain kinds of people as "symbolic assailants." That is, "persons whose gesture, language, and attire . . . the policeman has come to recognize as a prelude to violence."[45] Policemen create for themselves a whole series of danger signs which they use to identify symbolic assailants and other potential lawbreakers. Such signs vary, but as List 12.1 indicates, there are many.

The personal dispositions of the police, it has also been often noted, lead many to political ultraconservatism. Former Los Angeles police chief William H. Parker, himself a favorite of political conservatives throughout the country, described the political ideologies of the nation's peace officers as "conservative, ultraconservative, and very right wing." On the basis of interviews with policemen, Skolnick concluded, "It was clear that a Goldwater type of conservatism was the dominant political and emotional persuasion of police. I encountered only three policemen who claimed to be politically 'liberal,' at the same time asserting that they were decidedly exceptional."[46]

The rotten apple view of human nature has the important conse-

List 12.1   Suggestions About Persons to be Subjected to Field Interrogation

1. Suspicious persons known to the officer from previous arrests, field interrogations, and observations.

2. Emaciated-appearing alcoholics and narcotics users who invariably turn to crime to pay for cost of habit.

3. Person who fits description of wanted suspect as described by radio, teletype, daily bulletins.

4. Any person observed in the immediate vicinity of a crime very recently committed or reported as "in progress."

5. Known trouble makers near large gatherings.

6. Persons who attempt to avoid or evade the officer.

7. Persons showing exaggerated unconcern over contact with the officer.

8. Persons who are visibly "rattled" when near the policeman.

9. Unescorted women or young girls in public places, particularly at night in such places as cafes, bars, bus and train depots, or streetcorners.

10. "Lovers" in an industrial area (make good lookouts).

11. Persons who loiter about places where children play.

12. Solicitors or peddlers in a residential neighborhood.

13. Loiterers around public rest rooms.

14. Lone male sitting in car adjacent to schoolground with newspaper or book in his lap.

15. Lone male sitting in car near shopping center who pays unusual amount of attention to women, sometimes continuously manipulating rearview mirror to avoid direct eye contact.

16. Hitchhikers.

17. Person wearing coat on hot days.

18. Car with mismatched hub caps, or dirty car with clean license plate (or vice versa).

19. Uniformed "deliverymen" with no merchandise or truck.

20. Many others. How about your own personal experiences?

Source: Adapted from Thomas F. Adams, "Field Interrogation," *Police* (March-April 1963), p. 28.

quence of putting the policeman at odds with many of the groups he is called on to police. Because the policeman learns to look for and anticipate violence from the symbolic assailant, and because the symbolic assailant is often identified by his deviance in sometimes quite superficial matters, the policeman is led to suspicion of any behavior which is outside the conventional. The assumptions of the policeman's working personality lead him to treat the black, the brown, and the long-haired as enemies. This, it should be understood, is not so much a result of the fact that policemen are themselves rotten apples, but because policemen represent in a very heavy-handed way the deficiencies of our conventional wisdom and our social order. James Baldwin, eminent black essayist and novelist, captures the situation well:

> . . . the only way to police a ghetto is to be oppressive. None of the Police Commissioner's men, even with the best will in the world, have any way of understanding the lives led by the people they swagger about in twos and threes controlling. Their very presence is an insult, and it would be, even if they spent their entire day feeding gumdrops to children. They represent the force of the white world, and that world's real intentions are, simply, for the world''s criminal profit and ease, to keep the black man corralled up here, in his place. The badge, the gun and the holster, and the swinging club make vivid what will happen should his rebellion become overt. Rare, indeed, is the Harlem citizen, from the most circumspect church member to the most shiftless adolescent, who does not have a long tale to tell of police incompetence, injustice, or brutality. . . .
>
> It is hard, on the other hand, to blame the policeman, blank, goodnatured, thoughtless, and insuperably innocent, for being such a perfect representative of the people he serves. He, too, believes in good intentions and is astounded and offended when they are not taken for the deed. He has never himself, done anything for which to be hated — which of us has? And yet he is facing, daily and nightly, people who would gladly see him dead, and he knows it. There is no way for him not to know it: there are few things under heaven more unnerving than the silent, accumulating contempt and hatred of a people. He moves through Harlem, therefore, like an occupying soldier in a bitterly hostile country; which is precisely what, and where he is, and is the reason he walks in twos and threes.[47]

Varieties of Police Behavior:
Watchman, Legalistic, Service

Let me exemplify some variations possible in police behavior by telling of my own puzzling experiences with the policemen of two different kinds of cities. When I moved from Manhattan, Kansas, to San Diego, California, it became immediately apparent to me that police are not the same in every city. After two years without a violation in Manhattan, I found that in San Diego I could hardly keep out of trouble. Within a few short months, I was ticketed for jaywalking, field interrogated, and fined because I had parked my car in my driveway so that the rear of the car blocked the sidewalk. It could be that this is just another chapter in the old "country boy comes to the city" story; but the accumulated evidence of political scientists shows that there are indeed substantial differences in enforcement patterns among American cities.

Variations in the style of law enforcement, as we might expect, are not random, but are associated with the character of the political environment of a city. That is to say, police departments, like the total judicial process of which they are a part, adapt to the urban environment in which they are set.[48]

What styles of police adaptation to urban environment commonly occur in America? James Q. Wilson's study of police behavior in eight cities suggests that there are three major styles of law enforcement: the watchman style, the legalistic style, and the service style.[49]

As Table 12.2 shows, the *watchman style* police department places central emphasis on the peacekeeping role, more interested in informal adjustment of disputes than in issuing citations or making arrests. In those cities in which the watchman style operates (Wilson found Albany and Newburgh, New York to be good examples), police administrators seek to influence the exercise of discretion by the individual policeman so that many common minor violations are simply ignored. Juveniles, for example, are expected to misbehave, and their infractions — unless they are serious — are usually ignored or treated informally. Blacks, too, are thought to deserve a less strict law enforcement because, to the police, their conduct suggests a low level of public and private morality. In line with this view, the choice of leaving blacks

Table 12.2   Varieties of Police Behavior

Style	Defining Characteristics	Political Structure/Style Commonly Assocd.	Examples
Watchman	Emphasis on "peacekeeping" role	Caretaker	Albany, Amsterdam, and Newburgh, New York
Legalistic	Emphasis on "law enforcement" role	Reformed Cities: Council - Manager	Oakland, California; Highland Park, Illinois
Service	Balance between peacekeeping and enforcement roles; less likely to make arrest than legalistic style departments.	Amenities-Seeking	Brighton and Nassau County, New York

Source: Compiled from James Q. Wilson, *Varieties of Police Behavior* (Cambridge: Harvard University Press, 1968), Chap. 5-8.

alone becomes preferable to making numerous arrests. When blacks commit serious crimes, of course, they are to be dealt with in the more formal law enforcement mode. Motorists are seldom ticketed for minor traffic violations unless they annoy others or insult the police authority. It is interesting to note also that the watchman police style usually ignores vice and gambling. In short, the police emphasize good order over law enforcement.

The watchman style fits with the urban machine (for example, Albany, New York). As Wilson says, the watchman style of police system "is led by politicians who appeal to a predominantly working class and lower middle class constituency on the basis of party loyalty, ethnic identification, and exchange of favors, personal acquaintanceship, and the maintenance of a low tax rate."[50]

The *legalistic style* of law enforcement, on the other hand, is most usually found in reformed cities. In both Oakland, California, and Highland Park, Illinois, where Wilson found the legalistic style to be in operation, it emerged as a result of appointments of new police chiefs made by city managers who had come to the city with a mandate for change.[51] The legalistic style is distinguished by its emphasis on its law enforcement role. The legalistic police department issues citations and makes arrests with much greater frequency than does the watchman-type police department. Traffic citations are made at a high rate; juvenile offenders are detained and arrested in greater numbers; vigorous action is taken against vice and crime, whether the accused are making disturbances or not; and there are a large number of misdemeanor arrests even when, as with petty larceny, public order is not breached. In other words, in the legalistic-style city, the police will act as if there were a single standard of conduct expected of all residents, irrespective of their subculture. The law is uniformly enforced, but cultural pluralism is ignored. Blacks, juveniles, and drunks are more likely than others to commit particular crimes; as a result, the law falls more heavily on them and they experience it as "harrassment."

A third style of law enforcement which Wilson has discerned is characterized by a police force which strikes a balance between its peacekeeping and law enforcement roles. The *service style* of law enforcement occurs in cities in which the police take seriously all requests for either law enforcement or peacekeeping but are less likely to respond by making an arrest or other formal sanction than where the legalistic style prevails. The police intervene more frequently but less formally than in watchman cities. Wilson found that the service style prevailed commonly in homogeneous, middle-class cities in which there was a high level of apparent agreement among citizens on the need for public order, but in which there was no administrative demand for a legalistic style. Such cities often are crucially shaped by an amenities-seeking image of the role of local government.

Wilson acknowledges that these are tentative classifications of police style, that there may be other styles not enunciated, and that a number of cities probably have police departments that combine two styles. The central point is, however, amply underscored by the typology — that police behavior varies significantly and systematically from city to city. Equal treatment may be desirable or undesirable (depending on one's own value position); what *is* certain is that the value of equal treatment collides with the value of adapting law enforcement to the particular mix of subgroups present within the city.

SUMMARY

The first point of citizen contact with the law is with local police and courts. These courts of first resort are themselves important participants in the adjustment of conflicts. In general, local judicial machinery is over-burdened and organizationally cumbersome. The police have a great deal of discretion in the exercise of their functions and that discretion gives them a powerful political role.

It is not possible to assess the ultimate justice of the courts of first resort. But accounting for some variation from city to city, it is possible to discern a broad pattern of discrimination against racial minorities and social deviants by both courts and police.

NOTES

1. Reported in *Life* Magazine (November 19, 1971), p. 28.
2. These survey results were reported in *Life* Magazine, January 14, 1972, pp. 28A ff. As good social scientists, we should remind ourselves that a mail survey of this type is subject to severe bias, since those who return such questionnaires are those who are self-selected generally from the highly concerned group.
3. See his concurring opinion in *Mapp vs. Ohio* 367 U.S. 643; 81 S. Ct. 1684, 1689 (1961).
4. For an interesting discussion of the use and abuse of the search warrant, see Ed Cray, *The Big Blue Line: Police Power vs. Human Rights* (New York: Coward-McCann, 1967), pp. 41-55.
5. Figures were taken from President's Crime Commission, *Task Force Report: The Courts* (Washington, D.C.: U.S. Government Printing Office, 1967), pp. 31, 154.
6. Reported in James R. Klonoski and Robert I. Mendelsohn, eds., *The Politics of Local Justice* (Boston: Little, Brown, 1970), p. xvi. Original source is "City Courts Facing a Growing Crisis," New York *Times* (February 12, 1968), p. 35.
7. In states such as Louisiana, Texas, and California, they may also be involved with

the application of rules of law derived from the Roman law tradition imparted by the Spanish settlers of these areas.

8. Wallace S. Sayre and Herbert Kaufman, *Governing New York City* (New York: Russell Sage Foundation, 1960), p. 522.

9. In special circumstances, however, many state courts render what are called advisory opinions on a hypothetical set of facts presented to them by specified competent sources, usually legislative or administrative officers.

10. Carl A. McCandless, *Urban Government and Politics* (New York: McGraw-Hill, 1970), pp. 244-248.

11. See Klonoski and Mendelsohn, *Politics of Local Justice*, Section 4.

12. See Stewart Nagel, "The Tipped Scales of American Justice," *Trans-action* (May-June 1966), pp. 4-9.

13. President's Commission on Law Enforcement and Administration of Justice, *The Challenge of Crime in a Free Society* (Washington. D.C.: U.S. Government Printing Office, 1967), p. 133.

14. George F. Cole, "The Politics of Prosecution," in *New Perspectives in State and Local Politics*, ed. James A. Riedel (Waltham, Mass.: Xerox College Publishing, 1971), pp. 267-284, 272.

15. Ibid., pp. 272-273.

16. President's Commission on Law Enforcement and Administration of Justice, *Challenge of Crime*, p. 128.

17. On this point, see Klonoski and Mendelsohn, *Politics of Local Justice*, p. xvi. They say, "In recent decades a concern for equality has moved steadily to the center of discussion in debates concerning the qualities of a just society."

18. This line of study is suggested and some research strategies for pursuing it by James R. Klonoski and Robert I. Mendelsohn, "The Allocation of Justice: A Political Approach," *Journal of Public Law* 14 (November 2, 1965): 326-342.

19. Ibid., p. 339.

20. Ibid.

21. Ibid., p. 340.

22. Ibid.

23. These three types seem not to be exhaustive. A mass-bar variation of the elite-bar type might be possible, for example. Such a system would find the rhetoric of impartial justice more aligned with the practice of providing equal treatment to the minorities and the poor. Communal systems could exist in other variations than this one, which seems based on the small, sometimes oppressive Southern town. Building a political and legal system biased toward the desires of the community members does not necessarily mean that outsiders will be abused. It may be that we fail to understand the more subtle varieties of judicial process at the local level simply because we fail to differentiate an adequate range of types.

24. See Charles E. Ares, Anne Rankin, and Herbert Sturz, "The Manhattan Bail Project: An Interim Report on the Use of Pre-Trial Parole," *New York University Law Review* 38 (1963): 67-92.

25. Stuart S. Nagel, "Tipped Scales of American Justice." More detailed analysis can be found in an article by the same author, "Disparities in Criminal Procedure," *UCLA Law Review* 14 (1967): 1272-1305.

26. Note that this is a figure of the federal courts. The comparable figure for the local courts is not available; however, the Nagel study generally found little difference in the distribution of justice figures between the state courts and the federal courts.

27. Nagel, "Tipped Scales of American Justice," p. 5.

28. See Nathan Goldman, *The Differential Selection of Juvenile Offenders for Court Appearance* (New York: National Research and Information Center of the National Council on Crime and Delinquency, 1963).

29. Nagel, "Tipped Scales of American Justice," p. 8.

30. Arthur Niederhoffer, *Behind the Shield: The Police in Urban Society* (Garden City, N.Y.: Doubleday, 1969), p. 1.

31. Ibid., p. 39.

32. Ibid., Chap. 5. Also see David H. Bayley and Harold Mendelsohn, *Minorities and the Police* (New York: Free Press of Glencoe, 1969); and John H. McNamara, "Uncertainties in Police Work: The Relevance of Police Recruiters' Backgrounds and Training," in *The Police: Six Sociological Essays*, ed. David J. Bordua (New York: John Wiley and Sons, 1967), pp. 163-252.

33. A. James Reichley, "The Way to Cool the Police Rebellion," *Fortune* Magazine (December 1968), p. 113. As of 1970 the average pay was nearly $8,000 per year.

34. Jerome H. Skolnick, *The Politics of Protest* (New York: Ballantine Books, 1969), pp. 253-255.

35. Statement of Commissioner Michael Murphy in New York *Times* (February 23, 1964), p. 45.

36. See Chris Gugas, "Better Policemen Through Better Screening," *Police* 6 (July-August 1962): 54-58.

37. Captain Paul H. Bohardt, "Tucson Uses New Police Personnel Selection Methods," *FBI Law Enforcement Bulletin* 28 (September 1959): 8-12.

38. Neiderhoffer, *Behind the Shield*, p. 41.

39. Sol Braun, "The Cop as Social Scientist," New York *Times Magazine* (August 24, 1969), p. 69.

40. James Q. Wilson, *Varieties of Police Behavior* (Cambridge: Harvard University Press, 1968), p. 18.

41. Ibid., p. 31.

42. Thomas R. Brooks, "New York's Finest," *Commentary* 40 (August 1965): 29-30.

43. Skolnick, *Politics of Protest*, p. 259.

44. Ibid.

45. Jerome Skolnick, *Justice Without Trial: Law Enforcement in Democratic Society* (New York: John Wiley and Sons, 1967), p. 45.

46. Ibid., p. 61.

47. James Baldwin, *Nobody Knows My Name* (New York: Dell Publishing Co., 1962), pp. 61-62.

48. This observation and much of the discussion contained in this section, unless otherwise noted, is from James Q. Wilson, *Varieties of Police Behavior*, p. 233.

49. Ibid., Chap. 5, 6, and 7.

50. Ibid., p. 236.

51. Ibid., p. 258.

Policy in
the Urban Setting

Public policy is made when an issue is resolved. Even such a seemingly simple statement is subject to misunderstanding. The meaning of "issue," for example, as we discussed in connection with the problems of issue selection in community power studies, is subject to important misconceptions. It is commonly presumed that issues are fights: "common connotations of 'issue' include some amount of controversy or confusion."[1]

In Part Four we use "issue" in a broader sense. We assume that an issue can be a relatively quietly proposed and disposed question. It may be settled by administrative decision making, for instance, in a conventional way and without public hostility or even discussion. In addition, we assume that there are a number of latent issues in cities — that is, subjects which have the potential to pose questions that would require public conflict management should they arise. Frey calls these "suppressed issues," a term which connotes some effort to prevent the issue from becoming manifest.[2] Conflict over issues, then, may be: (1) latent; (2) conventional, when "established means of political expression are used to influence the outcome"[3]; and (3) rancorous, when the conflict involves a high level of hostility and when it is framed in personal terms. Opponents in rancorous conflicts usually see one another as being "vicious," "dirty," and often as "refusing to play by the rules." As Gamson defines rancorous conflict, it is "characterized by the belief that norms about the waging of political conflict . . . have been violated."[4]

The nature of the public policy process — the process of creating and enacting public policy — is not self-evident either. Public policy contains five major components. First, there is a decision on *a particular object or set of objects*, that is, some designated part of the environment which is to be affected. Second, there is *a desired course of events* or, in other words, a particular sequence of behaviors desired in the object. Third, there is *a selected line of actions* which are deliberately chosen to bring about the desired course of events. Fourth, there is *a declaration of intent* or some statement of the policy makers as to what they intend to do, how, and why. And finally, there is *an implementation of intent*, actions which are taken in the direction of the particular set of objects in pursuance of the choices and declarations.[5] Clearly, this conception of the policy process does not involve simple administration, but is itself a political process.

Finally, when we say that public policy resolves an issue, there is no intent to imply that the matter is finally settled. The enactment of a particular public policy may stir new conflicts, or it may only temporarily satisfy the parties to the previous conflict.

In this section we shall examine how the urban political process seeks to manage conflict, using some comparative and case studies. Here, we shall put together the components we have analytically distinguished and discussed in the preceding chapters. A process is always greater than (or at least different from) the sum of its parts. None of us could understand the operation of the human body if all we knew of it was what we could learn from each part being passed by us on a conveyor belt; part of the reality of the body is how it works when assembled and acting. So it is with a political process. In Chapter 13, then, we shall consider some of the comparative attempts to study urban policies and issues. Chapter 14 illustrates the process with three case studies of actual urban issues so that components and dynamics can be seen whole. And finally, Chapter 15 discusses the major features of the most central urban policies.

NOTES

1. Andrew McFarland, *Power and Leadership in Pluralist Systems* (Stanford: Stanford University Press, 1969), p. 122.
2. Frederick W. Frey, "Comment: On Issues and Non-Issues in the Study of Power," *American Political Science Review* 65 (December 1971): 1088.
3. William A. Gamson, "Rancorous Conflict in Community Politics," *American Sociological Review* 31 (February 1966): 71.
4. Ibid.
5. Austin Ranney, "The Study of Policy Content: A Framework for Choice," in *Political Science and Public Policy*, ed. Austin Ranney (Chicago: Markham, 1968), p. 7.

Chapter 13

Comparative Public Policies
and Issues

Peter Rossi observed in 1957 that most of the urban political research that had been done to that point had been case studies, that is, examinations of the particular events and processes in a specific single city or subarea. He urged at that time, that "research . . . should be extensive rather than intensive and comparative rather than the case study technique."[1] Political scientists have come to take Rossi's advice. Attempts to compare urban processes and to utilize aggregate data are particularly far along in the studies of relationships between public policy and environment (discussed in this chapter) as well as in the studies of urban decision making (discussed in Chapter 10).

This growing use of comparative research offers a number of advantages which the case study technique could not realize. For example, it is not enough to know that one community resolves an urban renewal question in a particular way. As careful students of politics, we want to know whether that is a *common* way of resolving that issue or whether unique situations and personalities, in that particular city, account for that outcome. Comparative study urges examination of a common variable in several cities or sub-populations, thus minimizing the impact of the unique. Comparative study generates a great deal of information. This would be a disadvantage if we had only the possibility of hand processing. But for contemporary researchers who are able to use statistical techniques and have access to computer technology, mountains of data are easily handled. Comparative technique, coupled with high-speed data processing, permits us to develop higher levels of generalization.

Comparative approaches will probably never entirely replace the case study, however. For some purposes we need to know and examine unique circumstances, particularly if we are interested in the sources of social and political change. For example, it may happen that the unique in one city may later become generalized to other cities. Another problem is that comparative studies require a paring down of the data, which results in the loss of descriptions of unique situations. It is also true that unique developments in a particular city could suggest alternative formulations of the theory a particular comparative analysis is seeking to verify. Finally, we should recognize that generalizations produced by aggregate data techniques sound to the non-specialist quite bland and uninteresting, stripped as they are of the drama and personalities which make local politics lively and interesting. Students of urban politics need not choose between comparative and case study approaches. Each has something useful to convey about an urban political process. Together, comparative and case study approaches will help us to understand more fully how urban politics works.[2]

PUBLIC POLICY AND ENVIRONMENT:
STATIC COMPARATIVE STUDY

Comparative study of urban political issues has generally not included a comparison of the dynamics of urban issues. However, as we saw in Chapter 4, a major research tradition has developed which associates urban environment and urban political structure with particular policy outcomes; the association is arrived at by a static rather than a dynamic formulation. Even so, this mode of comparative study has already made possible the partial testing of several explanations of the urban policy-making process. Comparative technique has been used to test the assumption that urban environment is a crucial determinant of which policies are adopted by a city.[3] Thus far, a number of studies have shown that social and economic cleavages in the city directly affect the content of a number of policies: educational policy and expenditure policy,[4] policies of cooperation or integration with neighboring municipalities,[5] decisions to change the form of government,[6] and urban renewal, for example.[7]

Thomas Dye's study of educational policies in sixty-seven large cities is a good illustration. Dye used the assumptions of a systems approach to specify expected relationships between environment, political structure, and educational policy outcomes. In general, he hypothesized that cities of higher socioeconomic status "know the value of education, are more sophisticated in judging the quality of educational services, and know how to make their demands felt in the political system."[8] Dye expected that structural characteristics, like the mode of choosing school board members, and the relationship between city government and the school district, would be less closely associated with educational policies. Tables 13.1 and 13.2 are his summaries of correlations between the selected environmental indicators and educational policy and also between educational structural variables and educational policy. Some of what these materials suggest could be put in proposition form:

1. Wealth (as measured by income, property value, and size of city) is the principal determinant of how much is spent on the education of each child.

2. Income and, secondly, property value are the most important determinants of local school support. The higher the median family income, the greater the local share of public school expenditures.

3. The higher the overall income level, the higher the school tax rate. Large nonwhite populations are associated with lower school tax rates.

Table 13.1   The Social Character of Cities and Educational Policy Outcomes

Educational Policy Outcomes	Urban Environmental Variables (see Note)											
	Size		Education		Occupa-tion		Income		Non-White		Property	
	Sim.	Par.	Sim.	Par.	Sim.	Par.	Sim.	Par.	Sim.	Par.	Sim.	Par.
Per Pupil Expenditures	.40*	.41*	-.04	-.13	-.01	-.02	.47*	.30*	-.39*	-.41*	.32*	.34*
Expenditures Relative to Income	-.14	.07	.15	.07	.14	-.02	-.11	-.06	-.09	-.02	-.39*	-.30*
School Tax Rate	.03	.04	.22	-.05	.25	.09	.29*	.25*	-.31*	-.16	-.10	-.16
Local School Support	.11	.03	.02	.11	-.08	-.17	.34*	.25*	-.17	-.08	.23	.06
Teachers' Salaries	.31*	.28*	-.05	-.17	-.02	.00	.42*	.29*	-.30*	-.26*	.19	.11
Teacher Turnover	.28*	.17	.15	-.01	.11	.04	.11	.08	-.08	.02	-.05	.14
Teacher-Pupil Ratio	-.03	-.02	-.07	.02	-.13	-.15	-.01	.11	.24*	.25*	-.02	-.17
Teachers without Degrees	.05	-.18	-.45*	-.31*	-.36*	.07	.02	.30*	.05	-.27*	.07	-.06
Teachers with Masters	-.01	.02	.23	.17	.15	-.06	.18	-.02	-.14	-.05	.21	.20
Drop Out Rate	-.12	-.05	.35*	.26*	.24*	-.06	.20	.10	-.04	.16	.07	.01
Private School Enrollment	.25*	-.04	-.45*	-.40*	-.36*	.07	.23	.38*	.07	-.01	.45*	.29*

Note: Figures are simple and partial correlation coefficients for 67 cities; partial coefficients show the correlations between policy variables and each environmental variable while controlling for all other environmental and structural variables; an asterisk indicates a significant relationship at the .05 level.

Source: Thomas R. Dye, "Governmental Structure, Urban Environment and Educational Policy," *Midwest Journal of Political Science* 11 (August 1967): 362.

Table 13.2   Structural Characteristics of School Systems and Educational Policy Outcomes

Educational Policy Outcomes	Structural Variables											
	School Board Selection		School Board Rep.		Assessor Selection		City Control of Budget		Form of Government		Type of Ballot	
	Sim.	Par.	Sim.	Par.	Sim.	Par.	Sim.	Par.	Sim.	Par.	Sim.	Par.
Per Pupil Expenditures	.07	-.15	.05	.01	.02	.01	.19	.23	-.07	.28*	.08	.12
Expenditures Relative to Income	-.27	-.11	-.05	-.11	.04	.09	-.02	.06	.35*	.25*	.02	.14
School Tax Rate	-.07	.10	.05	-.10	-.14	-.24	-.07	-.05	.11	.03	.07	.00
Local School Support	-.01	-.08	.05	-.03	-.06	.10	.10	.09	-.26	-.20	-.01	-.01
Teachers Salaries	-.02	-.08	-.05	-.09	.04	.00	.03	.03	-.01	.15	-.10	-.07
Teachers Turnover	-.28	-.23	.00	.10	.01	.00	.00	.11	.28*	.25*	.00	.15
Teacher-Pupil Ratio	-.02	.08	-.05	.07	.24	.27	-.33*	-.36*	-.04	-.15	-.23	-.16
Teachers Without Degree	.23	.09	.00	.06	-.22	-.23	.45*	.27*	-.32*	-.18	.41*	.23
Teachers with Masters	-.04	-.07	.11	.05	.09	.05	-.08	.00	-.06	-.02	-.02	.08
Drop Out Rate	-.09	-.03	-.03	-.01	.13	.09	-.09	.02	.02	-.06	-.08	.07
Private School Enrollment	.18	-.12	-.04	-.09	-.16	-.21	.11	-.08	-.48*	-.30*	.20	.12

Note: Figures are simple and partial correlation coefficients for 67 cities; partial coefficients show the correlations between policy variables and each structural variable while controlling for all other structural and environmental variables; an asterisk indicates a significant relationship at the .05 level.

Source: Thomas R. Dye, "Governmental Structure, Urban Environment and Educational Policy," *Midwest Journal of Political Science* 11 (August 1967): 374.

4. Variation in teachers' salaries is related to income level of the city. The higher the median family income, the higher the average classroom teacher's salary.

Dye found that the political structure of the school decision-making process had much less impact on educational policy than the environmental factors had. For example, there were no significant differences in educational outcomes between schools (1) whether school boards were elected or appointed, (2) whether school board members were selected from wards or at large, (3) whether the school board was free from budgetary control of the city, and (4) whether school board elections were partisan or nonpartisan.

Other comparative policy studies give political structures a more important place. Lineberry and Fowler, for example, argue that the environment is not a sufficient cause of a city's adopting a particular form of government.

They feel that a more sophisticated model would include political institutions as one of the factors which produce a particular form of local government; "We hypothesize that a causal model would include four classes of variables: socio-economic cleavages, political variables . . . political institutions . . . and political outputs."[9] James Clarke's study of forty-three Pennsylvania cities suggests that Lineberry and Fowler are correct. Clarke concludes that some of the political variables, such as types of proposal and cost, city hall response, and voter turnout, were important determinants of referendum outcomes.[10] Specifically, political explanations have also been found to be crucial in connection with fluoridation referenda[11] and urban transportation politics.[12]

Disagreement is usual in a young research tradition and should not be cause for frustration or alarm. Suspended judgment is one of those virtues every citizen of a democracy must cultivate. Meantime, ongoing inquiry must become more sensitive to a variety of criticisms. In general, those criticisms have moved toward the formulation that the causes of any particular urban policy are more numerous and varied than any of these studies have been able to control for. More specifically, critics have suggested that (1) the indicators of both the environmental and political processes under study are too crude to reflect adequately their effects on public policy. For example, to use per capita income as an indicator of wealth may mask important differences in the distribution of the wealth in compared cities. Additional studies must tell us whether those differences and other ones, have an important impact on policy.[13] (2) Case study and aggregate data studies have not been comparable because each has ignored certain variables, an omission which leads easily to exaggerating the importance of the variables that are examined. For example, most case studies do not discuss environmental variables at all, while most aggregate data studies ignore the political decision-making process as a potential explanation. (3) Comparative studies have not adequately recognized and controlled for differences in local policies and legal settings. Where there are federal or state policies affecting some of the cities or variables in the aggregate data, but not others, we simply cannot make meaningful comparison. What is needed are "synoptic measures" of the most significant elements of political process. Jacob and Lipsky say that at a minimum these indicators would include synoptic measures of the executive branch, the organization of the legislature, the strength of interest groups, and the linkages with other levels of government.[14]

Once we sophisticate our research techniques in these ways, we can expect some convergence in findings. The proposition which seems most likely to be verified is that *environmental factors are important determinants of certain policies which connect directly with the economic and social potentials of a city.* Policies on taxation and expenditure would be among those shaped by environment, while less routinized political questions — like fluoridation or elections — would be influenced more by political variables.

THE DEVELOPMENT OF URBAN ISSUES:
DYNAMIC COMPARATIVE STUDY

Studies of environment and public policy have not aimed to provide insight into the development of urban issues. The dynamics of urban issues are not well studied. Still, we have some important beginnings toward understanding how and why urban issues take the course they do. A first prerequisite to comparative issue study is the creation of a typology which would enable us to distinguish varieties of issues which arise in our cities.

A Typology Of Issues

Ernest Barth and Stuart Johnson suggest that local issues may be classified in accordance with five dimensions:[15]

1. *Unique - recurrent dimension.* Certain questions arise periodically in the life of a city. These perennial questions are likely to be handled by constituted public agencies having access to regularly allocated resources. Budget making, for example, is a perennial issue. At the opposite end of the continuum is the absolutely unique issue, such as a once-in-a-lifetime flood. There is no established procedure or structure to meet such a situation: resources must be developed and leadership mobilized for it.

2. *Salient - nonsalient to leadership.* Not everyone in a city cares about all the public questions that arise. Questions that are central to the interests of the city leaders and the organizational structures in which they hold positions — whether they be mayors, councilmen, or an economic elite — need to be distinguished from issues that are less important to urban leaders. When an issue is of great importance to public leaders but perceived to be of little importance to the general public, action taken on that issue may be unpublicized and directed through informal influence structures. But other issues may require public support and, therefore, will necessitate a public relations program initiated by the leadership and designed to convince a segment of the public of the worth of the program being undertaken.

3. *Salient - nonsalient to local publics.* This dimension refers to the importance which various local publics attach to a particular issue. Public questions of low interest to both leaders and the general public might either be

Marshall Henrichs

This ambiguous message posted in a city doorway serves to remind its readers of the recurrent and salient issue of minority-group needs.

simply neglected or be handled by professional organizers or lower echelon bureaucracies and leaders. When an issue is presumed to be highly salient to the public, potential decision makers are likely to concern themselves with the public relations of the decision.

4. *Effective action possible - effective action impossible.* There are certain issues which are presumed very important to both leaders and publics but which, at the same time, cannot be handled effectively. The local decision makers simply lack the resources — financial, political, technical or other kinds of resources. To illustrate, many Southern cities have desired to improve local education but have simply lacked the money to do so. Of course, whether action is possible or not also depends on the perceptions of the local leaders and public. Often it is claimed that the local government has no power to act in a particular area when, in fact, what is meant is that there is no will to act.

5. *Local - nonlocal dimension.* When an issue is perceived to concern program and problems that are properly dealt with by other organizations at the state or national level, then local leaders tend to look to those levels for guidance and direction in the development of programs. If, however, an issue is perceived as purely local, the range of policies considered will be determined by the local decision makers themselves without calling on experts or seeking directives from elsewhere.[16]

The Range of Political Issues

The *type of issue* and the *intensity of the conflict* that accompany an issue are prime factors to consider in developing theories of the dynamics of urban issues. For example, a number of public questions are recurrent, often annual, events and are characterized by *conventional* conflict. The adoption of the municipal budget and the periodic election of city officials are such issues. In fact, it is possible to get a good idea of the scope of issues raised in American urban life by relating the type of issue to the intensity of conflict, as is done for each of the five issue types in Table 13.3. There, an example is given for each possible configuration of the relationship between the type of issue and the intensity of the issue.

An example of a unique issue characterized by rancorous conflict is the occurrence of controversies over the performance of a particular city manager. It is, of course, quite possible that in particular cities different classifications of many of these examples would be possible. For instance, a latent issue such as the possibility of municipal ownership of public utilities could become manifest and be dealt with conventionally (as was the case in

Table 13.3   The Range of Urban Issues — By Type and Intensity of Conflict

		Intensity of Conflict		
		Latent	*Conventional*	*Rancorous*
Recurrence Dimension	*Unique*	Municipal ownership of public utilities	Referendum	Performance of a particular city manager
	Recurrent	Reform city government	Periodic elections; budgetary process	Ghetto rioting
Salience to Leadership	*Salient*	Increased taxes on local business	Tax policy; urban renewal	Accusations of industrial pollution of air
	Nonsalient	Desirability of progressive education	School text book choice	Sex education disputes
Salience to Publics	*Salient*	Urban growth	Zoning; planning; law enforcement	Neighborhood control; fluoridation; "law and order" controversies
	Nonsalient	Civil service policies	Hiring government consultants	Personal and jurisdictional disputes within local government organization
Possibility of Effective Action	*Possible*	Urban aesthetics; sign control	Location and use of city parks	"Subversive" teachers in local schools
	Impossible	River pollution from upstream source	Experimental education programs for poor (impossible where resources lacking)	Employment of more minority personnel in local business
Scope of Concern	*Local*	Growth and development policy	Planning; zoning; budgeting	Ghetto rioting
	Nonlocal	Use of formal voting registrars	Location of state highways in region	Federal court orders on integration

San Diego in the early seventies) or in some other city it could be dealt with rancorously. A rancorous conflict can be conventionalized, as when a sex education dispute is finally resolved by the local school administrators to the satisfaction of the parties. In other words, no one of these examples *must be* in the classification we have chosen to put it in, but often it is.

Despite the roughness of this classification scheme, it does help us understand the broad range of issues submitted to the urban political process. It further suggests that there may be several patterns of issue development, depending on the type and intensity of the issue. It also reminds us that there is a strong tendency to apply the term "issue" to only those conflicts which are rancorous. It is tempting to focus attention on the intense issues and to view the more conventional or latent issues as less interesting and important. Yet, as we review the range of issues, most of us would be inclined to assign great importance to many of the conventional and latent issues.

Rancorous conflicts deserve and receive careful observation, not only because they are the most dramatic, but also because rancorous conflicts often reveal many of the underlying strains in the body politic. Rancorous conflicts are symptomatic of the failure of conventional political processes to cope adequately with the needs of groups and individuals who feel strongly. So rancorous conflicts, while they may not always be concerned with the most fundamental issues that face the city, are still of great significance.

Whether or not a city is characterized by dramatic controversy depends on a number of factors peculiar to that setting: the nature of its economic structure, changes that occur over time, population shifts, the existence of heterogeneous values, and whether or not there are existing cleavages. All these factors influence the development of rancorous conflict.[17] Despite the obvious connection of rancorous conflict with the unique characteristics of the city in which it occurs, it *has* been observed that such controversies develop in similar patterns — more similar than we might expect.

The Dynamics of Rancorous Conflict

Once a controversy has begun, it follows a remarkably predictable pattern wherever it occurs. It is almost as though the controversy had a life of its own: "It is the peculiarity of social controversy that it sets in motion its own dynamics; these tend to carry it forward in a path which bears little relation to its beginnings."[18] It should be underscored that rancorous conflicts do not develop rationally; the actors definitely do not calculate their situations coolly and dispassionately, making moves and countermoves. Instead, the development of a rancorous conflict results to a great degree from involuntary and emotional responses. In other words, the actor in a rancorous conflict is like a person in a fight; he swings freely and often wildly.

James Coleman has discerned three fundamental transformations which take place as rancorous conflicts develop: first, the issues move from specific charges to more general ones; in that process, new and different issues are added to the original ones; and third, the participants in the controversy move from disagreement to antagonism in their responses to one another.

Specific to general

It is common for a controversy to start with a quite specific public question and then, as it heats up, it seems to expand to cover one or several general questions. In Scarsdale, New York, for example, the critics began by attacking the fact that particular books were in the school library; but as the controversy developed they began to focus on the whole educational philosophy of the school system. In Hutchinson, Kansas, opponents of a particular urban renewal project moved from specific opposition to parts of the plan to a discussion of the problems of federal dominance of localities to an eventual charge of Communist takeover of our governmental institutions.

Like most general tendencies, this tendency of a rancorous conflict to expand to larger issues does not occur in all cases. A number of specific political fights start and end with the same issue. Coleman suggests that the movement from specific to general issues occurs only in those cities in which there are cleavages of values or interests already in being. In other words, there must be a *reservoir of grievances.*[19] Where there is such a reservoir of grievances, usually a specific incident which is only one aspect or part of the underlying grievance is necessary to spark the broader controversy. Disputes that do not touch on that reservoir of grievances generally do not show this tendency to move from specific to general issues, but instead stay with the same issues throughout the controversy.

New and different issues

In cities where there is a reservoir of grievances, the development of a rancorous conflict is accompanied by the emergence of conflict over other issues, issues unrelated to the original one. Campaigns for elective office characteristically show this tendency: new issues multiply as the campaign becomes more intense. The tendency is apparent in other civic issues too. For example, a controversy in a small Midwestern city began in the later 1950s with a dispute over whether an alleged pornographic book should remain in the high school library; the dispute was soon expanded by those who were upset about the political content of books assigned by a particular English teacher; a bit later in this conflict, the qualifications, personality, and parentage of the principal were called into question.

In elections, as well as some other controversies, the addition of new issues may actually be a rational decision on the part of the antagonist, rather than an involuntary response. Participants raise additional issues to solidify opinion and to gain new allies and support by providing new bases of response. As the antiurban renewal forces gained strength in Hutchinson, Kansas, for example, the supporters of urban renewal found that many businessmen were remaining neutral. One of the pro-urban renewal people told the neutrals privately, "Look here, these are the same people who oppose seeking federal funds for a new airport. If they win here they can beat us on that too. And we both know you want that airport." This new issue, then, enticed a number of members of the business sector into active support of urban renewal.

As a controversy develops, each antagonist, whether arguing irrationally or cagily, seeks to bring to bear all the different arguments he can to justify his position to himself and to convince or overcome his opponent. The multiplication of issues serves the dual function of increasing solidarity among the like-minded and winning new adherents from uncommitted neutrals. Both these functions are vital; the first makes it easier to move allies into action, when that becomes necessary, by disposing of all their doubts and hesitancies; the second gains additional allies and potential resources, always important to the winning of the conflict.

Disagreement to antagonism

A final broad tendency in the development of rancorous conflict is the tendency for a dispute that begins dispassionately in simple disagreement to heat slowly to the level of personal slander, then rumor spreading, then direct hostility. Coleman notes that this is one of the most important aspects in the self-perpetuation of conflict. Once set in motion, hostility sustains conflict, even though the specific disagreements may be left behind. The original issues may be settled, but the controversy continues unabated. Beyond a certain stage, the antagonists disagree because they dislike one another, no matter what is at issue.

Coleman tentatively suggests that the explanation for the development of antagonism is essentially psychological. He suggests that we associate with each person we know certain beliefs, traits, attributes, and so forth, most of which are projections of our own, rather than characteristics of the person in question. As long as person A finds only one or a few of person B's characteristics objectionable, he is divided in his feelings toward him. A feels that B is neither wholly good nor wholly bad. But when A and B begin to quarrel, the process of argument itself generates new issues; A disagrees with more and more of his opponent's beliefs. Since these beliefs constitute B, as A perceives him, B's image grows still worse to A.

Thus the two processes — the first leading from a single issue to new and different ones, and a second leading from disagreement to direct antagonism —

Figure 13.1   Coleman's Seven Stages of Rancorous-Conflict Development

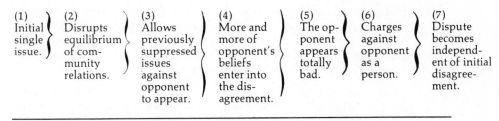

| (1) Initial single issue. | (2) Disrupts equilibrium of community relations. | (3) Allows previously suppressed issues against opponent to appear. | (4) More and more of opponent's beliefs enter into the disagreement. | (5) The opponent appears totally bad. | (6) Charges against opponent as a person. | (7) Dispute becomes independent of initial disagreement. |

Source: James Coleman, *Community Conflict* (Glencoe, Ill.: The Free Press, 1957), p. 11.

fit together perfectly and help carry the controversy along its course. . . . Once direct antagonism is felt toward an opponent, one is led to make public attacks on him.[20]

Coleman suggests that there is a seven-stage development of rancorous conflict. He diagrams those stages as shown in Figure 13.1. The full development of the controversy depends on the existence of a reservoir of grievances which the initial single issue calls into manifest dispute. Thus, the initial issue or "triggering incident" may seem minor by comparison to the controversy that follows it.

The dynamics of rancorous conflict are almost directly analogous to the dynamics of personal quarrels in which we have all engaged. We have all fought with people we have lived with, for example — parent, sibling, spouse, roommate, lover. No matter how compatible we are with one another, there are always irritations: he is too fastidious or he is not fastidious enough in personal appearance and housekeeping; she crowds me in bed; he uses my comb; she will not fix breakfast at the time I want it; her driving isn't up to my high standards; she is too friendly with other men, etc. All these problems are petty, and we are usually too cool and rational to be overwhelmed by any of them; but their weight increases over time. The reservoir of grievances presses against the dam of rationality.

> One morning after a fitful night, you get up to find your roommate's clothes draped across your desk and you have had enough. "Your stuff is in my way," you observe, "just like it always is." The initial single issue is joined.
>
> "How can you say that?" he heatedly replies.
>
> You could attempt to smooth the disruption at this point but you are angry, so you yell back some brilliant piece of repartee like, "Because it's true." This obviously disrupts the equilibrium of the relationship. Not sure that you have

just provided a definitive argument you continue, "How someone who is so picky about his car can be so sloppy about his clothes is beyond me."

That previously suppressed grievance is likely to spawn others as the argument progresses, especially since it now develops that your opponent also has a reservoir of grievances against you. He says, "You're a nut about your desk. You're fussy about all your possessions. In fact, you have lots of bourgeois values. I'll never be able to get along with you."

"Well, there are certainly a large number of things that I'm not pleased with about you all right," you reply, beginning to recite a long list from your reservoir of grievances. As you proceed to call more and more of his failures into account, you remind yourself of all the previous problems you have so magnanimously overlooked all this time. And as you do so, he begins to appear a totally bad person.

As your list is met by a counterlist rather than repentance, the only thing to do seems to be to renounce this bad person. Brilliance and clarity of argument are usually in evidence at this point too: "Well, you're just a rotten person. You always have been and you always will be. I don't know why I put up with you."

If, after you or he stalks out, the disruption does not heal in a few days, as most of this kind do — if this disruption, in other words, creates a complete fracture of the relationship over an extended period of time — then it is not uncommon for the parties to formulate their positions on other issues on the basis of (and in terms of) their dislike for one another. "Oh, he's a big supporter of Elliot Richardson. That settles it for me: I'm voting for the next Democrat who runs against Richardson for any office, no matter who it is."

The dispute has become entirely independent of the initial disagreement and it generates responses on subsequent issues.

There are always a number of difficulties in generalizing from personal relationships to social and political relationships. So this analogy should not be taken too seriously. In addition, as Coleman points out, the whole dynamic is not determined from the beginning: it can be interrupted, diverted, or consciously used. Unlike the personal fight, the social and political dispute may be affected by the structure of authority in a particular city, or by the social structure of a particular city.[21] But the essential dynamic is quite similar, especially the development of *polarization* as the controversy develops. In the case of a local conflict, that polarization may lead to the formation of new partisan organizations and side taking among the old organization, may facilitate the emergence of new local leaders and, thus, may alter the long-term structure of politics in the city.

After an examination of conflict in any setting, it always seems appropriate to remind ourselves that conflict in and of itself is neither good nor

An understanding of urban issues must begin with an understanding of the diverse needs and goals of those who use and inhabit the city.

bad. Its effect on a city may range from destructive to creative. Some conflicts leave communities torn apart and immobilized: all the leaders have been compromised, the integrity of all the social organizations has been dissipated, personal rapport has been destroyed among the operating elements of the city. The result may be that in an atmosphere of mutual suspicion no one is able to make a decision; and the result is governmental drift. In other instances, conflict may be cathartic: the participants need only to blow off steam by airing their grievances with one another. Once the tension has been released, business as usual can be restored with very little change in the structure of the political process or the character of public policy. Still other rancorous conflicts may result in the adaptation of the political process and public policy — the conflict having pointed out the need to change.[22] And finally, as Richard Sennett has pointed out, conflict can be creative, bringing to the surface long-repressed grievances and stimulating the emergence of new leadership and more effective policy. Conflict, in other words, may be the midwife of change, aiding in the birth of new political forms and greater citizen satisfaction and confidence.

SUMMARY

Comparative studies of both public policy and the dynamics of issues have produced sharpened understanding of the urban political process. Urban environmental characteristics, political structures, and processes seem to determine certain public policies. Study of the dynamics of urban issues is less well developed, but in James Coleman's formulation there is much insight and a number of hypotheses that deserve further investigation.

The parallels between personal quarrels and public conflicts are particularly provocative. The development of rancorous conflicts from specific to general issues, from a simple topic to many points of dispute, from mere disagreement to open hostility recurs often enough to invite more attention and study. Finally, we should again remind ourselves that even though the rancorous issues are the most exciting and easiest to study, a full understanding of urban policy requires that attention be paid to latent and conventional issues as well.

NOTES

1. Peter Rossi, "Community Decision-Making," *Administrative Science Quarterly* 1 (March 1957): 438.
2. It has been suggested that there is a need to merge the case study and aggregate approaches in one research strategy. Cf. James W. Clarke, "Environment,

Process, and Policy: A Reconsideration," *American Political Science Review* 63 (December 1969): 1172-1182.

3. Cf. Thomas R. Dye, "Governmental Structure, Urban Environment and Educational Policy," *Midwest Journal of Political Science* 11 (August 1967): 353-380.

4. Cf. Robert Lineberry and Edmund Fowler, "Reformism and Public Policies in American Cities," *American Political Science Review* 61 (September 1967): 701-716; Louis Masotti and Don Bowen, "Communities and Budgets: The Sociology of Municipal Expenditures," *Urban Affairs Quarterly* 1 (December 1965): 39-58.

5. Oliver Williams et al., *Suburban Differences and Metropolitan Policies* (Philadelphia: University of Pennsylvania Press, 1965); Thomas Dye et al., "Differentiation and Cooperation in a Metropolitan Area," *Midwest Journal of Political Science* 7 (May 1963): 145-155; Brett Hawkins, "A Note on Urban Political Structure, Environment and Political Integration," *Polity* 2 (Fall 1969): 32-48; also see the critique of this article by David Rosenthal in *Polity* 2 (Summer 1970): 540-545.

6. Lineberry and Fowler, "Reformism and Public Policies"; Charles Liebman, "Functional Differences and Political Characteristics of Suburbs," *American Journal of Sociology* 66 (March 1961): 485-490; and Clarke, "Environment, Process, and Policy."

7. Cf. Clarke, "Environment, Process, and Policy"; and Amos Hawley, "Community Power and Urban Renewal Success," *American Journal of Sociology* 68 (January 1963): 422-431.

8. Dye, "Governmental Structure, Urban Environment and Educational Policy," p. 357.

9. Lineberry and Fowler, "Reformism and Public Policies," p. 714.

10. Clarke, "Environment, Process, and Policy," pp. 1172-1182.

11. Robert Crain, Elihu Katz, and Donald Rosenthal, *The Politics of Community Conflict* (Indianapolis: Bobbs-Merrill Co., 1969).

12. Frank Colcon, "Decision-Making and Transportation Policy: A Comparative Analysis," (Southwestern) *Social Science Quarterly* 48 (December 1967): 383-397.

13. These criticisms draw heavily on the formulations of Clarke, "Environment, Process, and Policy," p. 486.

14. Herbert Jacob and Michael Lipsky, "Outputs, Structure and Power: An Assessment of Changes in the Study of State and Local Politics," *Journal of Politics* 30 (May 1968): 510-538.

15. Ernest Barth and Stuart Johnson, "Community Power and a Typology of Social Issues," *Social Forces* 38 (October 1959): 29-32. They base their typology on two major requirements. First, "the dimensions must be generic to all issues. Second, variations in each dimension must be theoretically relatable to variations in the patterns of influencing behavior." (p. 30). This means that their categories are tied to observable behaviors.

16. There is no need at this point to particularize the deficiencies of the typology. However, we should note that like so many of the typologies currently in use, it is not primarily a logical construct in that it does not create categories that are

both "mutually exclusive" and "jointly exhaustive." Instead, it reflects model variations which the researcher conceives to occur characteristically. Cf. Arthur L. Kallenberg, "The Logic of Comparison: A Methodological Note on the Comparative Study of Political Systems," *World Politics* 19 (October 1966): 69-82.

17. This observation and the following materials are largely taken from James Coleman, *Community Conflict* (New York: Free Press of Glencoe, 1957), pp. 6-7.

18. Ibid., pp. 9-10.

19. By "latent," there is no intention to imply that some other party consciously prevents the expression of the grievance, only that there has been — by choice or chance or inability to find the right channels — a failure to express openly and cathartically that grievance.

20. Coleman, *Community Conflict*, p. 11.

21. This is more fully discussed in Coleman, *Community Conflict*, Chap. 3.

22. For more complete discussion of these processes, see H. L. Nieburg, *Political Violence* (New York: St. Martin's Press, 1969), Chap. 4.

Chapter 14

Three Case Studies
in Urban Politics

While case studies have limited use, they nonetheless have an important place in the development of urban theory and in imparting a full understanding of city politics. For one thing, when we look carefully at a particular issue, we get a strong sense of the integrity of the process; we see the puzzle put together rather than scattered in its several parts. We are able to see the relationship and relative importance of each of the elements in the political process; perspective is gained. One element made visible by that perspective is the humanness of the political process. Case studies are little slices of life in which we can at last recognize ourselves in the participants. The outcomes of political interactions are not just abstract "outputs"; rather, they are quite concrete authorizations and prohibitions by which fortunes and careers can be made or broken, the lives of citizens can be destroyed or made more bearable, anxieties can be created or laid to rest, personal growth of citizens and leaders can be facilitated or retarded. In the case study, then, we can see and feel the ponderous importance of politics.

The issues that appear in this chapter have been selected from the large number of case studies written by political scientists and political participants. There is no attempt to be representative — geographically or by subject or any other criterion — in this selection. A representative selection would contain a larger and more ordinary array; it would be accurate but dull. What follows, then, are three case studies of issues marked by dramatic and rancorous confrontations.

A FIGHT OVER LOCATION OF A THRUWAY
IN UPSTATE NEW YORK

In the late 1950s the New York Thruway, a federally funded superhighway, was in the process of being surveyed and built. Location of a freeway is a political act as well as a feat of engineering and construction; hence, characteristically, political controversies blossom by the proposed roadway along with the wildflowers. Such a controversy developed in Hillcrest, New York. Hillcrest is a small (population 3000 at the time of the controversy), unincorporated, middle-class suburb of Binghamton. Such suburban places, we immediately suspect, are dominated by amenities-seeking citizens — a suspicion that seems congruent with the perspectives of the residents as well. One resident said of Hillcrest, for example, "although it is small, there is an unusually strong community spirit among its middle-class homeowners. We have a progressive board of education and two new schools of which we are very proud. . . . "[1]

The dispute began rather inconspicuously. Surveyors had been seen sighting along the quiet streets of the area. The first announcement that plans were being considered for building the freeway came when a brief legal notice was printed in the newspaper announcing that a public hearing would be held in the county courthouse to discuss the route of a federal superhighway through Broome County. Most people were too busy with the holidays to respond to the notice, but about one hundred turned out for the hearing.

At the public hearing, the District Engineer provided a technical description of a beautiful and useful expressway that was to cost one million dollars a mile. He displayed a map of Broome County. Hillcrest wasn't even marked on it, but a wide black line cut a swath through the county very close to where Hillcrest would be. When he was finished, the engineer called for statements from organizations. Representatives from the local Chamber of Commerce, banks, unions, and auto clubs spoke. Each was enthusiastic about the new highway and detailed the economic advantages that would accrue to the area — tourists would need restaurants, motels, service stations; business and industry would be stimulated by the close proximity of a major transportation route.

At the public hearing, the supervisor of the nearby town of Fendon, Robert Ford, was the closest thing to a political spokesman for the unincorporated town of Hillcrest. He was cautious, and he and the town attorney declared that they could say nothing unless they knew specifically where the route was to go in relation to Hillcrest. A number of private citizens also spoke at the hearing, showing much greater anxiety. The school board attorney argued, "This hearing is inadequate by law. Even today the route does not deal with specific localities."[2] But the District Engineer insisted that "details cannot be given now. The route could go one way or the other."[3]

The specific route was important to the residents of Hillcrest. A mile variation in the freeway's location could mean the difference between bisecting the town and bypassing it. Other participants in the hearing pressed the District Engineer for a specific route but failed and left the hearing feeling frustrated and helpless. According to Polly Praeger, who was to become a leader in the opposition to the thruway, those who were disturbed by the prospect of the highway splitting the town in half felt overwhelmed from the beginning. What chance did they have against the state Department of Public Works and the United States Bureau of Public Roads?

Hillcrest's homeowners were particularly threatened by the prospect of the thruway. Many began to flee the central city of Binghamton to be away from intensive business uses; others feared that their homes would be condemned as part of the thruway site. The Hillcrest Community Association, composed largely of middle-class homeowners, had in the past existed mainly to sponsor youth programs. Mrs. Praeger, drawing on her experience in working with the League of Women Voters, urged the Hillcrest Community Association to organize to oppose the routing of the freeway through Hillcrest. She asked them to write a letter of protest to John W. Johnson, superintendent of public works for New York State — claiming improper conduct of the hearing and requesting permission to have a statement from Hillcrest made a part of the record. The Association appointed a committee which drafted what they considered a very restrained letter. In general, the letter made clear (1) that the Association was in favor of the general program of construction of the thruway and (2) that the Association was not seeking to have the route changed from one area to another to protect the homes of Association members at the expense of the homes of others. But (3) they felt that the hearing had not been an adequate forum for the expression of the Association's views.

The response of the Department of Public Works was a minor victory for the Hillcrest Community Association; it acknowledged that the original notice in the newspaper had not prescribed the general location of the route of the thruway as Department regulations required. The letter also assured the Association that the Department of Public Works would "attempt to consider such changes in alignment as may be possible, in order to minimize destruction of property and still maintain an economical route for the project." Still, followup visits to the district office resulted in no more specifics as to where the thruway would be located. Polly Praeger was the first opponent of the thruway to see such a map. She happened to be in Albany for a meeting, and just on a chance she decided to visit the Department of Public Works to try to get the information. Her state senator made an appointment for her. She was not able to see anyone in command but did see an Assistant Deputy Engineer who, to her surprise, spread a large scale map of Hillcrest before her eyes. No one knows for sure whether the assistant simply made a mistake, whether Albany had been willing to divulge that information all along, or whether there had been a recent change of position.

The map confirmed what everyone had feared. In addition to the six-lane highway projected through Hillcrest, there were four access roads and four traffic circles. The map indicated that Hillcrest would be thoroughly remade. The city's water wells would have been destroyed. The highway would require confiscation of a third of the new elementary school property, some of the buildings of the Wyoming Conference Children's Home, and approximately one hundred new houses. The loss of the houses alone would subtract at least half a million dollars in assessed valuation from the town's tax roles. There was also an estimated loss of a million dollars in assessed valuation to the Board of Education. In addition to being faced with a heavier tax burden, residents who were to be displaced by the thruway would find it difficult to move from one section of Hillcrest to another because all available land had already been developed. Those people who remained would be separated into little islands by the limited access expressway, finding it difficult to associate with people on the other side of the expressway or interchange. In addition, their taxes would be greatly increased because of the revenue losses just mentioned.

The maps later made available for the homeowners' inspection also contained a line referred to as "Alternate A" which went outside Hillcrest and outside a neighboring village of Port Crane as well. When representatives of the homeowners approached the District Engineer to ask why Alternate A could not be built, the District Engineer explained, "No one would use it." But the opponents argued that it was only seven miles from Alternate A access to the courthouse at the center of the downtown area. People would drive seven miles to have access to a seventy-mile-an-hour expressway. The District Engineer still disagreed. Pressed, the engineers finally came up with two major reasons for the choice of the Hillcrest route: first, Hillcrest was closer to Binghamton by three miles, and second, Alternate A had one sharper curve and hill. "For these arguments, we could not see having our community ruined," commented Polly Praeger.

Although the homeowners felt that the engineers' reasons were inadequate, they did not make public charges of corruption or attack the process — they refrained, in other words, from initiating rancorous conflict. (In fact, said Mrs. Praeger, ". . . I think if they had ever told us categorically that Hillcrest was the only possible way that the road could be constructed from the engineering point of view, we would, as public-spirited citizens, have given up the fight.") But they were unconvinced. The Hillcrest Community Association pressed on, encouraging other local organizations to take a public stand. Eventually, an ad hoc committee was created, composed of a number of voluntary associations in the town: that ad hoc committee included Rotary, Kiwanis, churches, the American Legion, the PTA, the town board, the Board of Education, the Children's Home, and garden clubs. In addition, there was organized a subcommittee of prominent engineers who lived in Hillcrest and worked for such companies as General Electric, Ansco, and Link Aviation. As in a rancorous conflict, the issues began to broaden: what began as a local protest over the conduct of the public hearing became a plea for more imaginative planning.

The opponents did a great deal of research and held interviews with experts who might have information favorable to their cause. They kept Albany and Washington bureaucracy and legislators apprised of what they were doing. In addition, they held a number of meetings in the town, one of which was attended by about five hundred residents. As a result, they were beginning to attract broader public attention. The two Binghamton newspapers, the *Press* and the *Sun*, were covering the controversy in detail and publishing letters to the editor. Some of those letters were in favor of the prime route for the freeway and accused the ad hoc committee of obstructing progress. But the Binghamton *Sun* editorially supported the cause of the opponents:

> [The] offer of organized citizens of Hillcrest to withdraw their op-position . . . if it can be shown that the alternative they have proposed would be less direct, more expensive or impractical for any other reason, reflects a genuine regard for the principle of "greatest good for the greatest number" . . . such an attitude puts the whole issue up to the engineers. . . . Less easily understood is the reluctance . . . of the Department of Public Works in putting all the cards face up on the table. We are told that there are some things we do not understand, that once revealed could easily justify the uprooting and virtual annihilation of a community. . . . But Hillcrest is unusual. . . . To slash a wide pathway through the heart of such a neighborhood would be to discourage something our country can't afford to lose. But it isn't on sentiment that this opposition has developed. On the basis of hard, cold fact the Hillcrest Committee has presented its case in workmanlike fashion. The points raised . . . are of sufficient importance to everyone to merit definite rebuttal.

Amidst this growing opposition, the state decided to deliver on its offer to restudy the route and hold an "informational" meeting at which their decision would be announced to the people of Hillcrest. Eight hundred residents gathered to hear that decision. The atmosphere of the meeting was highly charged and the audience expectant and intent. Then came the climax: Hillcrest was still the recommended route. The engineers claimed that it would be cheaper than the alternate route by $9,500,000. They calculated that figure on the basis of two elements: (1) they projected that even if the alternate route were chosen, there would still be need for a $5,000,000 six-lane bridge because of the terrain around Hillcrest, and (2) they figured that if the highway were built three miles farther out, the resulting additional cost to the road users would amount to $4,500,000 over a twenty-year period. In the discussion that followed, Polly Praeger spoke for the ad hoc association: she denied the need of a new bridge; she argued that road users' costs were not properly costs to the taxpayers; and she asserted that if the state insisted on including social costs, then it should also admit other social and economic costs incurred by the people of Hillcrest. Despite these objections, the state adjourned the meeting without reconsidering its position.

In exchanges of correspondence that followed the informational meeting, the Director of Public Relations of the State Department of Public Works in Albany showed some irritation that the people in Hillcrest were not willing to acquiesce in the decision of the department: "We would be most interested to know whose judgment is used to substantiate your challenge of the validity of the District Engineer's analysis . . . [and your challenge that the] 'so called users' costs' are based on questionable premises. This unsupported verbal gymnastic smacks of plain rabble rousing. . . . " Even so, the Public Relations officer assured the ad hoc committee that they were giving the matter a truly impartial review and that their determination would be based on sound engineering and economical judgment in a spirit of good will and without malice.

Since they were making very little headway with the state bureaucracy, the ad hoc committee began to focus its efforts on the elected representatives. Congressman W. Sterling Cole had earlier blasted the public hearing as a "Star Chamber procedure" and had vowed to work for reconsideration by the Bureau of Public Roads. United States Senator Jacob Javits agreed to look into the matter. A petition drive produced over one thousand signatures which, along with telegrams and letters, were sent to Governor Harriman. The Governor's office replied that he was concerned and had been in touch with the State Department of Public Works. State Senator Warren M. Anderson, after attending a meeting of the ad hoc committee, decided that the objections were valid and arranged a meeting between some of the committee and Public Works Superintendent Johnson in Albany. In the meantime, the committee had a professor of community and county planning at Harper College, Dr. Seymour Z. Mann, prepare an "impartial" overview, the results of which were generally supportive of the position of the ad hoc committee. This overview was presented at the conference of Superintendent Johnson and members of the ad hoc committee. At that meeting Superintendent Johnson at last ordered the full review of the thruway location which the ad hoc committee had been requesting.

On October 20, 1957, the results of that review were announced: Hillcrest was to be bypassed by the new thruway. The ad hoc committee had won.

This case study illustrates a particular kind of issue. The controversy was initiated outside the town itself by state and national decision makers. This nonlocal situation, then, limited the possibilities for effective action within the town itself because the controversy was set in intergovernmental activities and relationships. The issue was unique rather than recurrent, hence, established groups had to be refocused and mobilized in unfamiliar ways. The middle-class suburban setting produced greater participation than might occur in other settings; such an issue was, of course, highly salient to the homeowning public of Hillcrest, but apparently less so to its elected and business leaders. It is also significant to note that this issue remained what we have called a conventional conflict: although there was considerable heat in the exchanges between the ad hoc committee and the highway engineers, the ad hoc committee refrained from attacking the rules of the game or crying corruption and the controversy was fought within established procedures.

ELGIN CRULL RESIGNS AS CITY MANAGER
OF DALLAS

The Crull case is a marked contrast to the freeway location fight in Hillcrest. The decision of the city manager to resign was almost entirely a local matter and was, apparently, much more salient to the leadership of the city than it was to the public. Like the Hillcrest issue, this issue was unique rather than recurrent, and it too represents a conventional rather than a rancorous conflict. Set in the city, this case study raises questions about the character of the mayor-council form of government and, therefore, about the broader issue of the reform movement itself.

Elgin Crull, the city manager of Dallas, submitted his resignation to the city council on June 6, 1966, after fourteen years of service. According to the press, he was to become an executive of one of the biggest banks in Texas. The council unanimously praised Crull's long service, accepted his resignation, and appointed his assistant to succeed him. The resignation appeared to much of the city as another case of a good man going on to a better job. But the most significant events leading to the resignation were largely hidden from the public. The more careful examination of the circumstances surrounding the resignation, reported by Bruce Kovner, reveal a quite different story.[4]

Crull began his career as a newspaperman for the Dallas *Dispatch-Journal* as the city hall reporter. When the city manager at that time found that he needed someone with detailed knowledge of the politics of the city, he persuaded Crull to become his assistant. Six years later, Crull succeeded him as manager. In other words, Crull had not followed what has become the normal career pattern for professional city managers: he had not been trained in engineering or administration and had not followed the pattern of working his way up from the managership of a small city to a medium-sized one to a large one. In Dallas at the time, however, this nonprofessional pattern was more an asset than a liability. The city preferred a homegrown product to an outsider who might not be sympathetic to the special qualities and values of Dallas life.

Crull's point of view suited Dallas. He was, a local newspaper said, "An impregnable rock against extravagance and waste." He believed that city government should do only what was clearly essential, and it should do that in the most economical way possible. He was not indifferent to the kinds of human problems that are legitimately the province of local government; but he believed, as apparently most of Dallas did, that the best way to improve such matters was to keep government interference and costs at a minimum. Moreover, Crull was a local who had a caretaker image of city government. He had been appointed by a city council controlled by conservative businessmen who wanted such qualities in a manager.

Things went well for Crull for a number of years, until the city council's composition began to change. Changes in the council probably reflect some alteration in the outlook of the business sector of Dallas and a growth in the number of amenities-seeking citizens. The council became less interested in economy and more interested in projects to improve the city. People began to call Manager Crull not "economical" but "tight fisted."

These changes in the outlook of Dallas citizens and leaders were embodied in J. Erik Jonsson. Jonsson was a wealthy and prestigious businessman who had come to Dallas from New Jersey during the Depression and had risen to prominence there and nationally as the Chairman of the Board of Texas Instruments, one of the country's largest manufacturers of electronics equipment. Jonsson had not run for public office but was known to be interested in public service. So in 1964, when the mayor resigned, the city council appointed Jonsson to the council, then made him acting mayor.

Whereas Crull had throughout his career dealt mainly with Dallas people through personal contact, Jonsson by contrast had always been oriented to a worldwide network of businessmen, professionals, and government officials who were in some way a part of his company's environment. What went on at MIT, on Wall Street, or in other countries was as real to him as anything in Dallas. Crull was a local, Jonsson a cosmopolitan.

One of the implications of these differing orientations was that to Jonsson most problems appeared to have technical solutions; there was no point in arguing about them: the intelligent thing to do was to employ researchers who would find the right solution. To Crull, problems seemed to consist of differences of opinion and conflicts of interest that had to be worked out by patient discussion and compromise, a process that could not be eliminated by research. Another point of contrast was that Jonsson, looking at things from the perspective of the fast-growing electronics industry, thought of all changes as progress and was eager to invest large sums in order to hasten its coming. Crull, from his experience as city manager, felt certain that change meant trouble.

As acting mayor in a council-manager form, Jonsson found that the powers of his office were almost entirely ceremonial: he was to preside over council meetings and to represent the city on public occasions. This is all in keeping with the intent of the reform movement to transfer control from "politicians" to "professionals." The mayor was without staff and authority for the very purpose of restricting him to broad matters of policy, leaving the manager alone to manage the city's business without interference.

Jonsson's first four days as mayor were something of a surprise. Many had assumed that, since he was such a busy executive and had been appointed rather than elected, he would remain in the background. Far from it. He was front-page news almost every day, visiting the city departments, calling on the council to prepare for the challenge of the future, appointing an "emergency committee" on traffic safety, and urging the public to make Dallas great. Jonsson was careful not to violate the prescription of his role, however. He visited only the city departments over which the council had direct control; in his speeches he showed that he was aware of the distinction between administration and policy, and he spoke only of policy matters. Initially, even Crull was satisfied that the mayor knew the rules of the game and meant to abide by them. He said later that Jonsson "damn near strangled himself trying to keep out of my way."

It became clear, however, that if Jonsson was to accomplish anything he would not long be able to keep out of the manager's way. Soon after taking office, for example, the mayor turned his attention to traffic safety. The year before, Dallas had had about one hundred traffic deaths. This was a small number for a city of its size, but the mayor was shocked and wanted to do something to save lives. The regulation of traffic was, of course, the responsibility of the police, and they were under the direct jurisdiction of the manager. To get anything done, Jonsson would have to persuade, cajole, or bully Crull. This was the way it had to be with everything. A comprehensive program of any kind was out of the question since the best that the mayor could hope for was to persuade the manager to take action on some fragment of the larger issue. Sometimes, even that was impossible. Jonsson ran for the mayor's seat in the spring of 1965 on a campaign proposal called "Goals for Dallas." The idea was that the "best minds" would be brought together to solve the problems of Dallas by the methods of research and analysis that had worked so well in big business. Jonsson's victory was overwhelming — he won 73 percent of the vote — and he regarded his victory as a popular mandate to carry out "Goals for Dallas."

Crull was opposed to "Goals for Dallas." He was sure that it would lead to undertakings outside the city government's proper sphere, and he doubted the ability of the mayor's experts to find workable solutions for the city's problems. The fact that Jonsson and some of his business friends had offered to put up most of the needed money made him even more skeptical: "He who pays the piper," he remarked, "usually calls the tune." He probably also realized that "Goals for Dallas" could be realized only if there were some changing of the role of city manager.

The budget became another source of conflict. Legally, it was the manager's responsibility to prepare it and the council's responsibility to pass on it. In practice, in Dallas as elsewhere, once the manager made his budget public, it was very difficult for the council to make any significant changes. This is partly because the budget is complex and time often short, but also because the public is likely to suspect that there are narrow political motives behind any council attempt to change the document. The difficulty in amending a budget works to the advantage of a manager and his department heads and against the council. As the mayor explained:

> The people in the administration are trying to build careers for themselves. It is only natural that they would build up ways of concealing things from the Council or try to get things done in their own way. The chief way of doing this is by giving the Council only a very short time to examine the budget.

The mayor and the manager were clearly on collision courses. The manager became convinced that the mayor's program was one he could not support or carry out. "It's not true that a city manager can work with any council," he told an interviewer. "You can't do a good job at what you don't believe in." The mayor continued to press: "The council must enforce its will," he told the same interviewer. "If the manager won't go along, you get rid of him."

The showdown between Jonsson and Crull came on August 9, 1965, at an informal meeting of the city council in one of the city's plush private clubs. At the mayor's urging, the council had compelled Crull to raise the tax rate by two cents; this would bring in about $500,000 in new revenue — enough to finance a few of the mayor's projects. Though the amount was not large, the manager's sense of fiscal integrity was violated. From the mayor's perspective the central question was one of control: Who was to run Dallas? In the course of the conversation at the club, the manager was criticized for his unwillingness to appropriate money for new projects or to support ser-vices at high enough levels. The manager defended himself against these criticisms on the grounds that the budget and the principle of fiscal integrity placed certain limits on what could be done. According to the recollection of one who was present, Mayor Jonsson was not entirely pleased with the manager's response and said so.

> Jonsson: We ought to tell the City Manager what services we want and he'll tell us how much it will cost. If he tells us what the budget is to be, he's making policy. We need to look ahead ten years. We need a ten year cash flow picture for basing a capital improvements program.
>
> Crull: The public doesn't understand long-term programs.
>
> Jonsson: Elgin, you are no longer running the farm. This city is a big business. We are exploring and we need your help. But we find a kind of passive resistance on your part. You're always telling us how *not* to do it.

Crull found it difficult to argue with a man who had recently received 73 percent of the vote, especially since it was evident that most of the other councilmen agreed with him. Crull concluded that his usefulness as manager of Dallas had ended, and he soon began looking for another job.

SCHOOL DECENTRALIZATION IN NEW YORK CITY

The final case study deals with a more complex issue. It describes the rancorous and recurrent struggle for neighborhood control of schools, par-ticularly the controversy which came to a head in the Ocean Hill-Brownsville District (JHS 271), a poor and predominantly black area of New York City. The struggle for neighborhood control of schools, as with many rancorous conflicts, brought to the surface a large number of additional value conflicts and interest conflicts. The prospect of greater citizen participation in local education profoundly threatened the control of the professional educators — top-level administrators, educational bureaucracy, and teachers alike. In the Ocean Hill-Brownsville dispute, we also have an example of conflict which does not remain cool but necessarily involves the educational bureaucracy of the state as well as the governor and state legislature. Because the conflict became so intense and because the values involved were of such broad in-terest, the issue became salient to both the general public and the public leaders of New York City and the state.

Background

Much of the impetus for school reform in New York City came from the frustrations of the school integration forces. Most of the earlier coalition for integration — poverty workers, parents, and ministers — gave up integration as a goal and moved to neighborhood control.[5] They had reason to believe, after all, that integration in New York City was a hopeless cause. They had failed to get the site they wanted for IS 201 in Harlem, which would have facilitated integration; and schools were becoming increasingly more segregated in the large cities of the North. New York's school segregation had increased in the five years preceding the IS 201 controversy and the prointegration forces had been unable to secure any meaningful action on any of their proposed plans.

The failure to make significant moves toward integration can be at least partially explained by the development of the urban school system in New York in the two decades prior to 1967; education in New York City had become insulated from public controls.[6] Important sources of potential power within the city had abandoned their interest and involvement in public education. Bureaucratization and professionalization were contributing factors: the specialized educational bureaucracy monopolized power through its control of expertise. The often-heard claim of the professional that he is the only one who can make competent judgments had been accepted, and contributing to this attitude was the change in the mayor's role to one of noninvolvement in educational matters.

Small wonder that much of the criticism of the neighborhood control forces was aimed at the operation of the educational system itself — a characteristic, incidentally, which qualifies this dispute as a rancorous conflict. For example, one circular distributed in Harlem warned that "the present structure of the New York City school system, not responsible or accountable to the minority community, is guilty of educational genocide." In the neighboring borough of Queens, the predominantly black Federation of Parents Clubs demanded that teachers be rated according to the scores their students achieved on standardized tests. Between 1963 and 1967, over a dozen parent boycotts occurred at various ghetto schools. At one point, a self-styled Peoples' Board of Education — which included a Catholic priest, a Protestant minister, and a black, former school integration leader — proclaimed itself the true Board of Education. Until they were arrested, the Peoples' Board of Education sat in the board members' seats for two days. These demonstrations had a common theme: parents wanted a substantial say in the running of the schools. Both school administrators and teachers saw the demonstrations as much more threatening: "What the parents are asking for is a revolution,"

Superintendent of Schools Bernard Donavan remarked, "and that doesn't happen overnight."

Development of the Issue

By midwinter of 1967, the politics of school decentralization was in full swing. Mayor John Lindsay began to break with the usual stance of non-involvement in educational policy. He was convinced that the public schools had to show "demonstrably better results" for the city's billion dollar investment. During a parent boycott of PS 125, the mayor had let it be known that, in principle, he believed parents should have a voice in the selection of the principals and should be given the right to interview candidates for such supervisory posts as principal and district superintendent. Still, the mayor lacked political resources to implement his desires; his major educational function was to appoint members of the city Board of Education. Since 1961, even that power to appoint was somewhat diluted since the choice was made from a list supplied by a screening panel composed of civic group representatives.

Even so, Lindsay publicly committed himself to school reform and sought additional resources, seeking authorization for his initiatives from the state legislature in the spring of 1967. Bypassing both the city Board of Education and the state education department, the mayor obtained legislation which gave him the power to reorganize the public school system into five school districts. In one sense, the law Lindsay obtained was a clever maneuver aimed at getting the city a larger proportion of funding; for, when the city was considered a conglomerate of five school districts rather than one school district, it stood to gain an additional $108 million in aid. But the law went beyond simple reorganization; it was a mandate to the mayor that

> increased community awareness and participation in the educational process is essential to the furtherance of education innovation and excellence in the public school system within the city of New York. . . . The legislature . . . declares that the creation of educational policy for the public schools within such districts will afford members of the community an opportunity to take a more active and meaningful role in the development of educational policy closely related to the diverse needs and aspirations of the community.[7]

The mayor was instructed to present a plan to the legislature by December 1967. He appointed a six-member blue ribbon committee headed by the president of the Ford Foundation, McGeorge Bundy, to draw a reorganization plan. No obvious holders of power in the school system were included on the committee. The United Federation of Teachers (UFT), a teacher's union of more than 40,000 members which was the official bargaining agent for the city's teachers, was not represented on the panel. Neither was the Council of Supervisory Associations (CSA), an organization of more than 3000 members representing persons in school supervisory positions such as high school and junior high school principals, assistant principals, high school department chairmen, the members of the board of examiners, assistant superintendents, and associate superintendents. Naturally, the professional educators became still more anxious when they found they were to be excluded from the panel. This exclusion proved to be a significant element of the controversy and of the subsequent failure of the panel to have its recommendations for decentralization enacted.

Initially, the new law evoked angry protest from the city's educational establishment because it empowered the mayor, rather than the Board of Education, to prepare the study. An organization representing local school parent associations decried the "destruction of the city's school system," feeling that, "badly as the city's schools need funds, [the law] was too high a price to get them"; State Commissioner of Education Allen's immediate reaction was that the mayor had exerted a "measure of political control"; the Association of Assistant Principals thought school children would now be "political pawns"; the Congress of Parents and Teachers feared that "every politician in the city [will now decide] on how our children will be educated"; and the New York *Times* found an "outrageous element in the act of legislative blackmail" that will signal a "forceful reassertion of political fiat as a controlling factor in the schools."[8]

Since no hard lines had yet formed, Mayor Lindsay moved to placate rising fears. He held a special meeting which included representatives of every educational interest group and assured his audience that he had not the slightest intention of running New York's school system. During this same period, the Board of Education approved a plan to experiment with greater neighborhood involvement in three school districts — IS 201, Ocean Hill-Brownsville, and Two Bridges. Coming when it did, the action gave the impression that the city board favored reorganization along decentralized lines.

Participants and Coalitions

Still, even before the Bundy panel had released its decentralization recommendations, alliances began to form. Black school activists, academics, some of the more radical white educational groups, and the mayor pressed for school decentralization. On the other side, the professional educational organizations (CSA and UFT) and the Board of Education submerged their traditional differences and united in opposition to the growing demand for neighborhood control of schools. More broadly, the decentralization alliance seemed to unite the city's upperclass with the city's underclass, both of whom had little faith in the schools. The antidecentralization forces largely reflected the coalition between the newly emergent middle-class white civil servants and the labor unions. Thus, the school decentralization issue brought the UFT into collaboration with one of its past rhetorical foes, the CSA: even though CSA was an arm of management, the UFT shared with the CSA the common objective of professional control of school decision making. The Bundy plan, presented to the mayor in the fall of 1967, solidified these emerging alliances. Essentially, it recommended that the school system of the city be subdivided into between thirty and sixty autonomous school districts, each with elected school boards, and each having assigned powers over budget, personnel, and curriculum. It proposed changes that would result in admitting more minority group members into teaching and supervisory positions. As to the structure of the local boards, the Bundy plan recommended that the majority of members on each board be elected by parents of children in the schools.

The Bundy report was sharply criticized, especially by the educators. The lone dissenting member on the Bundy panel explained his criticism of the report: "serious problems must arise in recasting, in one single stroke, the largest educational system in the world."[9] The professional groups saw the plan as an attempt to "balkanize" the city system and argued that local control would impede school integration. The UFT and CSA became major opponents of the bill which, based on the recommendations of the Bundy report, came before the state legislature during its 1968 session. The UFT reportedly spent somewhere between $125,000 and $500,000 in a public relations campaign that included hundreds of school meetings, newspaper ads, and radio spots.

The decentralization forces split, however, over the degree of decentralization each group wanted. They also lacked organization and funds and, thus, were hampered in their attempts to press for a meaningful bill. The two most influential civic educational organizations — the United Parents Association (UPA) and the Public Education Association (PEA) — presented their own drafts of a decentralization bill which departed significantly from the Bundy model by minimizing the delegation of power to the local districts. Various ideological differences between and among black and white reform groups diluted their collective strength. Finally, an umbrella coalition — the Citizens Committee for Decentralization of the Public Schools — was formed in early spring, 1968. The ad hoc group was nominally under the chairmanship of Radio Corporation of America President Robert Sarnoff and was established to lobby for the mayor's version of the Bundy plan. Even after the creation of this ad hoc committee, there was difficulty putting together a coherent position. The mayor did not play as forceful a role in pushing for passage of his bill as he had earlier indicated he would. Further, the Citizens Committee provided little financial or institutional push.

The UFT and the CSA, on the other hand, performed more smoothly. As discussion meetings were set up throughout the city, their membership covered everyone, both on the platform and in the audience. Their approach was blunt: they raised fears about the abolition of the merit system of teacher appointment and about black racism, and they expressed concern with the terrible problem ghetto districts would have in securing personnel, even though they had previously squashed plans to aid that process. This, of course, had the effect of formulating the issue along explosive racial lines.

In the spring of 1968, a more diluted decentralization bill was worked out by State Commissioner of Education Allen and the Board of Regents. But once again the effects of the UFT, coupled with a minimum of leadership from both the governor and the mayor, resulted in the defeat of the legislation. In their legislative campaign, the UFT pressed hard that it would organize against legislators who voted for the compromise. After the defeat of the compromise plan, the legislators, who all were up for re-election in the fall, postponed action for a year, empowering the city school board to draw up another decentralization plan. To placate the decentralization forces, the legislators increased the membership of the nine-member city Board of Education to thirteen, thus opening the way for the mayor to appoint a more decentralization-minded board.

The Teachers Strike

When the legislative battle was postponed until 1969, a second phase in the campaign developed in the fall of 1968: the school system was struck for thirty-six days. During the strike new issues were added and old ones fanned. The decision of the UFT to escalate their battle against decentralization, with Ocean Hill-Brownsville as the target, was probably made the previous spring. At that point, the district had ordered the involuntary transfer of nineteen educators. Arbitrary movement of teachers and administrators from one school to another had long been a source of irritation to the teachers, especially those who did not care to teach in predominantly black schools. At a meeting of the Education Committee of the Urban Coalition held that spring, the president of UFT, Albert Shanker, is alleged to have proclaimed that he would destroy the Ocean Hill-Brownsville Governing Board and its administrator, Rhody McCoy. During the spring the union had struck only the Ocean Hill-Brownsville District, with 350 teachers boycotting the district's schools. By September, the union decided to move to a citywide strike. In the midst of that citywide strike in October 1968, the UFT added still another issue to the controversy by announcing openly that the cost of settlement of the strike would be abolition of the Brownsville District.

UFT leadership was, of course, acting at this point to protect the newly gained power over policy which they had won in their 1967 contract. However, most of UFT's public statements focused on the issue of due process for the nineteen involuntarily transferred teachers who, according to the 1967 contract, were to be transferred only with their approval or in negotiation with the union. Still, as the strike proceeded it became clear that the union was not staying with that narrow formulation of the issue. As Marilyn Gittell argues, "Each union maneuver seemed directed at securing a confrontation with the opposition."[10] A UFT campaign charging racial extremism and anti-Semitism in Brownsville heightened fears and tensions. Leaflets and flyers, distributed throughout the city by the UFT and also by the CSA, quoted from materials purported to have been circulating throughout the Ocean Hill-Brownsville District. A representative sample of that inflammatory literature is contained in Illustration 14.1. Some of the alleged content of the hate literature later proved to be false; little of it was ever proved to have come from the district. Nonetheless, mass circulation of this kind of material fed existing fears and latent racism. The atmosphere of the city became more charged with each day of the strike. The Jewish population, having been drawn into the conflict, became more militant in its demands for redress. Jewish leadership in the city either joined the UFT and CSA or sat tight, providing no opposition or rational evaluation of the circumstances. The Board of Rabbis, generally a politically conservative body, became the spokesman for what was accepted as Jewish opinion.

The Board of Education joined in the confrontation by directing that schools be opened, even if this meant breaking in (custodians were supporting the strike). Black parents throughout the city, along with small groups of white parents and teachers, opened schools; generally, however, white parents joined the picket lines. In some areas of the city, "freedom schools" were held for white children while black children were in the public schools. There were reports that both UFT militants and black militants were shouting racial epithets and, in some cases, were violent in their actions.

Although Mayor Lindsay was on public record as committed to the preservation of the Ocean Hill-Brownsville District and to school decentralization, he nonetheless moved during this period to a position of arbiter, attempting to balance the interests of both sides during the strike. This pitted him against the UFT and CSA and created a political stalemate because of the commitment of the professional groups to abolish the district. Lindsay's position was made additionally difficult because of the solid support that labor in general gave to the UFT. In fact, the central labor council threatened at one

Illustration 14.1. An example of hate literature.

CITIZENS, PARENTS, TEACHERS: The following are excerpts from "educational literature" placed in the teachers' letter boxes and posted on pupils' bulletin boards in the Ocean Hill-Brownsville schools:

We demand that only black or Puerto Rican teachers are employed in our schools. We demand that we have the right to hire and fire all personnel. All outsiders-teachers (baby sitters) must be released as soon as Negro or Puerto Rican educators are available. Any teacher who belongs to the UFT or any other hostile group must be discharged. We demand that only locally controlled police can enter our schools. All supplies, wherever possible, must be purchased locally from friendly sources. All repairs must be given to black or Puerto Rican contractors. All "whitey" textbooks must be burnt and replaced by decent educational material. "Whitey" art and John Birch-type social studies must be replaced by African arts and crafts and African history.

> Some supervisors and we know who you are
> Plotting and scheming well you've gone too far
> We didn't ask you here and we don't want your kind
> One thing we learned and we learned it from you
> And it's screw the next man before he can screw you
> So here Judas pimps we'll give you a clue
> Shape up or ship out before this "Fall"
> Or all you mothers against the wall

point to call a general strike, according to reports from the mayor's office. Lindsay appeared to have no great political leverage in dealing with the situation; his influence was effective only on the Ocean Hill-Brownsville board, and he used that to force them to accept the teachers back as a part of the strike settlement. It is apparent, in retrospect, that the mayor had underestimated the strength of the union and of the strong leadership provided by Albert Shanker. He had equally underestimated the extent of latent racial feeling that could be aroused among whites. As the strike progressed, however, there could be no question of the mass support for the UFT: a city-wide decentralization rally produced a crowd of only 5000 to 6000 people, while two days later a UFT rally marched 40,000 people around city hall.

When the strike was finally settled, its terms indicated that the usual

If African-American History and Culture is to be taught to our Black
Children it Must Be Done by African-Americans Who Identify With
And Who Understand The Problem. It is Impossible For the Middle East
Murderers of Colored People to Possibly Bring to This Important Task
The Insight, The Concern, The Exposing of the Truth That is a *Must* If
The Years of Brainwashing and Self-Hatred That Has Been Taught To
Our Black Children By These Bloodsucking Exploiters and Murderers Is
to Be Overcome. . . . Get Out, Stay Out, Staff Off, Shut Up, Get Off Our
Backs, Or Your Relatives In The Middle East Will Find Themselves Giv-
ing Benefits To Raise Money To Help You Get Out From Under The
Terrible Weight Of An Enraged Black Community

FLASH! The Board of Education last night approved an evening adult
program at JHS 271 in Ocean Hill-Brownsville that features courses on
revolution, how to stage demonstrations, and "self-defense."

A course on "The History and Examination of Revolutionary Struggle"
will be taught by Herman Ferguson, convicted of conspiracy to murder
moderate civil rights leaders. Since Mr. Ferguson is currently in jail, the opening session of the course last night was taught by Oliver Leeds, former chairman of the Brooklyn chapter of the Congress of Racial Equality.

IS THIS THE KIND OF TEACHING MATERIAL WE WANT IN
AMERICAN PUBLIC SCHOOLS?

Council of Supervisory Associations
186 Joralemon Street
Brooklyn, N.Y. 11201
October 17, 1968

power sources had maintained their position. The professional coalition of
teachers and supervisory staff succeeded in negotiating a trusteeship status
for the district, which was just short of killing it outright. The Ocean Hill-
Brownsville governing board and the unit administrator were suspended; and
pending negotiation, involuntary transfers of teachers were in the future to be
covered by arbitration machinery.

The Outcome

When the 1969 session of the state legislature convened, there was a
clear indication that the protracted strike had produced a polarization of

forces. The school policy-making power was more obvious. The lines of battle had been drawn in public. While no one could now question the power of UFT and CSA, the decentralization supporters once again began to proclaim the divisions and weaknesses of the organizations. The demonstration districts had become the nucleus of the grassroots movement for neighborhood control and their experience had led them to a more extreme position. Decentralization no longer seemed adequate to them. The Ocean Hill-Brownsville confrontation had indicated that only more neighborhood control over local resources (jobs and contracts, for example) would provide sufficient power to influence school policy. However, the political power of the decentralization coalition had further eroded. The decentralization groups lobbied infrequently and ineffectively in Albany.

Undoubtedly, the neighborhood groups' lack of knowledge of legislative politics is part of an explanation for the fact that effective pressure was not brought to bear, even when it could have produced some minimal results. However, even if they had had the knowledge and will to lobby the legislature effectively, it is doubtful whether the groups could have exerted strong influence. These groups lacked the political resources — financial and organizational ones in particular — to impress legislators. Certainly, events during the 1969 session indicated that the elected state and city officials were extremely responsive to those groups which were able to command substantial resources, such as the unions and school professionals. Union financial support for election campaigns was an important factor in the officials' decisions. Only the more radical Reformed Democrats from Manhattan's upper West Side and the Harlem legislators remained a solid force for decentralization legislation. Early in the legislative session, the Republican leadership was prepared to lend its support to a strong decentralization bill but was soon swayed by the regular city Democrats who wanted to compromise with the UFT. Stanley Steingut, the Brooklyn Democratic party leader, led the downstate opposition to the stronger bill. Many of the opponents of decentralization, at this point, had larger stakes in the political struggle — the defeat of Mayor Lindsay in the upcoming election. They hoped that a resounding defeat of both his Board and his decentralization plans would embarrass him and could block his re-election.

The proponents of decentralization repeated their 1968 roles. The mayor again chose to moderate his position: he, too, was worried about his re-election. The governor seemed unwilling to enter the controversy; he wanted a bill, but its content seemed less important. He was finally accused by neighborhood groups of buying off the Harlem delegation with legislation creating a Harlem hospital. CORE leaders were informed about the hospital concession in a private meeting with the governor before he signed the weak decentralization bill; apparently, as a result, CORE agreed not to criticize the governor's action on decentralization.

The policy output of the three-year period of the politics of decentralization in New York came in that 1969 legislation. The legislation passed in the last day of an extended session and accomplished for the UFT-CSA what they were unable to achieve by their strike. The bill not only abolished the three demonstration school districts, it provided a new series of protective devices to guarantee centralization and professionalism.

SUMMARY

These three case studies do not by any means exhaust the range of urban issues. In fact, there are at least two important variations not covered here which we must understand if we are to have a working concept of urban politics in action. One type is the small, mundane, day-by-day urban issues which receive very limited attention from both the public and scholars but which, when taken all together, compose the total policy — a petition for a zoning variance on a piece of urban property, the budgetary decision as to whether to spend $18,000 to $20,000 a year on an administrator's salary, and so forth. Those questions can appear quite dull to the uninitiated or the uninvolved. But each has its own kind of drama and each contributes to the totality of urban policy, just as the skeletons of polyps contribute to the building of a coral reef.

The other kind of issue we need to understand is the latent issue. By definition, a latent issue is visible only when it is in the process of becoming manifest or when it has moved against a still background. For example, when I was studying Wichita, Kansas, I noted that the plants of several national firms were located just outside the boundary of the city. So I asked several people I interviewed there why such valuable property, which could yield additional revenues to the city, had not been annexed. I was generally told that it would not be worth the fight and that the revenues realized would cost too much of the good will of the business leaders of those firms. Thus, at that time, the annexation of the property was still a latent issue, a potential source of conflict and political management; but it was no less real on account of its latency. Eventually, a time would come when a decision for or against annexation would probably have to be made formally and definitively. Latent issues rarely go on indefinitely in latency.

The three issues that we have examined in case study form provide a strong sense of the flesh and blood, often the life and death drama, of urban politics. At the same time, they make it possible for us to see the several elements of urban politics at work — the setting out of which issues come, the processes by which urban conflicts are represented, and the processes by which conflicts are managed and urban policy is created. Such an understanding is necessary to produce more comprehensive and comprehensible scholarship, but it should also help the local leader and local participant to anticipate the direction of events and to understand the dispositions of participants in those future urban conflicts in which he participates.

NOTES

1. Polly Praeger, "Extinction by Throughway: The Fight to Save a Town," *Harpers Magazine* 217 (December 1958): 61-71. Unless otherwise indicated, the material in this section is taken from this article.
2. Ibid., p. 61.
3. Ibid.
4. This case study is taken almost verbatim from Kovner's report, "The Resignation of Elgin Crull," in *Urban Government: A Reader in Administration and Politics*, ed. Edward C. Banfield (New York: Free Press of Glencoe, 1969, 2nd ed.), pp. 316-321. Unless otherwise indicated, all quotations and observations contained in this section are from that source.
5. This account is based almost entirely on Marilyn Gittell, "Education: The Decentralization-Community Control Controversy," in *Race and Politics in New York City*, ed. Jewel Bellush and Steven M. David (New York: Praeger Publishers, 1971), pp. 134-163. Also see Maurice Berube and Marilyn Gittell, *Confrontation at Ocean Hill-Brownsville* (New York: Praeger Publishers, 1969). I acknowledge the aid of Phyllis Green, a graduate student at California State University at San Diego, in compiling this case study.
6. This point is documented and discussed by Marilyn Gittell in *Participants and Participation: A Study of School Policy in New York City* (New York: Praeger Publishers in cooperation with the Center for Urban Education, 1967, especially Chap. 4 and 5.
7. New York State Legislature, 1967 Session. Chapter 484 of the Sessions Laws of 1967.
8. All quoted in Gittell, "Education . . . " p. 148.
9. Ibid.
10. Ibid.

Chapter 15

The Content
of Urban Policy

Not much can be learned from a general textbook about the *content* of policy in a particular city. For that information, the researcher must submerge himself in the authorizing state law, ordinances, and practices of his city. But there are some widely shared policy patterns which we can review in such subjects as taxes and expenditures, education, and transportation. These patterns can help us see two things: how policies influence city living and how the different levels of government affect the policies ultimately formulated.

TAXING POLICIES

Cities raise most of their revenues themselves. A study made in the 1960s indicated that, despite the development of grants-in-aid, local governments raised about 80 percent of their own monies. Among the four major revenue sources — locally collected taxes, consumer charges for public services, borrowing, and intergovernmental aid — all but the last one rely on the ability of the local citizenry to raise the money for local government.

The property tax is the most important source of city income. In 1968-69 the property tax provided 34.5 percent of the total revenues for the municipal governments.[1] Counties, school districts, and other special districts are even more heavily dependent on the property tax. Relatively few cities make much use of sales or income tax. (In 1968-69, sales and income taxes amounted to only about 16.7 percent of the revenues of city governments.) These proportions seem relatively stable over time; in fact, the reliance of city government on the property tax was about the same through the 1960s as it was in 1900.[2]

State aid is the second most important source of revenues for local governments. All city governments in 1968-69 received 19.5 percent of their total government revenues from state aid programs. Such aid usually takes the form of grants for the support of specified activities such as welfare, schools, or roads. State grants may also be open ended, allowing the local officials discretion as to how to use the aid for general expenses of the city.

In total, federal aid is small when compared to state aid, amounting to 4.7 percent of local government revenues. Federal aid, while proportionately small, nonetheless has contributed to the maintenance of certain significant local programs in education, housing, planning, airport construction, health and hospitals, and highway construction. These particular programs may or may not continue to receive the same levels of support under the federal revenue-sharing program, which gives the local decision makers a lump sum of federal aid for use as they see fit.

The cities also raise some money through borrowing and service charges. In 1968-69, local governments raised $9 billion in charges for services and utility revenues and another $4.2 billion by taking on long-term debts.

Much has been said about the relative fairness of local tax structures. Two observations seem most important. First, it must be remembered that the ability to select tax sources is not entirely in the hands of the city decision makers. In fact, most states severely circumscribe the taxing powers of their local units. Most states, for example, forbid their cities to collect sales or income taxes. Tax and debt limitations are also commonly imposed by the states. As a result, cities are left with little discretion in revenue sources; the property tax is the only major tax allowed by all states. The fact that the property tax produces most of the bread and butter for the local government leads to a second observation about the fairness of local taxation. Reliance on property taxes contributes to the tendency of local tax to be *regressive*. (Regressive taxes are those which take larger percentages of the income of the poor than of the rich citizens.) The federal income tax, by contrast, tends to be *progressive* in this sense. A study in the 1960s of tax burdens assessed the impact of the total tax burden — national, state, and local — on taxpayers. The study concluded that people earning more than $15,000 a year paid about 34% of their incomes in taxes; those earning $10,000-15,000 paid about 22% of their incomes. Those with incomes less than $2000 a year, clearly those already living in poverty, were required to pay 21% of their incomes in taxes.[3] Thus, the *total* tax burden must be seen as regressive; that is, the poor do pay a smaller percent of their income in taxes, but they are actually not able to afford even that amount. A truly progressive tax would *pay* people in poverty — or at least abstain from taxing them.

Table 15.1   City Government Expenditures in 1966-1967

Expenditure Item	Amount (millions of dollars)	Percentage of Total Expenditures	Per Capita Amount
Total general expenditures	$19,172	100.0	$164.75
Education	3,120	16.3	26.81
Police and law enforcement	2,042	10.7	17.55
Highways	2,013	10.5	17.30
Fire protection	1,294	6.7	11.12
Public welfare	1,270	6.6	10.91
Sewage	1,124	5.9	9.66
Health and hospitals	1,038	5.4	8.92
Parks and recreation	913	4.8	7.85
Housing and urban renewal	861	4.5	7.40
Sanitation other than sewage	797	4.2	6.85
Interest on debt	735	3.8	6.32
General control	540	2.8	4.64
Financial administration	328	1.7	2.82
General public buildings	312	1.6	2.68
All other	2,784	14.5	23.93

Source: U.S. Bureau of the Census, *City Government Finances in 1966-67* (Washington, D.C.: U.S. Government Printing Office, 1968), p. 1.

SPENDING POLICIES

A budget is a statement of the priorities of the city government. For that reason, it reflects the culture of the city — what it values as well as, by implication, what it is willing to neglect. City government spending helps shape the local environment and has particular impact on the economic system. Need we qualify its importance further?

When it is read as a statement of priorities, Table 15.1 shows that the city governments of the country as a whole grant the most value to education, law enforcement, and highways, expending about 37 percent of their budgets for those activities. These figures, of course, mask considerable variation from city to city:[4] there exist wide differences in the priorities of the cities. New York City spends nearly one-third of its total budget on schools. Cities in the South, Midwest, and West have typically created special school districts with their own separate budgets. But in general, education is the leading city governmental expenditure. More of the specifics of each of these spending patterns are discussed in other sections of this chapter; we have already discussed law enforcement in Chapter 12.

The federal system in which the city is embedded is an important influence on the priorities of local government spending. As a result, the budget is not the statement of priorities of an independent unit, but is "distorted" toward the functions for which there is aid available from a higher government. For example, the city has to pay only one-third of the total costs of an urban renewal project; while it may have to pay all the costs of upgrading police or firemen's salaries. Needless to say, for political figures, who always want to show large gains for little expenditures, this situation disposes them toward the grant-in-aid programs, even if they do not represent the highest priority needs of the city.

EDUCATIONAL POLICIES

Our governments at all levels spend more on education than on any other domestic program. We spend more only on national defense. (In 1969 it was $45 billion for education and $81 billion for defense.) Like defense, education has contributed notably to the economic growth of the country. Each year, a large educational expenditure makes up a significant portion of the GNP; and each year, the educational system provides business and industry with thousands of people who are trained for occupational roles.[5] Those of us who are devoted to the concept of education as humanizing agent, rather than job training agent, think that education has contributed more than enough to the economic system. Despite our criticism and that of other factions with other grievances, it has been found that urban residents are fundamentally content; a recent six-city study showed that 90 percent were "satisfied" with their schools. Those discontent tended to be members of minority groups.[6]

By contrast to defense, education is characterized by decision making that is decentralized. There is a deeply held view that there should be neighborhood control of the public schools. As a result, there are nearly 22,000 local school districts which have substantial autonomy although they operate within regulations established by state governments. Most of these local school districts are organized much like the council-manager form of government. There is a "lay" board which makes educational policy and a superintendent who is a professional administrator. Much of what we have said above about the limitations of the council-manager form can also be applied to the organization of the school district: many of those difficulties are a result of the effort to separate administration from politics, and this effort is nowhere stronger than in education. The belief in nonpartisan, apolitical education is one of the central ideological doctrines of American education.[7] As we have seen, the plea for nonpolitics often masks a drive to have politics in another form. In the case of education, we can get some idea what form politics takes by examining (1) the characteristics of the lay school board members, and (2) the powers of the teachers and school bureaucracy.

The School Board

School board elections are characteristically held separately from other elections. This allows candidates to emphasize both their own independence from partisan concerns and the autonomy of school governance from controversial issues. One indirect outcome of this practice is a low voter turnout: and a 1958-1962 analysis of 48 suburban school districts in the Chicago area found that an average of 9 percent of the eligible voters showed up at the polls.[8] In school districts where there is more conflict over education, it has been found that turnout is somewhat higher.[9] But school board elections are hardly the showcase of American democracy.

What kinds of people are recruited to become school board members? The consistent finding of empirical studies is familiar: men with above-average formal education who are in business, managerial, or professional occupations are considerably overrepresented on school boards.[10] In addition, there is some evidence that school board members "represent a 'conservative' point of view which is consequently endorsed as the accepted system of values in the schools, but which is compatible with only a selected segment of the community."[11] This tendency is greatest in the city schools, where the minority group members, whose proportion in the total population of the community is higher than elsewhere in the nation, are glaringly underrepresented on the board.

Administrators and Teachers

The school board makes its most important impact on school policy when it chooses a superintendent. The board retains legal authority to make policy decisions, but it is widely accepted procedure for the superintendent to bring to the board the policy alternative he prefers. The American Association of School Administrators, a group representing the interests of the profession, justifies the centralization of the policy recommendation function in the hands of the superintendent on the grounds that he alone possesses the expertise to comprehend the feasible policy alternatives and can best anticipate their impact on the school system. Superintendents usually have the resources to maintain their power; they are full-time officers while board members are part-time, they are usually in office longer than most board members, and they have a staff and control of information which board members do not.

The result of this practice is the virtual insulation of public education from the political process. Some will, of course, argue that this is the desirable situation. A study of six urban school districts expresses a more negative assessment:

> Public education . . . has over the years become perhaps the most nonpublic of governmental services. Public school systems have removed decision-making from the agents closest to the school child — the teachers and parents. . . . The concept of public accountability has been abandoned.[12]

The insulation of public education is the result of many factors, most prominent of which is bureaucratic centralization. Centralization is necessitated by the size of the school system and the ideological rationale of professionalism, which is to some degree a product of the vested interest of the educationalists.

Teachers, by contrast to administrators, have very little power and a minimal role in policy matters. There are many parallels between the role of the public school teacher and that of the policeman. Both perform important public functions, and both see themselves as receiving low pay and relatively little public esteem. Both are able to exercise authority largely because of the discretion they have as a result of their being the decision makers on the spot. Most new teachers are somewhat surprised at their relative subordination in the educational hierarchy, however; and this discovery may differ greatly from the more "realistic" (lower) expectations of a new policeman. The teachers come from a college education which has emphasized professionalism, telling them that they are sufficiently advanced in learning to participate in the most far-reaching decisions. Presumably, too, they are attuned to the most recent developments in education. They are quickly confronted with the realization that they are tightly circumscribed by an educational bureaucracy which has taken unto itself important processes, such as control of the curriculum.[13]

Additional occupational strains for teachers result from the fact that they are generally recruited from the middle class. Although they are middle class and the public thinks of them as such, their salaries are seldom as high as blue-collar wages. As a result, teachers suffer from what sociologists call status inconsistency. The high proportion of women in the teaching profession also affects the social status of teachers. Women are generally paid lower wages in private jobs than are males doing comparable work.

The overwhelming tendency is for teachers, whether male or female, to be politically conservative. Particularly in the classroom, teachers rarely address controversial subjects. Discussion of the American political process is often undertaken just to emphasize a faith that borders on chauvanism. A major study of teacher handling of the subject of politics found:

Table 15-2.   Extent of Elementary School Segregation in Selected Systems, 1965 - 1966.

City	Percentage of Blacks in 90-100% Black Schools	Percentage of Blacks in Majority Black Schools	Percentage of Whites in 90-100% White Schools
Mobile	99.9	99.9	100.0
San Francisco	21.1	72.3	65.1
Marietta	94.2	94.2	100.0
Baltimore	84.2	92.3	67.0
St. Louis	90.9	93.7	66.0
Cincinnati	49.4	88.0	63.3
Providence	14.6	55.5	63.3
Houston	93.0	97.6	97.3

Source: U.S. Commission on Civil Rights, *Racial Isolation in the Public Schools* (Washington, D.C.: U.S. Government Printing Office, 1967), pp. 4-5, Table 1.

The classroom operates basically to reinforce a belief in the desirability of maintaining the status quo. It is very doubtful that the classroom experiences of students encourage them toward radical politics. If there is brain washing in the high schools, it is clearly not for indoctrination in socialism; rather, it appears aimed at the production of optimistic, uncritical citizens.[14]

Urban school districts in both the North and South have struggled with the problems of racial balance in the schools for at least twenty years; yet it remains probably the single most difficult policy question, consuming time and resources and generating conflicts from latent to rancorous. The study of the Ocean Hill-Brownsville dispute in New York City (see Chapter 14) illustrates many of the issues and complexities of racial policies in the public schools. These kinds of situations seem unavoidable, given the level of school segregation in both Northern and Southern cities (see Table 15.2).[15]

TRANSPORTATION POLICIES

After education and law enforcement, cities spend most on highways. As we saw in the earlier discussion of urban environment, the car has in many ways created the modern city; the newer cities of the West, particularly, show the spreading influence that the automobile makes possible. Urban transportation policies are importantly shaped by the other units of the federal system. Building and maintenance of local roads has mostly been a local respon-

Marshall Henrichs

Intersections like this one are fast disappearing from the American urban scene; not all four of the visible transportation means are still operational.

sibility, but the federal government began a program of assistance to highway construction in 1916. It was not until 1944 that the present direction of the federal highway program was clarified. In that year Congress began to create what became the interstate transportation system. No significant funding of the program was made until the mid-1950s. But in 1956, the Congress established the dominance of the federal government in the formulation of transportation policy by assuming 90 percent of the cost of highways built under its terms. At the same time, the Congress restricted the power of local governmental units to determine the routes of new highways by giving that power to the Bureau of Public Roads. The program of the new bureau was going to have its most dramatic impact on cities; specifically, in 1956 it called for the reorientation of the federal highway program from its earlier emphasis on rural road building to the creation of an interurban highway system. Since then, the routes of interstate highways have worked dramatic changes on the cityscape, easing automobile traffic within and through cities. But these gains have, of course, had their costs. New highway routes have torn neighborhoods apart, altering personal and social patterns and generating political conflicts.[16]

Another cost of increased use of the automobile has been the well discussed problem of air pollution. Automobiles generate about 60 percent of the
pollution in all cities, and about 88 percent in Los Angeles. In an important
sense, then, the policies on pollution have been necessitated by the increased
building of roads which encourage more automobile use.

Because many feel that the costs of increased automobile use are too
high, there has emerged a coalition of groups who wish to reorient urban
transportation policies toward the building of alternative modes. So far, rail
systems have won the favor of that coalition. But the "rail coalition" is
relatively lacking in political power; it tends to be not well organized and is
miscellaneously composed of some central-city commercial groups, ecology
organizations, newspapers, some politicians and commuters, and of course
the railroads themselves. The "road coalition" is more coherent and, so far,
more successful: it is composed of state and federal highway officials,
truckers, automobile associations, construction companies and their
suppliers, construction-related unions, petroleum interests, bus companies,
and most of the business interests that would benefit from the particular kind
of growth that highway building generates.[17] Needless to say, the "road
coalition" usually wins its policy goals.

Only in San Francisco has a new mass transit system been developed,
the Bay Area Rapid Transit System (BART). It took BART much longer to get
into operation than had been expected, and it is still too soon to assess its
overall effectiveness. Its most enthusiastic supporters saw it as "the solution"
to metropolitan transportation problems. Within its 75-mile network, which
includes surface track, elevated lines, and subways, it links into a single
automated system commutation in San Francisco, Alameda, and Contra Costa
counties. BART has not been as immediately successful as had been hoped:
labor disputes and increasing costs plagued its construction, and some early
bugs in the technology of the system have continued to give trouble. When
fully operational, the system may yet attain a substantial increase in the
numbers of commuters it carries, as well as a further reduction of commuting
time.

POVERTY POLICIES

More ink but less money is spent on urban poverty policies than on
most other city policies.

Poverty is a relative concept and not easily defined. Some, who would
just as soon do very little about poverty, delight in pointing out that those
who are considered poor in this country would be considered quite comfor-

table in more underdeveloped countries. But many who make this point, like most of us, have no first-hand experience of the life style of the poor.[18] For our purposes, there is no need to debate the relative meanings of poverty; we can simply accept the baseline figure provided by the U.S. Bureau of the Census, which assumes that a family of four requires $3553 a year to meet minimum nutritional, housing, and other needs. By that standard, about 12.5 percent of our citizens were "poor" in 1971. The proportions of poor are greatest among the black and the old.

In understanding the distribution of poverty, it is important to dispense with several myths:

1. *Most of the poor are unemployed.* Because most of the poor are . . . either aged or under eighteen years of age, this statement is literally true. But the overwhelming majority of employable poor are in fact employed, though at wages so low as to keep them below the poverty line. . . . Among the poor, 87 percent of white and 91 percent of black male family heads work.

2. *Most of the poor are on welfare.* In 1965 only 20 percent of poor people received public assistance and 82 percent of them were still poor (below the official poverty line) even with this assistance.

3. *Most of the poor are black.* Although a much larger *proportion* of blacks are poor than whites, a much larger *number* of whites are poor. In fact, two-thirds of the poor are white.

4. *Most of the poor live in large central cities.* Among blacks there is more poverty in the central cities, but many more white poor people live in the suburbs than in the central cities.[19]

The traditional approach of poverty policy is through the *welfare system*; and the guidelines and funds for the several programs of the welfare system are a result of the complexities of federalism. Speaking broadly, welfare programs are based either on the social insurance principle or on the provision of categorical assistance to the "deserving poor." Major programs currently in being include: old age insurance; survivors' insurance; disability and health insurance; aid to the blind, disabled, and aged; vocational rehabilitation; aid to families with dependent children; workmen's compensation; child health and maternal services; unemployment compensation; mental health services; and general relief.

Though a great deal of money is spent on the welfare programs, almost everyone agrees that they are unsatisfactory. The recipients in many programs complain of the inadequacy of the support and the paternalism of the supporters. Social workers themselves decry the red tape and complexity of their work and complain that they have too many cases, many of which are underfinanced. A number of critics outside the welfare system complain that it encourages people not to work; each has a pet story of a "welfare cheat." Most recent reform efforts have been responsive to those who want to catch the welfare cheat. One critic has described the resulting current situation succinctly: "The welfare system is designed to save money instead of people and tragically ends up doing neither."[20]

Marshall Henrichs

Despite all the studies and plans, life for the poor seems not to change much.

A second approach to creating policy to deal with poverty was undertaken in the mid-1960s and is in the process of abandonment in the early 1970s. It is loosely referred to as the *economic opportunity* program. With their many and controversial components, the economic opportunity programs were the result of President Lyndon Johnson's "war on poverty." There was no single coherent set of theories of poverty that was the foundation of the Economic Opportunities Act of 1964; it was a compromise program, and many feel that that fact doomed it from the start. Others insist it was the radical politics engendered by some of the programs which were its undoing. In any case, the Nixon administration began to disassemble the Office of Economic Opportunity when it came into office, cutting it back strenuously and shifting some of its functions to other federal agencies in 1972.

There were several components of the war on poverty programs contained within the Office of Economic Opportunity: the Job Corps was designed to provide vocational education and job training for youth; the Volunteers in Service to America (VISTA) was to be a domestic version of the Peace Corps; the Head Start Program was the most clearly successful element of the package — it provided preschool training for "disadvantaged" youth; the Neighborhood Youth Corps gave work experience and vocational training to youths living at home. The OEO also was to administer the controversial community action programs.

Community action programs aimed to provide federal assistance to help urban and rural areas mobilize their resources to combat poverty. The federal government was to pick up 90 percent of the funding of these CAAs (Community Action Agencies). The governing boards were to consist of representation from three sectors of the geographical region: *public agencies*, to include city government, school systems, and private welfare agencies; *private groups*, to include business, labor, religious groups, and minority group leaders; and *representatives of the poor* themselves. The participation of the poor was a result of the belief that there should be what was called "maximum feasible participation" of the poor in their own program.[21] The CAAs were expected to convene neighborhood meetings, survey the target areas, and hire the poor in the CAA itself as ways to maximize their participation. Much criticism has been directed at the efforts of certain CAAs on the grounds that they organized the poor to confront established powers. However, that role of the CAA occurred rather infrequently; as one study put it:

> Except for a very small number of communities, the community action program does not involve a predominant commitment to the strategy of giving power to the poor, or deliberate confrontation with established powers, of pur-

posefully created conflict. . . . This approach is found only in San Francisco, Syracuse and Newark of the thirty-five communities studied.[22]

One can, of course, understand the reasons for criticism of the mobilization efforts in the poverty areas; it seems contradictory for governments to pay people to conflict with them. Such a view is short sighted, however; it ignores the position that conflict develops skills and a sense of competence in the participants and provides grounds for ongoing contact, bargaining, and eventual integration between the poor and the government. It should not be a surprising finding that emerges from the examination by James Vanecko of the CAAs of fifty cities. He found that those CAAs which emphasized neighborhood organization and mobilization had the greatest impact in changing the policies of institutions serving the poor.[23] Perhaps it was this very kind of success which convinced many decision makers to withdraw or withhold their continuing support of this means of coping with poverty.

PLANNING POLICIES

Our review of the intellectual environment of the city leads us to conclude that the predominant orientation of city planners is antiurban. The reform movement which gave us city planning departments usually gave us planners with an antipolitics outlook. (Probably, many planners would just as soon not be discussed in a book about city politics.) Partly because we cannot take the antipolitics pose too seriously, partly because I have up to this point oversimplified the picture of planning, and partly because of contrary contemporary developments in planning, we need now to discuss the city planner.

First, it should be emphasized that planners have not given the city its characteristic form through acts of their will and power; urban environmental forces, particularly the economic and technological forces, have done that. Planners do engage in efforts to identify the correct goals of the city and to determine the resources available to reach these goals, as well as to specify the constraints on achieving them.

Organizationally, the planning staff is either a quasi-independent agency — usually called a planning commission — or a staff agency assisting the mayor or manager. There has been a long-standing debate among planners as to whether they should favor organizational proposals which would insulate them from the political process or those which would place the planning function within politics by locating it under the chief executive. The trend is toward a more political organizational location for planning, but there is little clear evidence that this enhances the planners' influence.[24]

Sign ordinances are but a small part of land-use planning, but the need for them is sorely apparent in the areas of urban sprawl.

Marshall Henrichs

At a minimum, planners gather and process information — a function which gives them one of their most important resources. One of the most visible products of city planning is the *land-use plan*, which reflects technical studies of existing land use and projects economic growth patterns. The plan suggests suitable municipal policies to promote city goals with respect to land use. Zoning is the principal tool for implementing the land-use plan; its function is to prevent "nonconforming uses." Land-use plans also include rules and regulations for subdivisions, specifying lot sizes, sidewalk and street construction, and required setback distances from streets. Building codes for industrial and commercial construction are also usually formulated by the planning staff.

The most grand of planning efforts is *master planning*, or comprehensive planning as it is sometimes called. Nearly every city has developed a master plan, partly because so much federal legislation makes cities eligible for various forms of aid only if they have one. The master plan has no less a goal than to provide a set of maps and policy statements which will both anticipate and determine the long-run course of development of the city. In practice, the bridge between the broad goal and the specifics of implementation is nearly impossible to build. I have already argued that such a form of planning is misconceived. But even if it were not, it would be almost impossible to attain. Just some of the problems and barriers include: (1) differing groups have competing goals which inhibit overall goal setting; (2) the sheer complexity of a city makes it impossible to understand it and manage it *today*, not to mention in its future; (3) such plans are not self-implementing, and planners generally lack the power to enforce them; and (4) the customary emphasis on the physical development of the city generally does not adequately consider the social and personal needs of its residents.

Master planning is an outgrowth of what has been described "environmental determinism" in planners;[25] that is, that the environment shapes all other realities — social, political, etc. But it would be an oversimplification to ascribe this viewpoint to all planners. One assessment suggests there are four types of planners: technicians, brokers, mobilizers, and advocates.[26] The *technician* is one who is most anxious to be insulated from politics and tends to withdraw from controversy. He shows more interest in the details of information gathering and emphasizes his expertness, neutral competence, and professionalism.[27] The *broker* deemphasizes his role as neutral expert and instead permits himself to be seen as a primarily political figure. He advises and negotiates with the political officials of the city. The planner who acts as a *mobilizer* is one who actively seeks support for his plans and policies among the active groups and influentials of the city. The *advocate* planner argues that he should fully embrace the political process and actively represent the interests of particular groups, in a kind of public defender stance; this role springs from the assumption that "any group which has interests at stake in the planning process should have those interests articulated in the form of a plan. . . . "[28] In many ways, planning is a function which is still in the process of defining itself.

SUMMARY

This brief overview of several important urban policies is no substitute for careful examination of the complex specifics that attend them. It has suggested certain highpoints, however. Certainly the importance of other levels of government in setting the terms of urban policies should be clear by now. It is also obvious that the reform movement lives among many of those charged with administering urban policies. There is a strong attempt on the part of many to insulate their functions from politics; this is especially true in the case of education, but by no means is restricted to it. The community action programs of the war on poverty in several cities entirely disregarded this dominant apolitical stance — and found themselves criticized and without funds. Planners have so far not seriously violated that norm; but advocacy planning, if it continues to develop, may provide another example of administration which recognizes and acts upon its political interests.

NOTES

1. U.S. Bureau of the Census, *City Government Finances 1968-69* (Washington, D.C.: U.S. Government Printing Office, 1970), Table 1, p. 5.
2. Ira Sharkansky, *The Politics of Taxing and Spending* (Indianapolis: Bobbs-Merrill 1969).
3. Gabriel Kolko, *Wealth and Power in America* (New York: Frederick A. Praeger, 1964), p. 37.
4. Cf. Louis F. Masotti and Don R. Bowen, "Communities and Budgets: The Sociology of Municipal Expenditures," *Urban Affairs Quarterly* 1 (1965): 22-38.
5. See Fritz Machlup, *The Production and Distribution of Knowledge in the United States* (Princeton: Princeton University Press, 1962).
6. Basil G. Zimmer and Amos Hawley, *Metropolitan Area Schools* (Beverly Hills: Sage Publications, 1968).
7. Philip Meranto, *School Politics in the Metropolis* (Columbus, Ohio: Charles E. Merrill, 1970).
8. David Minar, *Educational Decision-making in Suburban Communities* (Washington, D.C.: U.S. Office of Education, Cooperative Research No. 2440), 1966; also David Minar, "The Community Basis of Conflict in School System Politics," *American Sociological Review* 31 (December 1966): 822-835.
9. Minar, "Community Basis of Conflict," p. 824.

10. For a summary of studies dating from 1927, see Keith Goldhammer, *The School Board* (New York: Center for Applied Research in Education, Inc., 1964).

11. Meranto, *School Politics in the Metropolis*, p. 9. Also see Keith Goldhammer, "Community Power Structure and School Board Membership," *American School Board Journal* (March 1955), pp. 23-25.

12. Marilyn Gittell and Edward T. Hollander, *Six Urban School Districts: A Comparative Study of Institutional Response* (New York: Frederick A. Praeger, 1968), pp. 196-197.

13. A good discussion of the power of the educational bureaucracy in New York City is David Rogers, *110 Livingston Street* (New York: Random House, 1968).

14. Harmon Ziegler, *The Political Life of American Teachers* (Englewood Cliffs, N.J.: Prentice-Hall, 1967), p. 20.

15. For discussion of the distribution of segregation in school systems see Thomas R. Dye, "Urban School Segregation: A Comparative Analysis," *Urban Affairs Quarterly* 4 (December 1968): 141-165.

16. There are many examples of this; one is contained in Chapter 14 in a case study depicting the fight over location of the New York Thruway in an upstate town. More lengthy discussions are to be found in Herbert Gans, *The Urban Villagers* (New York: Free Press of Glencoe, 1962), and Alan Lupo, Frank Colcord, and Edmund P. Fowler, *Rites of Way: The Politics of Transportation in Boston and the U.S. City* (Boston: Little, Brown 1971).

17. For discussion of the coalitions see Jameson W. Doig, *Metropolitan Transportation Politics in the New York Region* (New York: Columbia University Press, 1966) Chap. 2; and Frank C. Colcord, Jr., "Decision-making and Transportation Politics: A Comparative Analysis," *Social Science Quarterly* 48 (December 1967): 383-398.

18. Reading is often the intellectual's substitute for experience; of course there is none that is valid. But here are a couple of books that come close to conveying the sense of frustration that pervades the lives of many poor people. John T. Hough, *A Peck of Salt* (Boston: Little, Brown, 1970; and Nancy Sirkis, *One Family* (Boston: Little, Brown, 1970).

19. Robert Lineberry and Ira Sharkansky, *Urban Politics and Public Policy* (New York: Harper & Row, 1971), p. 281.

20. Quoted in National Advisory Commission on Civil Disorders, *Report* (Washington, D.C.: U.S. Government Printing Office, 1968), p. 252.

21. This phrase has been subject to a variety of interpretations, leading one of the creators of the antipoverty programs to write his clarification, in Daniel P. Moynihan, *Maximum Feasible Misunderstanding* (New York: Free Press of Glencoe, 1969).

22. Howard W. Hallman, "The Community Action Program: An Interpretive Analysis," in *Power, Poverty and Urban Policy*, ed. Warner Bloomberg and Henry J. Schmandt (Beverly Hills: Sage Publications, 1968), p. 289.

23. James Vanecko, "Community Mobilization and Institutional Change: The Influence of the Community Action Program in Large Cities," *Social Science Quarterly* 50 (December 1969): 609-630.

24. Francine Rabinowitz, *City Politics and Planning* (New York: Atherton Press, 1969).

25. David C. Ranney, *Planning and Politics in the Metropolis* (Columbus, Ohio: Charles E. Merrill, 1969), p. 20.
26. Rabinowitz, *City Politics and Planning*, Chap. 4.
27. Alan Altschuler, *The City Planning Process* (Ithaca, N.Y.: Cornell University Press, 1965), p. 335.
28. Paul Davidoff, "Advocacy and Pluralism in Planning," *Journal of the American Institute of Planners* 31 (December 1965): 331-338.

PART FIVE

A Closing Note:
Politics and Community

The American city was the offspring of industrialism, and it has continued to grow and develop in response to the needs of the industrial and business interests within it. Technological change has affected the rate and some of the shape of that development but has not fundamentally altered the close relationship of city and economy. The elements of urban existence are profound and too numerous to detail, but this book has traced many of their implications for urban governance. Many of the conflicts within the urban culture result from the impact of economic forces on the social systems; the plight of the minorities is, in most of its aspects, traceable to the failures of the free market to adequately distribute its products. The transformations of the family and the development of functional dependencies as a substitute for full, face-to-face, friendship relationships is a social mirror image of the economic principle of specialization and division of labor. These and many other developments have produced much of the conflict that urban decision makers are called on to manage.

Democracy is not totally compatible with capitalism. There is always the potential that either the economic system will overwhelm the political system or vice versa. The pluralists have documented the fact that more than just the economic groups have access to the urban political process, and for this reason we must acknowledge that the economic system has not attained a stranglehold on urban politics. Still, it seems that pluralist democracy in America is only partially realized. The reform movement and the decisional

characteristics of city councilmen, managers, and mayors, for example, contradict many of the expectations of the pluralists. But even if pluralism were
to become more fully realized within the American urban political process, it
would still not be sufficient. What is lacking isn't peculiar to the political
process: every organization from the church to the PTA recognizes that people in general do not take an active participative role in their affairs. Why they
don't is a long story too, but here is one explanation I consider to be central —
one, perhaps, that points toward a course of action for those among you who
are concerned enough to act. As we saw in Chapter 2, the rise of urbanism has
meant a loss of community. It has long been the conservative social
philosophers, such as Burke, Kirk, and Nisbit, who have emphasized the importance of community in preserving and transmitting values. Their perspective ties those values rather too much to traditional institutions — particularly
family and church — than is necessary; but the need they cite for secular- and
nonfamilial-based communities should not be overlooked. It seems to me that
the rebuilding of such communitarian social settings within cities is the first
order of business in achieving the kind of urban self-renewal that all the
federally and foundation-supported projects have failed so far to accomplish.
The restoration of urban community seems to be the first step toward a more
humanized pluralism.

Before formulating any proposal for the reintroduction of viable, active communities into urban political life, we should first recognize that, like
most good ideas, it has already been discussed a good deal. So I will briefly
review four proposals for the restoration of democratic community: the
neighborhood movement, countercultures, the global village, and the survival
community.

THE NEIGHBORHOOD MOVEMENT

The neighborhood movement aims to make the boundaries of the
neighborhood synonymous with the boundaries of community. As one advocate puts it, "The physical area must be suitable for organizing self-rule; its
means must accord with the actual capacities of local power; and its
organizational form must serve the purpose of local liberty."[1]
Saul Alinsky, for example, through his Industrial Areas Foundation
(IAF) has organized neighborhoods into relatively autonomous political units,
able to utilize their own leadership and to pursue effective action. His community organization efforts are undertaken because, as he says, "I do not
believe that democracy can survive, except as a formality, if the ordinary
citizen's part is limited to voting — if he is incapable of initiative and unable to
influence the political, social, and economic structures surrounding him."[2]

Marshall Henrichs

The community atmosphere of this neighborhood gathering makes a positive argument for the potential of urban living.

Most of Alinsky's organizing efforts thus far have been undertaken in poor and black areas, but they are more broadly applicable.

In organizing a neighborhood, Alinsky insists that it is necessary to appeal to the immediate self-interests of the residents and to their resentment and distrust of the outside world to stimulate local action and to facilitate the development of indigenous leadership. Once invited by local people to enter a neighborhood, Alinsky usually tried to follow a rather standard pattern: (1) listen to the residents to find out their grievances; (2) spot indigenous local leadership; (3) get the leaders together and suggest ways in which power might be used to solve their grievances; and (4) demonstrate that power can be used effectively by starting with limited, quick-action goals but gradually extending them. In this way, local residents are drawn into political action and encouraged to believe their action can be effective. As a result of this involvement in common enterprise, citizens develop a sense of personal importance while their ongoing interaction facilitates a sense of community.

Alinsky has many critics. The most vocal among them decry his militancy and his "trouble making." Others criticize his strategies and style rather than his goals. Milton Kotler is one such critic who agrees that neighborhoods must be organized, but dislikes Alinsky's "military" style. Kotler prefers the creation of *neighborhood corporations* as an alternative. As the name implies, the neighborhood corporation is a neighborhood chartered by the state and legally constituted to be governed by its own public authorities. There are approximately seventy neighborhood corporations around the country at present.[3] Kotler recommends as a model the East Central Citizens Organization (ECCO) in Columbus, Ohio, with which he is associated. ECCO is essentially a poverty area within the city of Columbus and was originated early in 1965 when the neighborhood incorporated in order to assume control of a settlement house. The corporation's activities have diversified since that time. ECCO is democratically organized; that is, the fundamental authority of the corporation is "derived from its membership, which meets in assembly to elect the council members and chairman and to transact legislative business over the law, programs and budget of ECCO."[4] Kotler is enthusiastic about the community-building character of ECCO.

> One might say that having deliberative authority has liberated the political spirit of the residents for internal government and external struggle against the city on such issues as police conduct, administration of public schools, jobs, welfare, and many other issues of public interest. ECCO residents are now orators and officials, and practical political wisdom is developing in a community where earlier the only expressions were frustration and escape.[5]

COUNTERCULTURES

By contrast to the neighborhood organization, the counterculture need not have a territorial base. Instead it is composed of peoples, perhaps widely dispersed, who are becoming increasingly likeminded in their negative response to the technological, bureaucratic, and rationalistic nature of contemporary American culture. Countercultures have been described as special instances of what sociologists call subcultures.[6] A subculture is a group of people who vary consistently from the norms of society in beliefs, values, and behavior. Countercultures overlap familiar subcultures, but their uniqueness among subcultures "lies in their resistance to assimilation, their resistance to officialdom's demands, and the political salience of their life and struggles."[7]

Countercultures continue to multiply in America — disaffected youth, blacks, women's liberationists, etc. Still, comprehensive strategies and goals have yet to evolve. In a discussion of the "New Radicals," Paul Jacobs and Saul Landau express the fear that "without a long range commitment or ideology, community organizing is rarely more than an experiment in frustration."[8] But most of the countercultures are dedicated to experimentation rather than ideology. Their members are groping for new life styles, new forms of expression and understanding. As a result, they have much less concrete answers than do the neighborhood organizers to the question, how do we facilitate the growth of community in urban America? Answers range from advocacy of violent revolution to plans for the complete restructuring of Americans' world view. Theodore Rozak is an expansive proponent of countercultures who asserts that their primary purpose is "to proclaim a new heaven and a new earth so vast, so marvelous that the inordinate claims of technical expertise must of necessity withdraw in the presence of such splendor to a subordinate marginal status in the lives of men."[9]

THE GLOBAL VILLAGE

A still different concept of community is that the entire world has been for some time in the process of becoming integrated into a single community. The popularizer of this view is Marshall McLuhan. McLuhan's vision of the growth of the community is without territorial base. He sees its growth as inevitable but difficult to perceive. The growth of the global village, as he characterizes it, is an unanticipated consequence of the development of our "electric" technology. Technology enables the high-speed processing and transmission of information. The result is that each of us receives an extraordinary number of messages in any given time period. The barrage of information comes at us from throughout the world and in no particular sequential order. According to McLuhan, the inevitable result is that the old categories of analysis which erected barriers between human beings are inevitably broken down. Our sense of privateness is lost and we are left with a much fuller knowledge of our world and our fellow beings and they of us than we have had throughout the entire "mechanical" age. Television, for example, bombards us with images, some real, some imaginary. Within the confines of a half-hour newscast we characteristically receive images from the jungles of Vietnam, from Europe, from Washington, D.C., from our own city, and from picnics with the Pepsi generation. As McLuhan puts it, "We know too much about one another to be strangers."

Writing from a perspective similar to McLuhan's, Robert Theobald, a British economist, has observed that there is little in the contemporary city deserving of preservation or praise — that those cities are archaic, having been created primarily to "move people and goods." Now the central task of the city has become to move information.[10] Theobald's vision then, is that there is developing a "communications city," and it is within this setting that "we must discover the new vision of community in an electronic, communications era." Theobald's predictions as to the form that communities of the future will take are enticing. He suggests "the community will be diverse but will always involve a living, learning experience. Life will essentially be learning. In the 1970's we will create genuine learning communication centers in the home.

One will be able to call up facts, figures, and all the data required for the solution of his problem. The potential of cable television is extremely interesting here, because it provides much of the technology for the communication city."[11] Here Theobald is prophesying very much in the same vein that R. Buckminster Fuller has, that in the future we will combine the university and the community.[12]

SURVIVAL COMMUNITIES

Finally, Richard Sennett, a sociologist, has suggested that we need to create "survival communities." We have earlier in the book mentioned his view that urban dwellers tend to insulate themselves from contact with social types different from themselves. As a result, he says, most Americans fail to mature socially, because they have not had to face the conflict and compromise which face-to-face social relationships make necessary to survival. Most Americans grow up — without maturing — into "purified identities"; that is, they crystallize a rigid self-concept, taken on to make themselves distant from and above others. This rigid identity is embraced so as to give the self immunity to the pain of conflicting and tangled events that might otherwise confuse and perhaps overwhelm us.[13]

The antidote for purified identity is the survival community, which would force us to "experience . . . the friction of differences and conflicts. . . . The need is for men to recognize conflict, not to try to purify them away in a solidarity myth. . . . "[14] Such face-to-face groups must be consciously created, Sennett insists; they will not arise spontaneously. This is because the people and the system are in a "conspiracy with each other to establish a comfortable slavery to the known and routine." Sennett does not say how or who, but insists that diverse types must be forced together and denied access to the institutionalized modes of conflict management, police, etc., so that they can work through their differences.

This seemingly drastic prescription is within the same spirit as much of Alinsky's insight, except that Alinsky did not have to create survival communities when he worked with the poor and black. Most of them were already "mature" in the sense Sennett prescribes. But Sennett recognizes what Alinsky discovered relatively late in his career, that the central stumbling block in achieving solutions to many of the problems of the city is the attitudes and institutions of the middle class. Yet Sennett is inconsistent in his attitudes toward city living: after decrying the coerciveness of the contemporary institutions and the tendency of the city planner to impose his own values on the cityscape, Sennett proceeds to insist on imposing the survival community.

It is clear, then, that there is ample speculation about the need for, and means of, restoring community in an urban setting. The range of these ideas — from survival communities to global villages — provides significant evidence that our longing for a shared life and destiny has not died. We may yet resolve our material needs with our social and personal lives in a humanized pluralism.

NOTES

1. Milton Kotler, *Neighborhood Government: The Local Foundations of Political Life* (Indianapolis: Bobbs-Merrill Co., 1969), p. 39.
2. Saul Alinsky, as quoted in Charles E. Silverman, *Crisis in Black and White* (New York: Vintage Books, 1964), p. 63.
3. Kotler, *Neighborhood Government*, p. 44.
4. Ibid., p. 46.
5. Ibid., p. 49.
6. Much of this discussion draws on Harlan Lewin, "Seed Time of the New Republic: Ideology, Identity and Social Change," in *American Government and Politics*, ed. Ronald C. Moe and William A. Schultze (Columbus: Charles E. Merrill, 1971), pp. 559-571.
7. Ibid., p. 564.
8. Paul Jacobs and Saul Landau, *The New Radicals* (New York: Random House, 1966), p. 72.
9. Theodore Roszak, *The Making of a Counter Culture* (Garden City, N.Y.: Doubleday, 1969), p. 240.
10. Robert Theobald, *An Alternative Future for America* (Chicago: The Swallow Press, 1968), p. 138.
11. Ibid., p. 53.
12. R. Buckminster Fuller, *Education Automation* (Carbondale, Ill.: Southern Illinois University Press, 1952).
13. Richard Sennett, *The Uses of Disorder: Personal Identity and City Life* (New York: Alfred A. Knopf, 1970), pp. 5-6.
14. Ibid., p. 139.

Index

Activists: 31 - 32
Adams, Henry: 98
Addams, Jane: 181
Ad hoc groups: 128
Adrian, Charles: 117, 165, 167, 169
Advertising: 85, 124
Advisory Commission on Intergovernmental Relations (ACIR): 236, 241
Agger, Robert: 265 - 266
Alford, Robert: 86, 88, 89, 93 - 94
Alinsky, Saul: 114, 394, 395, 398
Allen, James E.: 366, 368
American Association of School Administrators: 379
American Proportional Representation League: 206
Anderson, Warren M.: 358
Anomie: 61 - 62
Antiurbanism: 96 - 100, 387
Appellate courts: 309
Arvey, Jake: 281
Ash, Solomon: 82
Atlanta (Ga.), elite in: 256 - 257
At-large elections: 213 - 215, 216
Authority: family attitudes, 75 - 80; structure and source, 10 - 12
Axelrod, Morris: 63
Axial development, theory of urban growth: 55

Bachrach, Peter: 262 - 263
Baldwin, James: 326
Banfield, Edward: 44, 66 - 67, 116, 120, 125, 146, 147, 158 - 162, 198, 218, 219, 250

Baratz, Morton: 262 - 263
Barth, Ernest: 340
Basic activities: 51
Bauer, Catherine: 99
Bauer, Raymond: 85
Bay Area Rapid Transit System (BART): 383
Beard, Charles: 204, 206
Behavioralism: 15
Bell, Wendell: 63, 64
Bipolar council: 279 - 280
Blacks: 5; absentee fathers, 64 - 65; anomie, 62; as colonials, 135 - 136, 147; courts and, 315, 317; leadership styles, 140 - 144; and metropolitan reorganization, 250; perceptions of government, 76 - 78; and police, 326; poverty, 383 - 387; separatism, 143 - 150; voting, 139 - 140
Bloc grants: 239
Bloomberg, Warner, Jr.: 91
Boosterism: 165
Boston (Mass.), voting in: 182 - 183
Brandeis, Louis: 305
Breakage effect, political attitudes: 81, 83
Brown, H. Rap: 143
Bundy, McGeorge: 365
Bureaucracy, discretion: 295 - 296
Burgess, Ernest W.: 46, 52, 54
Burney, LeRoy E.: 4
Business, political participation: 115 - 126, 177; bankers, 121 - 122; diversity, 119 - 126; lawyers, 122 - 123; real estate interests, 123; small, 120
Byrne, Gary: 79

401